Stage 2

Management Science Applications

Examination Text

British Library Cataloguing-in-Publication Data

A catalogue record for this book is available from the British Library.

Published by AT Foulks Lynch Ltd
6 Avonmouth Street
London
SE1 6NX

ISBN 0 7483 3206 5

Acknowledgements

We are grateful to the Chartered Institute of Management Accountants, the Chartered Association of Certified Accountants and the Institute of Chartered Accountants in England and Wales for permission to reproduce past examination questions. The answers have been prepared by AT Foulks Lynch Ltd.

CONTENTS

PREFACE

This is the second edition of this text and has been specifically written for paper 7, Management Science Applications for the new syllabus CIMA examinations.

The text has been written to cover the syllabus in great detail giving appropriate weighting to the various topics. More than that, however, we have analysed the syllabus guidance notes and the various clarifications issued by CIMA to ensure that all the appropriate items contained therein have been incorporated into the text.

We have also analysed the May 1995 examination and the August 1995 Syllabus Guidance Notes and where appropriate have responded to any topics where we considered the text needed expansion or clarification.

Our texts are, however, very different from a reference book or a more traditional style text book. The texts are targeted very closely on the examinations and are written in a way that will help you assimilate the information easily and give you plenty of practice at the various techniques involved.

Particular attention has been paid to producing an interactive text that will maintain your interest with a series of carefully designed features.

- **Activities**. The text involves you in the learning process with a series of activities designed to arrest your attention and make you concentrate and respond.

- **Definitions**. The text clearly defines key words or concepts and where relevant we do of course use CIMA's official terminology. The purpose of including these definitions is **not** that you should learn them - rote learning is not required and is positively harmful. The definitions are included to focus your attention on the point being covered.

- **Conclusions**. Where helpful, the text includes conclusions that summarise important points as you read through the chapter rather than leaving the conclusion to the chapter end. The purpose of this is to summarise concisely the key material that has just been covered so that you can constantly monitor your understanding of the material as you read it.

- **Self test questions**. At the end of each chapter there is a series of self test questions. The purpose of these is to help you revise some of the key elements of the chapter. The answer to each is a paragraph reference, encouraging you to go back and re-read and revise that point.

- **End of chapter questions**. At the end of each chapter we include examination style questions. These will give you a very good idea of the sort of thing the examiner will ask and will test your understanding of what has been covered.

All in all a study text that is focused on the examination which will teach you, involve you, interest you and help you revise - in fact an Examination Text.

THE SYLLABUS

ABILITIES REQUIRED IN THE EXAMINATION

Each examination paper contains a number of topics. Each topic has been given a number to indicate the level of ability required of the candidate.

The numbers range from 1 to 4 and represent the following ability levels:

Ability level

Appreciation

To understand a knowledge area at an early stage of learning, or outside the core of management accounting, at a level which enables the accountant to communicate and work with other members of the management team.

1

Knowledge

To have detailed knowledge of such matters as laws, standards, facts and techniques so as to advise at a level appropriate to a management accounting specialist.

2

Skill

To apply theoretical knowledge, concepts and techniques to the solution of problems where it is clear what technique has to be used and the information needed is clearly indicated.

3

Application

To apply knowledge and skills where candidates have to determine from a number of techniques which is the most appropriate and select the information required from a fairly wide range of data, some of which might not be relevant; to exercise professional judgement and to communicate and work with members of the management team and other recipients of financial reports.

4

EXAMINATION PROCEDURE

UK Legislation

The examination will be set in accordance with the provisions of relevant UK legislation passed and case law established up to and including 1 June preceding the examination. Specially relevant to the following papers: Business Environment; Business and Company Law; Financial Accounting; Financial Reporting; Business Taxation. (This ruling will be effective from and including the May 1995 examination.)

Statements of Standard Accounting Practice and Financial Reporting Standards

The examination will be set in accordance with relevant Statements of Standard Accounting Practice and Financial Reporting Standards issued up to and including 1 June preceding the examination. Specially relevant to the following papers; Financial Accounting; Financial Reporting. (This ruling will be effective from and including the May 1995 examination.)

Exposure Drafts

The examinations will be set in accordance with material contained in Exposure Drafts issued up to and including 1 June preceding the examination. Specially relevant to the following papers: Financial Accounting; Financial Reporting.

Stage 2, Paper 7: MANAGEMENT SCIENCE APPLICATIONS

Syllabus overview

This syllabus has three main strands: an appreciation of the management of operations; the use of relevant applied management science techniques; and the application of basic managerial economics. The main focus of these uses and applications will be on how management accountants can and do use this knowledge in their various roles, eg, as specialists, as members of management teams, as providers of management services, as users of specialist advice and as members of project teams.

An acquaintance with relevant computing and IT is expected. This syllabus will build on accounting, economic and quantitative knowledge gained at Stage 1.

Aims

To test the candidate's ability to:

- appreciate the basic management of operations

- apply relevant management science techniques in practical business situations

- understand how some techniques of managerial economics are used in business decision making

- derive management information from data to help solve problems.

Content	Ability required	Chapter where covered in this text
7a MANAGEMENT OF OPERATIONS (study weighting 15%)		
The nature and characteristics of operations management in production and service industries	1	1
The relevance of the product life cycle	2	1
An introduction to Value Analysis; pareto curves	2	1
Production processes: types and implications; facility layout	1	1
The management of capacity: factors affecting capacity; short, medium and long-term planning	2	1
Production control: networks, critical path analysis; batch and mass-assembly control	2	2
The control of work: sampling methods, method study and work measurement	3	4
Special factors affecting the service industries	2	1

Content	Ability required	Chapter where covered in this text
7b **QUALITY CONTROL AND STOCK CONTROL (study weighting 20%)**		
Aspects of quality: quality control, assurance, and management	2	5
Control charts for individual units, averages, range and proportions	3	5
The concept of total quality management; costs of quality, waste	1	5
Analysis of simple tables to provide meaningful information; the chi-squared test	3	6
Stock policy: simple systems, economic order quantity (EOQ) and economic batch quantity (EBQ) models; effect of discounts	2	7
7c **APPLICATIONS OF FINANCIAL MATHEMATICS (study weighting 15%)**		
The use of present value tables	2	8
Calculation and appraisal of annuities, loans and mortgages	3	9
Discounting: net present value and internal rate of return	3	8
Investment analysis and appraisal. Depreciation and capital replacement	3	8, 9
The use of spreadsheets for these methods	1	9
7d **DECISION MAKING (study weighting 20%)**		
Simple decision trees; drawing tree diagrams and identification of optimal decisions using expected values	3	10
Linear programming: graphical solution for two-variable problems; formulation and interpretation (only) of two-plus-variable models	2	11
Simulation; application of simple probability distributions and random numbers to problems of budgeting, queues, stocks, accidents, etc	3	12
The use of the computer in these techniques	1	12
7e **FORECASTING (study weighting 15%)**		
Cost, demand and sales forecasting; qualitative methods	2	13, 14
Applications of least squares linear regression	3	13
Exponential smoothing	2	15
Learning curves	2	15

SYLLABUS GUIDANCE NOTES

Stage 2, Paper 7: MANAGEMENT SCIENCE APPLICATIONS

Managers need usable information on which to base plans and practical business decisions. Such information itself often requires problem recognition, management skills and analytical thinking. This syllabus incorporates these requirements, and demands the application of this knowledge and skill in a variety of business settings.

The syllabus will be assessed with a largely practical examination, including a substantial case study element. Thus, candidates will be required 'to practise on the patient', albeit at a fairly straightforward level. The examination paper will contain descriptive and analytical questions, and the emphasis will always be on 'applications' rather than on theory.

It is important that candidates, especially those who have been exempted from Stage 1, appreciate that this syllabus builds on the economic, quantitative and accounting skills developed at Stage 1, and that a minimum level of numeracy is assumed. However, there will also be a strong emphasis on understanding and interpretation, with a commitment to reporting technical results to managerial colleagues in clear and concise English.

(a)   MANAGEMENT OF OPERATIONS (study weighting 15%)

Part of this section is general background information eg, the function of the operational manager and the nature of operations management, the characteristics of production and service industries, and the scope of operations. Only general knowledge of the product life cycle is expected (infancy, growth, maturity, saturation and decay) and it should be appreciated that, as products and services develop throughout their life, so the nature of the operations and management decisions surrounding them will also develop.

A knowledge of value analysis, as opposed to value engineering which is carried out at the initial design stage of the product's life, is essential. Also, candidates must have the ability to carry out a Pareto analysis (80/20 rule), together with the drawing of Pareto curves or equivalent diagrams to show the relative profitability of a group of products.

An appreciation of different production processes is required, ie, continuous flow, mass assembly, batch, job or project, plus the implications for products, operations, resources and capital investment. Candidates need to have only an appreciation of 'facility layout', ie, equipment, work people, raw materials, rather than detail of mathematical designs.

Differences between capacity, efficiency and productivity should be known. The factors affecting capacity (eg, demand, inputs, machinery) should be studied, and the short, medium and long-term planning implications. This links with Forecasting in section (e) of this syllabus.

Under 'production control' candidates will be required to know about networks, carry out a critical path analysis, and handle simple scheduling problems in batch control. 'The control of work' section of the syllabus includes method study, work study, standard times and bonus schemes. A knowledge of the use of basic sampling methods to establish satisfactory 'work sampling' is required eg, standard errors and confidence intervals for means and percentages. The ability to calculate a sample size for a given level of precision is required. This follows on directly from Stage 1. Questions on this topic could require answers in essay or report format, as well as requiring demonstration of the application of techniques.

(b)   QUALITY CONTROL AND STOCK CONTROL (study weighting 20%)

Candidates should be able to demonstrate some general knowledge about quality management, current trends towards quality improvement, the nature of the inspection process and acceptance sampling. Particular aspects of process control which need to be understood include p-charts, x charts and R charts, and how they are constructed and interpreted. An awareness of total quality management (TQM) is expected, including the relationship between costs and quality conformance. Students should be aware that TQM is largely about the elimination of waste, whether in manufacturing or service industries.

The section on stock control requires a knowledge of the basic economic order quantity model (EOQ), and the economic batch quantity model (EBQ) in which stock is replenished gradually, and an understanding of the limitations of these models in practice and the effects of lead times and simple discounts.

Within the broad context of 'control' it is useful to be able to prepare tables of results for management, where statistically significant data, ie, data with real meaning, is separated from data that is affected only by chance. The chi-squared test is a flexible method for doing just that. It is an easy test for candidates to learn and has wide applicability.

Candidates may be requested to perform calculations in all these areas. However, as much weight will be given to the understanding and application of the methods as to the mechanics of the calculations.

(c)   APPLICATIONS OF FINANCIAL MATHEMATICS (study weighting 15%)

A key skill of the management accountant is the ability to handle the time value of money, usually with compound interest. Thus, the use of the two basic formulae is necessary, namely (i) the value ($£V$) of a single investment of $£X$ after n years at $r\%$ rate of interest per year and (ii) the sum ($£S$) of a series of regular amounts $£A$ for n periods at $r\%$. This area of the syllabus will build on knowledge acquired at Stage 1.

(i) $V = X(1 + r)^n$

(ii) $S = A(1 - r^n)/(1 - r)$

All other relevant formulae are also included in CIMA Mathematical Tables. However, the ability to choose the appropriate formula for a given problem on, say, annuities, loans or mortgages, is a skill best learned by practising on examples.

The use of present value tables is necessary for discounting cash flows. Candidates will be expected to be able to compare investments using the criterion of net present value (NPV), to know the importance of a positive NPV and to estimate the approximate internal rate of return (IRR). Almost any financial context may be used in the examination paper but, in addition to those areas cited in the previous paragraph, depreciation and capital replacement are also obvious topics for applications.

(d) DECISION MAKING (study weighting 20%)

There are three main areas in this section: decision trees, linear programming and simulation.

Decision trees

Management decision makers have to contend with, by intuition or by formal process, the elements of decision logic, ie, the understanding and structuring of a problem, the use of probability to measure uncertainty, the setting up of decision trees to establish sequence, and the use of expected values as a basis for comparing possible outcomes. The syllabus covers the formal process of decision-making via the use of trees and expected values and candidates will be expected to apply the skills described in the following paragraph.

In a decision tree there are two types of 'event': random outcomes which are not under management's control, and decision points, which are controllable. After mastering this distinction, candidates should concentrate on ensuring that a decision tree accurately reflects the order of real-life events. Then, and only then, should probabilities and payoffs be added to the diagram.

The tree is evaluated by working from right to left, ie, the 'rollback' technique, calculating expected values at 'random outcome points' and selecting at decisions points the option with the largest expected profit.

Linear programming (LP)

Candidates will be required to analyse fully only two-variable problems. They must know how to formulate a LP problem from descriptive information, including the setting up of an objective function and constraints in mathematical terms. Only graphical solutions are expected, though an ability to solve two linear equations, as a check, is helpful. A detailed understanding of the results is essential eg, how sensitive is the answer to small errors in the assumptions, how much slack is there in the system, and so on. If there are more than two variables in a problem no analysis will be needed, but the ability to formulate the problem and to interpret the results will be expected.

Simulation

Only the use of elementary probability is required under this section.

(e) FORECASTING (study weighting 15%)

Every management accountant must be able to prepare, analyse and interpret simple forecasts. This section requires specific knowledge of, and skill in, linear regression analysis, the business meaning of the coefficients a and b in $Y = a + bX$ in the particular context of the problem, and their role in forecasting. The limitations and assumptions behind the analysis, not the theory, must be understood. The relevance of the correlation coefficient, r, must be appreciated, and the use of $100 \times r$-squared must be learned. (This latter measures the amount of the variance in Y, the 'response' variable, that can be attributed to the 'independent' variable, X. Thus, in some sense, a correlation coefficient of 0.7 is about 'twice' as strong as one of 0.5, because 49% is approximately twice the size of 25%.)

Practical problems in managerial situations do not limit themselves to regression analysis and quantitative issues. A simple treatment of qualitative problems is expected eg, Delphi techniques and the 'pooling' of subjective information. Candidates should not forget the time series methods learned in Stage 1 because comparisons between methods is often needed, along with an ability to select the most appropriate technique for a given situation. Simple applications of single exponential smoothing are required, of which moving averages are a special case, including how to calculate forecasts. Double exponential smoothing methods are **not** required. Candidates are expected to have a very elementary knowledge of learning curves.

(f)   MANAGERIAL ECONOMICS (study weighting 15%)

Candidates should already be familiar with the concepts of elasticity from Stage 1. In particular, they should be able to relate sales revenue to elasticity, to know what factors are likely to affect the price elasticity for a product, to distinguish between price, income and cross elasticity of demand, and to apply the concept of elasticity to practical problems. In addition, some understanding of the link between production volume and cost is required, along with the various categories of cost and the distinction between economic efficiency and technical efficiency.

Some integration with the economics, quantitative methods and accounting material covered at Stage 1 is expected through the simple application of elementary calculus to practical problems involving revenue, cost, profit and pricing.

WE CLARIFY THE SYLLABUS FURTHER

We maintain regular contact with the CIMA examiners to ensure that our texts are in line with the latest thinking and to clarify any points that may arise.

Below we reproduce the questions and answers on the Management Science Applications syllabus.

1 **At what level will linear programming be examined?**

Linear programming is a key part of the syllabus. Students will be expected to set up, solve and interpret 2-variable problems. Students need to be aware that more than 2-variable problems exist, but they will not be required to provide solutions.

2 **How far will the use of elementary calculus be examined?**

This appears in section 7f Managerial Economics. Students would be expected to understand elementary differentiation (the difference between x and y).

3 **Will students be asked to contrast NPV and IRR, or use each in isolation?**

Only a general appreciation of these topics would be required.

4 **Should students be using computers (including spreadsheet packages) as part of this syllabus?**

Questions in the examination will be based on outputs from standard packages, which require familiarity with such packages. However, neither management nor information technology skills can be effectively examined in a paper based environment. Students would be expected to gain 'hands-on' experience in parallel with the examinations through the practical experience requirements. Currently, however, the Record of Practical Experience (RPE) is the only vehicle for assessing this experience. It was acknowledged that this was an area of weakness in the qualification which needed addressing. There was a suggestion for incorporating a 'hands on' IT test into the syllabus; however, this would pose a logistical problem for an international student body.

5 **What is expected under 'pricing policies in practice' in section 7f?**

Students will be expected to isolate a particular price from a range of prices and identify the maximum profit price. This can be achieved by use of a graph, table or algebra using elementary differential calculus. It should be noted that in the Operational Cost Accounting paper, only an awareness of pricing and demand will be required - there will be no testing of calculus.

6 **Will decision trees include Bayes Theorem?**

No.

7 **What sort of questions will be set on stock control?**

Usually on differing re-order levels.

8 **Is the poisson distribution examinable _at any stage_ in the syllabus - ie, CQM, MSA, or any other paper? Because formulae and tables are still in the formulae booklet.**

Not per se. But under 'simulation' the poisson distribution is relevant eg, mean = variance = m, and the use of tables

9 **Is the binomial distribution examinable _at any stage_ in the syllabus - ie, CQM, MSA, or any other paper? Because formulae and tables are still in the formulae booklet.**

Not per se. It is, of course, a special case of the normal distribution

10   The normal distribution is obviously to be studied (because of the sampling aspects), although it is not mentioned in the syllabus anywhere, but will the normal distribution be examined in CQM or MSA *in its own right?* (ie, as in the previous stage 1 syllabus)

        No. Only as applications in sampling etc.

11   The 'Queuing theory' formulae are still given - is queuing theory examinable in any part of the CIMA syllabus?

        Not 'in its own right'. But under 'simulation' a simple application could appear.

12   Could the examinations board or relevant examiners please point out any differences in the syllabuses of CQM and MSA with regard to:

        (a)   **Financial Mathematics, and**

        (b)   **Regression and correlation.**

        The **level** is higher (**more** understanding) and **coverage** is wider (more use/applications)

13   The formula book contains formulae for AQL, LTPD, OC curve, producers risk and consumers risk, but these are not specifically mentioned on the syllabus for MSA. Are they examinable?

        These are **not** stated mathematically. An awareness of their existence and relevance is required in 'quality control'.

14   In the last set of questions and answers, the MSA examiner stated that tables needed for range charts would be in the book, but they are not. Range charts *are* on the syllabus. Will they be examined, and if so how?

        Calculations are **not** required. Knowledge and awareness of - yes.

Table 1

LOGARITHMS

	0	1	2	3	4	5	6	7	8	9	1	2	3	4	5	6	7	8	9
10	0000	0043	0086	0128	0170	0212	0253	0294	0334	0374	4	9	13	17	21	26	30	34	38
											4	8	12	16	20	24	28	32	37
11	0414	0453	0492	0531	0569	0607	0645	0682	0719	0755	4	8	12	15	19	23	27	31	35
											4	7	11	15	19	22	26	30	33
12	0792	0828	0864	0899	0934	0969	1004	1038	1072	1106	3	7	11	14	18	21	25	28	32
											3	7	10	14	17	20	24	27	31
13	1139	1173	1206	1239	1271	1303	1335	1367	1399	1430	3	7	10	13	16	20	23	26	30
											3	7	10	12	16	19	22	25	29
14	1461	1492	1523	1553	1584	1614	1644	1673	1703	1732	3	6	9	12	15	18	21	24	28
											3	6	9	12	15	17	20	23	26
15	1761	1790	1818	1847	1875	1903	1931	1959	1987	2014	3	6	9	11	14	17	20	23	26
											3	5	8	11	14	16	19	22	25
16	2041	2068	2095	2122	2148	2175	2201	2227	2253	2279	3	5	8	11	14	16	19	22	24
											3	5	8	10	13	15	18	21	23
17	2304	2330	2355	2380	2405	2430	2455	2480	2504	2529	3	5	8	10	13	15	18	20	23
											2	5	7	10	12	15	17	19	22
18	2553	2577	2601	2625	2648	2672	2695	2718	2742	2765	2	5	7	9	12	14	16	19	21
											2	5	7	9	11	14	16	18	21
19	2788	2810	2833	2856	2878	2900	2923	2945	2967	2989	2	4	7	9	11	13	16	18	20
											2	4	6	8	11	13	15	17	19
20	3010	3032	3054	3075	3096	3118	3139	3160	3181	3201	2	4	6	8	11	13	15	17	19
21	3222	3243	3263	3284	3304	3324	3345	3365	3385	3404	2	4	6	8	10	12	14	16	18
22	3424	3444	3464	3483	3502	3522	3541	3560	3579	3598	2	4	6	8	10	12	14	15	17
23	3617	3636	3655	3674	3692	3711	3729	3747	3766	3784	2	4	6	7	9	11	13	15	17
24	3802	3820	3838	3856	3874	3892	3909	3927	3945	3962	2	4	5	7	9	11	12	14	16
25	3979	3997	4014	4031	4048	4065	4082	4099	4116	4133	2	3	5	7	9	10	12	14	15
26	4150	4166	4183	4200	4216	4232	4249	4265	4281	4298	2	3	5	7	8	10	11	13	15
27	4314	4330	4346	4362	4378	4393	4409	4425	4440	4456	2	3	5	6	8	9	11	13	14
28	4472	4487	4502	4518	4533	4548	4564	4579	4594	4609	2	3	5	6	8	9	11	12	14
29	4624	4639	4654	4669	4683	4698	4713	4728	4742	4757	1	3	4	6	7	9	10	12	13
30	4771	4786	4800	4814	4829	4843	4857	4871	4886	4900	1	3	4	6	7	9	10	11	13
31	4914	4928	4942	4955	4969	4983	4997	5011	5024	5038	1	3	4	6	7	8	10	11	12
32	5051	5065	5079	5092	5105	5119	5132	5145	5159	5172	1	3	4	5	7	8	9	11	12
33	5185	5198	5211	5224	5237	5250	5263	5276	5289	5302	1	3	4	5	6	8	9	10	12
34	5315	5328	5340	5353	5366	5378	5391	5403	5416	5428	1	3	4	5	6	8	9	10	11
35	5441	5453	5465	5478	5490	5502	5514	5527	5539	5551	1	2	4	5	6	7	9	10	11
36	5563	5575	5587	5599	5611	5623	5635	5647	5658	5670	1	2	4	5	6	7	8	10	11
37	5682	5694	5705	5717	5729	5740	5752	5763	5775	5786	1	2	3	5	6	7	8	9	10
38	5798	5809	5821	5832	5843	5855	5866	5877	5888	5899	1	2	3	5	6	7	8	9	10
39	5911	5922	5933	5944	5955	5966	5977	5988	5999	6010	1	2	3	4	5	7	8	9	10
40	6021	6031	6042	6053	6064	6075	6085	6096	6107	6117	1	2	3	4	5	6	8	9	10
41	6128	6138	6149	6160	6170	6180	6191	6201	6212	6222	1	2	3	4	5	6	7	8	9
42	6232	6243	6253	6263	6274	6284	6294	6304	6314	6325	1	2	3	4	5	6	7	8	9
43	6335	6345	6355	6365	6375	6385	6395	6405	6415	6425	1	2	3	4	5	6	7	8	9
44	6435	6444	6454	6464	6474	6484	6493	6503	6513	6522	1	2	3	4	5	6	7	8	9
45	6532	6542	6551	6561	6571	6580	6590	6599	6609	6618	1	2	3	4	5	6	7	8	9
46	6628	6637	6646	6656	6665	6675	6684	6693	6702	6712	1	2	3	4	5	6	7	7	8
47	6721	6730	6739	6749	6758	6767	6776	6785	6794	6803	1	2	3	4	5	5	6	7	8
48	6812	6821	6830	6839	6848	6857	6866	6875	6884	6893	1	2	3	4	4	5	6	7	8
49	6902	6911	6920	6928	6937	6946	6955	6964	6972	6981	1	2	3	4	4	5	6	7	8

LOGARITHMS

	0	1	2	3	4	5	6	7	8	9	1	2	3	4	5	6	7	8	9
50	6990	6998	7007	7016	7024	7033	7042	7050	7059	7067	1	2	3	3	4	5	6	7	8
51	7076	7084	7093	7101	7110	7118	7126	7135	7143	7152	1	2	3	3	4	5	6	7	8
52	7160	7168	7177	7185	7193	7202	7210	7218	7226	7235	1	2	2	3	4	5	6	7	7
53	7243	7251	7259	7267	7275	7284	7292	7300	7308	7316	1	2	2	3	4	5	6	6	7
54	7324	7332	7340	7348	7356	7364	7372	7380	7388	7396	1	2	2	3	4	5	6	6	7
55	7404	7412	7419	7427	7435	7443	7451	7459	7466	7474	1	2	2	3	4	5	5	6	7
56	7482	7490	7497	7505	7513	7520	7528	7536	7543	7551	1	2	2	3	4	5	5	6	7
57	7559	7566	7574	7582	7589	7597	7604	7612	7619	7627	1	2	2	3	4	5	5	6	7
58	7634	7642	7649	7657	7664	7672	7679	7686	7694	7701	1	1	2	3	4	4	5	6	7
59	7709	7716	7723	7731	7738	7745	7752	7760	7767	7774	1	1	2	3	4	4	5	6	7
60	7782	7789	7796	7803	7810	7818	7825	7832	7839	7846	1	1	2	3	4	4	5	6	6
61	7853	7860	7868	7875	7882	7889	7896	7903	7910	7917	1	1	2	3	4	4	5	6	6
62	7924	7931	7938	7945	7952	7959	7966	7973	7980	7987	1	1	2	3	3	4	5	6	6
63	7993	8000	8007	8014	8021	8028	8035	8041	8048	8055	1	1	2	3	3	4	5	5	6
64	8062	8069	8075	8082	8089	8096	8102	8109	8116	8122	1	1	2	3	3	4	5	5	6
65	8129	8136	8142	8149	8156	8162	8169	8176	8182	8189	1	1	2	3	3	4	5	5	6
66	8195	8202	8209	8215	8222	8228	8235	8241	8248	8254	1	1	2	3	3	4	5	5	6
67	8261	8267	8274	8280	8287	8293	8299	8306	8312	8319	1	1	2	3	3	4	5	5	6
68	8325	8331	8338	8344	8351	8357	8363	8370	8376	8382	1	1	2	3	3	4	4	5	6
69	8388	8395	8401	8407	8414	8420	8426	8432	8439	8445	1	1	2	2	3	4	4	5	6
70	8451	8457	8463	8470	8476	8482	8488	8494	8500	8506	1	1	2	2	3	4	4	5	6
71	8513	8519	8525	8531	8537	8543	8549	8555	8561	8567	1	1	2	2	3	4	4	5	5
72	8573	8579	8585	8591	8597	8603	8609	8615	8621	8627	1	1	2	2	3	4	4	5	5
73	8633	8639	8645	8651	8657	8663	8669	8675	8681	8686	1	1	2	2	3	4	4	5	5
74	8692	8698	8704	8710	8716	8722	8727	8733	8739	8745	1	1	2	2	3	4	4	5	5
75	8751	8756	8762	8768	8774	8779	8785	8791	8797	8802	1	1	2	2	3	3	4	5	5
76	8808	8814	8820	8825	8831	8837	8842	8848	8854	8859	1	1	2	2	3	3	4	5	5
77	8865	8871	8876	8882	8887	8893	8899	8904	8910	8915	1	1	2	2	3	3	4	4	5
78	8921	8927	8932	8938	8943	8949	8954	8960	8965	8971	1	1	2	2	3	3	4	4	5
79	8976	8982	8987	8993	8998	9004	9009	9015	9020	9025	1	1	2	2	3	3	4	4	5
80	9031	9036	9042	9047	9053	9058	9063	9069	9074	9079	1	1	2	2	3	3	4	4	5
81	9085	9090	9096	9101	9106	9112	9117	9122	9128	9133	1	1	2	2	3	3	4	4	5
82	9138	9143	9149	9154	9159	9165	9170	9175	9180	9186	1	1	2	2	3	3	4	4	5
83	9191	9196	9201	9206	9212	9217	9222	9227	9232	9238	1	1	2	2	3	3	4	4	5
84	9243	9248	9253	9258	9263	9269	9274	9279	9284	9289	1	1	2	2	3	3	4	4	5
85	9294	9299	9304	9309	9315	9320	9325	9330	9335	9340	1	1	2	2	3	3	4	4	5
86	9345	9350	9355	9360	9365	9370	9375	9380	9385	9390	1	1	2	2	3	3	4	4	5
87	9395	9400	9405	9410	9415	9420	9425	9430	9435	9440	0	1	1	2	2	3	3	4	4
88	9445	9450	9455	9460	9465	9469	9474	9479	9484	9489	0	1	1	2	2	3	3	4	4
89	9494	9499	9504	9509	9513	9518	9523	9528	9533	9538	0	1	1	2	2	3	3	4	4
90	9542	9547	9552	9557	9562	9566	9571	9576	9581	9586	0	1	1	2	2	3	3	4	4
91	9590	9595	9600	9605	9609	9614	9619	9624	9628	9633	0	1	1	2	2	3	3	4	4
92	9638	9643	9647	9652	9657	9661	9666	9671	9675	9680	0	1	1	2	2	3	3	4	4
93	9685	9689	9694	9699	9703	9708	9713	9717	9722	9727	0	1	1	2	2	3	3	4	4
94	9731	9736	9741	9745	9750	9754	9759	9763	9768	9773	0	1	1	2	2	3	3	4	4
95	9777	9782	9786	9791	9795	9800	9805	9809	9814	9818	0	1	1	2	2	3	3	4	4
96	9823	9827	9832	9836	9841	9845	9850	9854	9859	9863	0	1	1	2	2	3	3	4	4
97	9868	9872	9877	9881	9886	9890	9894	9899	9903	9908	0	1	1	2	2	3	3	4	4
98	9912	9917	9921	9926	9930	9934	9939	9943	9948	9952	0	1	1	2	2	3	3	4	4
99	9956	9961	9965	9969	9974	9978	9983	9987	9991	9996	0	1	1	2	2	3	3	3	4

Table 4   **AREA UNDER THE NORMAL CURVE**

This table gives the area under the normal curve between the mean and a point Z standard deviations above the mean. The corresponding area for deviations below the mean can be found by symmetry.

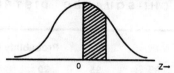

$Z = \dfrac{(x-\mu)}{\sigma}$	0·00	0·01	0·02	0·03	0·04	0·05	0·06	0·07	0·08	0·09
0·0	·0000	·0040	·0080	·0120	·0159	·0199	·0239	·0279	·0319	·0359
0·1	·0398	·0438	·0478	·0517	·0557	·0596	·0636	·0675	·0714	·0753
0·2	·0793	·0832	·0871	·0910	·0948	·0987	·1026	·1064	·1103	·1141
0·3	·1179	·1217	·1255	·1293	·1331	·1368	·1406	·1443	·1480	·1517
0·4	·1554	·1591	·1628	·1664	·1700	·1736	·1772	·1808	·1844	·1879
0·5	·1915	·1950	·1985	·2019	·2054	·2088	·2123	·2157	·2190	·2224
0·6	·2257	·2291	·2324	·2357	·2389	·2422	·2454	·2486	·2518	·2549
0·7	·2580	·2611	·2642	·2673	·2704	·2734	·2764	·2794	·2823	·2852
0·8	·2881	·2910	·2939	·2967	·2995	·3023	·3051	·3078	·3106	·3133
0·9	·3159	·3186	·3212	·3238	·3264	·3289	·3315	·3340	·3365	·3389
1·0	·3413	·3438	·3461	·3485	·3508	·3531	·3554	·3577	·3599	·3621
1·1	·3643	·3665	·3686	·3708	·3729	·3749	·3770	·3790	·3810	·3830
1·2	·3849	·3869	·3888	·3907	·3925	·3944	·3962	·3980	·3997	·4015
1·3	·4032	·4049	·4066	·4082	·4099	·4115	·4131	·4147	·4162	·4177
1·4	·4192	·4207	·4222	·4236	·4251	·4265	·4279	·4292	·4306	·4319
1·5	·4332	·4345	·4357	·4370	·4382	·4394	·4406	·4418	·4430	·4441
1·6	·4452	·4463	·4474	·4485	·4495	·4505	·4515	·4525	·4535	·4545
1·7	·4554	·4564	·4573	·4582	·4591	·4599	·4608	·4616	·4625	·4633
1·8	·4641	·4649	·4656	·4664	·4671	·4678	·4686	·4693	·4699	·4706
1·9	·4713	·4719	·4726	·4732	·4738	·4744	·4750	·4756	·4762	·4767
2·0	·4772	·4778	·4783	·4788	·4793	·4798	·4803	·4808	·4812	·4817
2·1	·4821	·4826	·4830	·4834	·4838	·4842	·4846	·4850	·4854	·4857
2·2	·4861	·4865	·4868	·4871	·4875	·4878	·4881	·4884	·4887	·4890
2·3	·4893	·4896	·4898	·4901	·4904	·4906	·4909	·4911	·4913	·4916
2·4	·4918	·4920	·4922	·4925	·4927	·4929	·4931	·4932	·4934	·4936
2·5	·4938	·4940	·4941	·4943	·4945	·4946	·4948	·4949	·4951	·4952
2·6	·4953	·4955	·4956	·4957	·4959	·4960	·4961	·4962	·4963	·4964
2·7	·4965	·4966	·4967	·4968	·4969	·4970	·4971	·4972	·4973	·4974
2·8	·4974	·4975	·4976	·4977	·4977	·4978	·4979	·4980	·4980	·4981
2·9	·4981	·4982	·4983	·4983	·4984	·4984	·4985	·4985	·4986	·4986
3·0	·49865	·4987	·4987	·4988	·4988	·4989	·4989	·4989	·4990	·4990
3·1	·49903	·4991	·4991	·4991	·4992	·4992	·4992	·4992	·4993	·4993
3·2	·49931	·4993	·4994	·4994	·4994	·4994	·4994	·4995	·4995	·4995
3·3	·49952	·4995	·4995	·4996	·4996	·4996	·4996	·4996	·4996	·4997
3·4	·49966	·4997	·4997	·4997	·4997	·4997	·4997	·4997	·4997	·4998
3·5	·49977									

Table 6 **THE CHI-SQUARED DISTRIBUTION (χ^2)**

Degrees of freedom	Probability level %						
	99	95	20	10	5	1	0·1
1	0·0^{3}157	0·00393	1·64	2·71	3·84	6·63	10·83
2	0·0201	0·103	3·22	4·61	5·99	9·21	13·81
3	0·115	0·352	4·64	6·25	7·81	11·34	16·27
4	0·297	0·711	5·99	7·78	9·49	13·28	18·47
5	0·554	1·15	7·29	9·24	11·07	15·09	20·52
6	0·872	1·64	8·56	10·64	12·59	16.81	22·46
7	1·24	2·17	9·80	12·02	14·07	18·48	24·32
8	1·65	2·73	11·03	13·36	15·51	20·09	26·12
9	2·09	3·33	12·24	14·68	16·92	21·67	27·88
10	2·56	3·94	13·44	15·99	18·31	23.21	29·59
11	3·05	4·57	14·63	17·28	19·68	24.73	31·26
12	3·57	5·23	15·81	18·55	21·03	26.22	32·91
13	4·11	5·89	16·98	19·81	22·36	27.69	34·53
14	4·66	6·57	18·15	21·06	23·68	29.14	36·12
15	5·23	7·26	19·31	22·31	25·00	30.58	37·70
16	5·81	7·96	20·47	23·54	26·30	32.00	39·25
17	6·41	8·67	21·61	24·77	27·59	33.41	40·79
18	7·01	9·39	22·76	25·99	28·87	34.81	42·31
19	7·63	10·12	23·90	27·20	30·14	36.19	43·82
20	8·26	10·85	25·04	28·41	31·41	37.57	45·31
21	8·90	11·59	26·07	29·62	32·67	38.93	46·80
22	9·54	12·34	27·30	30·81	33·92	40.29	48·27
23	10·20	13·09	28·43	32·01	35·17	41.64	49·73
24	10·86	13·85	29·55	33·20	36·42	42.98	51·18
25	11·52	14·61	30·68	34·38	37·65	44.31	52·62
26	12·20	15·38	31·80	35·56	38·89	45.64	54·05
27	12·88	16·15	32·91	36·74	40·11	46.96	55·48
28	13·56	16·93	34·03	37·92	41·34	48.28	56·89
29	14·26	17·71	35·14	39·09	42·56	49.59	58·30
30	14·95	18·49	36·25	40·26	43·77	50.89	59·70
40	22·16	26·51	47·27	51·81	55·76	63.69	73·40
50	29·71	34·76	58·16	63·17	67·50	76.15	86·66
60	37·48	43·19	68·97	74·40	79·08	88.38	99·61
70	45·44	51·74	79·71	85·53	90·53	100.4	112·3
80	53·54	60·39	90·41	96·58	101·9	112.3	124·8
90	61·75	69·13	101·1	107·6	113·1	124.1	137·2
100	70·06	77·93	111·7	118·5	124·3	135.8	149·4

The entry in the table is the value of χ^2 which would be exceeded with the given probability by random variations if the null hypothesis were true.

Table 7 SIGNIFICANT VALUE OF THE CORRELATION COEFFICIENT

If the calculated value of r exceeds the table value of r_α, a significant correlation has been established at the α significance level.

d.f.	$r_{.1}$	$r_{.05}$	$r_{.02}$	$r_{.01}$	$r_{.001}$
1	·98769	·99692	·999507	·999877	·9999988
2	·90000	·95000	·98000	·990000	·99900
3	·8054	·8783	·93433	·95873	·99116
4	·7293	·8114	·8822	·91720	·97406
5	·6694	·7545	·8329	·8745	·95074
6	·6215	·7067	·7887	·8343	·92493
7	·5822	·6664	·7498	·7977	·8982
8	·5494	·6319	·7155	·7646	·8721
9	·5214	·6021	·6851	·7348	·8471
10	·4973	·5760	·6581	·7079	·8233
11	·4762	·5529	·6339	·6835	·8010
12	·4575	·5324	·6120	·6614	·7800
13	·4409	·5139	·5923	·6411	·7603
14	·4259	·4973	·5742	·6226	·7420
15	·4124	·4821	·5577	·6055	·7246
16	·4000	·4683	·5425	·5897	·7084
17	·3887	·4555	·5285	·5751	·6932
18	·3783	·4438	·5155	·5614	·6787
19	·3687	·4329	·5034	·5487	·6652
20	·3598	·4227	·4921	·5368	·6524
25	·3233	·3809	·4451	·4869	·5974
30	·2960	·3494	·4093	·4487	·5541
35	·2746	·3246	·3810	·4182	·5189
40	·2573	·3044	·3578	·3932	·4896
45	·2428	·2875	·3384	·3721	·4648
50	·2306	·2732	·3218	·3541	·4433
60	·2108	·2500	·2948	·3248	·4078
70	·1954	·2319	·2737	·3017	·3799
80	·1829	·2172	·2565	·2830	·3568
90	·1726	·2050	·2422	·2673	·3375
100	·1638	·1946	·2301	·2540	·3211

d.f. = degrees of freedom

Table 11

PRESENT VALUE TABLE

Present value of 1 ie $(1 + r)^{-n}$ where r = discount rate, n = number of periods until payment.

Periods (n)	Discount rates (r)									
	1%	2%	3%	4%	5%	6%	7%	8%	9%	10%
1	0·990	0·980	0·971	0·962	0·952	0·943	0·935	0·926	0·917	0·909
2	0·980	0·961	0·943	0·925	0·907	0·890	0·873	0·857	0·842	0·826
3	0·971	0·942	0·915	0·889	0·864	0·840	0·816	0·794	0·772	0·751
4	0·961	0·924	0·888	0·855	0·823	0·792	0·763	0·735	0·708	0·683
5	0·951	0·906	0·863	0·822	0·784	0·747	0·713	0·681	0·650	0·621
6	0·942	0·888	0·837	0·790	0·746	0·705	0·666	0·630	0·596	0·564
7	0·933	0·871	0·813	0·760	0·711	0·665	0·623	0·583	0·547	0·513
8	0·923	0·853	0·789	0·731	0·677	0·627	0·582	0·540	0·502	0·467
9	0·941	0·837	0·766	0·703	0·645	0·592	0·544	0·500	0·460	0·424
10	0·905	0·820	0·744	0·676	0·614	0·558	0·508	0·463	0·422	0·386
11	0·896	0·804	0·722	0·650	0·585	0·527	0·475	0·429	0·388	0·350
12	0·887	0·788	0·702	0·625	0·557	0·497	0·444	0·397	0·356	0·319
13	0·879	0·773	0·681	0·601	0·530	0·469	0·415	0·368	0·326	0·290
14	0·870	0·758	0·661	0·577	0·505	0·442	0·388	0·340	0·299	0·263
15	0·861	0·743	0·642	0·555	0·481	0·417	0·362	0·315	0·275	0·239

Periods (n)	Discount rates (r)									
	11%	12%	13%	14%	15%	16%	17%	18%	19%	20%
1	0·901	0·893	0·885	0·877	0·870	0·862	0·855	0·847	0·840	0·833
2	0·812	0·797	0·783	0·769	0·756	0·743	0·731	0·718	0·706	0·694
3	0·731	0·712	0·693	0·675	0·658	0·641	0·624	0·609	0·593	0·579
4	0·659	0·636	0·613	0·592	0·572	0·552	0·534	0·516	0·499	0·482
5	0·593	0·567	0·543	0·519	0·497	0·476	0·456	0·437	0·419	0·402
6	0·535	0·507	0·480	0·456	0·432	0·410	0·390	0·370	0·352	0·335
7	0·482	0·452	0·425	0·400	0·376	0·354	0·333	0·314	0·296	0·279
8	0·434	0·404	0·376	0·351	0·327	0·305	0·285	0·266	0·249	0·233
9	0·391	0·361	0·333	0·308	0·284	0·263	0·243	0·225	0·209	0·194
10	0·352	0·322	0·295	0·270	0·247	0·227	0·208	0·191	0·176	0·162
11	0·317	0·287	0·261	0·237	0·215	0·195	0·178	0·162	0·148	0·135
12	0·286	0·257	0·231	0·208	0·187	0·168	0·152	0·137	0·124	0·112
13	0·258	0·229	0·204	0·182	0·163	0·145	0·130	0·116	0·104	0·093
14	0·232	0·205	0·181	0·160	0·141	0·125	0·111	0·099	0·088	0·078
15	0·209	0·183	0·160	0·140	0·123	0·108	0·095	0·084	0·074	0·065

Table 12 **CUMULATIVE PRESENT VALUE OF £1**

This table shows the Present Value of £1 per annum, Receivable or Payable at the end of each year for *n* years.

Present (n)	Interest rates r									
	1%	**2%**	**3%**	**4%**	**5%**	**6%**	**7%**	**8%**	**9%**	**10%**
1	0·990	0·980	0·971	0·962	0·952	0·943	0·935	0·926	0·917	0·909
2	1·970	1·942	1·913	1·886	1·859	1·833	1·808	1·783	1·759	1·736
3	2·941	2·884	2·829	2·775	2·723	2·673	2·624	2·577	2·531	2·487
4	3·902	3·808	3·717	3·630	3·546	3·465	3·387	3·312	3·240	3·170
5	4·853	4·713	4·580	4·452	4·329	4·212	4·100	3·993	3·890	3·791
6	5·795	5·601	5·417	5·242	5·076	4·917	4·767	4·623	4·486	4·355
7	6·728	6·472	6·230	6·002	5·786	5·582	5·389	5·206	5·033	4·868
8	7·652	7·325	7·020	6·733	6·463	6·210	5·971	5·747	5·535	5·335
9	8·566	8·162	7·786	7·435	7·108	6·802	6·515	6·247	5·995	5·759
10	9·471	8·983	8·530	8·111	7·722	7·360	7·024	6·710	6·418	6·145
11	10·37	9·787	9·253	8·760	8·306	7·887	7·499	7·139	6·805	6·495
12	11·26	10·58	9·954	9·385	8·863	8·384	7·943	7·536	7·161	6·814
13	12·13	11·35	10·63	9·986	9·394	8·853	8·358	7·904	7·487	7·103
14	13·00	12·11	11·30	10·56	9·899	9·295	8·745	8·244	7·786	7·367
15	13·87	12·85	11·94	11·12	10·38	9·712	9·108	8·559	8·061	7·606

Present (n)	Interest rates (r)									
	11%	**12%**	**13%**	**14%**	**15%**	**16%**	**17%**	**18%**	**19%**	**20%**
1	0·901	0·893	0·885	0·877	0·870	0·862	0·855	0·847	0·840	0·833
2	1·713	1·690	1·668	1·647	1·626	1·605	1·585	1·566	1·547	1·528
3	2·444	2·402	2·361	2·322	2·283	2·246	2·210	2·174	2·140	2·106
4	3·102	3·037	2·974	2·914	2·855	2·798	2·743	2·690	2·639	2·589
5	3·696	3·605	3·517	3·433	3·352	3·274	3·199	3·127	3·058	2·991
6	4·231	4·111	3·998	3·889	3·784	3·685	3·589	3·498	3·410	3·326
7	4·712	4·564	4·423	4·288	4·160	4·039	3·922	3·812	3·706	3·605
8	5·146	4·968	4·799	4·639	4·487	4·344	4·207	4·078	3·954	3·837
9	5·537	5·328	5·132	4·946	4·772	4·607	4·451	4·303	4·163	4·031
10	5·889	5·650	5·426	5·216	5·019	4·833	4·659	4·494	4·339	4·192
11	6·207	5·938	5·687	5·453	5·234	5·209	4·836	4·656	4·486	4·327
12	6·492	6·194	5·918	5·660	5·421	5·197	4·988	4·793	4·611	4·439
13	6·750	6·424	6·122	5·842	5·583	5·342	5·118	4·910	4·715	4·533
14	6·982	6·628	6·302	6·002	5·724	5·468	5·229	5·008	4·802	4·611
15	7·191	6·811	6·462	6·142	5·847	5·575	5·324	5·092	4·876	4·675

Table 13   **R A N D O M   N U M B E R S**

03 47 43 73 86	36 96 47 36 61	46 98 63 71 62	33 26 16 80 45	60 11 14 10 95
97 74 24 67 62	42 81 14 57 20	42 53 32 37 32	27 07 36 07 51	24 51 79 89 73
16 76 62 27 66	56 50 26 71 07	32 90 79 78 53	13 55 38 58 59	88 97 54 14 10
12 56 85 99 26	96 96 68 27 31	05 03 72 93 15	57 12 10 14 21	88 26 49 81 76
55 59 56 35 64	38 54 82 46 22	31 62 43 09 90	06 18 44 32 53	23 83 01 30 30
16 22 77 94 39	49 54 43 54 82	17 37 93 23 78	87 35 20 96 43	84 26 34 91 64
84 42 17 53 31	57 24 55 08 88	77 04 74 47 67	21 76 33 50 25	83 92 12 06 76
63 01 63 78 59	16 95 55 67 19	98 10 50 71 75	12 86 73 58 07	44 39 52 38 79
33 21 12 34 29	78 64 56 07 82	52 42 07 44 38	15 51 00 13 42	99 66 02 79 54
57 60 86 32 44	09 47 27 96 54	49 17 46 09 62	90 52 84 77 27	08 02 73 43 28
18 18 07 92 46	44 17 16 58 09	79 83 86 19 62	06 76 50 03 10	55 23 64 05 05
26 62 38 97 75	84 16 07 44 99	83 11 46 32 24	20 14 85 88 45	10 93 72 88 71
23 42 40 64 74	82 97 77 77 81	07 45 32 14 08	32 98 94 07 72	93 85 79 10 75
52 36 28 19 95	60 92 26 11 97	00 56 76 31 38	80 22 02 53 53	86 60 42 04 53
37 85 94 35 12	83 39 50 08 30	42 34 07 96 88	54 42 06 87 98	35 85 29 48 39
70 29 17 12 13	40 33 20 38 26	13 89 51 03 74	17 76 37 13 04	07 74 21 19 30
56 62 18 37 35	96 83 50 87 75	97 12 25 93 47	70 33 24 03 54	97 77 46 44 80
99 49 57 22 77	88 42 95 45 72	16 64 36 16 00	04 43 18 66 79	94 77 24 21 90
16 08 15 04 72	33 27 14 34 09	45 59 34 68 49	12 72 07 34 45	99 27 72 95 14
31 16 93 32 43	50 27 89 87 19	20 15 37 00 49	52 85 66 60 44	38 68 88 11 80
68 34 30 13 70	55 74 30 77 40	44 22 78 84 26	04 33 46 09 52	68 07 97 06 57
74 57 25 65 76	59 29 97 68 60	71 91 38 67 54	13 58 18 24 76	15 54 55 95 52
27 42 37 86 53	48 55 90 65 72	96 57 69 36 10	96 46 92 42 45	97 60 49 04 91
00 39 68 29 61	66 37 32 20 30	77 84 57 03 29	10 45 65 04 26	11 04 96 67 24
29 94 98 94 24	68 49 69 10 82	53 75 91 93 30	34 25 20 57 27	40 48 73 51 92
16 90 82 66 59	83 62 64 11 12	67 19 00 71 74	60 47 21 29 68	02 02 37 03 31
11 27 94 75 06	06 09 19 74 66	02 94 37 34 02	76 70 90 30 86	38 45 94 30 38
35 24 10 16 20	33 32 51 26 38	79 78 45 04 91	16 92 53 56 16	02 75 50 95 98
38 23 16 86 38	42 38 97 01 50	87 75 66 81 41	40 01 74 91 62	48 51 84 08 32
31 96 25 91 47	96 44 33 49 13	34 86 82 53 91	00 52 43 48 85	27 55 26 89 62
66 67 40 67 14	64 05 71 95 86	11 05 65 09 68	76 83 20 37 90	57 16 00 11 66
14 90 84 45 11	75 73 88 05 90	52 27 41 14 86	22 98 12 22 08	07 52 74 95 80
68 05 51 18 00	33 96 02 75 19	07 60 62 93 55	59 33 82 43 90	49 37 38 44 59
20 46 78 73 90	97 51 40 14 02	04 02 33 31 08	39 54 16 49 36	47 95 93 13 30
64 19 58 97 79	15 06 15 93 20	01 90 10 75 06	40 78 78 89 62	02 67 74 17 33
05 26 93 70 60	22 35 85 15 13	92 03 51 59 77	59 56 78 06 83	52 91 05 70 74
47 97 10 88 23	09 98 42 99 64	61 71 62 99 15	06 51 29 16 93	58 05 77 09 51
68 71 86 85 85	54 87 66 47 54	73 32 08 11 12	44 95 92 63 16	29 56 24 29 48
26 99 61 65 53	58 37 78 80 70	42 10 50 67 42	32 17 55 85 74	94 44 67 16 94
14 65 52 68 75	87 59 36 22 41	26 78 63 06 55	13 08 27 01 50	15 29 39 39 43
17 53 77 58 71	71 41 61 50 72	12 41 94 96 26	44 95 27 36 99	02 96 74 30 83
90 26 59 21 19	23 52 23 33 12	96 93 02 18 39	07 02 18 36 07	25 99 32 70 23
41 23 52 55 99	31 04 49 69 96	10 47 48 45 88	13 41 43 89 20	97 17 14 49 17
60 20 50 81 69	31 99 73 68 68	35 81 33 03 76	24 30 12 48 60	18 99 10 72 34
91 25 38 05 90	94 58 28 41 36	45 37 59 03 09	90 35 57 29 12	82 62 64 65 60
34 50 57 74 37	98 80 33 00 91	09 77 93 19 82	74 94 80 04 04	45 07 31 66 49
85 22 04 39 43	73 81 53 94 79	33 62 46 86 28	08 31 64 46 31	53 94 13 38 47
09 79 13 77 48	73 82 97 22 21	05 03 27 24 83	72 89 44 05 60	35 80 39 94 88
88 75 80 18 14	22 95 75 42 49	39 32 82 22 49	02 48 07 70 37	16 04 61 67 87
90 96 23 70 00	39 00 03 06 90	55 85 78 38 36	94 37 30 69 32	90 89 00 76 33

14. FORMULAE AND SYMBOLS

General section

$\pm$ plus *or* minus; positive *or* negative

$\neq$ not equal

$\simeq$ or $\doteqdot$ approximately equal

$>$ greater than

$<$ less than

$a > b > c, c < b < a$ value of middle term lies between outer values

$\geqslant$ greater than *or* equal to

$\log_e N$; Natural logarithm of N. Note that if $e^x = N$, $\log_e N = x$

$\log N$ $\log_{10} N$ common (Briggsian) logarithm of N. Note that if $10^x = N$, $\log N = x$

$e^x = 1 + \dfrac{x}{1!} + \dfrac{x^2}{2!} + \ldots$

xy or $x.y$ product of x and y; x multiplied by y; $(x)(y) = xy$

$*$ multiplied by
$A * B$ A times B

$y = f(x)$ y is a function of x

dy/dx or $f'(x)$ differential coefficient of $y = f(x)$; 1st derivative

d^2y/dx^2 or $f''(x)$ 2nd derivative

x/y or $x \div y$ x divided by y

x^n x to power n; the product $xx \ldots$ to n factors; nth power of x

$\sqrt{x} = x^{1/2}$ square root of x

$\sqrt[n]{x} = x^{1/n}$ nth root of x

$x^{-n} = \dfrac{1}{x^n}$ reciprocal of nth power of x

$|x|$ absolute value of x (sign ignored)

Σx summed values of variable x

$\sum\limits_{i=1}^{n} x_i$ summed values of variable x over range x_1 to x_n inclusive

$x!$ factorial x; the product $1, 2, 3, \ldots x$

$P(n,x)$ $_nP_x$ number of permutations of x things from n

$C(n,x)$ $_nC_x$ ^nC_x number of combinations of x things from n

101_2 subscript $_2$ indicates binary number system

534_n subscript $_n$ indicates number system based on n

$\int f(x)dx$ indefinite integral of $f(x)$

$\int\limits_a^b f(x)dx$ definite integral of $f(x)$ between limits $x=a$, $x=b$

Sets and Probability

A=B   set A equals set B

ε   is an element of

⊂   inclusion; A⊂B means set A is included in set B

∩(cap) conjunction, intersection; A∩B defines all elements included in *both* A and B

∪(cup) Union; A∪B defines all elements in A *plus* all elements in B, no element being counted twice

A′ or $\overline{A}$ negation; the set of all elements *not* in A

n(A)   number of elements in set A

U   universe of discourse, sample space; note that for any set A+A′=U=1

Φ( )   null or empty set
p(A)   probability of event A

p(A|B)   probability of event A, given B

General Rules
P(A∪B)=P(A)+P(B)−P(A∩B)

P(A∩B)=P(A).P(B|A)=P(B).P(A|B)

Statistics and Quantitative methods

μ   population mean

$\overline{x}$ sample mean

$Q_1 \ldots Q_n$ first ... nth quantile

cum x cumulative total of variable x

d.f.   degrees of freedom

χ^2 chi-squared

F F ratio

t   Student's t-statistic

n number in the sample

N   population size

s   sample standard deviation

s^2 sample variance

σ   population standard deviation

σ^2 population variance

s/$\overline{x}$ coefficient of variation

r   coefficient of correlation

r^2 (or R^2)   coefficient of determination

E(X)   expectation of X
= probability * pay off

p($X=x_1$)   probability that X equals x_1

Distributions
Binomial Distribution

$Pr(x) = {}^nC_x.p^x.q^{n-x}$

$${}^nC_x = \frac{n!}{(n-x)!(x)!}$$

Mean = $n.p$

Standard deviation = $\sqrt{n.p.q}$

Normal Distribution

$$Z = \frac{x - \mu}{\sigma}$$

Poisson Distribution

$$Pr(x) = \frac{e^{-m}.m^x}{x!}$$

Where e = exponential constant
m = mean rate of occurrence
= variance

Descriptive Statistics

Arithmetic Mean

$$\bar{x} = \frac{\Sigma x}{n} \quad \text{or} \quad \bar{x} = \frac{\Sigma fx}{\Sigma f}$$

Standard Deviation

$$SD = \sqrt{\frac{\Sigma(x - \bar{x})^2}{n - 1}} \quad \text{or} \quad \sqrt{\frac{\Sigma(x - \bar{x})^2}{n}}$$

if n is 'large'.

$$SD = \sqrt{\frac{\Sigma f x^2}{\Sigma f} - \bar{x}^2} \quad \text{(frequency distribution)}$$

Index numbers

Laspeyres quantity $\quad 100 \times \dfrac{\Sigma Q_1 P_0}{\Sigma Q_0 P_0}$

Paasche quantity $\quad 100 \times \dfrac{\Sigma Q_1 P_1}{\Sigma Q_0 P_1}$

Laspeyres price $\quad 100 \times \dfrac{\Sigma Q_0 P_1}{\Sigma Q_0 P_0}$

Paasche price $\quad 100 \times \dfrac{\Sigma Q_1 P_1}{\Sigma Q_1 P_0}$

Time series

Additive Model:
Series = Trend + Seasonal + Random

Multiplicative Model:
Series = Trend * Seasonal * Random

Statistical inference

Estimated Standard Errors —

Sample mean: $\quad \dfrac{s}{\sqrt{n}}$

Sample proportion: $\quad \sqrt{\dfrac{pq}{n}}$

$\bar{x}_1 - \bar{x}_2$: $\quad \sqrt{\dfrac{s_1^2}{n_1} + \dfrac{s_2^2}{n_2}}$

Chi squared (χ^2)

$$\chi^2 = \Sigma \frac{(O - E)^2}{E}$$

Regression Analysis

The linear regression equation of Y on X is given by:

$Y = a + bX \quad$ or
$Y - \bar{Y} = b(X - \bar{X})$, where

$$b = \frac{\text{Covariance (XY)}}{\text{Variance (X)}} = \frac{n\Sigma XY - (\Sigma X)(\Sigma Y)}{n\Sigma X^2 - (\Sigma X)^2}$$

and $a = \bar{Y} - b\bar{X}$,

or solve $\Sigma Y = na + b\Sigma X$
$\Sigma XY = a\Sigma X + b\Sigma X^2$

Exponential $\quad Y = ab^x$
Geometric $\quad Y = aX^b$

Coefficient of Correlation (r)

$$r = \frac{\text{Covariance (XY)}}{\sqrt{\text{VAR(X).VAR(Y)}}}$$

$$= \frac{n\Sigma XY - (\Sigma X)(\Sigma Y)}{\sqrt{\{n\Sigma X^2 - (\Sigma X)^2\}\{n\Sigma Y^2 - (\Sigma Y)^2\}}}$$

Exponential Smoothing

New Forecast = Old Forecast +
A(Old Actual Sales –
Old Forecast)

or

= A(Old Sales) + (1 – A). Old Forecast

Queueing Theory — Simple Queues

Average time spent in *system* (i.e. both queueing and in the service point)

$$\frac{1}{\mu - \lambda} = \frac{1}{1 - \rho}\left(\frac{1}{\mu}\right)$$

Average number in the *system* (both queueing and in the service point)

$$\frac{\lambda}{\mu - \lambda} = \frac{\rho}{1 - \rho}$$

Average time spent in the queue

$$\frac{\rho}{\mu - \lambda} = \frac{\lambda}{\mu(\mu - \lambda)} = \frac{1}{\mu}\left(\frac{\rho}{1 - \rho}\right)$$

Average numbers in the queue

$$\frac{\rho\lambda}{\mu - \lambda}$$

Quality Control

AQL = acceptable quality level

LTPD = lot (batch) tolerance proportion defective

α (alpha) = producer's risk

β (beta) = consumer's risk

OC = operating characteristic curve

Statistical process control

UCL = upper control limit
($\bar{x}$ + 3 Standard Errors)

LCL = lower control limit
($\bar{x}$ – 3 Standard Errors)

UWL = upper warning limit
($\bar{x}$ + 1·96 Standard Errors)

LWL = lower warning limit
($\bar{x}$ – 1·96 Standard Errors)

Inventory Control

EOQ basic model $\sqrt{\dfrac{2CoD}{Ch}}$

EBQ (gradual replenishment)

$$\sqrt{\frac{2CoD}{Ch(1 - \frac{D}{R})}}$$

1 MANAGEMENT OF OPERATIONS

INTRODUCTION & LEARNING OBJECTIVES

Syllabus area 7a. The nature and characteristics of operations management in production and service industries. (Ability required 1).

The relevance of the product life cycle. (Ability required 2).

An introduction to Value Analysis; pareto curves. (Ability required 2).

Production processes: types and implications; facility layout. (Ability required 1).

The management of capacity: factors affecting capacity; short, medium and long-term planning. (Ability required 2).

Special factors affecting the service industries. (Ability required 2).

When you have studied this chapter you should be able to do the following:

- Discuss the nature of operations management.
- Appreciate the relevance of the product life cycle.
- Distinguish between use value and esteem value and use this distinction in the context of value analysis.
- Analyse distributions by Lorenz curves and Pareto curves.
- Discuss strategies for facility layout and capacity management.

---

1 THE NATURE AND CHARACTERISTICS OF OPERATIONS MANAGEMENT

1.1 Introduction

Definition Operations management is concerned with the design and operation of sys. manufacture, transport, supply or service. (Wild)

1.2 The function of the operations manager

The operations manager is concerned with the use of physical resources and the flow of those resources for the basic functions of production, supply, transport and service. Many operations managers will be involved in more than one of those four basic functions. For example, production will be concerned with delivery of raw materials and the despatch of finished goods. A hospital will have transport, provide medical services and need a wide variety of supplies.

Inevitably, the role of an operations manager will be influenced by the structure of the operating system and the nature of the activity.

The student should have already noticed the reference to the word 'service'. The syllabus requires consideration of the special factors affecting operations management in service industries. Where relevant, service industries have been introduced in the text.

If the system creates output stocks as in manufacturing, this creates problems that are different from situations where there are no such stocks eg, a service.

The objectives of the entity will also influence the operation and the choice of strategies. There will also be problems inherent with the system. For example, in manufacturing, jobbing will create different problems from those in batch or process production. However, there are common problems; these are capacity management, scheduling and inventory management.

2   PROBLEMS COMMON TO ALL INDUSTRIES

2.1   Capacity management

This is concerned with the matching of resources to demand.

Excess capacity will mean that there will be low resource productivity, and equipment and/or staff could be lying idle. Later on, you may be required to measure this in the form of a capacity variance or a return on capital employed.

By contrast, a shortage of capacity could mean the use of overtime to meet delivery schedules, quality problems because of corners being cut to meet deadlines or delays on delivery. Such a situation would manifest itself to a management accountant through rate variances for overtime, possible overhead expense variances, quality and possible penalty costs.

2.2   Inventory management

This is the planning and control of physical stocks. This could be inventory levels for production, the holding of stocks in a retail business, or the holding of spares.

The existence of output stocks may facilitate the provision of a high and rapid response customer service. However, we will see that such a provision has a cost, both in terms of holding the required stocks, and in measuring resource stewardship. Non-availability could mean idle time in production, loss of customers in retailing, and equipment lying idle as a result of the non-availability of spares.

Inventories will tie up considerable amounts of capital, and hence require striking a balance between obtaining the benefits of flexibility, high customer service and an insulation against demand fluctuations, and on the other hand minimising the costs of such stocks.

2.3   Scheduling

In its widest sense, operations scheduling is the timing of occurrences within the system, arrivals and departures to and from the system and the movement of inventories around the system. Inventory will influence the scheduling process, as well as being part of it.

A familiar example is a servicing facility. A garage workshop will know what is coming in, and what work is likely to need doing. It will thus advise customers when to bring their vehicles in and how long the work will take. Large and diverse inventories may not be held, but will be brought in when required. By contrast, there are industries where there are wide fluctuations in demand and the need to respond quickly will require buffer stocks of both raw materials and finished goods to be held and a willingness to work overtime on the part of employees to provide for a rapid response.

2.4   Operations management structure

Six basic system structures identified by Wild are given below. In the following diagrams the symbols have the following meanings:

O   =   function ie, manufacture, supply, transport or service

V   =   Physical storage, inventory or queue

====> =   Physical input or output flow, of materials, machines, labour

C   =   Customer for system

Manufacturing sector

(a)   Manufacture or supply from existing stock of raw material, to stock of finished goods, to customer.

V =====> O =======> V =======> C

This is where a manufacturing company holds raw material and component stock, which is manufactured into finished goods which are then held in a finished goods store to enable the manufacturer to supply from stock. These would be standard products for which there is a fairly regular and uniform demand - cables, electrical fittings, packaging containers etc.

(b)   Manufacture or supply from JIT source, to stock, to customer

================> O =======> V =======> C

Here the manufacturer buys in as required when he receives an order. This is a jobbing type of business with a strong element of customer "pull" rather than production "push." A jobbing engineering plant, making unique products would fit into this category.

(c)   Manufacture or supply, from stock direct to customer

V =======> O ===============>C

This is similar to (a) above, except that there is no holding of buffer stocks of finished goods. Raw materials and components are held in anticipation of demand.   The manufacturing process is likely to be to order.

(d)   Manufacture or supply, from JIT source direct to customer

===================> O ============>C

If we concentrate on supply, then we can envisage the extractive industries. Coal, ore, quarry stone or even oil and gas comes straight from the source of supply and is shipped to the customer. The generation of electricity is similar. Coal, oil, gas, or uranium is fed in and the electricity transmitted into the grid and to the customer.

Transport and service systems

(e)   Transport or service from stock, and service continues to be supplied to customers.

V ========> O ============> C ===================>

Here we see the influence of customer "pull". There has to be an ongoing demand for the service. The customer requests the service and it is supplied from a stock or a fleet of vehicles. Scheduled activities or a normal train service would be examples of this.

(f)   Transport or service from source to customer.

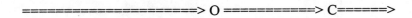

This suggests a specific demand, and in response to that demand, vehicles are laid on. A charter flight or an excursion train, subject to demand would fit into this category.

2.5   Inherent differences between manufacturing and the service sector

In manufacturing and supply (ie, retailing) the customers act directly upon output, "pulling" the system. By contrast, transport and services cannot respond unless the customer is already there, ie, "pushing" as well as ultimately pulling the system. A customer is a major physical resource for the system. Equally, a service company cannot build up "buffer" stocks in the same way as manufacturing. It can increase its capacity but it cannot store rides. In consequence it may force its customers to queue or tolerate overloading.

2.6   Influences on system structure

Four factors can be identified under this heading:-

(a)   The nature of the product or service and customer influence. Thus whether customers "push" (ie, queue) or "pull" (demand as in an emergency) will determine whether the structure is appropriate. Does the activity start by producing goods or offering a service, or can nothing happen until there is a customer?

(b)   If the structure is appropriate, is it feasible in terms of customer demand and predictability of demand? Unless the nature of the product/service required by future customers is certain, it will not be possible to operate in anticipation of demand and provide output stocks. The level of this knowledge will influence the level of stocks held and of rapidity of response.

These two points, based upon the influence of customers and the nature of demand are all beyond the direct control of operations managers and as such are external influences. There are, however, internal influences.

(c)   Desirability. This is influenced by objectives which are partly influenced by operations managers. A desirable structure may be one that gives priority to customers rather than resource productivity eg, a production line that can deliver to individual specification rather than a standard uniform product.

(d)   Change. A system may need to be changed over time. Competition may demand that the attitude to the customer changes which may alter the desirability. There may be a requirement to change capacity or inventories which will also change the system. A given system structure must thus be considered in the context of the current time period.

2.7   The scope of operations management

Operations management must ultimately satisfy the customer. This means satisfying a number of primary and secondary considerations. These are demonstrated in the table below.

Principal function	*Considerations of principal customer wants*	
	Primary	*Secondary*
Manufacture	Goods of a given, requested or acceptable specification.	Cost ie, purchase or obtaining cost. Timing: - from order to delivery.
Transport	Movement of a given, requested or acceptable specification.	Cost of movement. Timing: - duration or time to move; - time between request and commencement.
Supply	Goods of a given, requested or acceptable specification.	Costs and timing as in manufacture. Cost of treatment.
Service	Treatment of a given, requested or acceptable specification.	Timing: - duration of treatment; - wait or delay from time of request to commencement.

2.8   Conflicts and problems

(a)   The chief problem for operations management arises from the fact that operating systems must satisfy multiple objectives. Quality of customer service must be balanced with efficient use of resources. Failure to achieve this balance could lead to the entity failing in its operations, if not failing in the commercial sense. The diagram below illustrates the nature of the problem.

The customer service objective	*The area of potential conflict*	*The resource utilisation objective*
To provide agreed levels of customer service and satisfaction by providing goods or services with the right specification, at the right cost and at the right time.	To some extent and in some areas these objectives are in conflict. It is not usually possible to maximise performance on all aspects of these objectives.	To achieve adequate levels of resource utilisation or productivity ie, to achieve agreed levels of utilisation of materials, machines and labour.

Essentially, achieving the right balance is about finding the acceptable compromise. Achieving the specification is straightforward, but the market will put pressure on price and in turn, possibly put greater demands upon the specification. The right time will depend upon availability which could be a vital factor in the purchasing decision. These demands could be met with infinite levels of stock and variety of products. The cost, however, would be prohibitive. Thus specification has to be dictated by what can be achieved for an acceptable price and production levels based upon how long people are prepared to wait.

(b)   The scope of operations management identifies other potential problem areas. These are tabulated below.

You will notice that there are two basic classifications, the design and planning stage and the day-to-day operations and control.

Design/planning	Involvement in design/specification of the goods/service
	Design/specification of process/system
	Location of facilities
	Layout of facilities/resources and materials/handling
	Determination of capacity/capability/design of work or jobs
	Involvement in determination of remuneration system and work standards
Operation	Planning and scheduling of activities. Control and planning of inventories
	Control of quality
	Schedule and control of maintenance
	Replacement of facilities
	Involvement in performance measurement

2.9   Implications for the management accountant

The syllabus guidance notes emphasise that much of this is background information. To help the student relate to this material, we will illustrate from the table above how the management accountant might be affected by operations management tasks. Inevitably, some of this will relate to activities likely to be encountered further along in the course.

(a)   **Involvement in design/specification of product and process**

Later on, the student will encounter target costing. This is the production of a cost estimate from a competitive market price. The price the market will accept will dictate specification and hence development, production and after sales service and maintenance costs.

(b)   **Location of facilities**

This could be a capital budgeting decision. The input of the management accountant will be from the knowledge of the availability of grants, capital allowances, rent subsidies and local costs. The local reputation for hard work and productivity will also come into this decision frame.

(c)   **Control of quality**

Later on, the student will be introduced to quality costs. The control of quality will involve the costs of internal and external failure, appraisal costs and the costs (if needed) of prevention.

(d)   **Schedule and control of maintenance**

This could involve preparing the maintenance expenditure budget, monitoring and reporting costs of major overhaul against estimate and the evaluating the cost of a "crash" programme if a major repair is running late and the equipment will not be available with resultant loss of output or customer service.

(e)   **Replacement of facilities**

This might involve the accountant in a capital appraisal in order to assist the replacement decision making process.

(f)   **Involvement in performance measurement**

An essential part of the control process is monitoring performance against predetermined target, budget or standard. Conceptually, this can and must involve non-financial information, but the provision of cost against the activity-related data remains an important aspect of the control process and where the skills of the management accountant will be required.

3   THE RELEVANCE OF THE PRODUCT LIFE CYCLE

3.1   Introduction

The product life cycle is defined in the CIMA Terminology as "The pattern of demand for a product or service over time." (See figure below) The figure has also come from the Terminology. However, the additional comments in the figure have been taken from John Innes et al "Contemporary Cost Management" and R M S Wilson's "Strategic Management Accounting."

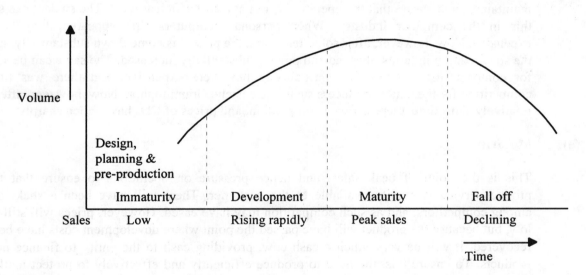

3.2   Detailed implications

(a)   **Planning and design**

Operations management will be involved in the design and specification of the good/service. The main input will be in determining the method of production or service delivery, which factory should manufacture the new product, or whether or not to manufacture "in house" or to franchise or sub-contract to another company.

Once these decisions have been made, the operations management will input into the choice of process depending upon production volume and related production time requirements. "Make or buy" decisions in regard to components, tools and moulds will also be taken at this time.

(b)   **Pre-production**

This is the time when the product is moving from final development to production. Test runs will be made to ensure that any potential problems in production are identified and eliminated. By this time, layout of facilities/resources and materials handling would be complete, but any "fine tuning" may be undertaken if required.

(c)   **Introduction and immaturity**

To reach this stage, a product/service must be available. This will require operations to have generated the appropriate outputs to meet the initial demand. If there are many outlets, such as with a motor car, then the production facility will be required to produce sufficient models so that every showroom has adequate numbers of the model for sale. For a large volume car, such as the Ford Mondeo or the Fiat Punto, this is an enormous task of production and distribution requiring until launch day, a high degree of secrecy.

(d)   **Development**

R M S Wilson divides this stage into growth and competitive turbulence. Sales will rise rapidly, requiring operations to produce and deliver the product/service. However, another influence will come into play. Where the product/service is innovative, the early period will be a time of few competitors. However, depending on ease of entry into the market, there will be a growing number of competitors. This will reduce the sales price and erode the profit level. Thus the emphasis upon operations will be to produce to a better specification in order to maintain market share, to ensure that quality specifications are met and maintained, and ensure that the operation is run at a cost efficient level. The student can see this in the computer industry. When personal computers first appeared, they were expensive. Now, however, after some ten years, the price has come down substantially, and the specification in terms of speed and power, substantially increased. The same can be said for compact discs. When first introduced, they were expensive, and there was little competition for the major producers such as Deutsche Grammophon. Now, however, after a relatively short time, there is fierce competition, and prices of CDs have fallen sharply.

(e)   **Maturity**

This is the point of peak sales, and hence pressure on operations to ensure that the product/service is readily available to the customer. There will have been a shake-out among competitors, and as such competition may have eased. However, prices will still be low, but because the product will have passed the point where development costs have been recovered, it will be very much a cash cow, providing cash to the entity to finance new products. To ensure this, the need to produce efficiently and effectively to protect market share and niche will remain.

Throughout the stages from introduction up to maturity, the student should have observed that there has been a switch in emphasis from operations management concerned with design and planning tasks such as location of facilities to operations and control tasks. As a product takes off in the market place, so the planning and scheduling of activities, inventory control, cost control and eventually machine maintenance will become pre-eminent.

(f)   **Decline**

Eventually, a product will pass maturity and go into decline. It will have been superseded by rival products with better more advanced technology, or it will no longer have the historic attraction to the customer. The impact for operations may be to scale down the level of activity, say reduce the number of lines and possibly the number of sites engaged in providing that product/service. If the product is to be replaced by a newer, more advanced model, then perhaps operations will make for a final run, build up enough stocks to satisfy demand for the remaining life span and concentrate activity on the introduction of the new product. At this stage, expenditures will be reduced quite substantially.

4 VALUE ANALYSIS

4.1 Introduction

Definition The CIMA Terminology defines value analysis as "a systematic inter-disciplinary examination of factors affecting the cost of a product or service, in order to devise means of achieving the specified purpose most economically at the required standard of quality and reliability." This wording in fact comes from BS 3138.

Wild (**Essentials of Production and Operations Management**) points out that value analysis is a term that is regarded as synonymous with value engineering. He differentiates between the two by stressing that value engineering is normally used in relation to new products, while value analysis refers to existing products. Peter Chalos (**Managing Costs in today's Manufacturing Environment**) quotes the Japanese use of value engineering in the target costing environment and there is an implication that the process continues right through the product life.

Considering the section on the product life cycle above, the student should expect to see the use of value analysis where the product/service is developing towards maturity.

4.2 Value analysis compared with cost reduction

Value analysis needs to be compared with conventional cost reduction. Wild emphasises that cost reduction techniques generally relate existing products with the emphasis upon manufacture at a lower cost by minimising the material used, changing design to facilitate easier, faster and cheaper manufacture and changing tolerances etc.

Value analysis is more comprehensive. It begins with an examination of the purposes or functions of the product and is concerned with establishing the means whereby these are achieved.

4.3 Principal objective

The principal objective is to increase profit in a competitive market place by means of a critical examination of areas of high cost with the purpose of eliminating those costs which do not add value to the product/service. These areas are material, production conversion cost, research and development and distribution. The student should pay particular attention to the absence of direct labour from this list. Direct labour in most manufacturing environments is down to less than 15% of the total cost and in many cases, is below 10%.

4.4 Types of value

Two types of value can be identified.

(a) **Use value**

This is related entirely to function, ie, the ability of a product to perform its specific purpose. A basic Ford Fiesta provides personal transport at a competitive price and is reasonably economic to run. The same may be said of most small volume cars, such as the Fiat Punto, the Volkswagen Polo and the Nissan Micra.

(b) **Esteem value**

This relates to status or regard associated with ownership. A Ford Fiesta will still provide a successful management accountant with reliable personal transportation. Indeed, it is even marketed as a small car for a successful person. However, such a person might want a car that says something about him/her. Thus he might move up to the top of the range Ford Scorpio. However, at that level and price range, cars associated with success and achievement become available, such as a Rover 800, Alfa-Romeo, BMW and even Mercedes-Benz.

Value is a function of both use and esteem. The result of value analysis is an improved value/cost relationship, giving a product which provides the necessary function with the essential qualities at a minimum cost.

4.5   The mechanics of value analysis

A team approach is the most appropriate and successful. This team should be drawn from:-

Design

Purchasing   (Maximum cost savings are often associated with the bought in goods and services.)

Marketing   (Important in the context of the esteem value of the product. Also marketing costs are now often 30% of the sales price.)

Production

Maintenance   (Could make the product more user friendly.)

Accounts

Such an approach is essential since value can be determined at any or all the stages between initial conception, through production to final delivery and after sales care. This also means that everybody gets together to talk about what is being done. Not to do this, argues Tom Peters, (**Liberation Management**) alienates the essential creative workers and induces misunderstandings and dysfunctional competitiveness. The following steps are recommended.

Step 1   Determine the function of the product

Step 2   Develop alternative designs

The relative importance placed by the customer upon the following will determine design or redesign objectives.

(a) Function
(b) Appearance
(c) Esteem associated with possession
(d) Intrinsic cost of materials and/or labour
(e) Replacement, exchange or disposal value

Step 3   Ascertain the costs

Step 4   Evaluate the alternatives

For existing products, the following questions will help to identify areas of potential value improvements:

(a) Which areas appear to offer the largest savings?

(b) What percentage of total cost is associated with bought out items?

(c)   What percentage of total cost is associated with labour?

A consideration of labour cost may be relevant here.   With the low content of traditional direct labour, scope for savings is limited.   However, by identifying "people cost" the value analysis exercise embraces indirect hourly paid workers such as store-keepers, conversion indirect salaried staff and the whole gamut of non-conversion salaried staff, many of whom add little value to the product or service.

(d)   What percentage of total cost is associated with materials?

Often the maximum cost saving associated with existing products relates to bought-in parts, materials and services.   The value of such purchased parts and materials can be investigated with a view to material or design changes by asking the following questions:

- How does it contribute to the value of the product?

- How much does it contribute to the total cost of the product?

- Are all its features and its specification necessary?

- Is it similar to any other part?

- Can a standard part be used?

- Will an alternative design provide the same function?

A simple example might be the fender on a car. Traditionally, these were made of steel, and coated with chrome to give that bright silver finish. No true all-American gas-guzzler was complete without such a fender to match its whitewall tyres. However, steel was heavy and expensive, so was chrome. Also, the cost of maintenance was high, and there was a tendency for such fenders to become very shabby if used as buffers.   Chrome also wore off causing the steel underneath to rust.

The idea to replace chrome on cheaper models with black plastic was tried. The effect did not look cheap, but rather sporting. The black contrasted well with the body colours and did not suffer from the drawbacks of chrome and steel. In these days of economy, it was cheaper and also lighter. It also rode collisions better, and was easier and cheaper to replace. Additionally, it did not detract from the value of the car.   The result was that most cars now have plastic fenders.

(c)   What marketing savings can be made?

Another example from marketing might be useful. A substantial cost of marketing cars is in the dealer network. In the United States, there are still too many of them, poorly managed, with high costs and dubious reputations. With the GM-Saturn range, GM have given dealers territories, made all the dealers look the same, insisted on the same standard of service, and encouraged many of the small family ("mom and pop") outfits to merge. By the year 2000, GM will have reduced its dealer network to 7,000 from the 14,000 in the 1970s. Those that remain will give a better service, enhance the image of the product and be cheaper to operate. (**Fortune** April 4 1994)

4.6   Implementing value analysis in practice

We have seen that there are four steps in the value analysis process (determine the function, develop alternative designs, ascertain costs and evaluate alternatives).

Developing alternative designs and techniques is a vital part of the process eg, alternative methods of achieving the required function as illustrated by the fender and dealership examples above. This is the creative aspect of value analysis, and may require "brainstorming" sessions. No reasonable or even ostensibly unreasonable alternative or suggestion should be rejected during this stage. The literature suggests that the session should be frenzied, chaotic, energetic, playful, intuitive and structured. It should be possible to come in at any time and at any level. The possibility of a back-to-back brainstormer, whereby employees meet either suppliers or customers should not be eliminated.

Among the objects to be considered at this stage might be:

(a)   eliminate parts or operations;

(b)   simplify parts or operations;

(c)   substitute alternative materials like plastic for chrome steel;

(d)   use standard parts or materials;

(e)   relax manufacturing tolerances; (Is the product being over-engineered for its place in the market?)

(f)   use standard manufacturing methods;

(g)   eliminate unnecessary design features;

(h)   change design to facilitate easier manufacture or maintenance; (Do we have to remove the dashboard to change a light bulb in the instrument panel?)

(i)   buy in rather than manufacture if it is cheaper;

(j)   use prefinished materials;

(k)   use prefabricated parts from cheaper specialists;

(l)   rationalise product ranges; (Or explore the possibility of putting different products on the same line. The Lexus is made on a standard Toyota production line.)

(m)   introduce low cost manufacturing processes;

(n)   rationalise the purchase of parts - single sourcing?

(o)   identify and eliminate material waste.

The above check list emphasises materials. However, what about procedures? Tom Peters illustrates how TIteflex, a US subsidiary of the British TI Group streamlined its procedures and facilitated faster order turnrounds.

Old system

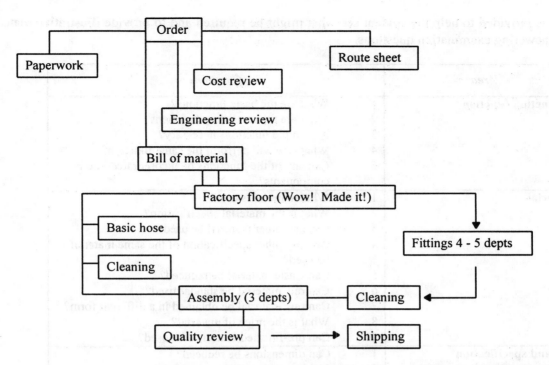

Under the old system, on the receipt of an order, paperwork was passed in turn through a further five departments. Some 50 pieces of paper were required just for one single order and this was before any manufacture instructions were given to the shop floor. When the order was eventually issued to the shop floor, it took six weeks to make. The student can readily imagine the cost of taking six weeks to process an order and the buffer inventories that such a slow process required.

The **new system** is as follows:-

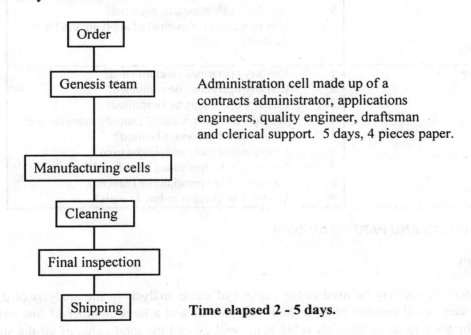

In contrast, the order is received by a cell of people who can handle all the required preparation work without a plethora of time consuming meetings and the passing of paper between separate departments. The result is delivery to the customer within two weeks.

Another example of changed procedures to improve productivity is Borg-Warner who removed their work-in-progress stores by re-coupling their production activities.

4.7   A value analysis checklist

This is provided to help the student see what might be required and to provide illustrative material for answering examination questions.

Area	Questions	
Production function	1	What are the basic functions?
	2	What are the secondary functions?
	3	Are all the functions necessary?
	4	What else will perform the same function?
	5	Can any of the functions be incorporated in other components?
Materials	1	What material is used?
	2	What is the material specification?
	3	Can any other material be used?
	4	Can any other specification of the same material be used?
	5	Can waste material be reduced?
	6	Can raw material be standardised?
	7	Can raw material be obtained in a different form?
	8	What is the price of material?
	9	Can pre-finished materials be used?
Size and specification	1	Can dimensions be reduced?
	2	Is the part oversize?
	3	If less expensive material is used, can size be increased?
	4	What tolerances are specified?
	5	Which tolerances are not critical?
	6	Can tolerances be increased?
	7	Can a standard part be used?
	8	What finish is required?
	9	Are the finish standards essential?
	10	Can an alternative method of applying the finish be used?
Manufacture	1	Can any operations be eliminated?
	2	Can any operations be combined?
	3	Can any operations be simplified?
	4	Would a different material simplify manufacture?
	5	Can standard processes be used?
	6	Can standard tools and jigs be used?
	7	Can assembly operations be reduced?
	8	Can assembly operations be reduced?
	9	Would it be cheaper to buy in parts?

5   LORENZ CURVES AND PARETO CURVES

5.1   Introduction

These two techniques may be used in the context of value analysis in the analysis of data where there are a very small number of large high value items and a large number of low value items. However, the total value of the high value items will exceed the total value of all the small value items by a considerable margin. Where such a situation occurs in practice, the identification of these groups enables special attention to be paid to the high value items, rather than waste time, effort and scarce resources on an indiscriminate allocation. Such areas that lend themselves to this type of analysis are inventory management, debtor control and sales records.

5.2   The Lorenz curve

This is a graphical method based upon a tabulation. The percentage of the cumulative frequencies at each class interval in a frequency distribution is correlated with the percentage of the cumulative total values of the items. The graphed line, called a Lorenz curve, is compared with the line of equal distribution to reveal the degree of inequality existing in the data.

5.3   Illustrative example

As the management accountant of Broadsword you are responsible for treasury management. You are thus concerned to make effective use of resources to chase up outstanding debtors. In order to see the distribution you wish to plot a Lorenz curve from the outstanding debtor balances.

Data:

Total value £	Number of debtors
<100	3,000
100 - <500	700
500 - <2,000	250
2,000 - <5,000	40
5,000 - <10,000	10
	4,000

5.4   Solution

The frequency distribution is tabulated in the form needed to provide the basic information for a Lorenz curve:-

Mid-points of values £	Frequency	Cumulative frequency Actual	%	Total value £k	Cumulative value £k	Total %
50	3,000	3,000	75	150	150	16.9
300	700	3,700	92.5	210	360	40.6
1,250	250	3,950	98.8	312.5	672.5	75.8
3,500	40	3,990	99.8	140	812.5	91.5
7,500	10	4,000	100.0	75	887.5	100.0

Drawing the curve, we get:-

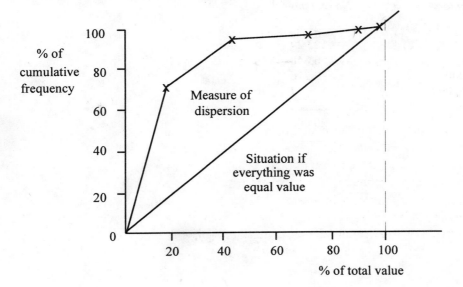

The graph clearly shows that 75% of the debtors account for only 17% of the outstanding items. _

As a general point, attention may be directed towards:-

(a)   Concentrating the effort on collecting the large items.

(b)   If there is an audit situation, the top 50 items could be 100% checked and then stratified sampling applied elsewhere.

(c)   In the case of inventory the storage resources and procedures applicable to classes of stock might be rationalised for the smaller value items especially if allied to the number of issues. JIT procedures would permit further rationalisation.

(d)   In an internal audit situation, the checks could be made more frequently on the large value classes under the continuous inventory control procedures.

5.5   Pareto curves

The student will have noticed in the Lorenz example above that 83% of the value of the debtors was contained in 25% of the invoices. This relationship is close to a common feature of debtor balances, wealth, income distribution and inventory: that of 80/20. This is the Pareto distribution named after an economist who first observed that the income of the wealthy few way exceeded that of the ubiquitous poor. In an organisational context, it may be observed that 80% of the value of all inventory will be tied up in only 20% of the volume. Put another way, 20% of all the high usage/high value items of inventory account for 80% of the costs.

Although high usage rate does not necessarily mean high stock levels, fast moving high usage items and expensive items are likely to incur greater storage costs than those that are slow-moving and inexpensive. As a result, it must be a primary objective of inventory control and value analysis to control effectively the fast moving/expensive inventory items in order to optimise resources and maximise potential savings.

5.6   Illustrative example

Boxer has analysed the value of inventory held in the store and it is desired to know whether or not it conforms to the Pareto curve.

The frequency distribution is:

Value of inventory £	No of items
<100	12,929
100 - <1,000	6,848
1,000 - <10,000	216
10,000 - <100,000	7
	20,000

5.7   **Solution**

Converting this data into a form more readily usable, we get:-

Midpoints of values £	Frequency	Cumulative frequency Actual	%	Total value £'000	Cumulative value £'000	Total %
50	12,929	12,929	64.6	646	646	10.8
550	6,848	19,777	98.9	3,766	4,412	73.7
5,500	216	19,993	99.9	1,188	5,600	93.6
55,000	7	20,000	100.0	385	5,985	100.0

A graph can now be sketched to ascertain whether the required 80/20 relationship appears to hold.

In practical terms, Pareto analysis can be used by companies to divide inventory into three distinct classes, A, B and C. A accounts for 80% of the value, B 13% and C 7%. Once this classification has been made, then the procedures appropriate for each category of inventory can be implemented. For group A, a comprehensive, regular and detailed 100% check and full stock control procedure is required. Less rigorous controls are required for B and a simple procedure for category C.

6   **PRODUCTION PROCESSES**

6.1   **Introduction**

The type of production process is determined primarily by the amount of repetition of the product. We will consider the traditional view first and then consider some of the developments as a result of technical progress in manufacturing.

6.2   **Job, unit or unique-product production**

This occurs when a customer requires a single product made to his specifications, eg, a ship or a suit. Demand can only be broadly forecasted and generally production schedules can be prepared only when the customer's order arrives. There is no production for stock and there are only limited stocks of materials kept. There must be a wider variety of machines and equipment available to do all types of work and the labour force must contain a wide variety of skills which may not be too easy to achieve.

As a result of her research, Joan Woodward widened the definition of a job or unit producer. She identified:-

-        the classic jobbing producer of single units to customer's orders;
-        production of technically complex units;
-        fabrication of large equipment in stages;

(This would equate to the traditional idea of contract work, such as shipbuilding or power station construction, where the job may be undertaken on site, invoiced as stages are completed and continue over more than one financial year.)

-        Production of small batches;
-        Production of components in large batches for subsequent incorporation into a variety of assemblies.

Woodward recognised that the latter categories overlapped into the traditional "batch" type of production.

The student should consider that job working could take the form of the assembly of standard products for individual customer needs. For example, Austin Reed provide a bespoke tailoring service. However, the service is offered within a range of cloths at a range of standard prices and designs. The suit is made to measure, but is only unique from the point that the customer may order slight detail differences, such as a longer jacket or revised layout of trouser pockets.

A garage also operates on a jobbing basis. Vehicles come in for routine services which require standard tools and skills. A stock of standard components such as lubricants, spark plugs and oil filters would be carried. However, any variation, such as the need to replace driving belts, worn tyres or a flat battery would be called off from suppliers as needed. As with the Austin Reed example, there is individual customer service for a standard range of products.

6.3   Batch production

This occurs where a quantity of products or components are made at the same time. There is repetition, but not continuous production. Production may be for stock, but if a batch is required to fulfil a special order the items are usually completed in one run. The choice and size of an economic batch is an important consideration and is discussed in more detail below.

Joan Woodward called this area large batch and mass production. In this category she identified:-

- production of components in large batches for incorporation into diverse assemblies;

This was the overlap area with small batch or jobbing.

- production of large batches, assembly line type;
- mass production;

- process production combined with the preparation of a product for sale by large batch or mass production methods.

This latter category overlapped with process production.

The famous management consultant, Peter Drucker, does not recognise "batch" production. Rather, he equates batch production as merely an extension of jobbing.

6.4   Mass production

Drucker defines this as "the assembly of varied products in large or small numbers out of uniform or standardised parts". The traditional or old style view stems from the famous Henry Ford quip that "the customer can have any colour car as long as it's black." Ford's view was that the essence of mass production was the manufacture of uniform products in a large quantity. There was to be no concession to diversity.

This however, is a complete misunderstanding.

The essence of mass production is to create a greater diversity of products based upon uniform parts. Drucker quotes the classic example of a Californian producer of cultivating machines. Each is unique. One example is a machine that performs all the operations required to successfully grow cucumbers. Yet each machine out of the range of over 700 different models is made up of entirely mass produced, uniform, standardised parts.

The essence of mass production is to produce what the customer wants from this range of standard parts.

Drucker quotes an interesting example from the electrical industry. At the start of the value analysis exercise, the company produced over 3,400 different models, each consisting of between 40 and 60 components. The first task was to eliminate the 1,200 products that were straight duplications. This still left 2,200 products requiring over 100,000 different components. After further product analysis, it was found that almost all the products fell into four categories, based upon the voltage they were supposed to carry. This enabled the number of components and component variations required to be substantially reduced. As a result today, there is the diversity of finished product, but each component is standardised with little variation on the basic theme.

Even at this early stage of study, the student should be able to see the magnitude of the cost savings in material that such an exercise can achieve.

6.5   Process production

Appleby uses the term "Flow production". Drucker emphasises that the chief characteristic of the process is that process and product become one. Traditionally, the oldest example of process production is the oil refinery. The end products that a refinery will obtain out of crude oil are determined by the processes it uses. It can produce only the oil distillates for which it is built and only in definite proportions. Any changes will require major plant modification. Other industries which fall into this category are chemicals, food processing and even glass production.

Joan Woodward identified the following in this group:-

-        process production combined with the preparation of a product for sale by large-batch or mass production methods

-        process of chemicals in batches

-        continuous flow production of liquids, gases and solid shapes.

The important point in Joan Woodward's analysis is the "continuous flow" and "solid shapes." Later on, the student will encounter "process costing" and its many misapprehensions. The Terminology definition is based upon Joan Woodward's view, with the emphasis upon "a sequence of continuous or repetitive operations or processes."

6.6   Variations

The demands of high technology and highly competitive markets have forced production lines to change from the stereotypes outlined above.

(a)   The use of either self-contained work groups or project teams who are responsible for the entire process. This is a break up of the mass production pattern into a number of small product lead groups. While this stems from the professional service industry, it has been incorporated into manufacturing.

(b)   The use of the manufacturing cell or cluster. This again is the breaking of the traditional layout into small specialist and accountable units. This has been achieved successfully at TIteflex, Asea Brown-Boveri and Johnsonville Foods.

One prime advantage is lower inventories and faster response when things go wrong. At Harley-Davidson, if the assembly cell finds that the custom handle-bars are not up to standard, the new organisation can quickly locate and rectify the problem. As a result, less scrap, less rectification and less inventory needs to be carried.

6.7   Organisational implications

The type of production will influence the type of organisation structure and level of complexity.

(a)   **Levels of authority**

Joan Woodward observed first that the number of levels of authority changed from unit to process production. In the unit environment, the median number of levels was three. In mass production it was four and in process production six. However, it is worth noting that while 75% of firms in unit and 52% in mass production were clustered around the median, it fell to 28% in process production. This statistic is reinforced by the fact that if a range between 5 and 7 is taken, the percentage increases to 72% and there is a pronounced skew towards larger numbers of levels of authority.

(b)   **Span of control of the first line supervision**

Here the median for the unit production firm was between 21 and 30 workers. For mass production, it was 41-50 and for process production it fell to 11-20. This should not be a surprise. Process production is highly capital intensive and frequently highly automated.

The ratio of managers and supervisors to total personnel also changed with the different types of production as the table below shows.

Ratio of management/supervision to total personnel

Firm size	400 - 500	850 - 1,000	3,000 - 4,600	(Numbers)
System of production				
Unit	1 : 22	1 : 35	1 : 26	
Mass	1 : 14	1 : 15	1 : 18	
Process	1 : 8	1 : 7	1 : 7	

(c)   **Impact on direct labour costs**

These decrease as production technology advances. Woodward observed a decline from 36% in unit production to 14% in process production. Advances in technology since have reduced the 36% to nearer 10%, with the range between 5 and 15%.

(d)   **Indirect people: traditional direct**

The ratio of indirect labour (of administrative and clerical staff) to traditional hourly paid has also changed. Advances in technology initially increased this ratio substantially. More recently, with delayering and sub-contracting, a reverse trend may be observed.

(e)   **Level of education**

The proportion of graduates (however defined) among supervisory staff increased also. Here Woodward gives a confusing definition. She heads her analysis "graduates", then switches to talking about professionally qualified people. In view of the time period (1950s), she was probably referring to the latter. Even so, a distinct pattern was observed. Unit-production employed qualified people in the R&D areas with the complexity of the product dictating the calibre of staff. By contrast, in the process industry, it was the process itself which governed the proportion of technically qualified staff.

(f)   **The span of control of the chief executive**

This widened considerably as the technology of the production advanced.

At the same time, greater flexibility of duties and responsibilities was more evident in the unit and process systems, and likewise, there was more written communication in the mass production system. Recent changes alluded to above will have increased the demands for flexible working and less bureaucratic communication. Specialisation of function was also most evident in the mass production system. This too will have changed somewhat with recent developments.

(g)   **Capital intensity**

Joan Woodward did not appear to cover capital investment in her famous survey. It is unlikely that she would have achieved a high correlation from the progression towards process production or from unit or unique production.

It will be self evident to the student that a process or continuous flow production environment such as an oil refinery, electricity generator, integrated steel mill or volume car production plant will be highly capital intensive. The demands of scale economies and the investment in the product mean that this is the only way. The electricity industry has to invest millions in production plant. High capital cost stations thus take the main load, with peak loads catered for by smaller stations that can be cut in or out quickly.

Mass or large batch production may vary in capital intensity. Newspaper and book printing is very much a large batch activity. Traditionally very labour intensive, demand now requires high-tech equipment. Short run publishers survive by being small and using very high levels of expensive equipment.

The unique producer, such as the local garage or bespoke tailor will not be very capital intensive, although the demands upon the former are changing this situation. Manufacturers are insisting that the local garage is capable of handling their vehicle, even if it is only a volume car like a Ford, Volkswagen or Fiat. However, the shipyard, or the contract constructor will be highly capital intensive, maintaining a large resource of plant and equipment.

7   **FACILITIES LAYOUT**

This comes under two headings: location and layout.

In addition, the syllabus guidance notes emphasise equipment, work people and raw materials, the traditional 3Ms: Machines, Men and Material.

7.1   **Location**

This will depend upon:-

(a)   **The availability of land**

Land of the right nature and price must be available. There must be provision for expansion. In this connection, there are various aid packages from local, national and European Community funds. Aid is usually dependent upon:

-        viability of the business entity and project,
-        contribution to UK output and innovation,
-        that the project could only go ahead with government support.

Regional enterprise grants may be available as well as Regional Selective Assistance. Loans may also be available from the European Community and ECSC loans if there is a possibility of employing redundant coal or steel workers. Additional incentives may be available for locating in Northern Ireland. The Japanese have located many of their European plants in UK special areas such as South Wales and Sunderland, while a Taiwanese textile manufacturer has located in Northern Ireland.

(b)   Availability of labour

Taking the "Men" aspect first, the availability of labour is a strong locational factor. This may be due to a pool of redundant workers from old industries such as the coal fields in the UK, Northern France and Belgium. It also may be that there is complementary labour available. The traditional locations for heavy industry had a pool of employable female labour, the wives of the heavy industry workers. The history of labour relations will also influence choice of location. Japanese choice has been influenced by the willingness to strike single union deals, while the unhappy history of labour relations in Dundee has caused the town to be rejected by would be investors (eg, Ford) and the closure of plants (Timex). In the United States, the siting of new car assembly plants in places such as Smyrna (Tennessee), away from the traditional areas of manufacture has been due to a policy to break the union stranglehold on the automobile industry.

(c)   Access to materials and markets

Traditionally, where heavy low value raw materials were used, there was an incentive to locate close to this resource. Thus the steel industry located near the coal fields or the ports (Port Talbot, Redcar and Dunkirk.). Now, however, much light manufacturing is footloose and needs to be close to labour and markets. The M4 corridor with its access to Heathrow for markets and a pool of labour is a popular choice.

7.2   Layout

There are two types of possible layout:

(a)   Product based layout where machines are laid out in accordance with sequences of operations to be carried out on the product. Traditionally this facilitated ease of moving material into and out of the stores. Now, with JIT systems, ease of frequent delivery from supplier and ready access to the line is crucial.

(b)   Process layout where machines are grouped in sections which depend upon the time of the operation performed. While this gives rise to congregation of specialist skills and possibly efficient working, it causes "decoupling". This gives rise to build ups of work in progress between machine groups and departments.

7.3   Some contemporary examples

Tom Peters (**Liberation Management** 1992) quotes a number of useful examples of efficient facilities layout.

(a)   Steelcase manufacture office equipment in Grand Rapids (Michigan). They have established a Corporate Development Centre to cut development time for new products. This building, which replaced three separate scattered sites, brings together designers, engineers, marketing and purchasing people. This functional diversity enables people from different disciplines to work together and see each other's viewpoints. To create spatial mobility, multiple work areas are used, individual workstations, common work areas and dedicated project rooms to enable experimentation.

(b)   The Coca-Cola/Schweppes Beverages plant at Wakefield, West Yorkshire is the largest of its kind in the world. It ships some 11,000 cans and bottles every hour. To facilitate teamwork, speed and efficiency the plant is designed so that all the 100 employees, including engineers and office workers are in sight of the shop floor. The plant is organised around cross-functional teams of five or six people. Workstations permit the placing of production workers and maintenance engineers side by side, while all the offices overlook the production or warehousing activity. With everybody close to the action, problems can be quickly corrected with the minimum of delay and cost.

(c)   Many forward thinking multinationals have closed their corporate and regional headquarters and dispersed whatever was needed into local centres of expertise as in CSC Europe, Business Area teams as in ABB and Practice Centers as at McKinsey. To create a more European and global culture, GM Europe has moved its slimmed down centre to Zurich, away from the parochial strait-jacket of Russelsheim.

(d)   Proximity to suppliers and markets to give flexible manufacturing is seen in Silicon Valley, California. Sun Microsystems buys in all its essential components from neighbouring companies, all on the leading edge of technology. It has not integrated its operations because products are unstable, product life cycles are too short and the technology is changing too fast. Rather, it concentrates its expertise and resources on co-ordinating the design of a final system, to advance a few critical technologies and to spread the costs and risk of new-product development through partnerships with suppliers such as Cypress Semiconductor and Texas Instruments.

7.4   The decoupling debate

The Ford plant at River Rouge (Michigan) in 1925 was a product layout plant. Ships and railcars delivered steady streams of iron ore, coal and limestone to blast furnaces which produced iron for castings for engine blocks and other parts. Everything was made in a continuous flow. Every department was co-ordinated into a continuous system of manufacture using conveyors. There was no warehouse or stores, material was delivered as required and used when it arrived. From raw material to despatch of completed vehicle took about 81 hours.

Coupled Processes River Rouge Plant 1925

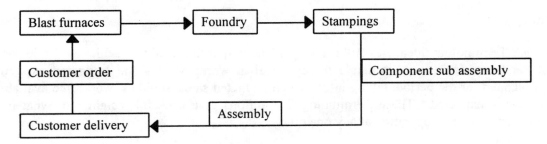

Such a system worked satisfactorily to produce one black car and one tractor. However, with the post-war demands for variety, the Americans decoupled all the processes and ran each process at a speed that produced the lowest unit costs. However, instead of producing for the customer, each unit produced vast amounts of work in progress, buffer stocks between each process. To achieve local scale economies, components were and still are shipped from central production areas to individual assembly plants.

The Japanese favour the original Ford system and the Toyota production lines emulate it. The emphasis is to manage processes not costs. Output is produced to satisfy demand based upon fast changeover. Thus the Toyota line can switch from a Carina to a Lexus and back again with minimum delay, and the two cars can even be built on the same line.

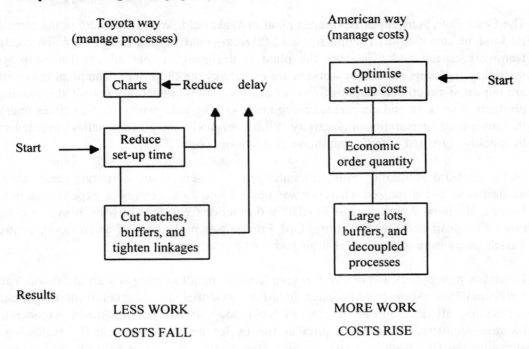

The student may be puzzled by the apparent high cost American operation. Cost-focused US manufacturers were geared by the 1960s to allow waste. (Henry Ford even regarded excess inventory and piles on the shopfloor as waste.) However, the parochial American (and British) view was that it did not matter. Every relevant (ie, domestic) competitor was doing the same thing, and excess costs could always be absorbed by higher production. Scale economies and volume of output were regarded as key imperatives of competition. By contrast, the Japanese were geared up to work in keeping with demand, to change over quickly, and to run balanced linked process with minimal interruption and rectification.

If the student requires another example, Borg Warner in the US have replaced their traditional batch production with a continuous flow from manufacturing cell to cell. This eliminates the piles of work-in-progress that hitherto littered the shopfloor and links production to customer demand.

8   CAPACITY MANAGEMENT

8.1   Definitions

The CIMA Terminology identifies **full** capacity - "the output that could be achieved if sales order, supplies and workforce were available for all installed workplaces" - and **budgeted capacity** - "output planned for the period, taking into account budgeted sales, supplies, workforce availability and efficiency expected." These Terminology definitions give a useful insight into what might affect the capacity of an operation at any one time.

Also from the Terminology, we can obtain a definition of **efficiency** - "a measure of output compared with input."

Another definition in this context is that of **productivity** - "a measure of efficient production."

8.2   Capacity management

This is one of the three inter-related problem areas of operations management. However, capacity management requires decisions about activity scheduling and inventory to be taken as a subsidiary activity.

The object of capacity management ie, the planning and control of system capacity is to match the level of operations with demand. Demand is uncertain, due either to uncertainties about the order book and/or about the availability of resources to meet the demand.

8.3 Short term implications

The short term aspect of capacity management is described by Wild as capacity control. This is defined as the "manipulation and deployment of given system resources to meet changes in demand levels." Wild sees this as activity scheduling and inventory management.

8.4 Capacity planning

This is a medium to long term problem. Essentially, it is necessary to determine an average level of demand/activity and plan for meeting variations above or below that average.

Example: A furniture remover will want to give a good service, and not keep customers waiting too long. However, demand will fluctuate. To avoid having too many idle drivers and vehicles around, capacity will be planned on an average basis, and when necessary, extra vehicles and drivers will be hired in. In this way, demand will be satisfied most of the time.

By contrast, the local firestation cannot keep its customers waiting, nor can it forecast demand accurately. It will maintain enough vehicles and manpower to deal with most situations, but in the event of a serious disaster, arrange for extra capacity from other depots or even other authorities.

8.5 Strategy for capacity management

(a) **Provide for efficient adjustment or variation of system capacity.**

Within certain limits, capacity can be changed. More resources can be provided or diverted as necessary.

Examples:

Resources	Capacity increase	Capacity decrease
All	Sub-contract some work Buy rather than make	Cancel sub-contracts Make rather than buy
Consumed material	Substitute readily available materials Increase supply schedules	Reduce supply schedules
Fixed machines	Defer maintenance Hire in	Subcontract or transfer out

(b) **Eliminate or reduce the need to make adjustments**

A temporary adjustment may be impossible. The process production systems already described fit into this category. Also, where highly specialised skills are required, it may be desirable to avoid the need for any changes in capacity.

In such a situation, the answer may be to avoid the adjustment situation. This could be achieved by having excess capacity and live with the problem of under used resources. This is ideal where customer satisfaction is of paramount importance. In a production environment, this can be achieved by holding "buffer" stocks of finished goods. An obvious example is the provision of disposable containers for ice cream and soft drinks. The demand for such products fluctuates wildly due to the vagaries of the British summer. As a result, the container manufacturers hold stocks, often at the expense of their customers in order to deliver quickly when the weather causes a dramatic change in demand.

An alternative for the service industry is to allow queuing. The Post Office has periods, such as at Christmas and on pension day when it is likely to be busy beyond its normal capacity. Being a monopoly, it can afford to let the customer queue. The transport industry can permit a certain amount of overcrowding. Rather than finance capacity just for it to remain idle, trains are overloaded when demand exceeds capacity.

8.6   Alternative strategies for different systems

This will be illustrated from four scenarios. In view of the syllabus stressing that the service sector must be included at every possible opportunity, two of the scenarios are deliberately taken from the service sector.

(a)   Manufacture or supply from stock, to stock and hence to customer. This is where raw materials and components are held, issued to manufacture and turned into finished goods which are then held before delivery to customer.

Such an organisation will aim for an efficient level of capacity and while it is feasible to maintain excess capacity, it is not normally necessary. Such a strategy might result in loss of customers, but it is regarded as unlikely. Nor is it considered likely that customers will have to wait. Both the loss of customer and the waiting are feasible and acceptable solutions, but can be countered by holding stock to cushion demand fluctuations.

(b)   Where a manufacturer delivers to the customer without holding finished goods. Fluctuations could be handled by increased capacity to avoid loss of customers. Since the product is not being delivered from a finished goods stock, the timing of delivery to the customer will be important in securing the order. Loss of orders or waiting for delivery may be acceptable. However, the risk of loss of future custom may mitigate against this strategy.

(c)   There is transporting or servicing from "stock". In such circumstances, it is normal to maintain excess capacity, even if it is old equipment only brought out to deal with peak loads. Where there is a monopoly, there is no risk of loss of customers, however, in a competitive world, there may be a loss of trade. This may be particularly the case where the customer cannot wait.

(d)   Transport or service from "stock" with customer "pull".

Here it could be possible to maintain excess capacity, but this is seen to be unnecessary. Rather, set an upper limit that accepts a possible loss of trade and queuing to reduce or smooth demand level fluctuations.

8.7   Capacity planning procedures

Capacity planning involves the determining of the capacity required in the system for meeting demand fluctuations.

(a)   **Determining capacity required**

The objective of this aspect of capacity planning is to determine what is required based upon demand. This will be especially important where it is necessary to hold inventories of resources or saleable products. When making a forecast, fluctuations will be expected but can be ignored. The average demand or the trend will usually suffice. If there is a deliberate strategy to increase capacity to cater for an expected demand then capacity will be increased. The following examples will illustrate the process.

Jobbing builder	Demand is measured on the basis of the order book, with capacity provided to meet demand. Some excess capacity may be provided, but the overall objective will be to maximise customer service with prompt and timely completion and an efficient use of consumable resources.
Fire service	Expected demand is forecast and since customers cannot queue, capacity is provided to meet maximum demand. In extreme cases there is a facility to adjust capacity by hiring in/out equipment. The primary objective will be high resource productivity.
Furniture removal	Again, demand can be predicted and capacity provided to meet average demand. Queuing of customers may result in a loss of trade. This can be dealt with by some capacity adjustment, hiring in when required. The objective will be to minimise customer queuing and the risk of loss of orders coupled to a high resource productivity.

In general, demand forecasting will depend upon the nature of the product or service. A highly capital intensive product such as a motor car will require a long period of capacity planning from introduction to final withdrawal. Lead times and availability of resources will also influence the capacity plan. As we have already seen, the position of the product in its life cycle will also influence the capacity required. Other possible influences might be the improvement of labour productivity due to the learning effect. This would reduce the amount of the direct labour resource required. By contrast, the reliability of the machinery might deteriorate over time, requiring extra resources. The economic operating level may also be relevant. This will identify the point where a given product can be produced at the lowest unit cost, but if this does not equate with customer demand, then it is pointless to produce for stock. This was the unhappy experience of the US automobile industry during the 1960s and contributed to its inability to meet Japanese competition.

A final point under this heading must be the impact of multi-channel systems, where more than one good or service is provided. In this case, demand for all outputs must be measured in common capacity related units. As budding management accountants, you should already be familiar with the "standard hour." Thus the demand for the products/service from such a system will be based upon the aggregation of the standard hours.

(b)   **Strategy for demand level fluctuations**

Two headings can be identified:

- adjustment of capacity
- avoidance of capacity adjustment

(i)   **Adjustment of capacity**

Make or buy/subcontract

This is an obvious option. However, it can cause higher unit costs due to subcontractor overheads and profit, as well as increased costs of transport, administration and inspection. Wild emphasises that such a solution is the least reliable, most expensive and least flexible at the time when it is most needed. The reason for this view is that when there is an upturn in demand it is frequently industry wide, and as a result, potential sub-contractors are likely to be busy.

In these days of world class manufacturing, it may be possible to obviate this problem by overseas sourcing. Differences in regional economies may permit sub-contracting in a part of the world where business is currently slack. However, this may compound the cost problems already alluded to above.

Workforce and hours changes

It may be possible to move the labour force around. Nowadays, with less risk of demarcation disputes this may be a feasible option. However, with less direct labour and limited scope for moving indirects into the operating area, this may not be an option. Wild is also doubtful that multi-skilled operatives are as efficient as the specialists.

A more practical option is the use of overtime to increase capacity. Overtime, shift premiums, higher supervision and support costs will increase the cost inputs. This may be further compounded by lower productivity, with more rectification and spoilt work. The longer hours may lead to more accidents, illness and greater absenteeism. However, this may be an alternative to recruiting and then having to lay-off.

A feasible alternative is to employ part-time workers who may work a "twilight shift" instead of overtime. Such employees would come in fresh and provide four to five hours extra daily per capita input. Where fluctuations can be predicted, such as a seasonal rush, sales seasons in retailing or the need for extending hours in financial services, many firms develop a pool of twilight or stand-by labour to be called in when needed.

Additional employees create a cost of recruitment and training, lessening if a pool exists. In Europe, full time employees also incur heavy employment costs, so the part time option has an added attraction.

If capacity has to be reduced, then lay-offs are an option, as is natural wastage, although this may not be an option when needed. In order to avoid loss of skills and a valuable workforce, short-time working or even tolerating some idle time may be a more satisfactory option. This will mean carrying a cost of underused capacity.

Deferred maintenance

In periods of high demand, resources may be stretched by postponing planned maintenance. This incurs the risk of high cost major breakdowns which could exacerbate the capacity problem, or the machinery not producing to specification. In periods of low demand, the maintenance could be brought forward, and idle direct workers employed to carry out the work.

Activity scheduling

The revision of activity schedules, possibly by doubling up orders can increase capacity. If a firm is making similar products for two customers, or has two orders, these could be done together and the excess material stored until required. The extra capacity is derived from reducing set up times.

(ii) Avoidance of capacity adjustment strategies

Refusing business

If an entity is working to full capacity, then it could always refuse orders. This could prove undesirable in the very long term.

Reducing service quality

If there is full capacity across an industry, or there is a monopoly situation, then lengthening queues or delivery times is an option. If a backlog develops, then when demand subsides, capacity utilisation will be maintained by clearing the backlog.

Adjusting inventory levels

Where there are fluctuations, such as in seasonal trade, then the periods of quiescence can be utilised to build up inventory, which then smooths out the peak periods. This is only an option where the product is suitable for a prolonged period of storage. The ability to meet demand at the peak period may result in improved customer confidence and market share. The trade off is the cost of holding inventory and the risks of deterioration.

Adjusting the price levels

Where prices are open to negotiation, then at times of peak demand, prices can be forced up. In the transport industry, the use of cheap fares utilises capacity in periods of low demand. These cheap fare options are not available when demand is likely to be high.

9 SELF TEST QUESTIONS

9.1 What customer wants must the operations management satisfy? (2.7)

9.2 Define 'value analysis'. (4.1)

9.3 Draw up a value analysis check list. (4.7)

9.4 What is a Pareto curve? (5.5)

9.5 Contrast batch, mass and process production. (6)

10 EXAMINATION TYPE QUESTION

10.1 The product life cycle

You are required to explain the product life-cycle concept and why it is important to a company planning for the development of new products. Illustrate your answer using examples with which you are familiar.

(25 marks)

11   ANSWER TO EXAMINATION TYPE QUESTION

11.1   The product life cycle

Many products pass through a number of stages in their history until they eventually decline in the face of outside competition or a change in consumer tastes. As illustrated below, it is very important to consider carefully when to start developing new products in order to achieve a steady rate of growth in both turnover and profits for the whole company.

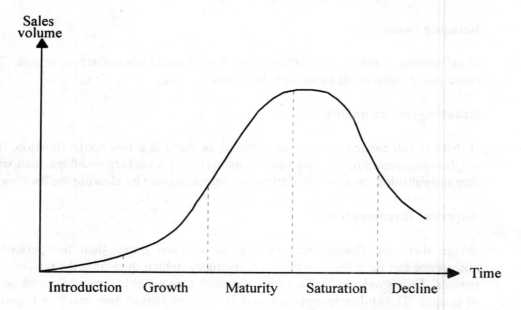

It should be noted that periods are only shown in the diagram as being of equal size for convenience. For example, product development may take three years but the product may be in decline for four years after market introduction. If this were the case, the product development of the second product would need to be started before market introduction of the first.

Some products have much longer life cycles than others - basic foodstuffs have much longer lives than more fashionable products such as clothes, although perhaps the days of the white loaf are numbered. The time required to develop a product also varies tremendously - forty years so far have been spent developing the fast breeder nuclear reactor and it is still not commercially viable. Conversely, it now takes about four years to develop a new car although the Mini took fifteen years.

It should also be realised that within an industry different products will have reached different stages which might not be typical of the industry as a whole. It is commonly believed that the electrical domestic appliance market has reached the maturity stage. However, although refrigerators are already in 90% of homes, microwave ovens have less than 15% ownership and it is consequently hardly surprising that the Japanese have decided to focus on this segment in order to enter the industry globally.

Marketing activities will change as a product passes through its life cycle. For example, strategic issues at the development stage of a grocery product would be concerned with such questions as 'What business are we in?' whilst marketing research would be concerned with new product testing. Marketing mix considerations would be at the planning stage although sales training would be taking place.

During the market introduction of the product the overall strategic decision would be whether to continue or to cancel. Marketing research would be directed at customer and consumer reactions which could lead to modifications to the product or to the pricing policy which could initially have been based on skimming or a penetration price. Promotion would be concentrating on the 'creation of demand' while the sales force would be dealing with unforeseen problems and gaining new distribution outlets.

In the growth stage the company can take risks with over-capacity and even with quality in order to establish a market position - profit margins will permit production inefficiencies. Strategic issues would include how to deal with private brands and marketing research would be focusing on brand share information. Price falls are likely and new variants would be introduced as a result of new product development. Promotion would be building up brand loyalty as the sales force battled for shelf space. Distribution would have to cope with the surge of demand as new outlets stocked up.

During maturity and saturation efficient use of plant and close attention to production costs become much more important. Strategy will be concerned with the introduction of new products and the relation of these to existing products. Marketing research will be looking for signs of market saturation and stagnation. Price will remain steady if no private brands exist; otherwise it will fall, particularly as large outlets pressure for special terms. 'Below the line' promotional expenditure will rise if private brands exist.

The decline stage will raise the question 'Do we wish to remain in business?' and how much will depend on the forecasts provided by marketing research. Prices would continue to fall and there would be greater promotional expenditure in an attempt to maintain sales.

It can therefore be seen that the product life cycle concept is not only a useful tool for analysing demand but is also valuable in managing the marketing mix during the introduction of a product and throughout its life cycle.

2 NETWORK ANALYSIS

INTRODUCTION & LEARNING OBJECTIVES

Syllabus area 7a. Production control: networks, critical path analysis; batch and mass-assembly control. (Ability required 2).

This chapter is concerned with the use of network analysis to illustrate the stages within a project and evaluate the effect of delays on the overall completion time.

When you have studied this chapter you should be able to do the following:

- Explain the use of networks.
- Draw a network.
- Distinguish between activities and events.
- Explain the use and meaning of floats.
- Analyse networks under conditions of uncertainty.
- Distinguish activity on line diagrams from activity on node diagrams.
- Explain how batch control may be achieved in practice.

---

1 CRITICAL PATH ANALYSIS (CPA)

1.1 Introduction

This chapter considers how management makes decisions about the progress of a project, once the decision to go ahead with it has been made.

1.2 Example

Hera Ltd has the opportunity to build a bridge to link the Isle of Wight with the mainland near Southampton. The decision process involved is in two parts:

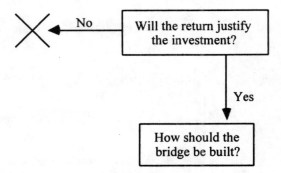

Decisions have to be made about the date of delivery of steel, how much cement is required, when should the fixers be brought into site, etc.

1.3   Definition

Definition   Critical path analysis – (CPA), or network analysis, may be defined as 'a quantitative technique for the control of projects. The events and activities making up the whole project are represented in the form of a graph.' (CIMA). It is a diagrammatic representation of the inter-relation over time of the activities involved in a project, and the subsequent analysis of those activities in terms of time, cost, and risk.

Note: that network analysis is essentially a planning and control technique.

Network analysis is also referred to as **critical path analysis**.

1.4   Problems in network analysis

There are five problems for the student to deal with:

(a)   Drawing the network.
(b)   Analysing the network in terms of time.
(c)   Analysing the network in terms of cost.
(d)   Analysing the network in terms of loading.
(e)   Analysing the network in terms of uncertainty.

The remainder of this chapter will be concerned with these problem areas. However, before commencing it is useful to look at some practical applications of network analysis.

1.5   Practical applications of network analysis

Network analysis is appropriate in any situation where there are series of activities in a complex project, some of which cannot be commenced until after others have been finished. Examples include:

(a)   construction projects;
(b)   scientific projects;
(c)   launching new products;
(d)   design and building of ships, aircraft, etc;
(e)   installing computer systems.

1.6   Drawing a network

Network analysis involves the construction of a diagram to show the interdependence of activities within a project. This diagram is the network of activities. It is the manager's equivalent of a conductor's orchestral score.

In the diagram, each activity is represented by an arrowed line and the start and finish of each activity by a circle (or node).

For example, part of the diagram in the operation of getting dressed might look like this.

The circles are **events** as distinguished from the **activities**. Putting on socks and putting on shoes are activities which take time. The states of having socks or shoes on, however, are events which take no time: events can be considered as being the start or finish of activities.

Students will note that the diagram above shows the two activities in their logical order, ie, shoes should not be put on before socks. Event 2 represents both the state of having socks on and the degree of completion of the overall project necessary before the activity of putting on shoes can commence.

1.7   Basic rules of networks

(a)   All events, except the first and last, must have at least one activity entering and at least one activity leaving them (this ensures that projects have just one initial and one terminal event).

(b)   Every activity must have an event at its start and finish: this allows each activity to have a unique identification.

(c)   Arrows are used to show the relationship between events: their lengths are no indication of the time taken for each activity.

(d)   Number the events from left to right, with arrows pointing from lower to higher numbers.

(e)   Dummy activities are used to enable the unique identification of each activity. Such activities take no time and use no resources – these are explained later.

(f)   No two activities must have the same start and finish events.

It is important to realise that in this context an event denotes inactivity – it is the state between activities.

1.8   A simple network

Consider the problem of making a cup of instant coffee (black with no sugar!)

–   assume that only one person is making the coffee in the quickest time.

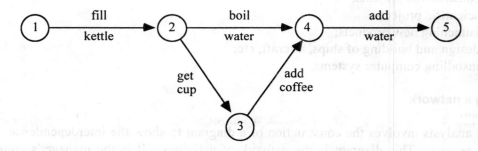

This is a very simple problem, but note the following points:

(a)   The pattern of activities flows from left to right.

(b)   Events are numbered from left to right so as to be able to uniquely identify any activity, eg, activity (3,4) is **add coffee**.

(c)   The network has one beginning and one ending event (1 and 5 respectively).

1.9   Dummy activities

Dummy activities are activities which take neither time nor resources. There are two types of dummy activity in networks:

(a)   Identity dummy activities.
(b)   Logic dummy activities.

1.10   Identity dummy activities

Identity dummy activities are used to enable each activity to be uniquely identified by the beginning and end events.

For example, consider the activity of making cement. This requires the purchase of cement and sand. Since these could be purchased simultaneously the relevant part of the network could be:

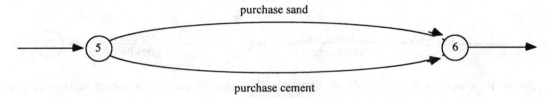

However, the result is that the notation (5,6) refers to either purchase sand or cement. In order to achieve a unique identification, a **dummy** activity is inserted (as a broken line), and the network becomes:

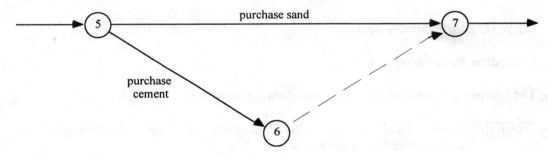

Now (5,6) is purchasing cement and (5,7) is purchasing sand.

The only purpose of the dummy activity (6,7) is to provide identification of the two activities.

1.11   Logic dummy activity

The logic dummy activity is illustrated by the following situation. Mr Smith walks from his office, leaves a package with the receptionist to be collected, then goes home. Mr Jones comes from his office, collects the package and also goes home.

Initially the network might be drawn as follows:

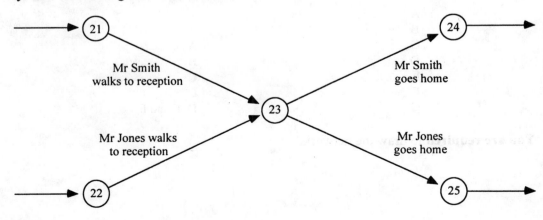

However, drawn this way, it appears that activity (23,24) (Mr Smith goes home) is dependent on activity (22,23) (Mr. Jones walking to reception). This does not accord with the facts as we know them, for Mr Smith does not need to wait for Mr Jones to come to reception before he can go home.

In order to tie in with the actual logic of the situation the network should be drawn:

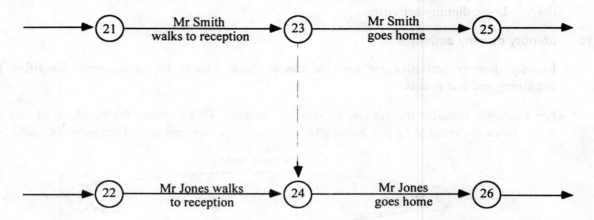

Note: it is assumed in the above example that this is part of a larger network; preceding and subsequent activities have been omitted for clarity.

This now accords with the actual logical relationship, ie, (24,26) depends both on (21,23) and (22,24) but activity (23,25) is only dependent on (21,23).

(23,24) is a logic dummy activity.

1.12   Procedure for drawing networks

The following procedure is useful when drawing networks:

Step 1   Draw a freehand rough network to follow the logic of the network. At this stage include dummies quite freely.

Step 2   Re-draw (still in freehand) eliminating the redundant dummies.

Step 3   Use the rough version from step 2 as a basis for a final network diagram.

1.13   Example

The following data is available regarding a project.

Activity	Dependent activity
A	–
B	A
C	A
D	B
E	C
F	C
G	D, E and F

You are required to draw the network.

1.14   Solution

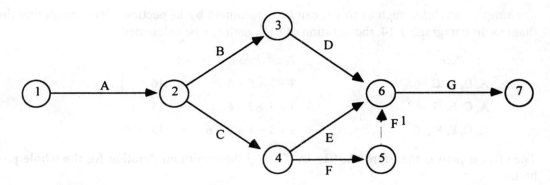

1.15   Activity

Draw the following network:

Activity	Dependent activity
A	–
B	–
C	A,B
D	C
E	A
F	D,E

1.16   Activity solution

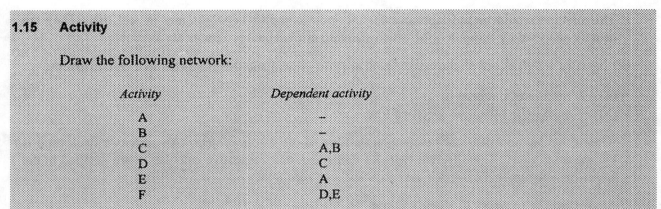

2   ANALYSING THE NETWORK

2.1   The critical path

The critical path is the path through the network with the longest total duration. It is critical in the sense that it determines how long the project will take and it is the most important piece of information to be obtained from an analysis of the network.

2.2   Example

The following additional data is available concerning the network in paragraph 1.13.

Activity	Normal duration (hours)
A	3
B	2
C	3
D	5
E	3
F	1
G	6

You are required to analyse the network in terms of time.

2.3 **Solution**

For simple networks, such as this it can be determined by inspection. By considering the network diagram in paragraph 1.14, the duration of each path can be calculated:

Path	Total duration (hours)		
A, B, D, G	$3 + 2 + 5 + 6$	=	16
A, C, E, G	$3 + 3 + 3 + 6$	=	15
A, C, F, F', G	$3 + 3 + 1 + 0 + 6$	=	13

The critical path is therefore A, B, D, G and the minimum duration for the whole project is 16 hours.

This method would be too laborious for the more complex networks met in real life. They are usually analysed by computer, for which standard critical path programs are available.

Logically activities not on the critical path are non-critical and therefore can, to a certain extent:

(a)   start late; and/or
(b)   take longer than the specified time

without having an effect on the completion time of the whole project. An activity's slack time is known as its float. The different types of floats and their respective calculation are detailed in the following section. Note, all critical activities have zero float.

2.4 **Analysing the network in terms of time**

This involves the following steps:

(a)   Establishing the **earliest event time** for each event.
(b)   Establishing the **latest event time** for each event.
(c)   Establishing the **floats** for each activity.
(d)   Establishing the **critical path and minimum project time**.

These are illustrated by the solution to the example.

2.5 **Solution**

Step 1   Working from left to right, calculate the earliest time by which each event can be achieved (ie, **all** activities leading to that event must be complete) – the earliest event time (EET) (shown in the boxes). Thus if event 2 can be reached no earlier than 3 hours from start, and B takes 2 hours, event 3 cannot be reached before $3 + 2 = 5$ hours.

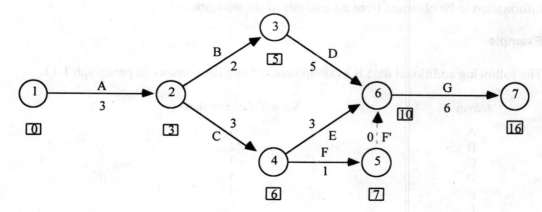

Note: that event 6 can be reached in three ways. To find the earliest event time for this event, take each route in turn and add the duration of the activity leading into the event to the earliest time of the previous event and take the **highest** result.

ie,   from event 3: $\boxed{5}$ + 5   =   10

         from event 4: $\boxed{6}$ + 3   =   9

         from event 5: $\boxed{7}$ + 0   =   7

The highest result is 10, which is therefore the earliest time of event 6.

Step 2   The EET of terminal event 7 is, in fact, the **minimum project time**. Further analysis will show that this is the time for the longest path through the network.

Step 3   Working back from right to left, enter the latest time by which each event must be achieved and thus the subsequent activities must begin, for the project still to be completed on time. This is the latest event time (LET).

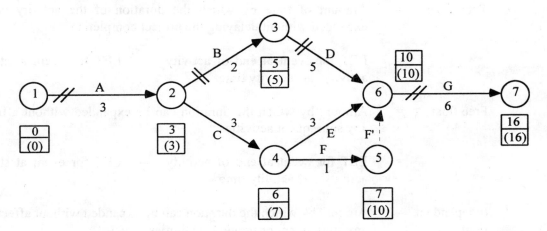

The LET for an event is the figure in brackets (other conventions are shown later).

For example, if event 7 is to be reached by 16 hours from the start and G takes 6 hours, then event 6 must be reached no later than 16 − 6 = 10 hours.

Note: that, going back, event 4 can be reached in 2 ways. To find the latest event time for event 4, subtract the durations of subsequent activities from the latest event times of the subsequent events and take the **lowest** result.

ie,   from event 6: $\boxed{(10)}$ − 3   =   7

         from event 5: $\boxed{(10)}$ − 1   =   9

The lowest result is 7 which is therefore the latest time of event 4.

Note: on the critical path earliest and latest event times are the same, hence 1-2-3-6-7.

Step 4 Calculate the **floats** on each activity.

There are three types of float:

(a) total float (sometimes called **interfering** float);
(b) free float;
(c) independent float.

Step 5 The critical path is the path through the network of those activities which have zero total float.

Note: there are several ways in which these floats are described. The above names are used throughout this text, as they are the most generally accepted. However, some writers use the term *free float* to describe the float which we define as 'independent float'. The student is therefore warned, when reading textbooks, to ensure the terminology is understood, and when writing examination answers, to define each float further by describing its calculation, as set out below.

Floats are calculated as follows:

Total float = Amount of time by which the duration of the activity can be expanded without delaying the project completion

= LET for event at end of activity – EET for event at start of activity – activity time

Free float = Amount by which the duration can be expanded without affecting any subsequent activities

= EET for event at end of activity – EET for event at start of activity – activity time

Independent = Amount by which the duration can be expanded without affecting
float any subsequent or previous activities

= EET for event at end of activity – LET for event at start of activity – activity time.

In symbol form:

$$\rightarrow \underset{\begin{array}{c}\boxed{E_i}\\\boxed{L_i}\end{array}}{\textcircled{i}} \xrightarrow{\quad D'n \quad} \underset{\begin{array}{c}\boxed{E_j}\\\boxed{L_j}\end{array}}{\textcircled{j}} \rightarrow$$

Total float = $L_j - E_i - D'n$

Free float = $E_j - E_i - D'n$

Independent float = $E_j - L_i - D'n$

where the symbols are as shown in the **diagram**.

Set the calculation out in tabular form as shown below.

Activity	Duration	Event at start		Event at end		Total float	Free float	Independent float
		Earliest time	Latest time	Earliest time	Latest time			
(i)	(ii)	(iii)	(iv)	(v)	(vi)	(vi)-(iii)-(ii)	(v)-(iii)-(ii)	(v)-(iv)-(ii)
A	3	0	0	3	3	0	0	0
B	2	3	3	5	5	0	0	0
C	3	3	3	6	7	1	0	0
D	5	5	5	10	10	0	0	0
E	3	6	7	10	10	1	1	0
F+F'	1	6	7	10	10	3	3	2
G	6	10	10	16	16	0	0	0

Note: that in the calculation of floats an identity dummy is best taken together with the activity it has helped to define.

The critical path is that chain of activities with zero total float, ie, A, B, D and G. In many projects there will be more than one critical path. Activities on critical paths are marked with a double line (as shown in step 3).

2.6   Explanation of floats

Activity C could be extended by 1 hour. To do so would place a constraint on E and F in that they would have to start 1 hour later. Hence the float is total but not free or independent.

Activity E could be extended by 1 hour. This would have no effect on the starting time of G, which is determined by when D finishes. Hence the float is free as well as total. It would, however, place a constraint on C in that C could not then be extended by 1 hour, hence it is not independent float.

Activities F + F' could be extended by 3 hours. Extending them by 2 hours would not place any constraint on the finishing of C or the starting of G. Hence there are 2 hours independent float.

It will be seen that independent float is a special case of free float, which, in turn, is a special case of total float.

2.7   Usage of floats

In addition to their use for identifying the critical path, floats are important for showing the effect on other activities if any activity takes longer than expected.

Perusal of the total float in the example indicates that in the case of activities (2,4), (4,5) and (4,6) the one day float is, in fact, the same day throughout. It may be used only once. Hence, if activity (2,4) is delayed by one day, no float is available for activity (4,5) and only 2 days for activity (4,6).

Usage of the total float of an activity therefore uses up the similar total floats on adjacent activities.

Usage of the free float of an activity does not affect subsequent floats, but does use up floats on preceding activities.

Usage of the independent float interferes with neither preceding nor subsequent activities.

2.8 Earliest and latest start and finish times

Event times relate to events, but start and finish times relate to activities. They can be calculated as follows:

Earliest start of an activity	=	Earliest time of the starting event
Earliest finish of an activity	=	Earliest start + duration of the activity
Latest finish of an activity	=	Latest time of end event
Latest start of an activity	=	Latest finish – duration of the activity

Taking activity F in the network in the example as an illustration:

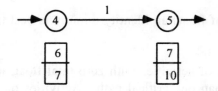

Earliest start	=	6
Earliest finish	=	$6 + 1 = 7$
Latest finish	=	10
Latest start	=	$10 - 1 = 9$

2.9 Shorthand for network analysis

It is often useful in answering questions on critical path analysis to use a convenient form of **shorthand**. One method is used above: EETs and LETs are contained in boxes beside the event nodes. A more tidy method is to use sub-divisions of the event node itself, eg:

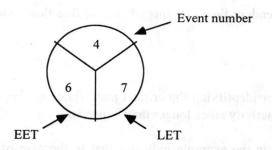

It is important to note that the student should not expect the examiner to be familiar with this, or indeed any one method of drawing networks. The student is therefore recommended to include a 'key' in his answer to assist the examiner in marking. (Drawing a 'T' in the circle rather than a 'Y' saves time.)

Sub-critical activities are activities which have a small float in relation to the length of the job as a whole: this means that a small change in their duration could easily render them critical.

2.10   Example

In the following network, what is the shortest time in which the project can be completed?

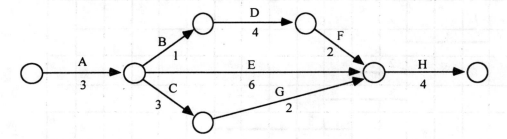

2.11   Example solution

Path	A B D F H:	3 + 1 +4 + 2 +4	=	14
	A E H:	3 + 6 + 4	=	13
	A C G H	3 + 3 + 2 + 4	=	12

Earliest completion is at time 14 determined by route A–B–D–F–H.

2.12   Analysing the network by loading

In practice, a project has to be carried out with a limited number of resource units, eg, men, or equipment. Thus, if certain activities require a certain number of men, it may be necessary to re-organise the project using the floats to **smooth the loading**.

2.13   Example

Using the same basic network from the example in 2.2, the following data on the number of men required for each activity is available.

Activity	No of men
A	4
B	2
C	3
D	3
E	2
F	2
G	5

You are required to analyse the network in terms of loading.

The stages in this solution following the construction of the network and the calculation of total floats, are:

Step 1   Draw a **Gantt chart** of the project.

Step 2   Add information on resources being used.

Step 3   Move activities within the float to minimise peak manpower requirements.

The Gantt chart for this problem is:

Time (hrs)	1	2	3	4	5	6	7	8	9	10	11	12	13	14	15	16
Activity																
A		4														
B				2												
C				3												
D							3									
E								2								
F							2									
G												5				
Men	4	4	4	5	5	6	7	5	5	3	5	5	5	5	5	5

Note: _____   denotes actual time required for an activity. The number on the line is the number of units of the resource required.

– – – –   indicates total floats on each activity.

The chart is constructed on the assumption that every activity starts as early as possible so that if it is to be moved, it can only be moved to the right. Thus A starts at the beginning of day 1 and finishes at the end of day 3. B cannot start until A has finished, so it must start at the beginning of day 4, etc.

The number of men is obtained by adding up the number of men required for each activity that is taking place at that time.

The Gantt chart highlights which activities are in progress at each time, on the assumption that each activity starts as early as possible.

Loading diagram

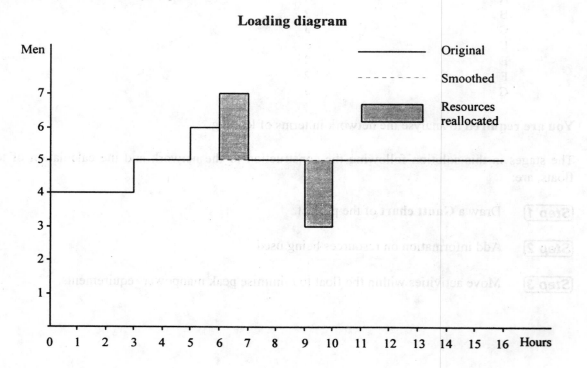

With activities starting as early as possible, 7 men are required on day 7. Activities with floats can be moved, within the limits of their floats, to try to reduce the maximum number required.

Smoothing is obtained very simply by moving resources used in activity F from day 7 to day 10. This can be achieved without extending the project, and as a result the peak manpower requirements is reduced from 7 to 6 men.

Note: take care when carrying out this type of exercise. The Gantt chart would suggest that activity C could be delayed by 1 hour without any other consequences. Remember that if C is delayed E and F are also delayed (see network). Although this has no effect on the project duration it would affect the loading diagram.

3   ANALYSING THE NETWORK UNDER UNCERTAINTY – PERT

3.1   Use of probability

The analysis so far carried out has been made on the assumption that times are known with certainty. In practice this will not be so, and the forecast of activity time will be the most likely outcome of a probability distribution.

The PERT technique has been developed to meet this problem (PERT = Project Evaluation and Review Technique). The forecaster is now required to give three time estimates relating to an activity within a network:

> the most likely time   L
>
> the most optimistic time   O
>
> the most pessimistic time   P

It is then assumed that the probability distribution of actual times follows a so-called Beta distribution. This is a theoretical probability distribution (just as the 'normal' and 'binomial' are and is very similar to the normal distribution) which has the parameters L, O and P. For this theoretical distribution it can be shown that:

> Mean activity time $= \dfrac{O + (4 \times L) + P}{6}$
>
> Standard deviation $= \dfrac{P - O}{6}$

3.2   Example

In a network, suppose the following data is available concerning one activity D.

> Most likely time, L   5
>
> Most optimistic time, O   4
>
> Most pessimistic time, P   7

Calculate the mean and variance assuming the distribution is a Beta distribution.

$$\text{Mean} \quad = \quad \frac{4 + (4 \times 5) + 7}{6} \quad \simeq \quad 5.16$$

$$\text{Standard deviation} \quad = \quad \frac{7 - 4}{6} \quad = \quad 0.5$$

The mean durations thus calculated should be used as activity durations for establishing the critical path, (for each activity use the mean NOT the most likely).

This data may then be used in further computations, and in simulating project outcomes. In particular, estimates of overall project duration can be made using:

Mean time for whole project   =   Sum of mean times of individual critical activities

Variance for whole project   =   Sum of variances for individual critical activities

Variance   =   (Standard deviation)^2

By assuming event times are normally distributed, it is possible to calculate the probability of any event being reached by a specified target date. If the probability is less than 0.4, it can be assumed that the target will not be achieved unless more resources are used. If the probability is greater than 0.6, the target date is so likely to be achieved that resources can be diverted to other uses if required.

3.3   Activity

Given the following data concerning Activity Q and assuming the distribution is a Beta distribution, calculate the mean and standard deviation of the activity time.

Most likely time   12 days
Most optimistic time   9 days
Most pessimistic time   16 days

3.4   Activity solution

$$\text{Mean} \quad = \quad \frac{9 + (4 \times 12) + 16}{6}$$

$$= \quad 12.17 \text{ days}$$

$$\text{Standard deviation} \quad = \quad \frac{16 - 9}{6}$$

$$= \quad 1.17 \text{ days}$$

4   ACTIVITY-ON-NODE DIAGRAMS

4.1   Network diagrams

The method that has been adopted of representing a network places the activities on the arrows, with activities separated from each other by events, represented by circles (or nodes). This is referred to as the **activity-on-arrow** or **activity-on-line** method.

An alternative method represents the activities by nodes (usually rectangular boxes in this method), the arrows then showing which activities are dependent on which other activities. This is called the **activity-on-node** method. This alternative method is shown as background information and students should not try too hard to study it in detail.

For example, consider the following simple network:

Activity	*Preceding activities*
A	–
B	A
C	A
D	B, C

Under the activity-on-line method, this would appear as:

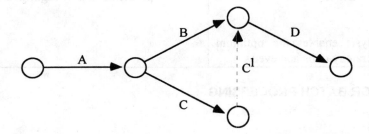

Using the activity-on-node method the network would be drawn as:

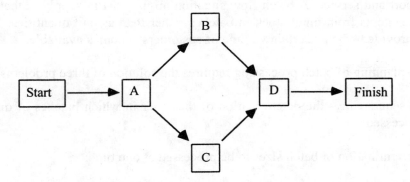

A network can be drawn using either method: analysis proceeds in the same way as for activity-on-line diagrams; earliest and latest event times are found; the critical path identified and so on.

It is important to realise that the two methods are merely different ways of achieving the same result. Although various advantages are claimed for each of the methods, there is little reason for preferring one method to the other and we have concentrated on the activity-on-line method.

4.2   Conclusions

Network analysis can be a powerful tool, but it is not without its drawbacks, which are summarised below:

Advantages	*Disadvantages*
(1) Visual aid for seeing inter-relationships.	(1) It is expensive, and may sometimes only show up what was obvious anyway.
(2) Provides a technique for planning and monitoring a project.	(2) Use is restricted to projects with a clearly defined beginning and end, and a logical relationship over time.
(3) Identifies critical and subcritical activities.	(3) Drawing a network does not solve problems; it only highlights them.
(4) Cost analysis enables the optimum cost and strategy to be achieved.	

5   SCHEDULING FOR BATCH PROCESSING

5.1   Introduction

Wild points out that batch processing can be applied to all four basic functions of production, supply, transport and service. A batch flow situation might exist in supply in that a function might seek to transfer items from input stock in batches rather than as unit quantities. Equally, transport may only be provided when a certain volume of customers becomes available.

In general the planning of batch processing requires the solution of three problems:

(a)   batch sequencing - the determination of the order in which batches of different items will be processed;

(b)   the determination of batch sizes to be processed at one time;

(c)   batch scheduling - the timing of the actual processing of the batches.

5.2   Batch sequencing

This will depend upon the cost of setting up which in turn may depend upon what has already been processed. If a similar product has just gone through, then it may be possible to save set up costs. Thus the first possibility is to identify those products that belong to a family of products and can be processed with the minimum amount of additional set-up costs or changes.

Thus if a sequence of these products can be identified, these should have priority, giving a straight clear production run. Items that do not fit into this family, or belong to another family group should then be set up separately.

Sequencing is important not only for the product. It is always possible that certain products or groups of products have the merit of being capable of processing on more than one machine. Such flexibility will mean that the product can be run on whatever suitable machine comes available.

5.3   Determination of batch sizes

This is a function of:-

(a)   stockholding;
(b)   processing;
(c)   set-up and preparation of machines and equipment.

This is studied later in this text in the chapter on stock control.

5.4   Batch scheduling

This can be done using a technique which was developed by the Goodyear Company in the 1940s and has been extensively used since, notably by the US military. It requires four stages:

(a)   the completion schedule;
(b)   the operation programme;
(c)   the programme progress chart;
(d)   analysis of progress.

The completion schedule is fairly self-explanatory. It is the time when the goods are required for delivery.

The operation programme is the lead time to completion. This dictates the time required to produce the goods for an on-time completion and if being assembled from components, the sequence of events. A simple product like a plastic container requires just one operation, so the programme is concerned with how long it will take to run the specific batch. If the product is more complicated, then there will be a sequence of operations possibly with a sub-sequence while components are being assembled and tested. A cable will require a single sequence, start with the copper or aluminium core and working through the various insulating covers. A guided weapon will have a sequence for the external casing in parallel with the assembly of components such as the guidance system, balance systems and the propulsion system.

Progress is monitored with the aid of a progress chart, measuring how many have been made compared with any target. Analysis of progress is achieved by working back from numbers delivered, to expected numbers to be delivered and whether or not targets or expectations will be achieved.

6   CHAPTER SUMMARY

This chapter has shown how network analysis may be used to illustrate and assist in the evaluation of a problem (often a project).

The drawing of the diagrams has been illustrated and the calculation of event times shown.

The issue of uncertainty has been tackled.

7   SELF TEST QUESTIONS

7.1   What is network analysis? (1.3)

7.2   State one practical application of network analysis. (1.5)

7.3   List the basic rules for drawing networks. (1.7)

7.4   What is an identity dummy activity? (1.10)

7.5   What is a logic dummy activity? (1.11)

7.6   What is the critical path? (2.1)

7.7   What is the meaning of a 'float' on an activity? (2.5)

7.8   What is the difference between a network chart and a Gantt chart? (2.13)

7.9   Explain the meaning of PERT. (3.1)

7.10   Explain the difference between activity-on-line and activity-on-node diagrams. (4.1)

8   EXAMINATION TYPE QUESTIONS

8.1   Installing a computer

The following information has been prepared as part of a plan to install a new mainframe computer:

Activity	Description	Preceding activities	Duration (days)	Number of men
A	Plan the installation	–	14	1
B	Prepare the site	A	20	3
C	Order hardware and await delivery	A	30	–
D	Install electrical services	B	6	2
E	Order air conditioning plant and await delivery	A	15	–
F	Install air conditioning	B, E	5	2
G	Install hardware	C, D, F	6	3

You are required

(a)   to construct a network and find the critical path and its duration;

(8 marks)

(b)   to represent the project by a suitable bar chart and construct a resource profile for the labour.

(12 marks)

(Total: 20 marks)

8.2   Engineering Instruments plc

Engineering Instruments plc has received an order for one of its products, for which it has quoted a delivery time of 30 days from receipt of order.   The project involves the processing of two components, X and Y, which are then assembled together and fitted into a purpose-built cabinet. The two unprocessed components are ordered specially from two independent suppliers, but the cabinet is made on the premises from raw materials already in stock. Construction of this cabinet commences as soon as the order is received from the customer.

Consider the following activities:

Activities	Description
A	Order and await delivery of X
B	Order and await delivery of Y
C	Process X
D	Process Y
E	Assemble X and Y
F	Make cabinet
G	Fit assembly in cabinet
H	Deliver to customer

The estimated duration parameters are as follows:

Activity	Duration (days) Most likely	Duration (days) Most optimistic	Duration (days) Most pessimistic
A	5	3	9
B	6	4	13
C	4	3	9
D	6	4	11
E	3	2	5
F	21	18	26
G	2	1	4
H	7	4	14

You are required

(a)   to construct a network for the project;

(b)   to calculate the probability of completing the project within the specified delivery time of 30 days.

(20 marks)

Tip: check that you have the correct network for (a) before starting (b). Part (b) requires an application of the normal distribution. If you are not happy with this technique, do not attempt this part of the question until you have studied the normal distribution in chapter 3.

9   ANSWERS TO EXAMINATION TYPE QUESTIONS

9.1   Installing a computer

(a)   **Network**

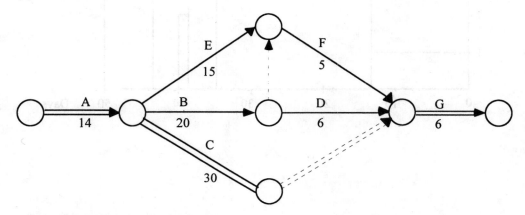

The numbers are the durations in days.

By inspection the critical path is A, C and G, indicated by a double line.

The duration is $14 + 30 + 6 = 50$ days

(b)   Bar chart

Days						10				20				30				40				50
Act.																						
A			1																			
B								3														
C								0														
D													2									
E								0														
F													2									
G																			3			
No. of men	1	1	1	1	1	1	1	3	3	3	3	3	3	3	3	3	4	4	4/2	0	0	3	3	3

Notes:

(1)   The dotted lines represent total float. 4 days total float has been shown for both B and D as calculation would suggest but if B is delayed, D must also be delayed.

(2)   The dummy activity after C is merely included to avoid making C a curve.

(3)   The number on each bar represents the amount of the resource required, ie, the number of men. These are added vertically each day to give the number of men required per day.

Resource profile. This is a histogram of the number of men required each day.

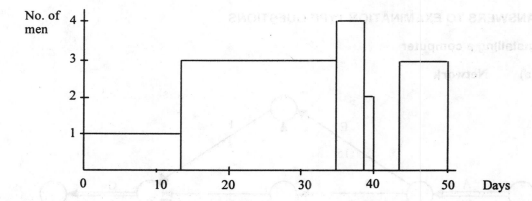

9.2   Engineering Instruments plc

Note: the giving of optimistic and pessimistic durations is a sure indication that the PERT approach is needed. Expected durations need to be calculated for inclusion on the network.

Arrow diagram

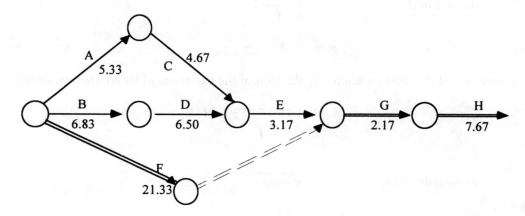

Calculation of expected durations

Activity	t_L	t_O	t_P	$\text{Exp } t = \dfrac{t_O + 4t_L + t_P}{6}$	
A	5	3	9	$\dfrac{(3+20+9)}{6}$	= 5.33
B	6	4	13	$\dfrac{(4+24+13)}{6}$	= 6.83
C	4	3	9	$\dfrac{(3+16+9)}{6}$	= 4.67
D	6	4	11	$\dfrac{(4+24+11)}{6}$	= 6.50
E	3	2	5	$\dfrac{(2+12+5)}{6}$	= 3.17
F	21	18	26	$\dfrac{(18+84+26)}{6}$	= 21.33
G	2	1	4	$\dfrac{(1+8+4)}{6}$	= 2.17
H	7	4	14	$\dfrac{(4+28+14)}{6}$	= 7.67

By inspection, the critical path is F, G, H, giving a total expected duration

$$= \quad 21.33 + 2.17 + 7.67$$

$$= \quad 31.17 \text{ days}$$

The variance of the total duration is the sum of the variances of the critical activities.

$$\text{Variance of F} \quad = \quad \left(\frac{t_p - t_o}{6}\right)^2$$

$$= \quad \left(\frac{26 - 18}{6}\right)^2$$

$$= \quad 1.78$$

$$\text{Variance of G} = \left(\frac{4-1}{6}\right)^2$$

$$= 0.25$$

$$\text{Variance of H} = \left(\frac{14-4}{6}\right)^2$$

$$= 2.78$$

The variance of the total duration = the sum of the variances of its component durations

$$= 1.78 + 0.25 + 2.78$$

$$= 4.81$$

$$\text{Standard deviation} = \sqrt{\text{Variance}}$$

$$= \sqrt{4.81}$$

$$= 2.19 \text{ days}$$

It is assumed that the total duration is normally distributed with a mean of 31.17 days and standard deviation of 2.19 days. Hence the probability of the duration not exceeding 30 days can be found as the shaded area in the diagram below:

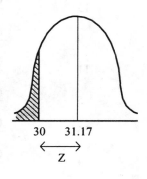

$$Z = \frac{30-31.17}{2.19}$$

$$= -0.53$$

Tabulated area from 30 to 31.17 = 0.2019

∴ Shaded area = 0.5 − 0.2019

= 0.2981 (≈ 0.3)

Hence the probability of the target date being achieved is 0.3.

3 PROBABILITY DISTRIBUTIONS

INTRODUCTION & LEARNING OBJECTIVES

Syllabus area.   There is no specific syllabus reference to this topic. However, the topics in syllabus area 7a on sampling, standard errors and confidence intervals that are covered in the next chapter, and also the topics in syllabus area 7b on process control including p-charts, x charts and R charts which are covered in chapter 5, can only be understood if you understand the material covered here.

Frequency or probability distributions can be either theoretical or observed. Theoretical frequency or probability distributions are mathematically defined from a theoretical situation. One distribution will be considered here: the normal distribution. The normal distribution is particularly important as sampling theory depends on it.

When you have studied this chapter you should be able to do the following:

- Recognise when to use the normal distribution.

- Apply the distribution to solve particular problems.

- Understand and be able to calculate confidently required outcomes by using the appropriate formulae.

---

1   NORMAL DISTRIBUTION

1.1   Introduction

When continuous data has been collected and a frequency distribution formed, it is often shown diagrammatically in a histogram, where the total frequency of the distribution is represented by the total area of the rectangles. When **comparing** histograms based on different sample sizes it is necessary to make the total area of each diagram the same or comparison is impossible. This is quite simply achieved by letting the area of each rectangle be equal to the **relative frequency** rather than the **absolute frequency** of the class.

If f_1 = frequency of the first class, then the relative frequency for the first class is $\dfrac{f_1}{n}$ or $\dfrac{f_1}{\sum f}$

where $n = \sum f$ is the total frequency. For the second class the relative frequency is $\dfrac{f_2}{n}$ etc.

A particular type of histogram that is commonly met is the bell-shaped diagram, ie, the highest column is in the centre of the histogram with decreasing columns spread symmetrically on either side of this peak. If the class intervals are **very** small, the histogram (figure 1) becomes a frequency curve (figure 2).

Figure 1

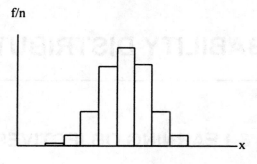

Figure 2

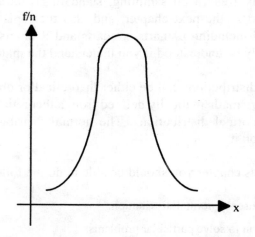

It is mathematically convenient to fix the total area under a histogram as one unit of area.

Since the area of the original histogram was one unit, the area under the curve will also be equal to unity. The **normal distribution curve** is a theoretical relative frequency curve which has a shape as in figure 2. Its actual shape can be defined mathematically, and therefore the area under any particular part of the curve can be computed, albeit with some difficulty.

1.2   Features of the normal curve

(a)   It is a mathematical curve, calculated from a complex equation, but which closely fits many naturally occurring distributions, such as heights of men.

(b)   It is symmetrical and bell-shaped.

(c)   Both tails of the distribution approach, but never meet, the x-axis. This is its chief difference from naturally occurring distributions. No man, for example, has an infinite height, (or a negative height).

(d)   The mean, median and mode lie together on the axis of symmetry of the curve.

(e)   The area under the curve is one unit of area and, by symmetry, the area to the left of the mean equals the area to the right of the mean which equals 0.5 units of the area.

1.3   Mathematical formula

Since the total area under the curve is one unit, the probability that a value of the variable lies between certain limits will be the corresponding proportion of the total area.

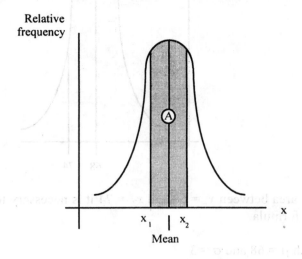

So the probability that x lies between x_1 and x_2 is the area A (shaded)

or $P(x_1 < x < x_2) = A$

This area can be found by using the normal distribution tables given at the front of the text and issued in the exam.

In order to use these tables it is necessary to know the mean (μ) and the standard deviation (σ) of the distribution being studied. Knowing these, the values (x_1 and x_2) of the variable can be standardised, ie, they can be expressed in terms of the number of standard deviations by which they differ from the mean. When the variable is transformed in this way, all normal distributions become identical, so that only the one set of tables is required.

The formula for calculating the standardised variables (usually given the letter z to distinguish them from the original data) is:

$$z = \frac{x - \mu}{\sigma}$$

1.4   Applications of the normal distribution

This distribution has many applications in life; eg, height, weight, intelligence of the population and other related matters have this type of distribution. However, one of its main uses is in sampling theory which will be studied in the next chapter.

In solving problems it is **always** advisable to **draw a sketch** of the distribution to ensure that the correct area is being calculated.

1.5   Example

A normal distribution has a mean of 68 and a standard deviation of 3. The area under the curve between the mean and 74 is calculated as follows:

First the curve is sketched and the required area shaded. It need not be to scale.

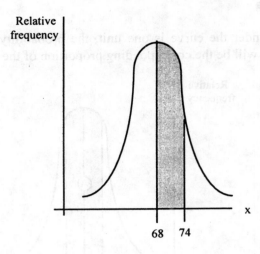

In order to find the area between $x_1 = 68$ and $x_2 = 74$ it is necessary to standardise the values of the variables using the formula.

For $x_1 = 68$ and with $\mu = 68$ and $\sigma = 3$

$$z_1 \;=\; \frac{68 - 68}{3} \;=\; 0$$

For $x_2 = 74$ and $\mu = 68$ and $\sigma = 3$

$$z_2 \;=\; \frac{74 - 68}{3} \;=\; 2$$

z_1 and z_2 simply measure the number of standard deviations between each value of the variable (ie, 68 and 74) and the mean, so 68 is zero standard deviations from the mean, since it is the mean, and 74 is two standard deviations above the mean (ie, $2 \times 3 = 6$ and $68 + 6 = 74$).

Standardising is a logical process that enables one set of standard normal distribution tables to be used. These tables give the area under the curve between the mean ($z = 0$) and the value calculated using the formula. (See Table 4 in the front of the text.)

From the table:

z_1 = 0   gives an area of 0, and
z_2 = 2   gives an area of 0.4772   (*Note* that the total area to the right of
                                                                    the mean is only 0.500)

∴   the probability that x lies between 68 and 74 is 0.4772 since that proportion of the area is enclosed between these limits. This is the shaded area in the sketch above.

∴ P $(68 < x < 74) = 0.4772$

It is not usual to standardise the mean as it will always result in a zero value and this is understood in the working.

1.6   Example

A normal distribution has a mean of 12, and a standard deviation of 3. The probability that a randomly chosen value of x lies between the values of 6 and 15 is calculated as follows:

Again, the curve is drawn and the appropriate area shaded.

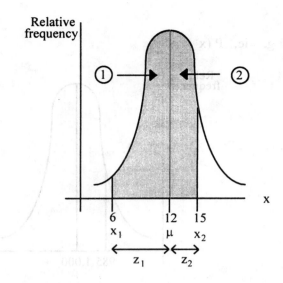

Since the area lies on both sides of the mean it is calculated in two steps.

Step 1   The area from 6 to the mean of 12 will be found; and

Step 2   the area from the mean of 12 to 15 will be found.

(a) $z_1 = \dfrac{6-12}{3} = \dfrac{-6}{3} = -2$ The minus sign merely indicates that 6 is 2 standard deviations below the mean. It can be ignored for the purposes of the calculation, since the distribution is symmetrical, and the area for $z = -2$ is therefore the same as for $z = +2$.

(b) $z_2 = \dfrac{15-12}{3} = \dfrac{3}{3} = 1$

From tables:

z_2	= 1	gives an area of	0.3413
z_1	= 2	gives an area of	0.4772
∴ total area			0.8185

∴   Probability that a randomly chosen value of x lies between the values of 6 and 15 is 0.8185

or $P(6 < x < 15) = 0.8185$

1.7   Example

Jam is packed in tins of nominal weight 1 kg (1,000 g). The actual weight of jam delivered to a tin by the filling machine is normally distributed about the set weight with a standard deviation of 12 g.

If the set, or average, filling of jam is 1 kg, calculate the proportion of tins containing:

(a)   less than 985 g;
(b)   more than 1,030 g;
(c)   between 985 g and 1,030 g.

1.8   Solution

(a)   Less than 985 g,   ie, $P(x < 985)$

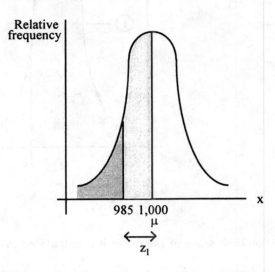

In order to calculate the proportion of tins containing less than 985 g it is necessary to find the area between 985 and 1,000 (lightly shaded) and subtract this from the area under half the curve, ie, 0.5.

$$\therefore z_1 = \frac{985 - 1,000}{12} = -1.25 \quad \text{(again the minus sign can be ignored)}$$

From the table $z_1 = 1.25$ gives an area of 0.3944, found in the row labelled 1.2 and the column headed 0.05.

$\therefore$ Area of darker shaded part of diagram $= 0.5 - 0.3944 = 0.1056$

So $P(x < 985) = 0.1056$

$\therefore$ Proportion of tins is 0.1056 (or 10.56%).

(b)   More than 1,030 g,   ie, $P(x > 1,030)$

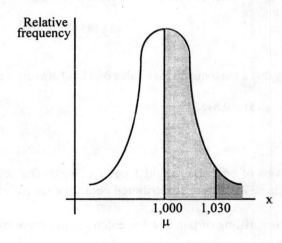

This is calculated in a similar way to part (a) ie, area under half the curve less area with light shading is the required area (shaded darkly).

$$z_2 = \frac{1,030 - 1,000}{12} = 2.5$$

From the table $z_2 = 2.5$ gives an area of 0.4938

∴   Area of dark shaded part of diagram = 0.5 − 0.4938

so P (x > 1,030) = 0.0062

∴   Proportion of tins is 0.0062 (or 0.62%).

(c)   Between 985 g and 1,030 g,   ie,   P (985 < x < 1,030)

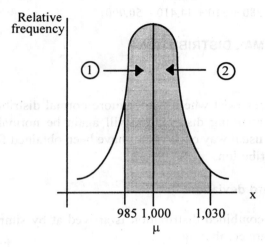

The area will again be calculated in two steps:

(i)   the area between the mean and 985;
(ii)   the area between the mean and 1,030.

These areas have already been calculated in (a) and (b).

Area 1 is 0.3944
Area 2 is 0.4938

So P (985 < x < 1,030) = 0.3944 + 0.4938 = 0.8882

∴   Proportion of tins is 0.8882   (or   88.82%).

1.9   Expected frequencies

These are derived in exactly the same way as in your earlier studies. The probabilities must be calculated first, and then the corresponding frequencies can be found.

1.10   Example

Considering the data of the previous example with jam tins, if 50,000 tins a week pass through the filling machine the number of tins expected to contain:

(a)   less than 985 g;
(b)   more than 1,030 g; and
(c)   between 985 g and 1,030 g,

is calculated as follows:

(a)   P (x < 985)   =   0.1056

∴   expected number of tins   =   50,000 × 0.1056

=   5,280

(b)   P (x > 1,030)   =   0.0062

       ∴   expected number of tins   =   50,000 × 0.0062

                                              =   310

(c)   P (985 < x < 1,030)   =   0.8882

       ∴   expected number of tins   =   50,000 × 0.8882

                                              =   44,410

(Check: 5,280 + 310 + 44,410 = 50,000)

2   COMBINED NORMAL DISTRIBUTIONS

2.1   Introduction

Many circumstances exist where two or more normal distributions are combined together. When this happens the resulting distribution will again be normal and therefore probabilities may be determined in the usual way once values have been obtained for the mean and standard deviation of the combined distribution.

2.2   Mean and standard deviation

The mean of the combined distribution is arrived at by simply adding together the means of the distributions that are combining.

In general terms:

$$\text{Mean } (A + B) = \text{Mean } A + \text{Mean } B$$

The same is not true of the standard deviation, although it is true for the variance of a distribution. Remember the variance of a distribution is the square of its standard deviation.

$$\text{Variance} = \sigma^2$$

$$\text{Variance } (A + B) = \text{Variance } A + \text{Variance } B$$

$$\therefore \quad \sigma(A + B) = \sqrt{\sigma_A^2 + \sigma_B^2}$$

2.3   Example

Over a period of time, a certain branch of Richquick Bank has analysed its daily note issue and found that demands for five pound, ten pound and twenty pound notes on any day of the week have approximately normal distributions with the following parameters:

Denominations	Number of notes	
	Mean	*Standard deviation*
£ 5	1,200	250
£10	600	100
£20	50	5

The demand for the three denominations are independent of one another.

What is the probability that the demand for cash exceeds £15,000 on any one day?

$$\text{Mean daily demand (£)} = 1,200 \times £5 + 600 \times £10 + 50 \times £20$$

$$= 6,000 + 6,000 + 1,000$$

$$= £13,000$$

$$\text{Standard deviation of demand} = \sqrt{(250 \times £5)^2 + (100 \times £10)^2 + (5 + £20)^2} \qquad \text{(£)}$$

$$= \sqrt{1,250^2 + 1,000^2 + 100^2} \qquad \text{(£)}$$

$$= \sqrt{2,572,500} \qquad \text{(£)}$$

$$= £1,603.90$$

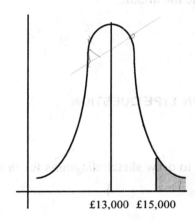

£13,000   £15,000

$$z = \frac{15,000 - 13,000}{1,603.90} = 1.2470 = 1.25$$

Since normal distribution tables are only produced for values of z to 2 decimal places, there is no point in calculating z more accurately (although σ should be found to several decimal places to avoid rounding). Since the normal distribution is not a triangle but a bell-shaped curve, there is little point in interpolating.

Area of tail (from tables)   =   0.3944

∴ Probability that demand is greater than £15,000 is 0.5 − 0.3944 = 0.1056.

3   CHAPTER SUMMARY

The normal distribution covered in this chapter is the most important probability distribution. In particular the next chapter shows how it is used in sampling theory.

The normal distribution applies to continuous variables, such as heights and weights, which can take any number as a value. This can be compared to discrete variables which can only take integer values 1, 2, 3 etc.

4   SELF TEST QUESTIONS

4.1   What are the features of the normal curve? (1.2)   *Bell shape*
Never touches axis
Area under curve = probability

4.2   What formula is used to calculate z in a normal distribution? (1.3)

$$Z = \frac{x - \mu}{\sigma}$$

5   EXAMINATION TYPE QUESTION

5.1   Workers' weekly wages

A group of workers has a weekly wage which is normally distributed with mean £120 and standard deviation £15.

Find the probability of a worker earning:

(a)   more than £110;
(b)   less than £85;
(c)   more than £150;
(d)   between £110 and £135;
(e)   between £125 and £135.

Find the limits which enclose the middle:

(f)   95%;
(g)   98%.

(20 marks)

6   ANSWER TO EXAMINATION TYPE QUESTION

6.1   Workers' weekly wages

Note: it is always advisable to draw sketch diagrams for this type of problem. They need not be to scale.

(a)

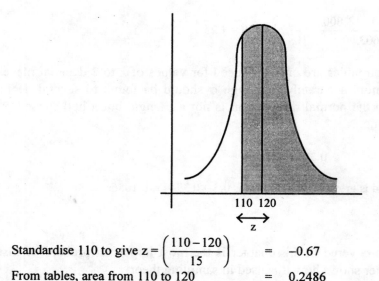

Standardise 110 to give $z = \left(\dfrac{110 - 120}{15} \right)$ = -0.67

From tables, area from 110 to 120   =   0.2486

(The negative value of z means that the area is to the left of the mean.)

$$P(> 110) \qquad = \quad 0.2486 + 0.5$$

$$= \quad 0.7486$$

(b)

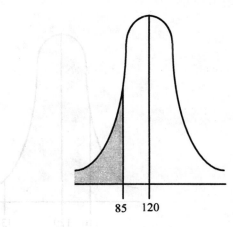

$$z = \frac{85 - 120}{15}$$

$$= -2.33$$

From tables, the area from 85 to 120 is 0.4901

$$P(< 85) = 0.5 - 0.4901$$

$$= 0.0099$$

(c)

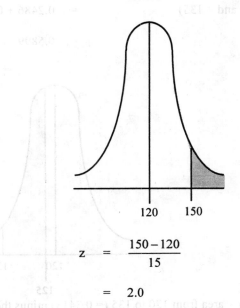

$$z = \frac{150 - 120}{15}$$

$$= 2.0$$

From tables, the area from 120 to 150 is 0.4772

$$P(> 150) = 0.5 - 0.4772$$

$$= 0.0228$$

(d)

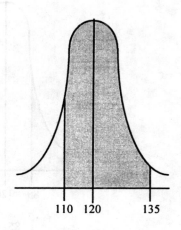

The area from 110 to 120 has already been found (0.2486)

For 135, $\quad z = \dfrac{135-120}{15}$

$$= 1.0$$

Area from 120 to 135 is 0.3413

Hence $\quad$ P(> 110 and < 135) $\quad = \quad 0.2486 + 0.3413$

$$= \quad 0.5899$$

(e)

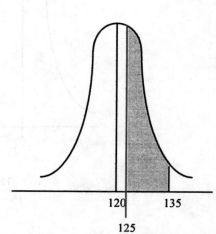

The required area = area from 120 to 135 (= 0.3413) minus the area from 120 to 125.

For 125, $\quad z = \dfrac{125-120}{15}$

$$= \quad 0.33$$

Area from 120 to 125 is 0.1293

Hence $\quad$ P(125 to 135) $\quad = \quad 0.3413 - 0.1293$

$$= \quad 0.212$$

(f)

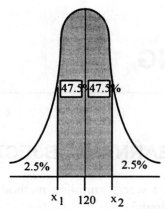

47.5% 47.5%

2.5%   2.5%

x_1 120 x_2

To find this, the tables must be used in the opposite way, ie, work outwards from the area found in the body of the table to find the value of z.

For an area of 0.475, z = 1.96

$$\frac{x_2 - 120}{15} = 1.96$$

$\therefore \quad x_2 = 120 + 1.96 \times 15 \quad = \quad 149.4$

By symmetry, the lower limit is given by $\dfrac{x_1 - 120}{15} = -1.96$

$\therefore \quad x_1 = 120 - 1.96 \times 15 \quad = \quad 90.6$

Hence the middle 95% lies between £90.6 and £149.4

(g)   For an area of 0.49, z = 2.33 (actual area = 0.4901)

$\therefore \quad \dfrac{x - 120}{15} = \pm 2.33$

$\quad x \quad = \quad £120 \pm £15 \times 2.33$

$\quad = \quad £(120 \pm 34.95)$

Hence the middle 98% lies between £85.05 and £154.95

4 SAMPLING

INTRODUCTION & LEARNING OBJECTIVES

Syllabus area 7a. The control of work: sampling methods, method study and work measurement. (Ability required 3).

It is often necessary to draw conclusions about a whole population by examining only a small sample taken from that population. In order to be able to do this successfully, it is very important that the sample is truly representative of the population.

The mean, median, standard deviation etc of the sample are known as **statistics**; the corresponding population values are called **parameters**.

From now on, it becomes important to distinguish carefully between sample data and population data. The usual method is to use Greek letters for the population parameters (μ = mean, σ = standard deviation) and English letters for the sample statistics ($\bar{x}$ for mean, s for standard deviation).

When you have studied this chapter you should be able to do the following:

- Understand the types of sampling methods.

- Estimate the mean and standard deviation of a population from sample data.

- Calculate a confidence interval for the estimate of a population mean.

- Determine the confidence interval for the estimate of a population percentage.

- Calculate the most appropriate sample size for producing these estimates.

- Understand how method study and work measurement are performed.

---

1 POPULATION AND SAMPLE

1.1 Definitions

Definition The term **population** is used to mean all the items under consideration in a particular enquiry. A **sample** is a group of items drawn from that population. The population may consist of items such as metal bars, invoices, packets of tea, etc; it need not be people.

Definition A **sampling frame** is a list of all the members of the population. It can be used for selecting the sample. For example, if the population is electors, the sampling frame is the electoral register.

The purpose of sampling is to gain as much information as possible about the population by observing only a small proportion of that population, ie, by observing the sample.

For example, in order to ascertain which television programmes are most popular, a sample of the total viewing public is interviewed and, based on their replies, the programmes can be listed in order of popularity with all viewers.

There are three main reasons why sampling is necessary:

(a)   The whole population may not be known.

(b)   Even if the population is known the process of testing every item can be extremely costly in time and money.

        For example, checking the weight of every packet of tea coming off a production line would be a lengthy process.

(c)   The items being tested may be completely destroyed in the process.

        In order to check the lifetime of an electric light bulb it is necessary to leave the bulb burning until it breaks and is of no further use.

The characteristics of a population can be ascertained by investigating only a sample of that population provided that the following two rules are observed:

(a)   The sample must be of a certain size. In general terms the larger the sample the more reliable will be the results.

(b)   The sample must be chosen in such a way that each member of the population has an equal chance of being selected. This is known as random sampling and it avoids bias in the results.

There are several methods of obtaining a sample and these are considered in turn.

1.2   Random sampling

A simple random sample is defined as a sample taken in such a way that every member of the population has an equal chance of being selected. To achieve this, every item in the population must be numbered in order. If a sample of, say 20, items is required then 20 numbers from a table of random numbers are taken and the corresponding items are extracted from the population to form the sample, (a table of random numbers, Table 13, is supplied in the exam), eg, in selecting a sample of invoices for an audit. Since the invoices are already numbered this method can be applied with the minimum of difficulty.

This method has obvious limitations when either the population is extremely large or, in fact, not known. The following methods are more applicable in these cases.

1.3   Systematic sampling

If the population is known to contain 50,000 items and a sample of size 500 is required, then 1 in every 100 items is selected. The first item is determined by choosing randomly a number between 1 and 100, eg, 67, then the second item will be the 167th, the third will be the 267th . . . up to the 49,967th item.

Strictly speaking, systematic sampling (also called quasi-random) is not truly random as only the first item is so selected. However, it gives a very close approximation to random sampling and it is very widely used, eg, in selecting a sample of bags of sugar coming off a conveyor belt.

There is danger of bias if the population has a repetitive structure. For example, if a street has five types of house arranged in the order, A B C D E A B C D E . . . etc, an interviewer visiting every fifth home would only visit one type of house.

1.4   Stratified sampling

If the population under consideration contains several well defined groups (called strata), eg, men and women, smokers and non-smokers, different sizes of metal bars, etc, then a random sample is taken from each group. This is done in such a way that the number in each sample is proportional to the size of that group in the population and is known as sampling with **probability proportional to size** (pps).

For example, in selecting a sample of people in order to ascertain their leisure habits, age could be an important factor. So if 20% of the population are over 60 years of age, 65% between 18 and 60 and 15% are under 18, then a sample of 200 people should contain 40 who are over 60 years old, 130 people between 18 and 60 and 30 under 18 years of age, ie, the subsample should have sizes in the ratio 20 : 65 : 15.

This method ensures that a representative cross-section of the strata in the population is obtained, which may not be the case with a simple random sample of the whole population.

The method is often used by auditors to choose a sample to confirm debtors' balances. In this case a greater proportion of larger balances will be selected.

1.5   Multi-stage sampling

If a nationwide survey is to be carried out, then this method is often applied.

Step 1   The country is divided into areas (counties) and a random sample of areas is taken.

Step 2   Each area chosen in Step 1 is then subdivided into towns and cities or boroughs and a random sample of these is taken.

Step 3   Each town or city chosen in Step 2 is further divided into roads and a random sample of roads is then taken.

Step 4   From each road chosen in Step 3 a random sample of houses is taken and the occupiers interviewed.

This method is used for example, in selecting a sample for a national opinion poll of the type carried out prior to a general election.

1.6   Cluster sampling

This method is similar to the previous one in that the country is split into areas and a random sample taken. Further sub-divisions can be made until the required number of small areas have been determined. Then every house in each area will be visited instead of just a random sample of houses. In many ways this is a simpler and less costly procedure as no time is wasted finding particular houses and the amount of travelling by interviewers is much reduced.

1.7   Quota sampling

With quota sampling the interviewer will be given a list comprising the different types of people to be questioned and the number or quota of each type, eg, 20 males, aged 20 - 30 years, manual workers. 15 females, 25 - 35, housewives (not working). 10 males, 55 - 60, professional men . . . etc. The interviewer can use any method to obtain such people until the various quotas are filled.

This is very similar to stratified sampling, but no attempt is made to select respondents by a proper random method, consequently the sample may be very biased.

1.8 Statistical enquiries

Many of the problems met in a business situation are capable of being treated statistically. The steps in a statistical enquiry are as follows:

Step 1 Define the problem. The population to be investigated must be clearly defined at this stage as well as the problem itself.

Step 2 Select the sample to be examined. The size of the sample and the method used to select the sample will have to be determined, and will depend on the degree of accuracy and budgeted cost of the enquiry.

Step 3 Draft the questionnaire. A pilot survey is conducted to test the questionnaire before it is finalised, as it cannot be amended once distributed.

Step 4 Collect the data. Data is collected in various ways where it has not already been collected for some other statistical purpose.

Step 5 Check the returned questionnaires. Responses to questionnaires are checked and sometimes coded before data tabulation can take place.

Step 6 Organise the data. Some data will need to be reorganised before it can be tabulated, ie, items counted or values totalled.

Step 7 Analyse and interpret the data. Information collected has to be presented in a form that is easy to understand, ie, tables, charts and graphs from which conclusions can be reached about the sample collected.

Step 8 Write the report. The conclusions arrived at in (7) above will form the basis of a report which will recommend a certain course of action.

1.9 Survey methods

Primary data can be collected in the following ways:

(a) **Postal questionnaire**

This allows respondents to remain anonymous if desired. The main disadvantage is that many people will not bother to return the questionnaire, resulting in a low response rate. Those who do respond may do so because they have a special interest in the subject, resulting in bias.

(b) **Personal interview**

Questions are asked by a team of interviewers. A set questionnaire is still used to ensure that all interviewers ask the same questions in the same way, to minimise interviewer bias. The response rate is usually higher than (a), but employment of trained interviewers is costly.

(c)   **Telephone interview**

Similar to personal interview, but only suitable where all members of the population have a telephone (eg, business surveys). It is cheap and produces results quickly.

(d)   **Observation**

Only suitable for obtaining data by counting (eg, number of cars passing a traffic census point) or measuring (eg, time taken to perform a task in work study).

1.10   Misleading statistics

Before leaving the topic of published statistics, it is necessary to mention a word of caution when dealing with statistical data.

All graphs, charts, tables, diagrams, etc must be carefully studied for units, scales, dates, etc.

All statements must be read and analysed for ambiguities and bias.

The following example may help to underline this last point.

1.11   Example

Badly worded statements can bring the subject of statistics into disrepute.

You are required to consider the following statements and:

(a)   explain briefly where they mislead or fail to make sense; and

(b)   re-word them in a more acceptable form.

(i)   'Nine out of ten people in this country would oppose a policy of state intervention in the Z industry'.

(ii)   'Unemployment up 10% . . .' as stated in newspaper A,

'Unemployment down 10% . . .' as stated in newspaper B, both on the same day.

(iii)   'There are 2.41 children per family in the country of Y'.

(iv)   '80% of car accidents occurred within three miles of the driver's home, therefore, longer journeys must be safer'.

1.12   Solution

(i)   (a)   The statement presumably gives the opinion of a **sample** of people, and the proportion of 'nine out of ten' must be an **average** figure. With the present wording, the statement implies, however, that **exactly** nine out of ten people in the population **as a whole** would oppose state intervention in the Z industry.

(b)   A better wording would be:

'In a sample of 2,500 people interviewed recently, about 90% said that they were opposed to state intervention in the Z industry'.

(ii)   (a)   Although the statements seem at first sight to be incompatible, this is not necessarily the case since no base dates are given. Also, it may be that one newspaper was quoting actual unemployment and the other was quoting seasonally adjusted values.

       (b)   The alternative wordings:

           'Unemployment up 10% since July 1988'; 'Unemployment down 10% since March 1993' renders the statements compatible.

(iii)   (a)   The figure of 2.41 is clearly an average: no family can have exactly 2.41 children. Further, the precise figure is not particularly helpful.

       (b)   An adequate wording would be:

           'On average, there are between two and three children per family in the country of Y'.

(iv)   (a)   Longer journeys might perhaps be safer, but such an inference cannot be drawn from the first part of the statement. If the majority of journeys are made within three miles of people's homes, then one would expect the majority of accidents to occur there.

       (b)   The false conclusion should be omitted so that the statement reads: 'The majority of car accidents occurred within three miles of the driver's home'.

2   THE THEORY OF SAMPLING (MEANS)

2.1   Unbiased estimates

Any sample statistic can be used to estimate the corresponding population parameter and this is then known as a **point estimate of the parameter**. The most commonly used statistics are the mean and standard deviation.

If one sample is randomly selected from a given population the mean $(\bar{x})$ of the sample will give the best (ie, unbiased) estimate of the population mean (μ).

When the standard deviation of a population is estimated from a sample rather than from measuring every member of the population, this is denoted by placing the symbol ^ over the symbol for standard deviation. Thus:

σ =   Exact population standard deviation, obtained by measuring every item in the population.

$\hat{\sigma}$ =   Population standard deviation estimated from a sample (called 'sigma hat').

s =   Sample standard deviation (ie, the standard deviation of the items in the sample).

It is a proven fact that the sample standard deviation tends to underestimate the population standard deviation. It is said to be a biased estimator. A better, unbiased, estimate is obtained by multiplying the sample standard deviation by:

$$\sqrt{\frac{n}{n-1}}$$

This is known as Bessel's correction. However, when $n \geq 30$, this correction factor makes little difference and its use is then optional:

$$\mu = \bar{x} \text{ for all values of } n$$

$$\hat{\sigma} = s \times \sqrt{\frac{n}{n-1}} \text{ for all values of } n$$

$$\simeq s \text{ for } n \geq 30$$

Note on formulae for calculating standard deviations

By definition, $s = \sqrt{\dfrac{\Sigma(x-\bar{x})^2}{n}}$ or $\sqrt{\dfrac{\Sigma x^2}{n}-\left(\dfrac{\Sigma x}{n}\right)^2}$

Applying Bessel's correction:

$$\hat{\sigma} = \sqrt{\frac{\Sigma(x-\bar{x})^2}{n}} \times \sqrt{\frac{n}{n-1}} \quad \text{or} \quad \sqrt{\frac{\Sigma x^2-\dfrac{(\Sigma x)^2}{n}}{n}} \times \sqrt{\frac{n}{n-1}}$$

$$= \sqrt{\frac{\Sigma(x-\bar{x})^2}{n-1}} \quad \text{or} \quad \sqrt{\frac{\Sigma x^2-\dfrac{(\Sigma x)^2}{n}}{n-1}}$$

Thus, when $n-1$ is used as the divisor for calculating the standard deviation, it is $\hat{\sigma}$ that is being calculated, not s .

2.2   Example

A random sample of 15 metal bars is taken from a day's production. The weights of the bars in kg are:

1,205, 1,205, 1,208, 1,215, 1,260, 1,270, 1,271, 1,272, 1,283, 1,286, 1,289, 1,290, 1,291, 1,292, 1,293.

Using this data, the best possible point estimates of the mean and standard deviation of the weights of *all* such bars are calculated as follows:

(a)   Estimate the mean of the population.

$$\bar{x} = \frac{\Sigma x}{n}$$

$$= \frac{1,205+1,205+1,208+...+1,293}{15} \text{ kg}$$

$$= \frac{18,930}{15} \text{ kg}$$

$$= 1,262 \text{ kg}$$

$\therefore \quad \bar{x} = 1,262$ kg. This is the mean of the sample and can be used as an estimate of the population mean.

ie, $\mu = 1,262$ kg. This is the estimate of the mean of the population based on the sample data

(b)   Estimate the standard deviation of the population

Step 1   Calculate the standard deviation of the sample.

$$x^2 \quad = \quad \begin{matrix} 1,452,025, & 1,452,025, & 1,459,264, & 1,476,225, & 1,587,600, \\ 1,612,900, & 1,615,441, & 1,617,984, & 1,646,089, & 1,653,796, \\ 1,661,521, & 1,664,100, & 1,666,681, & 1,669,264, & 1,671,849 \end{matrix}$$

$$\Sigma x^2 \quad = \quad 23,906,764$$

$$s \quad = \quad \sqrt{\frac{\Sigma x^2 - \frac{(\Sigma x)^2}{n}}{n}} \qquad = \qquad \sqrt{\frac{\Sigma x^2}{n} - \left(\frac{\Sigma x}{n}\right)^2}$$

$$= \quad \sqrt{\frac{23,906,764}{15} - \left(\frac{18,930}{15}\right)^2}$$

$$= \quad 33.77 \text{ kg}$$

Step 2   Estimate the standard deviation of the population using $\hat{\sigma} = s \times \sqrt{\dfrac{n}{n-1}}$

$$\hat{\sigma} \quad = \quad 33.77 \times \sqrt{\frac{15}{14}}$$

$$= \quad 34.96 \text{ kg}$$

or $$\hat{\sigma} \quad = \quad \sqrt{\frac{\Sigma x^2 - \frac{(\Sigma x)^2}{n}}{n-1}}$$

$$= \quad \sqrt{\frac{23,906,764 - \frac{(18,930)^2}{15}}{14}}$$

$$= \quad 34.96 \text{ kg as before}$$

$\therefore$ the unbiased estimate of the population standard deviation = 35 kg (2 sf.).

2.3   Further example

A further example illustrating when to use n and when to use $n - 1$ in the calculation of standard deviations:

A random sample of 5 wooden tables was selected from a large production run (the 'population'). The lengths of the 5 tables, in metres, were found to be:

1.25, 1.30, 1.32, 1.26, 1.21.

It is required to obtain

(a)   The mean length of the 5 tables selected (ie, the sample mean).

(b)   The standard deviation of length of the 5 tables selected (ie, the standard deviation of the sample).

(c)   The mean length of all tables in the production run (ie, the population mean).

(d)   The standard deviation of length of all tables in the production run (ie, the population standard deviation).

2.4   Solution

Note that as every table made in the large production run was not measured, it is not possible to calculate the exact mean and standard deviation of the population; they must be estimated from the sample of 5 selected, which is why the sample was taken.

Initial calculations:

$$\Sigma x \quad = \quad 1.25 + 1.30 + 1.32 + 1.26 + 1.21 = 6.34 \text{ metres}$$

$$\Sigma x^2 \quad = \quad (1.25)^2 + (1.30)^2 + (1.32)^2 + (1.26)^2 + (1.21)^2 = 8.0466 \text{ sq. metres}$$

(a)   The mean length of the five tables is $\bar{x}$, where

$$\bar{x} = \frac{\Sigma x}{n} = \frac{6.34}{5} = 1.27 \text{ metres (to 3 sig. figs.)}$$

This is the sample mean.

(b)   The standard deviation of length of the five tables is s. This is where n is used as the divisor, hence

$$s \quad = \quad \sqrt{\frac{\Sigma x^2}{n} - \left(\frac{\Sigma x}{n}\right)^2}$$

$$= \quad \sqrt{\frac{8.0466}{5} - \left(\frac{6.34}{5}\right)^2}$$

$$= \quad 0.0387 \text{ metres (3 s.f.)}$$

This is the sample standard deviation.

(c)   The estimated mean length of the whole production run is the same as the mean of the sample, hence

Estimated population mean = 1.27 metres.

(d)   The estimated standard deviation of length of table for the whole production run is $\hat{\sigma}$. This is where $n - 1$ is used as the divisor, hence

$$\hat{\sigma} \quad = \quad s\sqrt{\frac{n}{n-1}} = 0.0387 \times \sqrt{\frac{5}{4}}$$

$$= \quad 0.0433 \text{ metres (3 s.f.)}$$

This is the estimated population standard deviation.

In sampling theory, it is usually the estimated population standard deviation rather than the sample standard deviation that is required so if you are still in doubt as to which formula to use, use the one with $n - 1$ as the divisor, as this will more likely be the correct one.

2.5   Distribution of sample means

If two samples of the same size are drawn from a given population they will not be identical, even though each has been randomly selected. So if the mean of each sample is calculated, two different values will result, each of which could be used to estimate the population mean.

If a large number of samples of the same size (n) are drawn from a given population and the mean of each calculated, a distribution of values will be obtained. This is known as the **sampling distribution of the mean** or the **distribution of sample means.**

When large samples are taken (ie, $n \geq 30$) this distribution is found to be normally distributed irrespective of the form of the distribution of the parent population.

Furthermore, the mean of all the sample means is the population mean. So the distribution of sample means will be of the type:

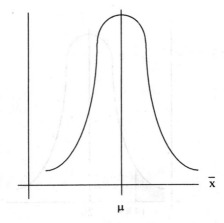

Any normal distribution is completely defined by its mean and standard deviation. To avoid confusion, the standard deviation of **this** sampling distribution is called the **standard error** and its value is $\dfrac{\sigma}{\sqrt{n}}$ (ie, the population standard deviation divided by the square root of the sample size).

The larger the sample size (n) the smaller will be the value of the standard error $\dfrac{\sigma}{\sqrt{n}}$ and the less dispersed will be the sample means about the population mean.

So the distribution of sample means is normal with mean μ and the standard deviation (or standard error) related to the population standard deviation as shown above and therefore the standardised variable becomes:

$$z = \frac{\bar{x} - \mu}{\frac{\sigma}{\sqrt{n}}}$$

The following points should be noted:

(a)   The population from which the samples are drawn need not itself be normally distributed. It is the sample means that are normally distributed about the population mean.

(b)   The standard error, $\dfrac{\sigma}{\sqrt{n}}$ of the means is **not** the sample standard deviation **nor** the population standard deviation; it is an entirely separate value that measures the spread (or dispersion) of the sample means. It happens to depend on σ and n which is not surprising, though this need not be proved at this level.

(c) n is the size of each sample and **not** the number of samples that are taken. In general, only one sample is available and all conclusions are based on the one set of data as will be seen shortly.

(d)   The main reason for taking samples is so that inferences can be made about the population under consideration. It is, therefore, very likely that σ will not be known and therefore s, the sample standard deviation, must be used to estimate σ.

(e)   It is assumed that the population is very large, so that any sample forms only a very small proportion of that population (less than 5%).

(f)   A further necessary assumption is that the sample size is ≥ 30.

2.6   Example

The mean length of a component is specified as 20cm with a standard deviation of 0.51cm. The probability that a sample of 100 rods will have a mean less than 19.85cm is calculated as follows:

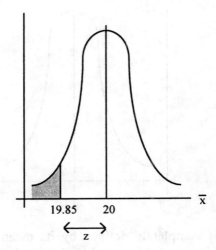

$\mu = 20$, $\sigma = 0.51$, $n = 100, \bar{x} = 19.85$

standard error $= \dfrac{\sigma}{\sqrt{n}} = \dfrac{0.51}{\sqrt{100}} = 0.051$ cm

Standardising: $z = \dfrac{19.85 - 20}{0.051}$

$= \dfrac{-0.15}{0.051}$

$= -2.94$ Area $= 0.5 - 0.4984$

$= 0.0016$

(ie, 19.85 is 2.94 standard errors below the population mean of 20.)

$\therefore P(\bar{x} < 19.85)$ $= P(z < -2.94)$ $= 0.0016$

$= 0.16\%$

2.7   Confidence intervals

Instead of giving just a point estimate of the population mean, it is possible to give a probable range of values in which the population mean lies and the probability that it does in fact lie within this range. This range of values is known as a **confidence interval**. The lower and upper limits of this interval are called **confidence limits, or precision limits**. The probability that the population value lies within this range is known as the **confidence level**.

In order to calculate the limits of a confidence interval, the following critical values must first be understood.

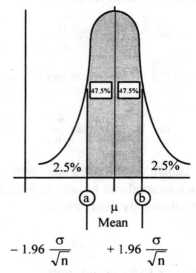

$$-1.96 \frac{\sigma}{\sqrt{n}} \qquad +1.96 \frac{\sigma}{\sqrt{n}}$$

95% of the area under any normal curve is contained within ± 1.96 standard deviations of the mean. This can be checked from normal curve tables. 1.96 standard deviations corresponds to 0.475 or 47.5 % of the area; twice this (remembering that the tables are one-sided) gives 95%.

So, for a sampling distribution, the range from $\mu - 1.96 \dfrac{\sigma}{\sqrt{n}}$ to $\mu + 1.96 \dfrac{\sigma}{\sqrt{n}}$

((a) to (b) above) contains 95% of all the sample means. Therefore, the probability that a sample mean lies within this range is 0.95 and the probability that a sample mean lies outside this range is 0.05. So ninety-five samples out of every 100 would yield a mean value in this range and only five samples in every 100 would yield a value outside this range.

Also:

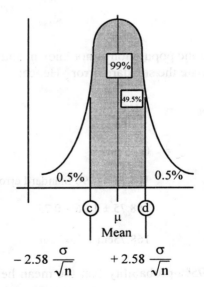

$$\mu - 2.58 \frac{\sigma}{\sqrt{n}} \qquad to \qquad \mu + 2.58 \frac{\sigma}{\sqrt{n}} \qquad ((c) \text{ to } (d) \text{ above})$$

99% of the area under any normal curve is contained within ± 2.58 standard deviations of the mean. So for a sampling distribution the range from

contains 99% of all sample means. Therefore, the probability that a sample mean lies within this range is 0.99 and the probability that it falls outside the range is 0.01. So out of every 100 samples ninety-nine would yield a value within the range and only one would give a value outside it.

It therefore follows that there is a 95% probability that the population mean lies within ± 1.96 standard errors of a sample mean, ie, in the range:

$$\bar{x} - 1.96 \frac{\sigma}{\sqrt{n}} \qquad \text{to} \qquad \bar{x} + 1.96 \frac{\sigma}{\sqrt{n}}$$

There is a 99% probability that the population mean lies within ± 2.58 standard errors of a sample mean, ie, in the range

$$\bar{x} - 2.58 \frac{\sigma}{\sqrt{n}} \qquad \text{to} \qquad \bar{x} + 2.58 \frac{\sigma}{\sqrt{n}}$$

These ranges of values are known as the 95% and 99% confidence intervals for the population mean. Any size of confidence interval can be set up, by using the appropriate number of standard errors, but these are two very commonly used values.

2.8   Summary

95% confidence limits $\qquad = \quad \bar{x} \pm 1.96$ standard errors

99% confidence limits $\qquad = \quad \bar{x} \pm 2.58$ standard errors

where the standard error $\qquad = \quad \dfrac{\sigma}{\sqrt{n}}$

If σ is not known, use $\hat{\sigma} \quad = \quad s\sqrt{\dfrac{n}{n-1}} \quad \cong s$ if n is large, say ≥ 30.

2.9   Example

The mean and standard deviation of the height of a random sample of 100 students are 168.75 cm and 7.5 cm, respectively. The 95% and 99% confidence intervals for the mean height of all students are calculated as follows.

2.10   Solution

As the standard deviation of the population is not known, and $n > 30$, the standard deviation of the sample can be used to calculate the standard error. Hence:

$$\text{Standard error} \quad = \quad \frac{7.5}{\sqrt{100}} \text{cm}$$

$$= \quad 0.75 \text{ cm}$$

The 95% confidence limits are $\qquad 168.75 \pm 1.96$ Standard errors

$$= \quad 168.75 \pm 1.96 \times 0.75$$

$$= \quad 168.75 \text{cm} \pm 1.47 \text{ cm}$$

This means that there is a 95% probability that the mean height of all students is between 167.28 and 170.22 cm.

The 99% confidence limits are $\qquad 168.75 \pm 2.58$ Standard errors

$$= \quad 168.75 \pm 2.58 \times 0.75$$

$$= \quad 168.75 \text{cm} \pm 1.94 \text{ cm}$$

This means that there is a 99% probability that the mean height of all students is between 166.81 and 170.69 cm.

It is important to note that it is impossible to infer an exact value of the population mean from a sample. We can only state that there is a specified probability that the population mean is within specified limits. This uncertainty is known as sampling error. The only way to eliminate sampling error and obtain an exact value for the population mean is to measure every item in the population.

The result of **increasing** the degree of confidence (from 95% to 99%) is that the precision of the estimate is reduced, ie, a wider interval is calculated for μ.

2.11   Sample size for a given error

$1.96 \, \dfrac{\sigma}{\sqrt{n}}$ and $2.58 \, \dfrac{\sigma}{\sqrt{n}}$ are known as **errors** in the estimates of μ. It is possible to reduce the size of this error by increasing the value of n, the sample size.

2.12   Example

In measuring the reaction time of individuals, a psychologist estimates that the standard deviation of all such times is 0.05 seconds.

Calculate the smallest sample size necessary in order to be (a) 95% and (b) 99% confident that the error in the estimate will not exceed 0.01 seconds.

(a)   95% confidence limits are $\bar{x} \pm 1.96 \, \dfrac{\sigma}{\sqrt{n}}$

$\therefore$ error in estimate $= 1.96 \, \dfrac{\sigma}{\sqrt{n}} = 1.96 \times \dfrac{0.05}{\sqrt{n}}$

and this must be less than or equal to 0.01 seconds.

$\therefore \quad 1.96 \times \dfrac{0.05}{\sqrt{n}} \quad \leq \quad 0.01$

$\therefore \quad \dfrac{1.96 \times 0.05}{0.01} \quad \leq \quad \sqrt{n}$

$\quad 9.80 \quad \leq \quad \sqrt{n}$

$\quad 96.04 \quad \leq \quad n \quad$ (squaring both sides to remove square root)

The sample size should be 97 since n must be greater than or equal to 96.04.

(b)   99% confidence limits are $\bar{x} \pm 2.58 \, \dfrac{\sigma}{\sqrt{n}}$

$\therefore \quad$ error in estimate $= 2.58 \, \dfrac{\sigma}{\sqrt{n}} = 2.58 \times \dfrac{0.05}{\sqrt{n}}$

and this must be at most 0.01 seconds.

$\therefore \quad \dfrac{2.58 \times 0.05}{\sqrt{n}} \quad \leq \quad 0.01$

$\quad \dfrac{2.58 \times 0.05}{0.01} \quad \leq \quad \sqrt{n}$

$\quad 12.90 \quad \leq \quad \sqrt{n}$

$\quad 166.41 \quad \leq \quad n \quad$ (squaring both sides)

The sample size should be 167.

By increasing the sample size from 97 to 167, we can be more confident that the mean reaction time is within the required limits.

2.13   Activity

A sample of 100 items from a production line has a mean length of 8.4 cm with standard deviation 0.5 cm.

What is the 95% confidence interval for the mean length of all items from that production line?

2.14   Activity solution

95% confidence interval $= \bar{x} \pm 1.96 \dfrac{\sigma}{\sqrt{n}}$

Using s to estimate σ,

95% confidence interval $= 8.4 \pm 1.96 \times \dfrac{0.5}{\sqrt{100}}$ cm

$= 8.4 \pm 1.96 \times 0.05$ cm

$\therefore \quad 8.302 < \mu < 8.498$ cm

3   THEORY OF SAMPLING (PROPORTIONS)

3.1   Introduction

It is often necessary to estimate a population proportion from a sample, rather than estimating a mean. For example, in public polls, sample enquiries are made to estimate the proportion of people in favour of Government policies. In consumer research, it may be required to estimate the proportion of consumers who would use a new product in order to estimate the demand. This type of enquiry is known as **sampling for attributes**, as the object is to estimate the proportion of the population who possess the attribute under investigation.

If $n \geq 30$, the normal distribution can be used as an approximation to this distribution, hence, provided the sample size is not less than 30, the theory is the same as that for means, except that a different formula is used for the standard error.

Standard error of a proportion $= \sqrt{\dfrac{pq}{n}}$

where p = proportion of the population possessing the attribute

q = $1 - p$ = proportion not possessing the attribute

n = size of sample

If the proportion of the population is not known, the proportion of the sample can be used as an estimate.

Note that to be consistent with the convention of using Greek letters for population parameters, π (pi) should be used rather than p. However, as the CIMA list of formulae uses p, it has been retained here.

3.2   Example

Past experience with an examination in Law has shown that only 50% of the students pass. The probability that 55% or more of a group of 200 students will pass is calculated as follows:

The population proportion is 50%, ie, $\dfrac{50}{100} = 0.5$. Hence:

$$p = 0.5, \quad \therefore\ q = 1 - 0.5 = 0.5 \quad \text{and} \quad n = 200$$

$$\text{Standard error} \quad = \quad \sqrt{\dfrac{pq}{n}} \quad = \quad \sqrt{\dfrac{0.5 \times 0.5}{200}}$$

$$= \quad \sqrt{0.00125}$$

$$= \quad 0.03536$$

Given sample proportion $=$ 0.55

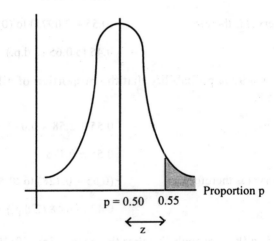

Standardising the value 0.55:

$$z \quad = \quad \dfrac{0.55 - 0.5}{0.03536}$$

$$= \quad 1.41 \qquad \text{Area} = 0.4207 \quad \text{(from table at front of text)}$$

$$\therefore \text{ the required probability} \quad = \quad 0.5 - 0.4207$$

$$= \quad 0.0793$$

The chances of 55% (or more) passing are 0.0793 or approximately 8 in 100.

3.3   Confidence intervals

The 95% and 99% confidence limits for the population proportion are obtained in the same way as those for the sample mean, using the formula for the standard error of a proportion, ie:

95% confidence limits $=$ sample proportion $\pm$ 1.96 SE

99% confidence limits $=$ sample proportion $\pm$ 2.58 SE

where   SE $=$ $\sqrt{\dfrac{pq}{n}}$

If the population proportion is not known, use the sample proportion to calculate the standard error.

3.4   Example

Calculate the 95% and 99% confidence limits for the proportion of all voters in favour of candidate A if a random sample of 100 voters had 55% in favour of A.

3.5   Solution

As the population proportion is not known the sample proportion must be used to calculate the standard error; Hence:

$p = 0.55,$ $\qquad q = 1 - 0.55 = 0.45$ $\qquad$ and $\qquad$ $n = 100$

$$\text{Standard error} \quad = \quad \sqrt{\frac{pq}{n}} \quad = \quad \sqrt{\frac{0.55 \times 0.45}{100}}$$

$$= \quad 0.04975$$

95% confidence limits $\qquad = \quad 0.55 \pm 1.96 \times 0.04975$

$$= \quad 0.55 \pm 0.0975$$

The 95% confidence interval is therefore $\qquad (0.55 - 0.0975)$ to $(0.55 + 0.0975)$

$$= \quad 0.45 \text{ to } 0.65 \text{ (2 d.p.)}$$

This means that there is a 95% probability that the proportion of all voters in favour of candidate A is between 45% and 65%.

The 99% confidence limits $\qquad = \quad 0.55 \pm 2.58 \times 0.04975$

$$= \quad 0.55 \pm 0.128$$

The 99% confidence interval is therefore $\qquad (0.55 - 0.128)$ to $(0.55 + 0.128)$

$$= \quad 0.42 \text{ to } 0.68 \text{ (2 d.p.)}$$

This means that there is a 99% probability that the proportion of all voters in favour of candidate A is between 42% and 68%.

There is obviously a very large sampling error, indicating that a larger sample should have been used.

Note again the nature of the inference that can be drawn from the sample. It does not follow that because 55% of the sample were in favour, 55% of the population will be in favour. We can only infer that there is a specified probability that the proportion will be within specified limits. If the candidate assumed from the sample result that he would win the election, he might well be disappointed.

3.6   Problems of sample size for a given error

The standard error and hence the error in the estimate can be reduced by increasing the sample size *n*.

At the 95% level, the error in the estimate is 1.96 standard errors and at the 99% level 2.58 standard errors.

3.7   Example

An advertising firm claims that its recent promotion reached 30% of the families living in the city. The company who hired the firm doubts this assertion and wishes to take a sample survey of its own. Calculate the sample size necessary to be at least 95% confident that the estimate will be within 3% of the true value.

Here, the only estimate available of the population proportion is 30% or 0.3. This value must therefore be used to calculate the standard error.

Hence: p = 0.3

q = $1 - 0.3 = 0.7$

Standard error = $\sqrt{\dfrac{pq}{n}}$

= $\sqrt{\dfrac{0.3 \times 0.7}{n}}$

but we require the value of n to be such that 1.96 standard errors = 0.03 (ie, 3%)

$\therefore$ 0.03 = $1.96 \times \sqrt{\dfrac{0.3 \times 0.7}{n}}$

$\therefore$ $\sqrt{n}$ = $\dfrac{1.96 \times \sqrt{0.3 \times 0.7}}{0.03}$

$\therefore$ n = $\dfrac{1.96^2 \times 0.3 \times 0.7}{0.03^2}$ (squaring both sides)

= 896.4

A sample size of 897 should be taken.

Note that in order to calculate the standard error, it is necessary to have an assumed value of the population proportion p. If the survey is completely new, there will be no means of knowing what value of p would be reasonable to assume. In this case, the method used is to take the worst possible case giving the highest standard error. This is when p = q = 0.5.

Thus in the previous example, if it was not valid to assume p = 30%, the calculation would be as follows:

Take $p = q = 0.5$

Standard error   = $\sqrt{\dfrac{0.5 \times 0.5}{n}}$ = $\sqrt{\dfrac{0.25}{n}}$

We require   0.03 = $1.96 \sqrt{\dfrac{0.25}{n}}$

n = $\left(\dfrac{1.96}{0.03}\right)^2 \times 0.25$

= 1,067.1

A sample of size 1,068 would be required.

3.8   Activity

In a random sample of 144 people, 63% preferred the flavour of a new brand of instant coffee to that of the other brands tested.

What are the 99% confidence limits for the proportion of the total population preferring the new brand?

3.9   Activity solution

Estimated $p = 0.63$, $q = 1 - 0.63 = 0.37$, $n = 144$

$$\begin{aligned}
\text{99\% confidence limits} \quad &= \quad \text{sample proportion} \pm 2.58 \text{ standard errors} \\
&= \quad 0.63 \pm 2.58 \sqrt{\frac{0.63 \times 0.37}{144}} \\
&= \quad 0.63 \pm 0.10 \\
\therefore \quad &\quad \quad 0.53 < p < 0.73 \\
\text{or} \quad &\quad \quad 53\% < p < 73\%
\end{aligned}$$

3.10   Illustration

A manufacturer of electric light bulbs needs to estimate the average 'burning life' of the bulbs he makes. A random sample of 100 bulbs was found to have a mean life of 340 hours with a standard deviation of 30 hours.

Calculate

(a)   the standard error of the mean;

(b)   the 95% and 99% confidence intervals for the population mean;

(c)   the sample size necessary to provide a degree of accuracy within 3 hours at the 95% level.

3.11   Solution

$\bar{x} = 340$ hours, $s = 30$ hours $= \hat{\sigma} \ (n > 30)$ $n = 100$

(a)   Standard error
$$\begin{aligned}
&= \quad \frac{\hat{\sigma}}{\sqrt{n}} \\
&= \quad \frac{30}{\sqrt{100}} \\
&= \quad 3 \text{ hours}
\end{aligned}$$

(b)   95% confidence interval for μ:

$$\begin{aligned}
\bar{x} &\pm 1.96 \times \frac{\hat{\sigma}}{\sqrt{n}} \\
&= \quad 340 \pm 1.96 \times 3 \\
&= \quad 340 \pm 5.88 \\
&= \quad 334.12 \text{ to } 345.88 \text{ hours} \\
&= \quad 334 \text{ hours to } 346 \text{ hours}
\end{aligned}$$

99% confidence interval for μ:

$$\bar{x} \pm 2.58 \times \frac{\hat{\sigma}}{\sqrt{n}}$$

$$= \quad 340 \pm 2.58 \times 3$$

$$= \quad 340 \pm 7.74$$

$$= \quad 332.26 \text{ to } 347.74 \text{ hours}$$

$$= \quad 332 \text{ hours to } 348 \text{ hours}$$

(c)   The error in the estimate = 3 hours

$$\therefore \quad 1.96 \times \frac{\hat{\sigma}}{\sqrt{n}} \quad = \quad 3$$

$$\therefore \quad 1.96 \times \frac{30}{\sqrt{n}} \quad = \quad 3$$

$$\therefore \quad \frac{1.96 \times 30}{3} \quad = \quad \sqrt{n}$$

$$19.6 \quad = \quad \sqrt{n}$$

$$384.16 \quad = \quad n$$

∴ it is necessary to use a sample of at least 385.

4   WORK STUDY

4.1   Incentive schemes and work study

In a previous chapter, value analysis, which was concerned with reducing cost on an overall basis, was considered. Work study, by contrast, is much more localised in concept, being primarily concerned with encouraging labour to improve efficiency and, hence, reduce labour costs. One of the ways in which labour can be encouraged to operate more efficiently is by offering incentives to workers for producing output at a higher rate than might normally be expected. To do this, it is of course necessary to decide on the level which would be considered just acceptable as well as establishing the incentives for working at a level above this minimum. The minimum acceptable level of working is called *allowed time* (ie, the time which will be allowed in doing a job) and this time is normally established by using work study methods.

4.2   Work study – the two aspects

There are basically two aspects to work study:

(a)   method study;
(b)   work measurement.

Each of these is considered below.

4.3   Method study

Method study is concerned with the most efficient use of resources and the best method of production to achieve this. Basically, the current methods are examined to establish their acceptability, and alternative methods are considered. If it is thought that the existing methods can be improved in any respect (eg, re-arrangement of the work or sequence of operations), then this improved method may be implemented. Some follow-up must, of course, be made to confirm that the improved method has achieved its aim.

4.4   Work measurement

Once the method of working has been satisfactorily determined, the work can be measured by timing. This can be of two methods:

(a)   *time study* where actual work being done is timed; or

(b)   *analytical estimating* for new work, to obtain estimates of the times.

In either case each operation will be considered in turn.

Once the work is measured, a total time for the job can be established having regard to fatigue of workers and their personal needs. This will establish the time allowed for the job. The incentive scheme is then prepared by considering how much time is likely to be saved under the scheme and the value of this time to the employer in terms of additional output. This will then give an indication of how much the employer should be willing to pay for the incentive scheme.

Various formulae have been established over the years to assist in the calculation of incentives, the most common being:

(a)   *Piece work* where an employee is paid on the basis of units produced rather than on a time basis.

(b)   The *Halsey* scheme under which an employee earns a bonus equal to the proportion of the time he saves on a job, eg:

$$\text{Bonus} = \tfrac{1}{2} \times \text{Time saved} \times \text{Basic wage rate}$$

The employee's total pay is, therefore: Basic wage + Bonus

(c)   The *Rowan* scheme, which is similar to the Halsey scheme but which places an upper limit on the bonus which can be earned, ie:

$$\text{Bonus} = \frac{\text{Time taken}}{\text{Time allowed}} \times \text{Time saved} \times \text{Basic wage rate}$$

4.5   Comment on bonus schemes

Even back in the 1940s, Weldon made the comment about the limited use of bonus schemes. In general the following guidelines should be followed:

(a)   There must be full discussion between employer, employees and their representatives before the scheme is introduced. Imposed schemes will be likely to cause more harm than good.

(b)   It must be readily understandable by the employees to avoid the suspicion that they are being cheated.

(c)   The bonus must be adequate enough to motivate them to greater effort.

(d)   There must be adequate and credible inspection, again to avoid the perception of operatives being cheated.

(e)   Employees must not be made responsible or penalised for an event that is beyond their control. This avoids disputes arising from the non-payment of bonuses. However, it could mean the provision of guaranteed bonuses if it is not possible to earn a bonus for certain uncontrollable reasons.

(f)   The bonus should be paid as quickly as possible after it has been earned.

(g)   There must be a reduction in unit costs.

(h)   It should be recognised that no bonus scheme is a ready made solution to the problems of badly managed or poorly equipped production areas.

(i)   However sophisticated the work study methods that establish the original rates, the actual rate fixing will still retain an element of judgement, with the result that the final setting up will involve negotiation and consultation with the unions. This could be protracted and if not satisfactorily resolved, could cause a serious sequence of disputes and stoppages.

4.6   Advantages and disadvantages

Advantages

(a)   Increased production, increased wages and a reduction in unit fixed overhead costs.
(b)   Improved productivity enables the firm to retain a competitive edge.
(c)   Operator morale is improved by rewards directly related to effort.
(d)   More efficient workers will be attracted by the lure of high wages.

Disadvantages

(a)   There are frequent problems in establishing performance rates and levels which lead to on-going disputes.

(b)   There is the ever present temptation to retime the job if the bonuses get too high.

(c)   Some schemes are highly complex and expensive to maintain.

(d)   Some groups of workers, although unskilled are able to earn high wages resulting in the erosion of differentials causing further unrest.

(e)   It could be argued that with direct labour costs in manufacturing down to under 10%, and much of the people cost fixed, traditional bonus schemes are now an irrelevance, and some form of profit sharing or share incentive is more appropriate.

4.7   Group Schemes

There are situations where groups of operatives work, rather than individuals. Traditionally, this was seen in coal mining or batch production lines, or these days where there are manufacturing cells. In such circumstances, a group scheme might be considered appropriate.

Advantages of group schemes

(a)   A greater team spirit is generated amongst the participating operatives.

(b)   Administration is cheaper because individual workers do not have to be tracked and recorded.

(c)   Indirect support workers could be included and recognised as part of the team.

(d)   The number of rates to be negotiated would be reduced.

(e)   A group scheme might form the foundation for more flexible working arrangements.

Disadvantages

(a)   The less direct contact may reduce the incentive.

(b)   Less industrious operatives can fail to 'pull their weight' yet still collect the bonus. Eventually this will cause friction, especially where there are well motivated and industrious operatives.

(c)   It is not always easy to apportion the amount of bonus between grades of operatives. This can result in a 'broad brush' rate being applied to all operatives which can exacerbate the effects of the situation already described above.

5   SELF TEST QUESTIONS

5.1   What is Bessel's correction? (2.1)

5.2   What is a distribution of sample means? (2.5)

5.3   What are confidence intervals? (2.7)

5.4   What confidence level is given by the interval $\bar{x} \pm 1.96$ standard errors? (2.8)

5.5   What is the formula for the standard error of a proportion? (3.1)

6   EXAMINATION TYPE QUESTIONS

6.1   Sampling computer records

A mail-order company is analysing a random sample of its computer records of customers. Among the results are the following distributions:

Size of order £	Number of customers
Less than 1	8
1 and less than 5	19
5 and less than 10	38
10 and less than 15	40
15 and less than 20	22
20 and less than 30	13
30 and over	4
Total	144

You are required

(a)   to calculate the arithmetic mean and standard deviation order size for the sample;

(10 marks)

(b)   to find 95% confidence limits for the overall mean order size for the customers and explain their meaning.

(6 marks)

(Total: 16 marks)

6.2   Mail-order customers

(a)   A simple random sample of 400 of a large mail-order company's customers showed that the mean value of orders in the first quarter of 19X7 was £31 with a standard deviation of £10.

Find 95% confidence limits for the population mean and interpret your answer.

(6 marks)

(b)   (i)   The sample of 400 comprises 80 pensioners. Find a 99% confidence interval for the population percentage of pensioner customers and interpret your answer.

(6 marks)

(ii)   What size of sample would have to be taken to be at least 95% confident that the population percentage of pensioner customers would be estimated to within ± 2%?

(8 marks)

(Total: 20 marks)

7   ANSWERS TO EXAMINATION TYPE QUESTIONS

7.1   Sampling computer records

Notes:

(i)   Take the upper group boundaries as 1, 5, 10 . . . etc.

(ii)   Close the final group by assuming the same interval as the previous group, ie, '30 and less than 40'.

Size of order (£)		Mid-point x	f	fx	fx^2
0 and less than	1	0.5	8	4	2.0
1 and less than	5	3.0	19	57	171.0
5 and less than	10	7.5	38	285	2,137.5
10 and less than	15	12.5	40	500	6,250.0
15 and less than	20	17.5	22	385	6,737.5
20 and less than	30	25.0	13	325	8,125.0
30 and less than	40	35.0	4	140	4,900.0
			144	1,696	28,323.0

$$\text{Mean} = \frac{\sum fx}{\sum f}$$

$$= \frac{1,696}{144}$$

$$= £11.78$$

$$\text{Standard deviation} = \sqrt{\frac{\sum fx^2}{\sum f} - \left(\frac{\sum fx}{\sum f}\right)^2}$$

$$= \sqrt{\frac{28,323}{144} - \left(\frac{1,696}{144}\right)^2}$$

$$= £7.61$$

Note: you are reminded that column 5 = column 2 × column 4.

(b)   Standard error $= \dfrac{\sigma}{\sqrt{n}}$

$$= £\frac{7.61}{\sqrt{144}}$$

$$= £0.6342$$

95% confidence limits   =   mean ± 1.96 standard errors

=   £(11.78 ± 1.96 × 0.6342)

=   £11.78 ± £1.24

=   £10.54 to £13.02

This means that there is a 95% probability that the mean size of all orders in April was between £10.54 and £13.02.

7.2   Mail-order customers

(a)   Standard error $= \dfrac{\sigma}{\sqrt{n}}$

$$= \frac{£10}{\sqrt{400}}$$

$$= £0.5$$

95% confidence limits   =   sample mean ± 1.96 standard errors

=   £(31 ± 1.96 × 0.50)

=   £31 ± 0.98

=   £30.02 and £31.98

This means that there is a 95% probability that the mean value of all orders lies between £30.02 and £31.98.

Note: a common mistake, particularly under the stress of examination conditions, is to omit to divide the standard deviation by $\sqrt{n}$ to obtain the standard error.

(b)   (i)   Standard error of a proportion $= \sqrt{\dfrac{p(1-p)}{n}}$

where p = population proportion. As the population proportion is not known and the sample is a large one, the sample proportion is used as an estimate. Hence;

$$p = 80/400 = 0.2$$

$$\text{Standard error} = \sqrt{\dfrac{0.2 \times 0.8}{400}}$$

$$= 0.02$$

99% confidence limits   = sample proportion ± 2.58 standard errors

$$= 0.2 \pm 2.58 \times 0.02$$

$$= 0.2 \pm 0.0516$$

Hence 99% confidence limits for the percentage

$$= (20 \pm 5.16)\%$$

This means that there is a 99% probability that the percentage of all customers who are pensioners is between 14.84% and 25.16%.

Note: to convert a proportion to a percentage, it is multiplied by 100. This applies equally to confidence limits for proportions.

(ii)   To be 95% confident that the proportion would be estimated to within ± 2%, we require

1.96 Standard errors of the proportion = 0.02 (ie, 2%)

If it is assumed that the population proportion is 0.2, as obtained from the sample,

$$1.96 \sqrt{\dfrac{0.2 \times 0.8}{n}} = 0.02$$

where n is the size of the sample.

This gives n $= \left(\dfrac{1.96}{0.02}\right)^2 \times 0.2 \times 0.8$

$$= 1{,}537$$

However, if it cannot be assumed that the population is 0.2, then the value of p that gives the highest standard error (p = 0.5) should be taken.

In this case

$$1.96 \times \sqrt{\frac{0.5 \times 0.5}{n}} \quad = \quad 0.02$$

$$\text{giving n} \quad = \quad \left(\frac{1.96}{0.02}\right)^2 \times 0.5 \times 0.5$$

$$= \quad 2,401$$

Notes:

(i)   The sample size must always be rounded to the nearest whole number above; rounding down will not achieve the required accuracy of sample prediction.

(ii)   In b (ii), strictly speaking, 2,401 is the correct answer, but it is doubtful whether a candidate would be penalised for the answer 1,537. You should make sure you understand the reason for the different answers.

5 QUALITY CONTROL AND CONTROL CHARTS

INTRODUCTION & LEARNING OBJECTIVES

Syllabus area 7b   Aspects of quality: quality control, assurance, and management. (Ability required 2).

The concept of total quality management; costs of quality, waste. (Ability required 1).

Control charts for individual units, averages, range and proportions. (Ability required 3).

This chapter looks at the qualitative aspects of quality control and related topics and the ways quality can be achieved.

When you have studied this chapter you should be able to do the following:

- Define the important aspects of quality.
- Understand what is meant by total quality management.
- Understand the inspection process and acceptance sampling.
- Classify the costs of quality.
- Prepare the various forms of control chart and discuss their role in quality assurance.

1 ASPECTS OF QUALITY, QUALITY CONTROL, ASSURANCE AND MANAGEMENT

1.1 Definitions

Quality may be defined simply as a degree or level of excellence. Excellence in this context may be interpreted as being in keeping with the specification.

This leads into Wild's definition.

[Definition]   The quality of a product or service is the degree to which it satisfies the customers' requirements.

This in turn is influenced by:-

Design quality: the degree to which the specification of the product/service satisfies customers' requirements.

Manufactured quality: the degree to which the product/service, when made available to the customer, conforms to specifications.

Quality control and assurance may be defined as a system of procedures which:-

- ensures only materials and components which conform to the given specifications are accepted from suppliers,

- ensures that during the conversion of these items only products which conform to specification are produced,

- ensures that only those products which conform to the specification are offered to the customer.

Quality assurance may go further than pure inspection on receipt. It can mean developing systems in partnership with suppliers to ensure flexible service, rapid feedback if there are faults and even assuring continued supply by appraising the financial health of the supplier.

1.2   Total quality management (TQM)

Total quality management (TQM) is the name given to programmes which seek to ensure that goods are produced and services are supplied of the highest quality. Its origin lies primarily in Japanese organisations and it is argued that TQM has been a significant factor in Japanese global business success. The basic principle of TQM is that costs of prevention (getting things right first time) are less than the costs of correction.

This contrasts with the 'traditional' UK approach that less than 100% quality is acceptable as the costs of improvement from say 90% to 100% outweigh the benefits.

Which view is correct is a matter of debate but the advocates of TQM would argue that in addition to direct costs the impact of less than 100% quality in terms of lost potential for future sales also has to be taken into account.

1.3   Features of TQM

The philosophy of TQM is based on the idea of a series of quality chains which may be broken at any point by one person or service not meeting the requirements of the customer. The key to TQM is for everyone in the organisation to have well-defined customers - an extension of the word, beyond the customers of the company, to anyone to whom an individual provides a service. Thus the 'Paint shop' staff would be customers of the 'Assembly shop' staff who would themselves be the customers of the 'Machine shop' staff. The idea is that the supplier-customer relationships would form a chain extending from the company's original suppliers through to its ultimate consumers. Areas of responsibility would need to be identified and a manager allocated to each, and then the customer/supplier chain established. True to the principle outlined above the quality requirements of each 'customer' within the chain would be assessed, and meeting these would then become the responsibility of the 'suppliers' who form the preceding link in the chain.

Quality has to be managed - it will not just happen. To meet the requirements of TQM a company will probably need to recruit more staff and may also need to change the level of services on offer to its customers, which includes 'internal' customers. This would probably entail costs in terms of the redesign of systems, recruitment and training of staff, and the purchase of appropriate equipment.

Thackray writing in **Management Accounting** (November 1990) indicated the following features of companies which follow TQM:

(a)   Absolute commitment by the chief executive and all senior managers to doing what is needed to change the culture.

(b)   People are not afraid to try new things.

(c)   Communication is excellent and multi-way.

(d)   There is a real commitment to continuous improvement in all processes.

(e)   Attention is focused first on the process and second on the results.

(f)   There is an absence of strict control systems.

The last two points appear to go against the central thrust of UK management accounting. The point being made is that concentrating on getting a process right will result in an improved result. A process is a detailed step in the overall system of producing and delivering goods to a customer. Improving a process without worrying about the short-term effects will encourage the search for improvement to take place, the improvement will more likely be permanent, and will lead to further improvements. A concentration on results and control generally means attaching blame to someone if things go wrong. Therefore employees would not have an incentive to pick up and correct errors but rather would be encouraged to try and conceal them.

1.4   Analysis and restructuring of resources

In many businesses, employees' time is used up in **discretionary activities**. Discretionary activities are activities such as checking, chasing and other tasks related to product failures. Some/most of this time may be capable of being redeployed into the two other categories of work:

(a)   Core activities, and
(b)   Support activities.

Core activities add direct value to the business. They use the specific skills of the particular employees being examined and are the reason for their employment. Support activities are those activities which clearly support core activities and are thus necessary to allow core activities to add value. The importance of this analysis can be seen in a quote from a US Chief Executive some years ago: 'The only things you really need to run a business are materials, machines, workers and salesmen. Nobody else is justified unless he's helping the worker produce more product or the salesman sell more product.'

Analysis of employees' time will provide a clearer view of the costs of poor quality and whether efforts in other departments could reduce the amount of time spent by a department further down the product chain on discretionary activities. For example, suppose there are seven processes from purchasing of raw materials through various stages of production to delivery of the product to the customer. If each process is 90% effective then there will be only a 48% success rate at the end of the seventh stage (90% × 90% × 90% etc). What happens in practice however may be that personnel employed in stage 4 of the process spend a lot of their time on discretionary activities trying to remedy the effect of defects at earlier stages. It is suggested that it would be more sensible for departments in the earlier stages to get things right the first time.

An example quoted in a **Management Accounting** article (May 1989) is of an office equipment supplier which analysed employees' time into core, support and discretionary activities. It was found that half of the salesmen's face-to-face selling time with customers consisted of listening to their complaints about poor customer service.

1.5   Quality circles

Quality circles consist of about ten employees possessing relevant levels of skill, ranging from the shop-floor through to management. They meet regularly to discuss the major aspect of quality but other areas such as safety and productivity will also be dealt with.

The main aim is to be able to offer management:

(a)   ideas connected with improvements and recommendations;
(b)   possible solutions and suggestions;
(c)   organising the implementation of (a) and (b).

The development of quality circles allows the process of decision making to start at shop floor level, with the ordinary worker encouraged to comment, make suggestions, as well as being allowed to put them into practice. Circle members experience the responsibility for ensuring quality, and have the power to exercise verbal complaint. Quality circles may be applied at any level of organisational activity, being used to cover all aspects and could conceivably involve all employees.

Jaguar, the established motor company, has effectively used this system resulting in the involvement of ten per cent of the workforce. A notable point here is that in one decade the number of quality inspectors required has been roughly halved. Clearly, quality circles are a practical means of gaining employee participation; they are not mainly for reducing costs although this aspect will be a major topic for discussion. Other benefits are increased awareness of shop-floor problems, members gain confidence over problem solving etc, greater output, improved quality and shop-floor participation.

Equally, putting this system into practice can prove difficult. The well established system of hierarchical management is difficult to penetrate, and to some organisations it would present extreme changes. Some systems may not be able to accommodate such change, eg, the armed forces or police force where a powerful hierarchy has developed.

1.6   Quality control

Quality control is the title given to the more traditional view of quality.

It may be defined as the process of:

(a)   establishing standards of quality for a product or service;

(b)   establishing procedures or production methods which ought to ensure that these required standards of quality are met in a suitably high proportion of cases;

(c)   monitoring actual quality;

(d)   taking control action when actual quality falls below standard.

The contrast with TQM is that less than 100% quality may be regarded as acceptable. Eradicating the costs of failure of a product should be weighed against higher prevention costs for example. Charts such as statistical control charts are often used to monitor quality in such instances especially in terms of the physical dimensions of the component parts of a product or the strength of a product.

1.7   Current trends towards quality improvement

In the late nineteenth century, Andrew Carnegie, the Scots born American steel entrepreneur, insisted that he was provided with a quality product to sell, for he knew that one adverse comment on his rails would have a serious detrimental effect upon customer confidence in his product.

Carnegie knew his customers very well and what they expected. He knew his industry well and kept in touch with technical trends and he knew his product.

The debate that accounting and management accounting especially has lost relevance centres on the view that western industry had lost this Carnegie ideal and replaced it with an obsession for accounting numbers. Businesses moved away from defining processes in terms of what people do or satisfaction that customers receive. The focus was on costs, profits and accounting relationships and accounting control.

What Johnson calls the Dark Age of American business history is now coming to an end with a refocussing of attention on the priorities established by Carnegie and others. R S Kaplan has identified a quality revolution that is moving through industry. New terms of competition have developed around quality, time-based competition, information technology and concurrent product-process design.

1.8   Trends in quality management

The traditional view of quality is through quality control and inspection. In short that meant keeping up to engineering standards and specifications. Recent competitive developments have proved that this was not enough. British and American cars could compete while they were competing against each other in a virtual closed system. Once that system was burst open by the onset of Japanese competition, then things had to change.

Quality is now about total delivery of the product or service. Tom Peters quotes a number of examples to illustrate what this means.

(a)   Caterpillar

Caterpillar aim to produce a better, more efficient crawler tractor than anybody else in the world. It also operates a system whereby there is a 48 hour parts delivery service anywhere in the world. If that is not maintained, the customer gets the part free. This requires a product that is reliable and does not fail. It means that customers come back and constantly specify Caterpillar tractors for whatever job is required. The product is expensive, more expensive than its alternatives, but the added reliability makes up for the price differential.

(b)   Hewlett-Packard

The famous HP3000 system ranks rightly at the top in terms of quality. However, the company does not rest on its laurels. Rather it strives to maintain its quality lead because if it does not, it will lose market share to the Japanese. (Tom Peters **In Search of Excellence**)

(c)   Service sector examples

Moving away from manufacturing and the production of a quality product to services, Tom Peters (**Liberation Management**) gives an interesting example. Both Federal Express and United Parcels are delivery services. Both have a philosophy of excellent delivery standards. United Parcels' slogan is "as reliable as taking it yourself." However, Peters argues that going beyond customer expectation is what impresses the customer and brings him back for more. The parcels delivery that goes the extra mile is the one that forcibly demonstrates quality.

Quality is not necessarily about Rolls-Royce engineering standards. It is about customer satisfaction. The product may have low quality and low value added, but if it does the job well and pleases the customer and is what the customer wants, then it will take the market.

2   THE NATURE OF THE INSPECTION PROCESS AND ACCEPTANCE SAMPLING

2.1   Introduction

Inspection is a process whereby a decision can be made about whether an item or a batch of items is acceptable or not in terms of the specification.

2.2   Location of inspection

It is rare to locate a formal inspection after every stage in the system. The cost of such a facility would be prohibitive. The problem is to optimise the cost of inspection by balancing its cost against the benefits of inspection and the risks of not inspecting. In practice, such decisions are a combination of empirical and quantitative rules.

(a)   Inspect before costly operations in order to avoid high rectification costs for defective items.

(b)   Inspect before any series of operations during which inspection will be difficult and/or costly.

(c)   Inspect after operations which generally result in a high rate of defectives.

(d)   Inspect before operations which would conceal defects previously caused.

(e)   Inspect before "point of no return" ie, after which any rectification would be impossible or very expensive.

(f)   Inspect before points at which potential damage may be caused, ie, before the use of equipment which would be damaged through the processing of faulty items.

(g)   Inspect before a change in quality responsibility eg, between departments.

2.3   Acceptance sampling

Inspection of each critical feature of every item to ensure that no defective items pass through is an ideal situation, but it may be uneconomical or even impossible.

(a)   Inspection may cause damage or even complete destruction of the items such as fuses or hand grenades.

(b)   The accuracy of inspection may be diminished after frequent repetition. Long periods of routine inspection may prove fatiguing and boring for the inspector, whose accuracy and judgement might then be affected.

(c)   Handling the item may result in deterioration.

(d)   Items may deteriorate rapidly prior to use, and lengthy inspection periods may be undesirable.

(e)   Inspection may be hazardous, even a dangerous procedure.

To avoid these problems, some form of sampling inspection is employed. In acceptance sampling, decisions about the quality of batches of items are made after inspection of only a portion of the items. If the sample conforms to the requisite quality levels, then the whole batch from which it came is accepted. If, however, the sample does not conform, then the batch is rejected or tested further. Such a procedure enables decisions about the quality of items to be made quickly, easily and cheaply. An element of risk remains: a greater or lesser proportion of defectives could always lead to the wrong conclusion being made about a batch. This may be achieved by taking a **single** sample lot from a batch, or **multiple** samples from the same batch. The items are then classified as either good or bad. This is **attribute sampling**.

Although **variable sampling** can be used to test compliance with exact dimensions, attribute sampling can be employed on quality of finish, performance or measurements.

In an ideal world, the customer would like 100% of products purchased to be acceptable. Since this is impractical, a lower standard must be accepted. Even so, only by 100% inspection can we be 100% sure that a batch conforms to the accepted standard.

3   COST OF QUALITY

3.1   Production quality

In recent times a great deal of attention has been devoted to quality issues in the UK. Although there has always been a general awareness of the need to ensure the satisfaction of the customer, it is the worldwide nature of competition that has focused attention on the need to act. Competitor pressure has often come from the Japanese, whose basic premise is that poor quality is unacceptable.

However, quality has a cost (either because quality is poor and incurs costs due to waste or customer rejection, or simply because the implementation of quality management itself has a cost) and it is useful to consider the extent of **quality related costs.**

3.2   Quality related costs

CIMA official terminology defines and analyses the types of cost related to quality. A report *'The effectiveness of the corporate overhead in British business'* Develin & Partners 1989, estimates that the average cost of waste and mistakes in the UK represents 20 per cent of controllable corporate overhead.

CIMA official terminology defines as follows:

(a)   **Quality related costs**

> **Definition**   Cost of ensuring and assuring quality, as well as loss incurred when quality is not achieved. Quality costs are classified as prevention cost, appraisal cost, internal failure cost and external failure cost.

(b)   **Prevention cost**

> **Definition**   The cost incurred to reduce appraisal cost to a minimum.

(c)   **Appraisal cost**

> **Definition**   The cost incurred, such as inspection and testing, in initially ascertaining and conformance of the product to quality requirements.

(d)   **Internal failure cost**

> **Definition**   The cost arising from inadequate quality before the transfer of ownership from supplier to purchaser.

(e)   **External failure cost**

> **Definition**   The cost arising from inadequate quality discovered after the transfer of ownership from supplier to purchaser such as complaints, warranty claims and recall cost.

3.3   Measurement of quality

Many companies in industrialised countries are adopting quality improvement as a primary corporate objective. As a management accountant this will impinge upon you in two ways. First, the implementation of TQM on all the company's functional activities. Secondly, and perhaps more important, where quality priorities are tied to enhancing the value of products/services which an entity provides to its customers. This covers a wide range of criteria. Measures that might be used to control and improve quality of performance include:

-    proportion of deliveries made on time,
-    number of sub-standard products,
-    the amount of reworks,
-    frequency and length of machine breakdowns,
-    the launch time of new products and
-    number and gravity of customer complaints.

3.4   Classification of quality costs

From the CIMA definition quoted above, we can classify the different costs of quality.

(a)   **Failure costs**

Costs required to evaluate, dispose of and either correct or replace a defective or deficient product. These can be sub-divided under two headings:-

Internal failure costs

Failure costs discovered before the product is delivered to customers. Examples include:

-    Rework or rectification costs,
-    Net cost of scrap,
-    Disposal of defective products, and
-    Downtime or idle time due to quality problems.

External failure costs

Failure costs discovered after the product is delivered to the customer. Examples include:

-    Complaint investigation and processing,
-    Warranty claims,
-    Cost of lost sales, and
-    Product recalls.

The student should note the opportunity cost of lost sales. It is argued by C D Heagy that introducing this factor makes total quality costs more accurate. She argues:

"By focusing part of the measurement of quality cost on lost sales, this improved model requires management to bring the market place into the quality decision process."

This emphasises another important feature of TQM, that it crosses the traditional functions within an organisation. Marketing and sales have to be concerned about the quality of the product they are presenting.

Product recalls do little for the image of the product/service. While it does show concern for quality and safety, it emphasises that a procedure failed somewhere and was not detected until too late.

(b)   Appraisal costs

Costs of monitoring and inspecting products in terms of specified standards before the products are released to customers. This is very much the traditional view of quality control. Examples might be:

- The capital cost of measurement equipment,
- Inspection and testing,
- Product quality audits,
- Process control monitoring, and
- Test equipment expense.

(c)   Prevention costs

Investments in machinery, technology, education and training programmes designed to reduce the number of defective products during production. Examples are:

- Customer surveys,
- Research of customer needs,
- Field trials,
- Quality education and training programmes,
- Supplier reviews,
- Investment in improved production equipment,
- Quality engineering, and
- Quality circles.

In western industrialised countries, products have always been considered defective if they do not conform to internally set and agreed specifications and standards. Today, however, a customer has a higher expectation of the product he is buying and his standards may be higher than that of the manufacturer. Much of the improvement in the quality of volume cars has been due to the Japanese competition arising from lower failure rates, and higher specifications for less money available on cars imported either from emerging producers or dumped from the former Eastern bloc. The customer of the future will expect a longer guarantee for his durable product, possibly even over life. Thus prevention will be about making design standards that conform to the expectations of customers in the form of "super-prevention costs". Indeed, W R Pasewark argues that for a product to gain world superiority, the speed of entry into the super prevention area will be a vital component of success.

4   TQM AND THE ELIMINATION OF WASTE

4.1   Introduction

Waste is defined in the Terminology as "discarded substances having no value." This is in contrast to scrap which is seen to have some value.

One school of thought in the current management accounting debate harks back to the way things used to be done. This is not a yearning for the "good old days", but rather a painful discovery that much of Japanese success is due to emulating the best of American and European practice.

4.2   Ford's pioneering approach

Ford identified three categories of "waste." Unlike the CIMA definition, he envisaged that all **material waste** had some salvage value. More critical was the **time waste**, since that could not be recovered or salvaged.

However, Ford identified a third category of waste, that of **holding inventories** of raw materials and finished goods in excess of requirements. Inventory has to be financed, it has a holding cost, it runs the risk of deterioration. All this commits resources that could be better used elsewhere. The Ford philosophy, later to be copied by Toyota aimed at eliminating waste in all its forms.

4.3   The impact of decoupling and the TQM response

The post-war western approach of decoupling operations to gain specialist scale economies has produced waste in the form of excessive piles of inventory being moved from isolated departments. Scale efficiencies and economies have undoubtedly been achieved. However, in the west, the cost has been higher levels of inventory.

There is a negative aspect to decoupling. The specialist production areas produce inventory. They absorb conversion overhead. Their output is measured in terms of overhead absorbed, not units delivered to customer. If waste is to be eliminated, then the accountants must create and use measures that do not encourage the wasteful build up of inventory. To the chagrin of financial accountants, that means getting rid of total absorption costing as part of the production control process. TQM means that accountants are involved, and their contribution to waste reduction may well mean new measures of performance. (It is a salutary point that much of the problems of western industry is blamed by H Thomas Johnson on management accountants' obsession with variable costs, contribution margin and the break even rate of output [not sales] rather than control of the fixed cost expense.)

4.4   How direct labour hours might mislead

As a management accountant you will quickly become familiar with standard costing, variance analysis and standard direct costs. These are designed to control the production process. Empirical evidence, however, shows that over emphasis on certain of these variances actually increases costs and waste. H Thomas Johnson identifies waste arising from longer runs which go into inventory, more scrap, more rectification, and longer lead times due to passing products backward and forward along production lines and in and out of stores. In addition, whereas the Japanese approach has always been to encourage change and improvement, the decoupled western approach makes no allowance for such an input.

4.5   The Japanese approach

The Japanese approach to control waste is not to produce for inventory, but to reduce the scale of operation to the level of demand, and use smaller machines at slower rates. They also ensured that they "got it right first time." This again was not a Japanese idea, but derived from the father of TQM, American W Edwards Deming.

4.6   A possible way forward

The student may perceive these ideas as controversial. However, there is a wind of change blowing through the profession, and the student has to be ready for it. Some of the ideas on these pages have been put forward by people such as Prof Michael Bromwich, a former president of CIMA. Such people are shaping the pattern of thinking and inevitably, the minds of examiners.

Johnson advocates that the TQM driven company must first have a leadership that inspires employee-driven (ie, self motivation, not coercion) customer service.

Secondly there must be performance measures developed by the accountants that motivate simplifying work and eliminating waste in all its forms.

4.7   The Impact of Just In Time (JIT)

JIT manufacturing can be described as a philosophy of management dedicated to the elimination of waste and the constant pursuit of improvement. In this context, waste goes beyond even the Henry Ford notions of excess to 'anything that does not add customer perceived value to a product.' (Drury **Standard Costing** 1992). The lead time involved in manufacturing and selling a product consists of process time, inspection time, move time, queue time and storage time. Only process time actually adds value to the product. The others only add costs.   Other research suggests that only 10% of the manufacturing lead time in the USA is actually value adding process time. Thus if lead times can be reduced, the cost of manufacturing can be substantially cut. As an example, Ford are looking to cut the lead time for the introduction of new models to 36 months against the current for the 1996 Taurus (next one up from the European Scorpio) of 42.

5   STATISTICAL PROCESS CONTROL   — omit —
confusing.

5.1   Introduction

Managers need to be confident that the processes under their responsibility are operating under control.   As the search for improved quality has grown keener in recent years, so the need for improved process control has grown more important.   Control charts are a common method of enabling managers to see the trend of output from their process.   The statistical theory studied earlier can then be applied to the chart and conclusions drawn.

5.2   Example of a control chart

The idea is that successive readings are taken from the process output and that these readings are then displayed on a chart, for example as below:

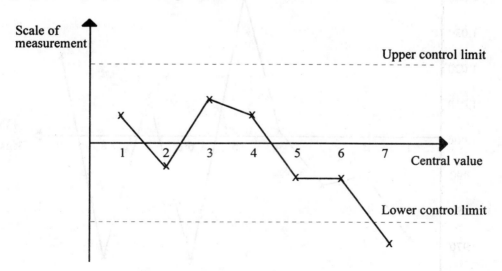

Once one of the control limits is breached, there is evidence that the process is out of control and management must take appropriate control action to remedy the process.

This 'evidence' can be quantified by statistical applications explained below.   It is possible to determine confidence limits on the hypothesis that the process is out of control once the control limits have been exceeded.

5.3   Types of control chart

Four types of chart can be prepared:

- a chart of individual unit results, called an x chart
- a chart of average results, called an $\overline{x}$ chart
- a chart of the range of observed results, called an R chart
- a chart of observed proportions, called a p chart.

The syllabus requires knowledge of each of these forms of control chart; they will be examined in turn in this chapter.

6   CHARTS OF INDIVIDUAL UNIT RESULTS

6.1   Introduction

The first idea might be to measure the result of every unit output from a system. For example a retailer might be trying to sell 1 kg bags of sugar but would be willing to accept some deviation from this standard weight. The first nine bags of sugar produced by a system might have weights as follows:

972g	991g	988g
1,002g	1,041g	967g
1,013g	968g	1,022g

To judge whether this system is under control, a control chart could be drawn up of the actual weights of bags output from the system.

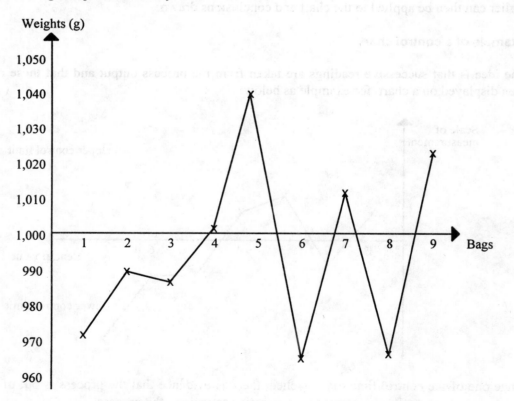

This clearly gives management an immediate visualisation of the output from the system but two very real problems exist for such a chart:

(a)   Measuring the output of each item is clearly impractical in a process such as bags of sugar where there is a high volume of throughput.

(b)   Any control limits (eg, at 960g and 1,040g) outside which the process may be believed to be going out of control can only be set arbitrarily. The advantage of the sampling analysis below is that it applies statistical theory to the problem to quantify the probability that a process is out of control, by calculating **confidence limits.**

6.2   Individually sampled units

The next idea might be to pick units, one at a time, from time to time at random, and measure these to judge if a system is under control. We can now start to apply statistical theory.

6.3   Example

KS Ltd manufacture tins of paint which should each contain 2 litres of paint. Eight individual tins have been selected from the morning's output; their volumes are as follows

Tins	Volume of paint (litres)
1	2.10
2	1.89
3	1.94
4	2.07
5	2.09
6	1.94
7	1.99
8	2.06

Is this evidence that the process is out of control?

6.4   Solution

First we calculate the mean and standard deviation of the sample.

x	$(x - \bar{x})^2$
2.10	0.0081
1.89	0.0144
1.94	0.0049
2.07	0.0036
2.09	0.0064
1.94	0.0049
1.99	0.0004
2.06	0.0025
___	___
16.08	0.0452

Mean of the sample $\bar{x} = \dfrac{\sum x}{n} = \dfrac{16.08}{8} = 2.01$

Standard deviation of the sample $s = \sqrt{\dfrac{\sum(x - \bar{x})^2}{n}} = \sqrt{\dfrac{0.0452}{8}} = 0.0752$

From our knowledge of statistical sampling:

Best estimate of population mean = 2.01 litres

Best estimate of population standard deviation

$$\sigma = s \times \sqrt{\frac{n}{n-1}} = 0.0752 \times \sqrt{\frac{8}{7}} = 0.0806 \text{ litres}$$

We can determine 95% confidence limits for the actual population mean from this sample data, recognising that this is a small sample (n < 30), so the t-distribution should be used rather than the normal distribution. If you are not familiar with the t-distribution from your earlier studies do not worry. You could use the normal distribution although this would not be as accurate.

With n = 8, there are 7 degrees of freedom and the tables of the t-distribution give a critical t-statistic of 2.365. We are therefore 95% confident that the actual population mean μ has the value

$$\mu = \bar{x} \pm (\text{Critical t-score} \times \sigma)$$

$$= 2.01 \pm (2.365 \times 0.0806)$$

$$= 2.01 \pm 0.19 \text{ litres.}$$

It is common to place 'warning' limits at the 95% confidence level and 'action' limits at the 99% confidence level. From the t-tables the 99% confidence limits would be

$$\mu = 2.01 \pm (3.499 \times 0.0806)$$

$$= 2.01 \pm 0.28 \text{ litres.}$$

These limits could be drawn on a control chart as below.

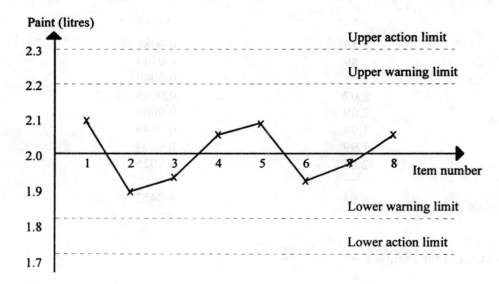

6.5 Conclusion on x charts

Conclusion Control charts can be drawn of individual units selected from a process, and control limits marked on the chart. When the limits are exceeded, there is evidence that the process is out of control. However, more powerful statistical theory can be applied to the alternative types of chart described below.

7   CHARTS OF AVERAGE RESULTS: $\overline{X}$ CHARTS AND R CHARTS

7.1   Introduction

In the preceding paragraph, **individual units** were repeatedly selected and introduced into the analysis. In practice, quality controllers generally select small samples of a **group of items** from time to time, rather than one-off items. The analysis then proceeds on the basis of the means calculated for the sample, and the variability of the sample members.

Variability can be measured in terms of standard deviations or ranges. Both are possible, though in practice it is more common to work with ranges since they are so much easier to calculate than standard deviations.

7.2   Using averages and standard deviations

Consider again the data in paragraph 6.4. Suppose this time that the 8 readings are the means of 8 samples of size 30 that have been selected at random from the process output. Any control chart drawn of a series of sample means is called an $\overline{x}$ chart.

Recall from your earlier studies the properties of a distribution of sample means:

- it is a normal distribution (as long as n $\geq$ 30)
- it has a mean of μ , the population mean
- it has a standard deviation of $\dfrac{\sigma}{\sqrt{n}}$, called the standard error of the mean.

Earlier we calculated for the data that:

Best estimate of μ = 2.01 litres
Best estimate of σ = 0.0806 litres

Therefore the standard error = $\dfrac{\sigma}{\sqrt{n}} = \dfrac{0.0806}{\sqrt{30}} = 0.0147$

Control limits could be drawn on the $\overline{x}$ chart at three standard errors above and below the mean, so that:

UCL	=	upper control limit = μ + 3 standard errors
LCL	=	lower control limit = μ − 3 standard errors

Similarly warning limits could be drawn at 1.96 standard errors above and below the mean, so that:

UWL	=	upper warning limit = μ + 1.96 standard errors
LWL	=	lower warning limit = μ − 1.96 standard errors

With the given numbers the warning limits would be set at

$$2.01 \pm (1.96 \times 0.0147)$$
$$= \quad 2.01 \pm 0.03 \text{ litres.}$$

These warnings limits are designed so that 95% of observed sample means are expected to lie within them, but we see from the observed results that only one of the observed means falls within these limits, suggesting that the process is out of control. Certainly most of the observed means lie outside the control limits set at

$$2.01 \pm (3 \times 0.0147)$$
$$= \quad 2.01 \pm 0.04 \text{ litres.}$$

7.3   Using averages and ranges

It is much quicker to calculate the range of a sample (the difference between the lowest value and the highest value) rather than the standard deviation (which requires the data for all values and involves squares and square roots), so most process control in practice involves calculations with the ranges of samples selected.

Suppose that we have a process with a standard output value of S. We can repeatedly take small samples of size n and calculate their means $\bar{x}$ and their ranges R. The mean of these ranges is calculated as $\bar{R}$.

Control limits are then set on a control chart as $S \pm A\bar{R}$, where A is read off from statistical tables that would be provided for you in the examination.

7.4   Example

A process manufactures 500g boxes of chocolates. Ten samples, each of five boxes of chocolates, have been selected at random from the day's production and the following calculations made:

Sample number	Sample mean	Sample range
	g	g
1	507	12
2	521	19
3	485	11
4	501	15
5	492	12
6	511	21
7	489	10
8	494	17
9	503	12
10	507	20

Determine suitable control limits for this process.

7.5   Solution

Control limits are $S \pm A\bar{R}$

$\bar{R}$ is the mean of the observed ranges ie,

$$\frac{12+19+11+......+12+20}{10} = \frac{149}{10} = 14.9g$$

Each sample contains 5 items. For n = 5, standard statistical tables can be looked up to find the appropriate value of A = 0.577.

Control limits should be set at $500 \pm (0.577 \times 14.9)$
                                     $= 500 \pm 8.6g$

If future samples of five boxes of chocolates have mean weights outside these limits, control action should be taken.

(Note: the standard values of A are calculated so that the limits represent three standard deviations above and below the mean of the distribution. Our control limits can therefore be called 3σ control limits.)

7.6   What if no standard is available?

If no value for S is known in a particular process, it is still possible to construct control limits from the sample data. This time the limits are set at

$$\overline{\overline{x}} \pm A\overline{R}$$

Where $\overline{\overline{x}}$ is the mean of the sample means

   A is the 3σ statistic read off statistical tables as before

   $\overline{R}$ is the mean of the sample ranges as before

7.7   Example

Consider again the data from paragraph 7.4, but this time we are not told that the boxes have a standard weight of 500g.

The control limits will now be set at

$$\overline{\overline{x}} \pm A\overline{R}$$

$\overline{\overline{x}}$ =   the mean of the observed sample means

$$= \frac{507 + 521 + \ldots + 503 + 507}{10}$$

$$= \frac{5,010}{10}$$

$$= 501g$$

The 3σ control limits would now be set at

$$501 \pm (0.577 \times 14.9)$$
$$= 501 \pm 8.6g$$

7.8   R charts

The standard statistical tables can also be used to set control limits on the range of samples taken from a process, so that a control chart can be drawn of observed ranges incorporating control limits. This type of chart is called an R chart.

Features of an R chart
*   the central value of the chart is $\overline{R}$, the mean of the sample ranges
*   the lower control limit is $B\overline{R}$, where B can be read from statistical tables
*   the upper control limit is $C\overline{R}$, where C can be read from statistical tables.

7.9   Example

Consider again the data from paragraph 7.4. To draw an R chart we must identify
*   central value = $\overline{R}$ = 14.9g as calculated above
*   lower control limit (with n = 5) = $B\overline{R}$ = 0 × 14.9g = 0g
*   upper control limit (with n = 5) = $C\overline{R}$ = 2.115 × 14.9g = 31.5g.

The R chart can now be drawn as below

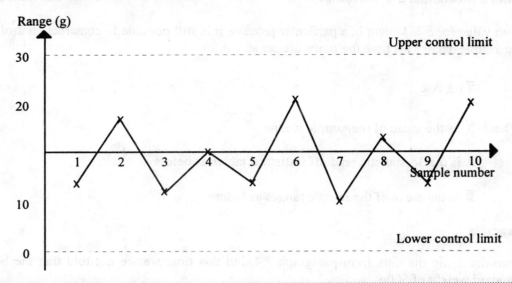

7.11   Activity solution

Central value = $\overline{R}$ = 20kg.
Lower control limit (with n = 10) = $B\overline{R}$ = 0.223 × 20 = 4.46kg.
Upper control limit (with n = 10) = $C\overline{R}$ = 1.777 × 20 = 35.54kg.

8   CHARTS OF PROPORTIONS: p CHARTS

8.1   Introduction

Certain variables must be **tested for attributes** rather than offering a continuous distribution. Samples can then be selected from the process output and the proportion with the attribute calculated for each sample. A control chart is then drawn for these proportions; this is a p-chart.

A typical example of attribute testing is to determine the number of defective items coming out of a process. This information is then used to estimate the proportion of defectives in a whole population. If the defective proportion is unacceptably high, the process is out of control.

8.2   Example

RM Ltd manufactures computer monitors and is concerned about the number of defective monitors that are rejected after a certain process.

25 samples, each of 100 monitors, are selected from a week's output and the number of defectives in each sample is recorded. These numbers are as follows

4	9	5	11	7
8	10	9	12	14
13	5	0	10	9
10	14	3	7	17
12	4	12	13	12

Draw a control chart for the proportion of defective monitors.

8.3   Solution

Total number of defectives = 4 + 9 + ... + 13 + 12 = 230
Total number tested = 25 × 100 = 2,500

∴ Estimated proportion defective $p = \dfrac{230}{2,500} = 0.092$

The standard error of a proportion is given by

$$\sqrt{\frac{p(1-p)}{n}} = \sqrt{\frac{0.092 \times 0.908}{100}}$$

$$= 0.029 \text{ monitors}$$

95% confidence limits can be set as warning limits at

$$p \pm 1.96 \sqrt{\frac{p(1-p)}{n}}$$
$$= 0.092 \pm 1.96 \times 0.029$$

$$= 0.092 \pm 0.057 \text{ monitors.}$$

The p-chart can now be constructed.

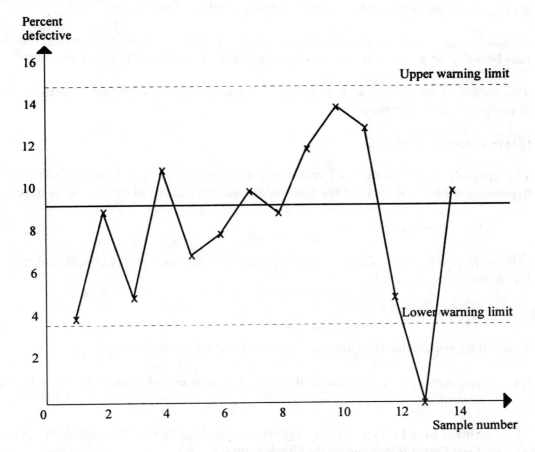

Note: the validity of having a lower warning limit in this sort of analysis is questionable, since the lower the number of defective units the better. However you are advised to include a lower warning limit in an examination answer unless advised otherwise in the question.

9   INTERPRETATION OF CONTROL CHARTS

Analysing a control chart is a matter of common sense. Any of the following might be evidence that a process is (or is about to be) out of control:

- points falling outside the control limits
- points consistently on one side of the central value
- a cyclical pattern of points
- significant numbers of points consistently close to the limits
- a trend in the points, either upwards or downwards.

Control charts can assist in forecasting that a process is about to go completely out of control. So long as control action is taken before the point of breakdown to solve the problem, large amounts of time and money can be saved in avoiding serious damage.

10   QUALITY CONTROL PROCEDURES

10.1   Use of a decision rule

A company can use the sampling theory studied earlier to test particular methods for deciding whether a process is out of control. For example, a jam manufacturer might have a process which is supposed to output jars of jam each holding 500g. It might additionally be known from long experience that the standard deviation of the output weights is 6g, ie, that $\sigma = 6$g.

The company tests whether the process remains under control by taking a random sample of 36 jars per hour from the output and calculating the mean weight of the sample.

A decision rule has been adopted that the process is believed to be in control if the mean weight falls between 497g and 503g, and outside these limits it is believed to be out of control.

This section of the text shows how such a decision rule can be appraised by drawing the operating characteristic curve for the rule.

10.2   Errors in statistical testing

The company wishes to test the hypothesis that the process is under control with $\mu = 500$g. The hypothesis to be tested is called the **null hypothesis** and is denoted by H_0. So we have:

H_0: $\mu = 500$g.

If the null hypothesis is rejected, we must accept the **alternative hypothesis** which is denoted by H_1. In the given case we have:

H_1: $\mu \neq 500$g.

You will appreciate that two possible errors could arise from the testing

(i)   The company may conclude that the process is out of control, when in fact it is still in control.

This is called a Type I error - rejecting a true hypothesis. The probability of committing a Type I error is denoted by the Greek letter α.

(ii)   The company may conclude that the process is under control, when in fact it is out of control.

This is called a Type II error - accepting a false hypothesis. The probability of committing a Type II error is denoted by the Greek letter β.

Conclusion   The errors that can arise in statistical hypothesis testing can be summarised in a table as below.

	Accept H_0	Reject H_0
H_0 is true	Correct decision is made	Type I error
H_0 is false	Type II error	Correct decision is made

10.3   How are α and β calculated?

Type I error

If the observed $\bar{x}$ fell below 497g while μ in fact was still 500g, a Type I error would arise.

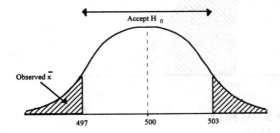

Since the distribution of sample means is a normal distribution, we can immediately state that

p (Type I error) $= \alpha =$ probability that $\bar{x}$ should exceed 3g away from the mean either side.

The standard deviation of the distribution of sample means is the standard error, calculated as

$$\frac{\sigma}{\sqrt{n}} = \frac{6}{\sqrt{36}} = 1 \text{ gramme}$$

So 497 and 503 represent respectively 3 standard errors below and above the mean of the distribution.

From tables, α $=$ $2 \times (0.5 - 0.49865)$
              $=$ $0.0027.$

Type II error

Consider the possibility that μ might have actually shifted to a value of 494g. What is the probability then that H_0 is accepted, ie, what is the probability that $\bar{x}$ will lie between 497 and 503g?

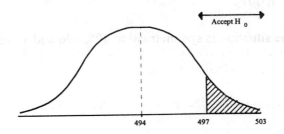

497 represents 3 standard errors above the mean
503 represents 9 standard errors above the mean, ie, a very remote possibility

$\therefore$ p ($\overline{x}$ lies between 497 and 503g)

= p (exceeding 3 standard errors from the mean)

= 0.5 – 0.49865 from tables

= 0.00135.

We can perform a similar analysis for the case where μ actually is 496g, and again for 498g.

μ = **496g**

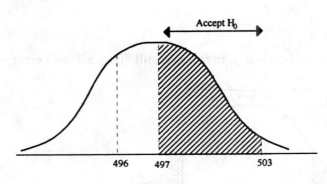

p (H_0 is accepted)   =   0.5 – 0.3413
                        =   0.1587

μ = **498g**

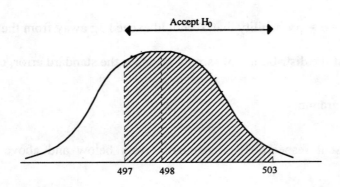

p (H_0 is accepted)   =   0.3413 + 0.5
                        =   0.8413.

When μ = 500, p (H_0 is accepted) has already been analysed when calculating α earlier.

So p (H_0 is accepted)   = $1 - \alpha$
                          = $1 - 0.0027$

                          =   0.9973

When μ = 502, 504 or 506g, the situation is symmetrical to 498, 496 and 494g.

So we can draw up the following table.

True value of μ	$\beta = Probability\ of\ accepting\ H_0$
g	
494	0.00135
496	0.1587
498	0.8413
500	0.9973
502	0.8413
504	0.1587
506	0.00135

10.4   Operating characteristic curves

The above table is used to analyse the effectiveness of this particular decision rule. The values of β calculated above are plotted on a graph against the values of the true μ to produce the operating characteristic curve (or OC curve) of this decision rule.

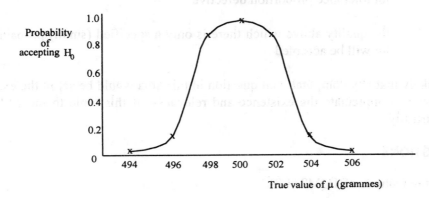

The graph shows the operating characteristic curve of the decision rule to believe that the process is under control as long as the sample mean lies between 497 and 503g.

Different decision rules will have differently-shaped OC curves. A good rule should have a high probability of accepting H_0 as long as the true value of μ is close to 500g, as in the above graph, so the tested decision rule appears reasonably good.

Conclusion   An operating characteristic curve gives an immediate picture of how good a decision criterion is in reliably keeping a process under control.

10.5   Acceptance sampling

When a manufacturer has agreed to supply a large number of certain parts regularly to a purchaser, the purchaser will wish to test each batch that he is supplied with to ensure that it is of satisfactory quality before he accepts it. As long as there is some attribute that can be tested for acceptability, the purchaser can adopt a decision rule for acceptance as described above. This process is called acceptance sampling or lot-by-lot sampling inspection.

100% inspection of the items in a batch is usually not practical or cost-effective, so a sampling approach must be adopted. You now know that any such sampling exercise contains a risk of giving the wrong answer, but both producer and consumer should be able to estimate the size of such risk.

The producer will want to know the probability of having a good lot rejected; you should recognise this as α, the probability of a Type I error. It should now be clear why, in an acceptance sampling situation, α is called the producer's risk.

At the same time, the consumer will want to know the probability of incorrectly accepting a bad lot; you should recognise this as β, the probability of a Type II error, and realise why β is called the consumer's risk.

If the levels of α and β are specified, and the size of the sample is agreed, standard statistical tables exist to give a decision rule that meets all the required criteria. Certain terms are used in the tables that may require explanation:

AQL	=	acceptable quality level
	=	the lowest quality at which the consumer will accept a lot with a specified probability
LTPD	=	lot tolerance proportion defective
	=	the quality above which there is only a specified (small) probability that a lot will be accepted

However it is unlikely that any computational question in this area would be set in the exam. What is important is that you appreciate the existence and relevance of this topic to the wider area of quality control generally.

11   SELF TEST QUESTIONS

11.1   What are the features of TQM? (1.3)

11.2   What are quality circles? (1.5)

11.3   What is acceptance sampling? (2.3)

11.4   What are the main quality costs? (3.4)

11.5   What are the four types of process control charts? (5.3)

11.6   Distinguish between a Type I and a Type II error. (10.2)

12   EXAMINATION TYPE QUESTION

12.1   Quality assurance

As senior product management accountant you have been informed by the MD that 'something drastic has to be done about quality'. In his view, quality is the responsibility of your department and he has suggested that you take a tougher line with those responsible for quality problems, raise quality standards, increase inspection rates, and give greater authority to quality control inspectors.

You are required:

(a)   to evaluate the suggestions made by the MD.

(10 marks)

(b)   to state what additional or alternative proposals you would offer.

(15 marks)

(Total: 25 marks)

13   ANSWER TO EXAMINATION TYPE QUESTION

13.1   Quality assurance

In general terms, the suggestions made by the MD reflect a mistaken view of quality and how it is assured.   His emphasis is 'reactive' rather than 'pro-active', is 'feedback' based rather than 'feedforward', and is concerned with quality control rather than quality assurance.

(a)   Specifically:

(i)   His initial statement that 'something drastic has to be done about quality' does not seem to be based on any kind of systematic analysis or measurement. Nor does it suggest that the MD understands the meaning of quality, which according to Crosby is 'conformity to requirements'.

(ii)   His statement that 'quality is the responsibility of your department' ignores the fact that quality is the responsibility of all staff at all stages, in all departments and at all levels.

(iii)   The 'tougher line' suggests a punishment orientated approach which contradicts the advice of Deming 'to drive out fear', and to seek co-operation.

(iv)   'Raising quality standards' without targeting particular areas, and without understanding why such quality improvement is necessary, is likely to be a costly and unproductive exercise.

(v)   'Increasing inspection rates' and 'giving greater authority to quality control inspectors' reinforces the 'control' approach, and the 'specialist' emphasis discussed earlier.

(b)   An alternative approach involves viewing quality control as part of a more strategic approach to quality - quality assurance. This requires:

(i)   An analysis of existing quality performance and problems. Such an analysis should involve all levels and all departments, and should concern itself with the customers, with the competition, with suppliers as well as the activities of the firm itself. Crosby advocates the creation of 'quality committees' composed of members drawn from different departments.

(ii)   Calculating the 'cost of quality', which involves measuring the costs of not 'getting it right first time', and includes 'prevention costs', 'appraisal costs', and 'failure costs'. Crosby advocates should identify a sizeable potential cost saving (or to quote Crosby 'quality is free').

(iii)   The careful selection and monitoring of suppliers, perhaps involving an 'active' rather than a passive relationship.

(iv)   The design of the product, to ensure an appropriate level of quality.

(v)   The installation of quality information systems which measure and feedback quality performance to those involved, and which can serve as the basis for targets.

(vi)   Quality improvement, perhaps involving the creation of quality circles.

(vii)   Quality staff, which involves investment in recruitment, selection, training, development, appraisal and reward.

In conclusion, such an approach is essentially long term, and requires a shift in thinking about quality at all levels. The essential ingredient in this cultural shift is a 'right first time' mentality which encompasses all activities that impinge on quality. In short, the MD and other staff need to be educated in 'total quality management'.

6 CHI-SQUARED TESTS

INTRODUCTION & LEARNING OBJECTIVES

Syllabus area 7b. Analysis of simple tables to provide meaningful information; the chi-squared test. (Ability required 3).

The chi-squared test provides a technique for controlling quality by comparing the results of different samples and evaluating whether there is a significant difference between them, and between them and the population they are meant to have come from.

When you have studied this chapter you should be able to do the following:

- Understand when the χ^2 test can be used.

- Make appropriate calculations for the χ^2 test.

- Apply the χ^2 test to different situations.

1 THE CHI-SQUARED TEST

1.1 Introduction

In many manual and automated production processes there is often a normal level of items that totally fail a quality control inspection and have to be discarded; an intermediate stage might occur in which, on reworking, an item might be expected to subsequently pass inspection. It is the job of management to monitor those levels of rejects and items needing reworking and to investigate ways of reducing those levels.

If items are produced on different production lines or by different production staff it is important to check that one line or one member of staff isn't falling behind the standard of the rest. To that end schedules or tables will be drawn up of items inspected. Below is one such table where, as far as the level of rejects and reworks is concerned, everything would appear to be running at a uniform level.

Week 1's output	Production line A	Production line B	Production line C	Total
Rejects	8 (2%)	10 (2%)	12 (2%)	30 (2%)
Reworks	16 (4%)	20 (4%)	24 (4%)	60 (4%)
Satisfactory	376 (94%)	470 (94%)	564 (94%)	1,410 (94%)
Total	400 (100%)	500 (100%)	600 (100%)	1,500 (100%)

Assuming that the normal level of rejects is 2% and of reworks is 4% then each line is as efficient as the other. Questions might be asked about the differing levels of output but not the rate of rejects etc.

Supposing now that in week 2 the same output levels are achieved and the same overall level of rejects, but they are distributed differently as follows.

Week 2's output	Production line A	B	C	Total
Rejects	6	9	15	30
Reworks	12	20	28	60
Satisfactory	382	471	557	1,410
Total	400	500	600	1,500

Overall production hasn't changed; the question that needs asking is, 'can one line be said to be working more efficiently with respect to rejects than the others?'. Clearly the answer is, 'In this week - yes - slightly'. What management needs to know is whether this difference is 'significant', whether it means anything, whether these differences are indicative of problems in production lines or whether they are simply the sort of variations that could be expected in figures such as these. A variety of 'significance tests' could be used to help management. The most useful in this case is the chi-squared (χ^2) test.

1.2 Contingency tables

In the context of a chi-squared test, the table of data above is referred to as a contingency table. A chi-squared test establishes whether the differences between observed frequencies (the nine figures which total 1,500) and expected frequencies (to be determined shortly) are more than can simply be due to chance.

In the case of the rejects example, expected frequencies would be based on a **null hypothesis** that there was **no difference** in the rate of rejects from different lines. (A null hypothesis inevitably states that there is no difference, it has been compared with the legal principle that a prisoner is innocent until proved guilty - there is no good or bad production lines until irrefutable evidence appears to the contrary.) If there was no difference in the rate of rejects then the frequencies would resemble those of week 1.

There is a difference between the frequencies in week 1 and week 2, and it has to be decided whether the difference is big enough to be significant.

1.3 χ^2 statistic

In order to decide whether the difference between observed frequencies (O) and expected frequencies, based on a null hypothesis, (E) are significant, rather than just finding a difference (O − E), a statistic, a measure, called the chi-squared is calculated:

$$\chi^2 = \sum \frac{(O-E)^2}{E}$$

In the previous instance O is represented by week 2's figures, E by week 1's figures.

The value of χ^2 is:

$$\chi^2 = \frac{(6-8)^2}{8} + \frac{(9-10)^2}{10} + \frac{(15-12)^2}{12} +$$

$$\frac{(12-16)^2}{16} + \frac{(20-20)^2}{20} + \frac{(28-24)^2}{24} +$$

$$\frac{(382-376)^2}{376} + \frac{(471-470)^2}{470} + \frac{(557-564)^2}{564}$$

$$= \frac{2^2}{8} + \frac{1^2}{10} + \frac{3^2}{12} + \frac{4^2}{16} + \frac{0^2}{20} + \frac{4^2}{24} + \frac{6^2}{376} + \frac{1^2}{470} + \frac{7^2}{564}$$

$$= 3.201$$

The next stage is to interpret this statistic, to see if a figure of 3.201 is sufficiently large to indicate that the production lines are operating at different levels of efficiency.

1.4   Degrees of freedom

When looking at either of the tables, the totals of the rows and columns were the same, as they must be for this test (a less contrived example will be shown later). However, given these totals, the arrangement of the nine figures in the body of the table was not completely random. Once it is known in week 2 that, with 30 rejects produced, 6 came from line A and 9 from line B, it automatically follows that 15 must have come from line C. Similarly if it is known that there were 60 reworks and 12 came from line A and 20 from line B, it follows that 28 must have come from line C. Furthermore, knowing the total output of each of the 3 lines, the total number of satisfactory items produced by each line can now be deduced.

In order to ascertain the make up of the table of 3 rows and 3 columns given that the total of the rows and columns is known, only 4 individual frequencies must be established; the rest can be found as 'balancing figures'. We say this '3 by 3' contingency table has 4 **degrees of freedom**. This parameter is important for chi-square tests.

In general for contingency tables:

Number of degrees of freedom, ν = $(\text{rows} - 1) \times (\text{columns} - 1)$

1.5 χ^2 tables

To determine whether a value for χ^2 is too large to merely suggest that differences in frequencies are due to chance three things are needed:

- χ^2 tables (as supplied by CIMA);

- the number of degrees of freedom, ν;

- a significance level (or probability level).

The χ^2 tables appear at the front of the examination text, the number of degrees of freedom in this case is 4 and, for the moment, a probability level of 5% will be assumed.

The χ^2 tables (4 degrees of freedom, probability level 5%) gives us a critical value for χ^2 of **9.49**.

As the notes at the bottom of the table show there is only a 5% chance that the calculated value for χ^2 would exceed 9.49 as a result of random variations if the null hypothesis were true. Put another way, since our calculated value for χ^2 is less than 9.49 we can be fairly confident that the null hypothesis is true - that there is no significant difference between the observed and expected frequencies; that there is no significant difference between the efficiencies of the three production lines; that the small differences that have been noted are purely due to chance.

1.6   Significance test method

Step 1   State the 'null hypothesis' (H_0).

H_0:   There is no difference between the efficiencies of the three production lines in week 2.

Step 2   State the 'alternative hypothesis' (H_1).

H_1:   There is a difference between the production line efficiencies in week 2.

Step 3   Tabulate observed frequencies leaving room for expected frequencies.

	Production line						Total
	A		*B*		*C*		
	O	E	O	E	O	E	
Rejects	6		9		15		30
Reworks	12		20		28		60
Satisfactory	382		471		557		1,410
Total	400		500		600		1,500

Step 4   Calculate expected frequencies, based on the null hypothesis, and insert them in the table. (Show workings for a few.)

Since the total split of output is in the ratio 2 : 4 : 94 then, based on the null hypothesis, this should be seen in each production line. The first figure (A's rejects) should be:

$$400 \times \frac{2}{100} = 8$$

The central figure (B's reworks) should be:

$$500 \times \frac{4}{100} = 20$$

All these should be calculated and tabulated.

Step 5   Calculate χ^2.

$$\chi^2 = \sum \frac{(O-E)^2}{E} \qquad (= 3.201)$$

Step 6   Determine the number of degrees of freedom.

$$v = (\text{rows} - 1) \times (\text{columns} - 1) = (3 - 1) \times (3 - 1) = 4$$

Step 7   Choose a probability (significance) level.

This may well be specified, if not choose 5% or 1%.

Step 8   Find the critical value for χ^2 from tables.

At the: 5% level, reject H_0 if $\chi^2 > 9.49$

1% level, reject H_0 if $\chi^2 > 13.28$

Step 9   Compare the calculated value for χ^2 with the table figure and decide whether or not to reject the null hypothesis.

Here H_0 cannot be rejected. There is insufficient evidence to suggest any real variation in the efficiency of the production line.

1.7   Example

Two factories (X and Y) using materials from the same supplier produce output for a given period classified into three grades, (A, B, C) as follows:

	Grade A	Grade B	Grade C	Total
		Output in tons		
Factory X	45	14	29	88
Factory Y	17	7	29	53
Total	62	21	58	141

Do these output figures show a significant difference (testing at both the 5% and 1% significance levels) between proportions of different grades produced by the two factories?

1.8   Solution

The above table is a 2 × 3 contingency table because it has two rows (Factory X and Factory Y) and three columns (Grades A, B and C). It classifies the data according to two attributes, the grade of product and the type of factory. The χ^2 test tests whether there is an association between the two attributes. The actual frequencies must be used, not proportions or percentages.

The null hypothesis is that there is no association between the attributes. If this hypothesis were true, we would expect the proportion of each grade to be the same at each factory. The best estimate of these proportions is $\dfrac{62}{141}$, $\dfrac{21}{141}$ and $\dfrac{58}{141}$ respectively.

The values expected if the null hypothesis is true are therefore obtained by splitting up the total for each factory in these proportions.

For factory X, the total is 88, giving:

Grade A: $E = \dfrac{62}{141} \times 88 = 38.7$

Grade B: $E = \dfrac{21}{141} \times 88 = 13.1$

Grade C: $E = \dfrac{58}{141} \times 88 = 36.2$

For factory Y, the total is 53, giving:

Grade A: $E = \dfrac{62}{141} \times 53 = 23.3$

Grade B: $E = \dfrac{21}{141} \times 53 = 7.9$

Grade C: $E = \dfrac{58}{141} \times 53 = 21.8$

The structure of these calculations should be noted, ie:

$$E = \frac{\text{Column total} \times \text{Row total}}{\text{Grand total}}$$

Placing the E values in the same cells as the corresponding observed values (O):

	Grade A O E	Grade B O E	Grade C O E	Total
Factory X	45 38.7	14 13.1	29 36.2	88
Factory Y	17 23.3	7 7.9	29 21.8	53
Total	62	21	58	141

Now, to calculate χ^2:

		O	E	O − E	$(O - E)^2$	$\dfrac{(O-E)^2}{E}$
Factory X	Grade A	45	38.7	6.3	39.69	1.03
	Grade B	14	13.1	0.9	0.81	0.06
	Grade C	29	36.2	-7.2	51.84	1.43
Factory Y	Grade A	17	23.3	-6.3	39.69	1.70
	Grade B	7	7.9	-0.9	0.81	0.10
	Grade C	29	21.8	7.2	51.84	2.38
	Total	141	141.0			$\chi^2 = 6.70$

Number of degrees of freedom $= (r - 1)(c - 1)$

where   r   =   number of rows
        c   =   number of columns

In this example, the number of degrees of freedom $\begin{aligned} &= (2-1)(3-1) \\ &= 1 \times 2 \\ &= 2 \end{aligned}$

From tables:

Reject H_0 at the 5% level if $\chi^2 > 5.99$

at the 1% level if $\chi^2 > 9.21$

The calculated value for χ^2 of 6.70 falls between these two. We reject H_0 at the 5% level but not at the 1% level.

One useful way of interpreting these two conclusions is to say that we are 95% sure that there is a difference in the output of the two factories but not 99% sure.

1.9   Yates' correction for one degree of freedom

χ^2 tests are prone to errors when there is only one degree of freedom, which will be the case with a 2×2 contingency table. A continuity correction must be applied. The effect of this is to decrease the modulus (ie, absolute value) of each $O - E$ by 0.5. This is illustrated in the following example.

1.10   Example

| | Machine output | | |
	Defective	Non-defective	Total
Machine A	25	375	400
Machine B	42	558	600
	67	933	1,000

Is there an association between the number of defectives and the machine used?

Solution

H_0: no association between number of defectives and machine used. Calculating the E values by the formula:

$$E = \frac{\text{Row total} \times \text{Column total}}{\text{Grand total}}$$

Class	O	E	$O - E$	Corrected $O - E$	$(O - E)^2$	$\dfrac{(O - E)^2}{E}$
A/Def	25	26.8	-1.8	-1.3	1.69	0.063
A/Non-def	375	373.2	1.8	1.3	1.69	0.005
B/Def	42	40.2	1.8	1.3	1.69	0.042
B/Non-def	558	559.8	-1.8	-1.3	1.69	0.003
					$\chi^2 =$	0.113

Degrees of freedom $=$ $(r - 1)(c - 1)$
$=$ $(2 - 1)(2 - 1)$
$=$ 1

From the χ^2 table, the critical value at the 5% level is 3.84.

As 0.113 < 3.84, H_0 is accepted, there is no association between the number of defectives and the machine used.

1.11   Correction for E ≤ 5

For any χ^2 test, all E values should be > 5, otherwise errors again become unacceptably large. If any class has an E value ≤ 5, it should be combined with another class - either combine two rows or two columns.

2   APPLICATION TO FREQUENCY DISTRIBUTIONS

2.1   Introduction

It is possible to apply the χ^2 test to problems not involving contingency tables but rather a frequency distribution such as the one shown below.

2.2   Example

A die is thrown 600 times and the following results are obtained:

Score	1	2	3	4	5	6
Frequency	80	90	100	105	110	115

Is there significant evidence of bias?

2.3   Solution

H_0:   the die is not biased
H_1:   the die is biased

The expected frequencies would each be 100, since:

$$P(1) = \frac{1}{6} \qquad \therefore \text{ expected frequency} = \frac{1}{6} \times 600 = 100$$

$$P(2) = \frac{1}{6} \qquad \therefore \text{ expected frequency} = \frac{1}{6} \times 600 = 100$$
... etc.

Score	Observed frequency	Expected frequency	O - E	$(O-E)^2$	$\dfrac{(O-E)^2}{E}$
1	80	100	-20	400	4
2	90	100	-10	100	1
3	100	100	0	0	0
4	105	100	5	25	0.25
5	110	100	10	100	1
6	115	100	15	225	2.25
Total	600	600			8.5

$$\therefore \chi^2 = \sum \frac{(O-E)^2}{E} = 8.5$$

2.4   Interpretation

Having calculated χ^2 as 8.5, it is now necessary to interpret this result.

$v = 6 - 1 = 5$, since again we are concerned with the degrees of freedom. In this sort of test the formula to use is that the number of degrees of freedom = number of frequencies − 1.

From the tables a selection of χ^2 values is:

degrees of freedom	*Probability level %*			
	10	*5*	*1*	*0.1*
5	9.24	11.07	15.09	20.52

These values actually mean:

$P(\chi^2 > 9.24)$	=	10%	or 0.10	ie, there is a 10% chance that purely random fluctuations would cause χ^2 to be greater than 9.24, etc.
$P(\chi^2 > 11.07)$	=	5%	or 0.05	
$P(\chi^2 > 15.09)$	=	1%	or 0.01	
$P(\chi^2 > 20.52)$	=	0.1%	or 0.001	

8.5 is less than the 10% critical value for χ^2; ie, the result is not regarded as significant. (Put more simply, it is not very surprising that a χ^2 value of 8.5 is obtained since this could quite easily have arisen from purely random fluctuations.)   Therefore there is no reason to conclude that the differences arose from bias rather than sampling fluctuations.

2.5   Activity

A large fashion house is investigating if its distribution of sales between outlets changed between 19X1 and 19X2. It has determined the number of units sold of one particular relatively expensive outfit at four representative outlets in both 19X1 and 19X2.

			Outlets		
Year	*A*	*B*	*C*	*D*	*Total*
19X1	100	150	80	70	400
19X2	110	225	115	50	500

Test at the 5% level, using the chi-squared goodness of fit test to see if there has been any change in the distribution of sales between outlets between 19X1 and 19X2.

2.6   Activity solution

H_0: no change from 19X1

H_1: there has been a change from 19X1

The actual observed frequencies (O) in 19X2 were:

A	*B*	*C*	*D*	*Total*
110	225	115	50	500

To obtain the expected frequencies for 19X2, assuming the same distribution as in 19X1, we need to multiply the 19X1 figures by $\frac{500}{400}$ to keep the same proportions but totalling 500 instead of 400.

Expected frequencies (E):

A	B	C	D
$100 \times \dfrac{500}{400}$	$150 \times \dfrac{500}{400}$	$80 \times \dfrac{500}{400}$	$70 \times \dfrac{500}{400}$
= 125	= 187.5	= 100	= 87.5

O	E	$(O - E)$	$(O - E)^2$	$(O - E)^2/E$
110	125	−15	225	1.80
225	187.5	37.5	1,406.25	7.50
115	100	15	225	2.25
50	87.5	−37.5	1,406.25	16.07
500	500	Observed chi-squared		27.62

Now $v = 4 - 1 = 3$, testing at 5% level, so the test value of chi-squared from tables is 7.81.

As the observed chi-squared value of 27.62 is greater than the test value of 7.81, reject the null hypothesis and accept the alternative hypothesis.

Conclusion   The distribution of sales between outlets has changed between 19X1 and 19X2.

The high value of chi-squared is caused by the values of 7.50 and 16.07 in the last column. It would seem that the high unit sales of outlet B have increased in proportion terms and the low unit sales of outlet D have decreased in proportion terms. The other two outlets have not changed significantly. The product seems to be established at B and not established at D.

3   GOODNESS OF FIT TO A NORMAL DISTRIBUTION

3.1   Introduction

For a normal distribution, the mean and standard deviation are required. Usually these must be estimated from the sample. The expected frequencies are then calculated using the appropriate areas of the normal distribution. There is now an additional constraint on the E values because they must have the correct standard deviation as well as mean. Hence:

Number of degrees of freedom = number of E values −3

3.2   Example

A sample of 65 sacks of fertiliser with nominal weight 1 kg were checked for weight with the following results:

Weight (g) x	No. of sacks f
< 1,060	6
≥ 1,060 and < 1,070	10
≥ 1,070 and < 1,080	16
≥ 1,080 and < 1,090	14
≥ 1,090 and < 1,100	10
≥ 1,100 and < 1,110	7
≥ 1,110	2
Total	65

Could this sample have come from a population with weights normally distributed?

3.3   Solution

From the above data, by the usual method of calculating mean and standard deviation from the midpoints of each class:

Mean (μ) = 1,081 g
Standard deviation ($\hat{\sigma}$) = 15.55 g

The null hypothesis is that the sample came from a normal distribution with mean 1,081 g and standard deviation 15.55 g.

The distribution can be represented diagrammatically as follows (not to scale):

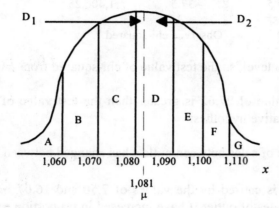

To find the expected values, areas A, B, C, D, E, F and G are required. They are found by the usual method for a normal distribution.

The calculation can be set out as follows, using the fact that:

$A = 0.5 - (B + C + D_1)$
$B = (B + C + D_1) - (C + D_1)$
$C = (C + D_1) - D_1$
etc.

x	$z = \dfrac{x - \mu}{\hat{\sigma}}$	Tabulated area*	Strip	Area of strip		
1,060	-1.35	0.4115	A	0.5 – 0.4115	=	0.0885
1,070	-0.71	0.2611	B	0.4115 – 0.2611	=	0.1504
1,080	-0.06	0.0239	C	0.2611 – 0.0239	=	0.2372
1,081	0	0	D_1	0.0239 – 0	=	0.0239
1,090	0.58	0.2190	D_2	0.2190 – 0	=	0.2190
1,100	1.22	0.3888	E	0.3888 – 0.2190	=	0.1698
1,110	1.86	0.4686	F	0.4686 – 0.3888	=	0.0798
>1,110		0.5	G	0.5 – 0.4686	=	0.0314

* Obtained from the table of the normal distribution.

The expected values are the probabilities multiplied by the total frequency (65). D_1 and D_2 are combined to give D.

Weight (g)	Probability	E = prob × 65	O	O – E	$\frac{(O-E)^2}{E}$
< 1,060	0.0885	5.8	6	0.2	0.007
≥ 1,060 < 1,070	0.1504	9.8	10	0.2	0.004
≥ 1,070 < 1,080	0.2372	15.4	16	0.6	0.023
≥ 1,080 < 1,090	0.2429	15.8	14	-1.8	0.205
≥ 1,090 < 1,100	0.1698	11.0	10	-1.0	0.091
≥ 1,100 < 1,110	0.0798	5.2)			
		) 7.2*	9*	1.8	0.450
≥ 1,110	0.0314	2.0)			
	1.0000	65.0		χ^2 =	0.78

* Combined because the last group (1,110 and over) has $E \le 5$.

Number of degrees of freedom = 6 – 3 = 3

Critical value of χ^2 from the χ^2 table at 5% level of significance = 7.81

As 0.78 < 7.81, H_0 is accepted.

The distribution of weights is normal with mean 1,081 g and standard deviation 15.55 g.

4   SELF TEST QUESTIONS

4.1   What is the formula for the chi-squared statistic? (1.3)

4.2   How are the expected values calculated in a contingency table? (1.6)

4.3   What is Yates' correction? (1.9)

4.4   How many degrees of freedom are there for a goodness of fit test to a normal distribution? (3.1)

5   EXAMINATION TYPE QUESTION

5.1   Cash flow and debtors

A company which has a range of profitable products is experiencing serious cash flow problems. The management accountant has decided to analyse the data relating to debtors, for she suspects that those debtors who owe more to the company are those who are taking longer to settle. A sample of 400 debts is produced and is analysed under the following headings:

(i)   Period outstanding **beyond** the normal credit period

1–2 weeks	slow
3–4 weeks	very slow
5–6 weeks	warning letter
7–8 weeks	legal action

(ii)   Amount of debt

£1,000–1,999	small
£2,000–2,999	medium
£3,000–3,999	large
£4,000–4,999	substantial

The clerks in the department have undertaken an examination of the 400 debts, and have produced the table below:

	Slow	Very slow	Warning letter	Legal action
Small	12	15	16	17
Medium	15	17	21	27
Large	17	26	26	41
Substantial	26	32	37	55

You are required:

(a)   to use the chi-squared test to substantiate or refute the suspicion of the management accountant;

(b)   to explain carefully what is meant by the term 'significance' in the present context, and how a 'hypothesis test' differs from a 'test of significance'.

6   ANSWER TO EXAMINATION TYPE QUESTION

6.1   Cash flow and debtors

(a)   Chi-squared test

(Tutorial note: the values used in a chi-squared test must be actual frequencies. These are the number of debts in each category. The information as to how these categories are defined is not used in the test.*)*

Calculate row and column totals of the numbers of debts:

	S	VS	WL	LA	Total
Small	12	15	16	17	60
Medium	15	17	21	27	80
Large	17	26	26	41	110
Substantial	26	32	37	55	150
Total	70	90	100	140	400

Null hypothesis: there is no association between age and size of debt.

If the null hypothesis is true, the numbers expected in each category (E) are given by:

$$E = \frac{\text{Row total} \times \text{Column total}}{\text{Grand total}}$$

These are calculated and inserted in the table below, together with the observed values (O), and the other data for obtaining chi-squared. For example, the expected number of small, slow debts is:

$$\frac{60 \times 70}{400} = 10.5$$

O	E	$O-E$	$\dfrac{(O-E)^2}{E}$
12	10.5	+1.5	0.2143
15	13.5	+1.5	0.1667
16	15	+1	0.0667
17	21	−4	0.7619
15	14	+1	0.0714
17	18	−1	0.0555
21	20	+1	0.0500
27	28	−1	0.0357
17	19.25	−2.25	0.2630
26	24.75	+1.25	0.0631
26	27.5	−1.5	0.0818
41	38.5	+2.5	0.1623
26	26.25	−0.25	0.0024
32	33.75	−1.75	0.0907
37	37.5	−0.5	0.0067
55	52.5	+2.5	0.0476

$$\chi^2 = 2.1398$$

No. of degrees of freedom $\quad = \quad$ (Rows − 1) (Columns − 1)

$$= \quad (4-1)(4-1)$$
$$= \quad 9$$

The critical value of chi-squared at the 5% level of significance, obtained from the tabulated distribution, is 16.92.

As the calculated value is less than the critical value, the null hypothesis is accepted. There is no evidence of an association between age and size of debt.

*(**Tutorial note:** if no level of significance is specified in the question, assume the 5% level.)*

(b) **Explanation**

The differences between the O and E values, and consequently the value of chi-squared derived from them, are said to be not significant because they are small enough to be explained by random sampling error. If the probability of this explanation being correct was less than 5%, resulting in a value of chi-squared greater than 16.92, the differences between the O and E values, and the value of chi-squared, would have been said to have been significant in being too great to be explained by random sampling error, and must therefore have been due to an association between age and size of debt.

A test of significance is used when a sample result differs from an anticipated population value or from another sample value, and it is required to know whether this difference is significant. The calculation of the test statistic requires an assumption to be made about the values of the population parameters. This assumption is usually to the effect that the difference is not significant, so that the population parameters can be estimated from the sample. The assumption is called the 'null hypothesis', and the test of significance then becomes a test of the truth of this hypothesis. Significance testing and hypothesis testing are therefore closely related terms, and are often used synonymously.

7 STOCK POLICY

INTRODUCTION & LEARNING OBJECTIVES

Syllabus area 7b. Stock policy: simple systems, economic order quantity (EOQ) and economic batch quantity (EBQ) models; effect of discounts. (Ability required 2).

When you have studied this chapter you should be able to do the following:

- Explain the principles and calculation of economic order quantities.

- Distinguish between situations requiring the use of economic order quantity and economic batch quantity models and make appropriate calculations.

- Explain the relationship between lead times, stock-outs and buffer stocks.

- Calculate the effects of discounts.

---

1 INVENTORY CONTROL

1.1 Inventory control systems

It is important that inventory levels are maintained at a high enough level to service the production facility and at the same time at a level which minimises working capital tied up in inventory. The following sections look at both the physical aspects of different control systems and the mathematical techniques supporting control.

1.2 Definitions

Throughout this chapter there are certain terms which will re-occur and it seems a good idea to begin by defining the important ones before commencing on the theory.

> **Definition**   **Lead time**: this is the time which elapses between the placing of an order for stock and its eventual delivery. Thus, a supply lead time of three months means that it will take three months from the time an order is placed until the time it is delivered into stores.

> **Definition**   **Stock-out**: a situation where there is a requirement for an item of stock, but the stores or warehouse is temporarily out of stock.

> **Definition**   **Buffer stocks**: to avoid stock-outs, it may be necessary to hold safety stocks or buffer stocks to meet unexpected high demand. Buffer stocks should only be required intermittently during the lead time between re-ordering an item and its re-supply. If there is excessive demand, or a delay in re-supply, the buffer stocks might be used. At all other times, buffer stocks represent 'excess' stockholding and give rise to 'extra' stockholding costs.

Definition   **Re-order quantity**: this is the number of units of an item in one order.

Definition   **Re-order level**: this is the balance of units remaining in stock, at which a new order for such units will be placed.

Definition   **Economic order quantity**: this is the optimal re-order quantity for an item of stock which will minimise costs assuming supplies are received immediately or lead time is constant and certain.

1.3 Two-bin system

Under this system the existence of two bins is assumed, say A and B. Stock is taken from A until A is empty. A is then replenished with the economic order quantity. During the lead-time stock is used from B. The standard stock for B is the expected demand in the lead-time, plus the buffer stock. When the new order arrives, B is filled up to its standard stock and the rest placed in A. Stock is then drawn as required from A, and the process repeated.

The same sort of approach is adopted by some firms for a single bin. In such cases a red line is painted round the inside of the bin, such that when sufficient stock is removed to expose the red line, this indicates the need to re-order. The stock in the bin up to the red line therefore represents bin B, that above the red line bin A.

In considering the costs of stock control, the actual costs of operating the system must be recognised. The costs of a continual review as implied by the two-bin system may be excessive, and it may be more economic to operate a **periodic review system**.

1.4 Periodic review system

Under this system the stock levels are reviewed at fixed intervals, eg, every four weeks. The stock in hand is then made up to a predetermined level, which takes account of likely demand before the next review and during the lead-time. Thus, a four-weekly review in a system where the lead-time was two weeks would require that stock be made up to the likely maximum demand for the next six weeks.

This system is described in some textbooks as the **constant order cycle system**.

1.5 Physical stocks and recorded stocks

The systems described above assume that physical stock counts are taken to arrive at re-order levels. Under the two-bin system this may be so, but increasing reliance is placed on stock records such as bin cards to show when the re-order point is reached. It is frequently found during physical stock checks that recorded stocks bear no relation to stocks actually held. The reasons for differences include:

(a)   breaking of bulk;
(b)   pilferage;
(c)   poor record-keeping.

The consequence of differences between physical and recorded stocks will be that the use of stock records for re-order purposes will be inadequate. Every effort must therefore be made to ensure that stock records are as accurate as possible, otherwise the stock control model will be rendered unreliable. However, more frequent stock counts will raise the cost of stockholding and the model will require further review.

The use of computers in business has resulted in increasing reliance on stock records as opposed to physical stock counts.

Conclusion

Advantages of two-bin system	*Advantages of periodic review system*
Stock can be kept at a lower level because of the ability to order whenever stocks fall to a low level, rather than having to wait for the next re-order date.	Order office load is more evenly spread and easier to plan. For this reason the system is popular with suppliers.

1.6   ABC inventory analysis

We have already looked at this technique earlier in this text, but it is worth looking at it again briefly here as it is another method of stock control.

This is a technique which divides stocks into sub-classifications based on an annual usage value and involves using different control systems for each classification.

It is based on **pareto** analysis which states that approximately 20% of the total quantity of stock lines may account for about 80% of the total value of stock.

The idea is to gear the quality of stock control procedures to the value of the stock and therefore to help ensure that the stock control methods adopted are cost effective.

1.7   Illustration

An example of ABC analysis is the classification of stock as follows:

	No of days' supply held in stock
Class A	2 days
Class B	5 days
Class C	10 days
Class D	20 days or more

Stock levels of high value category A items are kept low in order to save on holding costs.

The priority with category D items is to avoid stockouts, hence much higher stocks are held. The company could use the 'two bin system' for this category of items.

2   INVESTMENT IN INVENTORY

2.1   Inventory valuation methods

It may be asserted that the object of holding stocks is to increase sales and thereby increase profit. The implications of stockholding are that a wider variety of products is offered and that customer demand is more immediately satisfied because the product is available: both implications should prevent prospective customers from going elsewhere.

Although the above assertion is more identifiable when related to finished goods, the benefits of stockholding of materials and components may be similarly postulated.

Holding stock is an expensive business - it has been estimated that the cost of holding stock each year is one-third of its cost. Holding costs include interest on capital, storage space and equipment, administration costs and leases.

On the other hand, running out of stock (known as a stock-out) incurs a cost. If, for example, a shop is persistently out of stock on some lines, customers will start going elsewhere. Stock-out cost is difficult to estimate, but it is an essential factor in inventory control.

Finally, set-up or handling costs are incurred each time a batch is ordered. Administrative costs and, where production is internal, costs of setting up machinery will be affected in total by the frequency of orders.

The two major quantitative problems of re-order levels and order quantities are essentially problems of striking the optimum balance between two of the three costs categories above.

Essentially, three inventory problems need to be answered under either of two assumptions:

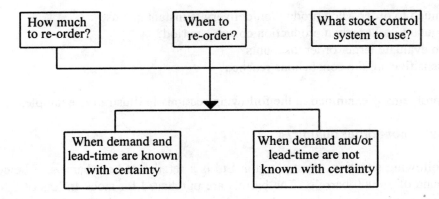

2.2   Pattern of stock levels

When new batches of an item in stock are purchased or made at periodic intervals, the stock levels will exhibit the following pattern over time:

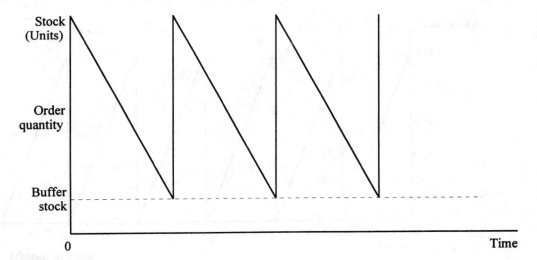

The questions asked are:

(a)   **How much to re-order?**

Large order quantities cut ordering and set-up costs each year. On the other hand, stock volumes will on average be higher, and so holding costs increase. The problem is balancing one against the other.

(b)   When to re-order?

A gap (known as the lead-time) inevitably occurs between placing an order and its delivery. Where both that gap and the rate of demand are known with certainty, an exact decision on when to re-order can be made. In the real world both will fluctuate randomly and so the order must be placed so as to leave some buffer stock if demand and lead-time follow the average pattern. The problem is again the balancing of increased holding costs if the buffer stock is high, against increased stock-out costs if the buffer stock is low.

2.3   Re-order quantities

Calculation involves four distinct problems:

(a)   How much to order when production/delivery is instantaneous?
(b)   How much to order when production covers a period?
(c)   How to evaluate larger order discounts?
(d)   How sensitive are the conclusions reached?

Each of these problems is examined in the following sections in illustrative examples.

2.4   Estimating lowest cost order quantity

Consider the following situation. Watallington Ltd is a retailer of beer barrels. The company has an annual demand of 30,000 barrels. The barrels are purchased for stock in lots of 5,000 and cost £12 each. Fresh supplies can be obtained immediately, ordering and transport costs amounting to £200 per order. The annual cost of holding one barrel in stock is estimated to be 10% of its cost ie, £1.20.

The stock level situation could be represented graphically as follows:

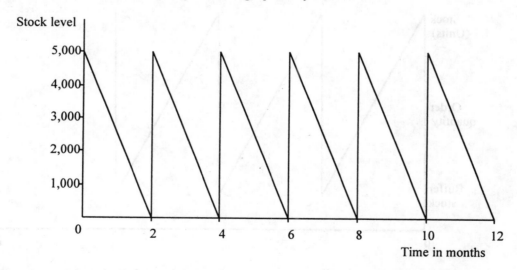

Thus, Watallington Ltd orders 5,000 barrels at a time and these are used from stock at a uniform rate.

Every two months stock is zero and a new order is made. The average stock level is $\dfrac{5,000}{2}$ barrels, ie, half the replenishment level.

Watallington's total annual inventory costs are made up as follows:

		£
Ordering costs	$\dfrac{30,000}{5,000} \times £200$	1,200
Cost of holding stock	$\dfrac{5,000}{2} \times £1.20$	3,000
Total inventory costs		4,200

30,000 barrels are purchased annually in lots of 5,000. If each order costs £200, the total ordering costs are £1,200. The cost of holding each barrel in stock was estimated at £1.20. With the average stock being half the replenishment level, the annual stockholding costs are £3,000 when ordering six times a year.

Compare these costs with those of ordering four, eight, ten and fifteen times a year.

A No of orders per year	B Annual ordering costs £(A × 200) £	C Order size 30,000 ÷ A barrels	D Average stock C ÷ 2 barrels	E Stockholding costs per annum £(D × £1.20) £	F Total inventory cost £(B + E) £
4	800	7,500	3,750	4,500	5,300
6	1,200	5,000	2,500	3,000	4,200
8	1,600	3,750	1,875	2,250	3,850
10	2,000	3,000	1,500	1,800	3,800
15	3,000	2,000	1,000	1,200	4,200

To minimise total inventory costs (column F), make between eight and fifteen orders a year, ie, order size should be between 3,750 and 2,000 barrels a time. A more explicit solution could be achieved by calculating costs at nine, ten, eleven, twelve, thirteen and fourteen orders per year.

However, rather than continue with the trial and error process, the results from the table could be shown graphically, plotting actual cost against size of order. Three curves result:

(a)   annual ordering costs curve (column B);

(b)   annual stockholding costs curve (column E);

(c)   total inventory costs curve (column F).

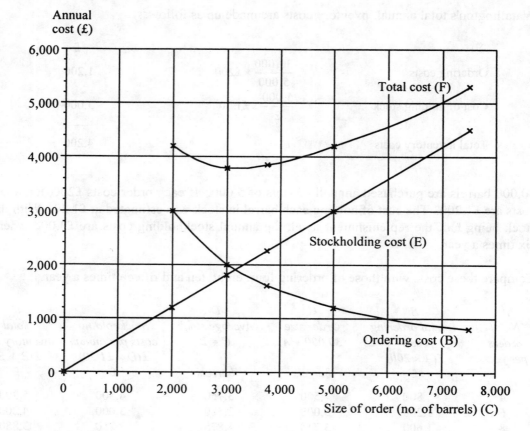

From the graph the order quantity which gives the lowest total cost is somewhere between 3,000 and 3,200 barrels. It is difficult to be much more accurate than this by reading the graph, however there is a mathematical model which can provide more accurate figures which we shall now look at.

3 ECONOMIC ORDER QUANTITY (EOQ)

3.1 Derivation of the model

We have already defined the EOQ earlier in the chapter, but it is worth repeating here to focus attention on what it is.

[Definition] The **economic order quantity** is the purchase order size which takes into account the optimum combination of stockholding costs and ordering costs.

It is possible to draw general conclusions from a typical situation, such as Watallington, applicable to all inventory problems. The following notation will be used:

x = re-order quantity

C_O = costs of making one order

D = expected annual sales volume (ie, demand)

C_h = cost of holding one unit in stock for one year.

The assumptions used in the model are as follows.

(a) Demand is certain, constant and continuous over time.

(b) No stock-outs.

(c)   All prices are constant and certain ie, there are no bulk order discounts.

(d)   Supply of the stock items is received all in one delivery and instantaneously after ordering or the supply lead time is constant and certain.

Since there are no stock-out costs, no buffer stocks and no bulk purchase discounts the only items of cost which vary with the size of the order are stock holding costs and ordering costs.

	Item	*Watallington*	*The general model*
(a)	Average stock	$5,000 \times \dfrac{1}{2} = 2,500$	$\dfrac{x}{2}$
(b)	Annual holding cost	$2,500 \times £1.2 = £3,000$	$\dfrac{xC_h}{2}$
(c)	Re-order cost per year	$\dfrac{30,000}{5,000} \times £200 = £1,200$	$\dfrac{C_oD}{x}$
(d)	Total costs	$£3,000 + £1,200 = £4,200$	$\dfrac{xC_h}{2} + \dfrac{C_oD}{x}$
(e)	Differentiate with respect to x and minimise		$\dfrac{C_h}{2} - \dfrac{C_oD}{x^2} = 0$
(f)	Economic Order, Quantity (EOQ).	$= \sqrt{\dfrac{2 \times £200 \times 30,000}{1.2}}$ $= 3,162$ barrels.	$x = \sqrt{\dfrac{2C_oD}{C_h}}$

Using the expression given for total cost above,

$$
\begin{aligned}
\text{Total cost} \quad &= \quad £(\frac{30,000}{3,162} \times 200) \quad + \quad (\frac{3,162}{2} \times £1.20) \\
&= \quad £(9.488 \times 200) \quad + \quad 1,897.2 \\
&= \quad £1,897.6 \quad\quad\quad + \quad 1,897.2 \\
&= \quad £3,795 \text{ to the nearest £ when 3,162 barrels are ordered at a time.}
\end{aligned}
$$

In practice, this would mean taking 9.488 orders a year, which is nonsense. It is more sensible to order in lots of 3,000 barrels at a total inventory cost of £3,800 per annum (see table) which is only £5 more than the theoretical minimum cost.

3.2   Activity

Calculate the economic order quantity given the following data:

Annual demand	5,000 units
Ordering cost	£150 per order
Annual holding cost	£2 per unit

3.3   Activity solution

$$\sqrt{\frac{2 \times £150 \times 5,000}{£2}}$$

= 866 units (to nearest unit).

4   ECONOMIC BATCH QUANTITY (EBQ)

4.1   Derivation of the model

> [Definition]   The **economic batch quantity** is the optimum size of a batch produced internally which minimises costs. It is the same model as the EOQ apart from that model's assumption of instantaneous re-supply; this time stocks are replenished gradually over a period of time.

In situations where stock is produced internally, a significant time-lag will elapse between the beginning and end of production of a batch. The 'saw-tooth' diagram then becomes:

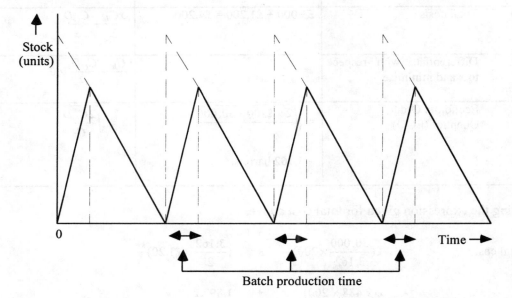

The result is that stock never reaches the level of buffer stock plus order quantity. The average stock is, as a result, less. This difference is a function of the rates of demand and production.

Maximum stock is now (ignoring buffer stock):

$$x(1 - \frac{D}{R})$$ where R is annual production rate.

The economic order quantity formula is modified to:

$$\sqrt{\frac{2C_oD}{C_h(1 - \frac{D}{R})}}$$

The solution is then referred to as the economic batch quantity (EBQ).

Notes:

(1) R is the annual production rate on the assumption that the product is produced continuously over the year.

(2)   when R is very large in relation to D, then $(1 - \dfrac{D}{R}) \approx 1$, ie, the original formula.

4.2   Example

Smoothy, who manufactures silk ties, asks you to estimate the size of the production run which will give him the lowest cost. You ascertain the following information.

Estimated demand = 9,000 pa (D).

Set-up costs of each production run = £50 (C_O).

Cost of each tie = £4.

Cost of holding one tie in stock for one year = 40p (C_h).

Current rate of production = 1,000 ties per month (R).

$$
\begin{aligned}
x \;\; &= \;\; \sqrt{\dfrac{2 C_O D}{C_h (1 - \dfrac{D}{R})}} \\[3mm]
&= \;\; \sqrt{\dfrac{2 \times 50 \times 9,000}{0.4(1 - \dfrac{9,000}{12,000})}} \\[3mm]
&= \;\; \sqrt{9,000,000} \\[2mm]
&= \;\; \underline{3,000}
\end{aligned}
$$

ie, the optimum production batch is 3,000 ties.

4.3   Activity

Calculate the economic batch quantity from the following data:

Annual demand	10,000 units
Machine set-up costs	£250 per production run
Production rate	1,500 units per month
Stockholding costs	£0.60 per unit per annum.

4.4   Activity solution

$$
\sqrt{\dfrac{2 \times 250 \times 10,000}{0.60(1 - (10,000 / 18,000))}}
$$

= 4,330 units.

5   SIMPLE DISCOUNTS

5.1   The effect of simple discounts on the EOQ

Frequently, discounts will be offered for ordering in large quantities. The problem is: if the order quantity to obtain discount is above what would otherwise be the EOQ, is the discount still worth taking? The problem may be solved by the following procedure:

Step 1   Calculate the EOQ ignoring discounts.

Step 2   If this is below the level for discounts, calculate total annual stock costs.

Step 3   Recalculate total annual stock costs using the order size required to just obtain the discount.

Step 4   Compare the cost of steps 2 and 3 with saving from the discount, and select the minimum cost alternative.

Step 5   Repeat for all discount levels.

5.2   Example

In the Watallington illustration, suppose additionally that a 2% discount is available on orders of at least 5,000 barrels and that a 2.5% discount is available if the order quantity is 7,500 barrels or above. With this information, would the economic order quantity still be 3,000?

	£
Step 1 and Step 2 have already been carried out, and it is known that total annual cost at EOQ =	3,795

Step 3   At order quantity 5,000, total cost

$$= \frac{xC_h}{2} + \frac{C_oD}{x}$$

	£
$\dfrac{5,000 \times 12 \times 0.98 \times 0.1}{2} + \dfrac{30,000 \times £200}{5,000} =$	4,140

Extra costs of ordering in batches of 5,000	(345)
Less: Savings on discount 2% × £12 × 30,000	7,200

Step 4   Net cost saving   6,855

Hence batches of 5,000 are worthwhile.

Similarly purchasing in batches of 7,500 results in:

	£
Total costs	5,187.5
Costs at 5,000, as above	4,140
Extra costs	1,047.5
Savings on extra discount (2½ – 2)% × £12 × 30,000	1,800
Net cost saving	752.5

It is concluded that a further saving can be made by ordering in batches of 7,500.

6   **EFFECTS OF UNCERTAIN LEAD TIMES AND DEMAND**

6.1   **When to re-order**

The second problem in inventory control is when to re-order. When demand and lead-time are known with certainty this may be calculated exactly.

Re-order level is when lead-time × demand exactly equals units in stock. On this basis, as the next delivery is made the last unit of stock is being sold. However, in the real world this ideal cannot be achieved. Demand will vary from period to period and lead times might be unpredictable depending on the reliability or otherwise of the supplier, hence re-order points must allow some buffer, or safety, stock.

The size of the buffer stock is a function of three factors:

(a)   Variability of demand and/or lead time.

(b)   Cost of holding stocks.

(c)   Cost of stock-outs (this is the cost of being asked for an item which is out of stock).

The problem may be solved by calculating costs at various levels, by the following procedure:

Step 1   Estimate cost of holding one extra unit of stock for one year.

Step 2   Estimate cost of each stock-out.

Step 3   Calculate expected number of stock-outs associated with each level of stock.

Step 4   Calculate EOQ, and hence number of orders per annum.

Step 5   Calculate total costs (stock-outs plus holding) per annum associated with each level of buffer stock, and select minimum cost option.

6.2   **Example**

Autobits Ltd is one of the few suppliers of an electronic ignition system for cars, and it sells 100 units each year. Each unit costs £40 from the manufacturer, it is estimated that each order costs £10 to handle and that the cost of holding one unit in stock for one year is 25% of the cost price. The lead time is always exactly one week. The weekly demand for units follows a probability distribution with a mean of 2, as follows.

Demand	Probability of demand
0	0.14
1	0.27
2	0.27
3	0.18
4	0.09
5	0.04
6	0.01

Autobits estimates that the stock-out cost, the cost of not being able to meet an order, is £20 per unit.

Autobits must estimate both how many units should be ordered at a time and when the orders should be placed.

Step 1   Annual cost of holding one unit: £10 (£40 × 25%).

Step 2   Cost of stock-out: £20

Step 3   Distribution of demand in lead-time is as shown above:

Hence, the **expected** level of demand in the lead-time is 2, and if buffer stock were zero, reordering would take place when stock fell to 2, ie, Buffer stock = (actual re-order level − 2).

Buffer stock of 4 (6 − 2) would mean that, on the basis of the observations, a stock-out would never occur. Thus, the range of buffer stock options is between 0 and 4 units, ie, re-order levels between 2 and 6.

A table can be prepared showing the relationship between buffer stock and actual demand in terms of stock outs.

Pay-off table in terms of stock-outs
(ie, no. of stock-outs per lead-time)

Re-order level	2	3	4	5	6
Actual demand during lead-time					
2 or less	0	0	0	0	0
3	1	0	0	0	0
4	2	1	0	0	0
5	3	2	1	0	0
6	4	3	2	1	0

Multiplying, then, by the probability of that level of demand occurring, the expected number of stock-outs is:

Expected number of stock-outs

Re-order level		2	3	4	5	6
Demand	*Probability*					
2 or less	0.68	0	0	0	0	0
3	0.18	0.18	0	0	0	0
4	0.09	0.18	0.09	0	0	0
5	0.04	0.12	0.08	0.04	0	0
6	0.01	0.04	0.03	0.02	0.01	0
Total = Expected stock-outs per order		0.52	0.20	0.06	0.01	Nil

Step 4

$$\text{EOQ} \quad \sqrt{\frac{2C_oD}{C_h}} \quad = \quad \sqrt{\frac{2 \times 10 \times 100}{10}} \quad = \quad \sqrt{200}$$

$$= \quad 14.142$$

$$= \quad 14 \text{ to nearest whole number}$$

$$\text{Orders per annum} = \frac{100}{14} = 7.142$$

Step 5

(i)	Re-order level	2	3	4	5	6
(ii)	Buffer stocks ((i) − 2)	0	1	2	3	4
(iii)	Annual cost of holding buffer stock ((ii) × £10)	0	£10	£20	£30	£40
(iv)	Stock-outs per order (per step 3)	0.52	0.20	0.06	0.01	Nil
(v)	Annual cost of stock-outs ((iv) × 7.142 × £20)	£74.28	£28.57	£8.57	£1.43	Nil
(vi)	Total buffer stock cost ((iii) + (v))	£74.28	£38.57	£28.57	£31.43	£40

It is concluded that the minimum cost solution is to hold a buffer stock of 2, ie re-order when stocks fall to 4.

Conclusion From the above analysis, it is apparent that increasing buffer stock is worthwhile if:

Reduction in annual stock-outs costs > Unit holding cost

or

(Stock-out cost × Orders per annum × Decrease > Unit holding cost
 in expected number of stock-outs per order)

6.3 Re-order levels with variable demand and variable lead times

Consider the Autobits Ltd example given in 6.2 but this time the company has a definite policy of ordering 7 times a year and lead time for deliveries as follows:

Days	*Prob.*
7	0.8
8	0.2
	―――
	1.0
	―――

You can assume that, if the lead time is 8 days, the demand on the eighth day is equal to the average of demand for the previous seven days.

You are required to calculate the total expected costs associated with reorder levels of 2, 4 and 6 and to recommend which of these levels should be adopted by Autobits Ltd.

Solution

Step 1   Identify the possible demand figures over the reorder period and the joint probabilities of these demand figures arising.

The tables below only include figures where the expected demand exceeds the reorder level. The analysis has been prepared taking into account incremental holding costs over those associated with a reorder level of 2.

(a)   **Re-order level = 2**

Demand	Lead time days	Excess over reorder level	Joint prob	Units
2.29	8	0.29	0.054	0.015
3.0	7	1.00	0.144	0.144
3.43	8	1.43	0.036	0.051
4.06	8	2.00	0.072	0.144
4.57	8	2.57	0.018	0.046
5.00	7	3.00	0.032	0.096
5.71	8	3.71	0.008	0.032
6.00	7	4.00	0.008	0.032
6.86	8	4.86	0.002	0.010
			Expected stock-out	0.569

Expected annual stock-out costs   £

0.569 units × 7 × £20   =   79.66
      ↑
given number of
orders per year

Incremental holding costs   =   0

                                  £79.66

Demand (D)	Prob of D	Lead time days	Prob	Joint prob	Total demand
0	0.14	7	0.8	0.112	0
		8	0.2	0.028	0
1	0.27	7	0.8	0.216	1.00
		8	0.2	0.054	1.14
2	0.27	7	0.8	0.216	2.00
		8	0.2	0.054	2.29
3	0.18	7	0.8	0.144	3.00
		8	0.2	0.036	3.43
4	0.09	7	0.8	0.072	4.00
		8	0.2	0.018	4.57
5	0.04	7	0.8	0.032	5.00
		8	0.2	0.008	5.71
6	0.01	7	0.8	0.008	6.00
		8	0.2	0.002	6.86
	1.00			1.000	

Note: the total demand figures are the appropriate demand figures for a lead time of 7 days and the demand figure plus one seventh thereof for a lead time of 8 days.

Step 2   Having established a full demand distribution an analysis similar to that conducted earlier in this section can be undertaken.

(b)   Re-order level of 4

Demand	Lead time days	Excess over reorder level	Joint prob	Units
4.57	8	0.57	0.018	0.010
5.00	7	1.00	0.032	0.032
5.71	8	1.71	0.008	0.014
6.00	7	2.00	0.008	0.016
6.86	8	2.86	0.002	0.006
			Expected stock-out	0.078

		£
Expected annual stock-out costs		
0.078 units × 7 × £20	=	10.92
Incremental holding costs 2 units × 10	=	20.00
		£30.92

(c)   Re-order level of 6

Demand	Lead time days	Excess over reorder level	Joint prob	Units
6.86	8	0.86	0.002	0.002
			Expected stock-out	0.002

		£
Expected annual stock-out costs		
0.002 units × 7 × £20	=	0.28
Incremental holding costs 4 × 10	=	40.00
		£40.28

From the above analysis it is concluded that a re-order level of 4 should be adopted, as at this level stock out costs and holding costs are minimised.

6.4   Feedback control

It is important that a stock control system should have some mechanism whereby re-order levels and re-order quantities are adjusted according to changes in demand or lead time supply. Consequently, a stock control system should incorporate a feedback system to make new rules for obtaining more effective control in the future.

Some feedback control systems are based on what is known as **exponential smoothing**, whereby the forecast for the next period is based on the forecast for the preceding period, as modified by the actual demand which occurred in that period, ie

$$\text{New forecast} = \text{Old forecast} + A\ (\text{Actual demand} - \text{Old forecast})$$

where A is a fraction between 0 and 1. Where conditions are relatively stable, the new forecast will be based on the old forecast, and thus impute a fairly low value to A (0.1 – 0.2). When conditions are more volatile, a higher value of A (0.5 – 0.7) will be used to emphasise more strongly the divergence of the old forecast from the actual demand.

More sophisticated stock control methods are possible through computerisation. As was pointed out earlier, if stock records are inaccurate, the stock control method will also be inaccurate.

7   LIMITATIONS OF THE MODELS IN PRACTICE

7.1   Unrealistic assumptions

Earlier in the chapter when we first defined the EOQ model it was shown that the model is based on certain assumptions eg, demand is certain, supply of stock is immediate or the supply lead time is constant and certain. Obviously in reality this is not the case. However, the models can still be of use if the results given by them are subject to sensitivity analysis.

7.2   Example - sensitivity to demand

Looking back at the example Watallington Ltd, suppose actual demand is 45,000 beer barrels per year. What is the cost of basing EOQ on 30,000 barrels per year?

(a)   When demand was 30,000 barrels per year the optimum reorder quantity was 3,000 barrels. Calculating the inventory costs at order quantity 3,000 units when demand is 45,000 barrels per year, the answer is:

$$\frac{45,000 \times 200}{3,000} + \frac{3,000 \times 1.2}{2} =$$

£
4,800

(b)   Now calculate the inventory cost using the correct re-order quantity for 45,000 barrels.

$$\text{EOQ at demand 45,000} \quad = \quad \sqrt{\frac{2C_oD}{C_h}}$$

$$= \quad \sqrt{\frac{2 \times 45,000 \times 200}{1.2}}$$

$$= \quad 3,873 \ (\text{round to } 3,750)$$

cost at order level 3,750

$$= \frac{45,000 \times 200}{3,750} + \frac{3,750 \times 1.2}{2} =$$

4,650

It is concluded that the extra costs incurred are only £150 pa ie, EOQ is insensitive to a change in demand of as much as 50%.

7.3   Example - sensitivity to ordering costs

Reverting to the original Watallington data, but assuming order costs are actually £350 per order. What is the cost of basing EOQ on an order cost of £200?

£

(a)   Inventory costs at order level 3,000 units

$$\frac{30,000 \times 350}{3,000} + \frac{3,000 \times 1.2}{2} =$$

5,300

(b)   EOQ at order cost £350

$$\sqrt{\frac{2 \times 30,000 \times 350}{1.2}}$$ =   4,183 (round to 4,000)

Costs at order level 4,000

$$= \frac{30,000 \times 350}{4,000} + \frac{4,000 \times 1.2}{2} =$$

5,075
_____

275

It is concluded that the extra costs incurred are only £275 pa, ie EOQ is relatively insensitive to a change in fixed order cost of as much as 75%.

7.4   Control levels

In a system where order quantities are constant, it is important to identify alterations to the estimates on which the EOQ was based. Thus, a reporting mechanism is incorporated whereby the stock controller is notified when the stock level exceeds a maximum or falls below a minimum.

Maximum level would represent the normal peak holding, ie buffer stocks plus the re-order quantity. If the maximum is exceeded, a review of estimated demand in lead-time is implied.

Minimum level usually corresponds with buffer stock. If stock falls below that level, emergency action to replenish may be required.

The foregoing levels would be subject to modification according to the relative importance/cost of a particular stock item.

7.5   The minimum level

The minimum level has been described above as being equal to the buffer stock. An alternative explanation is to describe it as the level below which stocks would not normally be expected to fall. This is equal to:

Re-order level – (Average usage per day × Average lead time (days))

7.6   The maximum level

The maximum level may be referred to as the level above which stock should not normally rise, it is given by:

Re-order level + Re-order quantity – (Minimum usage per day × Minimum lead time (days))

7.7   Activity

The following data relates to an item of raw material:

Cost of the raw material	£10 per unit
Usage per day	100 units
Minimum lead time	20 days
Maximum lead time	30 days
Cost of ordering material	£400 per order
Carrying costs	10% per annum

Note: assume that each year consists of 48 working weeks of five days per week.

You are required:

(i)   to calculate the re-order level;
(ii)   to calculate the re-order quantity;
(iii)   to calculate the maximum level;
(iv)   to calculate the minimum level.

7.8   Activity solution

(i)   3,000 units
(ii)   4,382 units
(iii)   5,382 units
(iv)   500 units.

8   CHAPTER SUMMARY

This chapter has considered the techniques used to optimise stock holding and inventory investment.

9   SELF TEST QUESTIONS

9.1   What is the definition of buffer stock? (1.2)

9.2   Why may there be differences between physical stocks and recorded stocks? (1.5)

9.3   Suggest three items included under the heading 'holding costs'. (2.1)

9.4   What is the 'lead time'? (2.2)

9.5   Explain the objective of using the EOQ model. (2.4)

9.6   What are the assumptions upon which the EOQ model is based? (3.1)

9.7   What is the difference between the EOQ model and the EBQ model? (4.1)

9.8   Discuss in five steps how bulk discounts can be incorporated into the analysis. (5.1)

9.9   What are the limitations of the EOQ model in practice? (7.1)

9.10   In respect of the EOQ model, how can sensitivity analysis be used? (7.2, 7.3)

10   EXAMINATION TYPE QUESTIONS

10.1   Computer bureau order quantity

It has been estimated that a computer bureau will need 1,000 boxes of line printer paper next year.

The purchasing officer of the bureau plans to arrange regular deliveries from a supplier, who charges £15 per delivery.

The bureau's accountant advises the purchasing officer that the cost of storing a box of line printer paper for a year is £2.70. Over a year, the average number of boxes in storage is half the order quantity (that is the number of boxes per delivery).

The ordering cost is defined as the delivery cost plus the storage cost, where the annual costs for an order quantity of x boxes will be:

Delivery cost:

$$\text{Number of deliveries} \times \text{Cost per delivery} = £\frac{100}{x} \times 15$$

Storage cost:

$$\text{Average stock level} \times \text{Storage cost per box} = £\frac{x}{2} \times 2.70$$

You are required

(a) to calculate the delivery cost, storage cost and ordering cost for order quantities of 50, 100, 150, 200 and 250 boxes;

(3 marks)

(b) to sketch these values for delivery cost, storage cost and ordering cost on the same graph; and

(5 marks)

(c) to estimate the order quantity which will minimise cost.

(2 marks)

(Total: 10 marks)

10.2   K & L Games Ltd

K&L Games Ltd is re-evaluating its stock control policy. Its daily demand for wooden boxes is steady at 40 a day for each of the 250 working days (50 weeks) of the year. The boxes are currently bought weekly in batches of 200 from a local supplier for £2 each. The cost of ordering the boxes from the local supplier is £64, regardless of the size of the order. The stockholding costs, expressed as a percentage of stock value, are 25% pa.

You are required

(a) to determine the economic order quantity and frequency of replenishment, and the annual saving to be made by implementing these;

(12 marks)

(b) to recommend whether or not it is worthwhile to make use of the local supplier's new quantity discount scheme, shown below.

Local Supplier's New Discount Scheme

Quantity	*Discount*
0 - 999	0%
1,000 - 4,999	5%
5,000 +	10%

(8 marks)

(Total: 20 marks)
(CIMA Nov 87)

11   ANSWERS TO EXAMINATION TYPE QUESTIONS

11.1   Computer bureau order quantity

(a)   **Calculation of cost associated with particular order quantities**

Order quantity x	Delivery cost $\dfrac{1,000}{x} \times 15$ £	Storage cost $\dfrac{x}{2} \times 2.70$ £	Ordering cost Delivery + Storage cost cost £
50	$\dfrac{1,000}{50} \times 15 = 300$	$\dfrac{50}{2} \times 2.70 = 67.50$	367.50
100	$\dfrac{1,000}{100} \times 15 = 150$	$\dfrac{100}{2} \times 2.70 = 135.00$	285.00
150	$\dfrac{1,000}{150} \times 15 = 100$	$\dfrac{150}{2} \times 2.70 = 202.50$	302.50
200	$\dfrac{1,000}{200} \times 15 = 75$	$\dfrac{200}{2} \times 2.70 = 270.00$	345.00
250	$\dfrac{1,000}{250} \times 15 = 60$	$\dfrac{250}{2} \times 2.70 = 337.50$	397.50

(b)   For graph see next page.

(c)   From the graph, the optimum order quantity is approximately **106 units**.

Note: from the figures calculated in (a) we can see that the order quantity of 100 units results in the lowest cost.

This would be the answer to give if we had not been required to prepare a graph.

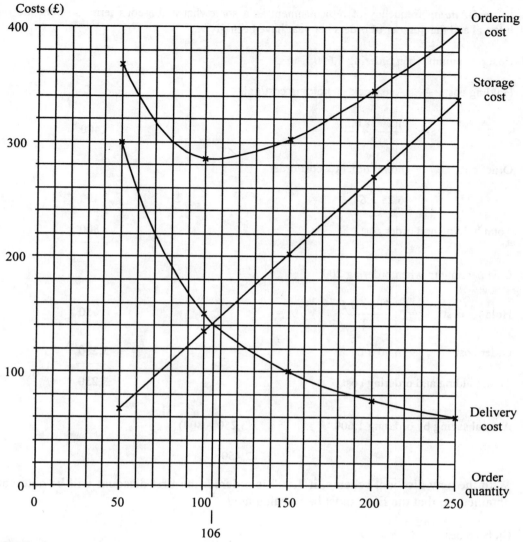

Costs (£)

106

11.2   K & L Games Ltd

(a)   Annual demand   =   40 × 250   =   10,000 boxes   =   D
Order cost   =   £64   = C_o
Holding cost per year per unit = 25% of £2 = £0.50   = C_h

$$EOQ = \sqrt{\frac{2C_oD}{C_h}} = \sqrt{\frac{2 \times 64 \times 10,000}{0.5}}$$

$$= 1,600 \text{ boxes}$$

Number of orders per year $= \dfrac{\text{Annual demand}}{\text{order quantity}}$

$$= \frac{10,000}{1,600}$$

$$= 6.25$$

Re-order interval $= \dfrac{1}{\text{no of orders}}$

$$= \frac{1}{6.25} \text{ yrs}$$

$$= \frac{250}{6.25} \text{ days}$$

$$= 40 \text{ days}$$

(Tutorial note: 'frequency of replenishment' is a somewhat ambiguous term, so both the re-order interval and the number of orders per year have been given.*)*

Cost per annum when ordering 1,600:

				£
Holding cost	=	Ave stock × holding cost/unit		
	=	$\dfrac{1,600 \times 0.5}{2}$	=	400
Order cost	=	no. of orders × cost/order		
	=	6.25 × 64	=	400
Total holding and order cost			=	800

Cost per annum when ordering 200:

				£
Holding cost	=	$\dfrac{200 \times 0.5}{2}$	=	50
Order cost	=	50 × 64	=	3,200
Total holding and ordering cost			=	3,250

Annual saving by ordering 1,600	=	£(3,250 − 800)
	=	£2,450

(b)   With the new discount scheme, if 1,600 is ordered, the first discount will be automatically obtained, so that the EOQ must be re-calculated.

C_h becomes   0.25 × 1.9

= 0.475

The EOQ becomes $\sqrt{\dfrac{2 \times 64 \times 10,000}{0.475}}$

= 1,642

The choice is therefore between ordering 1,642 and 5,000.

(i)   Order 1,642:

				£
Holding cost	=	$\dfrac{1,642 \times 0.475}{2}$	=	390
No of orders	=	$\dfrac{10,000}{1,642}$		
	=	6.09		
Order cost	=	6.09 × 64	=	390
Purchase costs	=	10,000 × 1.9	=	19,000
Total cost per annum			=	19,780

(ii)   Order 5,000:

The holding cost per unit becomes $0.25 \times 1.8 = £0.45$

Number of orders/year $= \dfrac{10,000}{5,000} = 2$

			£
Holding cost	$=$	$\dfrac{5,000 \times 0.45}{2}$ $=$	1,125
Order cost	$=$	2×64 $=$	128
Purchase cost	$=$	$10,000 \times 1.8$ $=$	18,000
Total cost per annum			19,253

Hence it is worthwhile to order 5,000.

(Tutorial note: always work to the minimum discount quantity. If more than the minimum is ordered, costs will increase until a further discount (if any) is obtained.*)*

8 COMPOUND INTEREST AND PRESENT VALUES

INTRODUCTION & LEARNING OBJECTIVES

Syllabus area 7c.   The use of present value tables. (Ability required 2).

Discounting: net present value and internal rate of return. (Ability required 3).

Investment analysis and appraisal. (Ability required 3).

When you have studied this chapter you should be able to do the following:

- Distinguish between simple and compound methods of calculating interest.
- Understand terminal value and net terminal value and why present values are more appropriate.
- Understand how and when to use present value tables.
- Calculate perpetuities and annuities.
- Understand and calculate IRR.
- Conduct investment analyses and appraisals using NPV and IRR techniques.

---

1 INTRODUCTION TO SIMPLE AND COMPOUND INTEREST

1.1 Simple interest

When money is invested it earns interest; similarly when money is borrowed interest is payable. The sum of money invested or borrowed is known as the **principal**.

With simple interest, the interest is payable or receivable each year but it is not added to the principal. For example, the interest payable (or receivable) on £100 at 15% pa for 1, 2 and 3 years will be £15, £30 and £45.

The usual notation is:

$$I = \frac{PRT}{100} \quad \text{or} \quad R = \frac{100I}{PT} \quad \text{or} \quad T = \frac{100I}{PR}$$

where P = principal in £

R = interest rate % pa

T = time in years

I = interest in £

1.2   Example

A man invests £160 on 1 January each year. On 31 December simple interest is credited at 12% but this interest is put in a separate account and does not itself earn any interest. Find the total amount standing to his credit on 31 December following his fifth payment of £160.

Year (1 January)	Investment (£)	Interest (31 December)
1	160	$\frac{12}{100} \times 160 = £19.20$
2	160 + 160 = 320	$\frac{12}{100} \times 320 = £38.40$
3	160 + 320 = 480	$\frac{12}{100} \times 480 = £57.60$
4	160 + 480 = 640	$\frac{12}{100} \times 640 = £76.80$
5	160 + 640 = 800	$\frac{12}{100} \times 800 = £96.00$
Total		£288.00

$$\text{Total amount at 31 December, Year 5} \quad = \quad £(800 + 288) \quad \text{(Principal \& simple interest)}$$

$$= \quad £1,088$$

1.3   Activity

Calculate:

(a)   the total amount of interest if a lump sum of £5,000 is invested for 5 years at 12% per annum simple interest;

(b)   the rate pa of simple interest if the amount of interest over 10 years on £800 is £400.

1.4   Activity solution

(a)   P   =   £5,000,   R   =   12,   T   =   5

$$I \quad = \quad \frac{PRT}{100} \quad = \quad \frac{5,000 \times 12 \times 5}{100} \quad = \quad £3,000$$

(b)   P   =   £800,   T   =   10,   I   =   £400

$$R \quad = \quad \frac{100 \times I}{PT} \quad = \quad \frac{100 \times 400}{800 \times 10} \quad = \quad 5\% \text{ pa}$$

1.5   Compound interest

With compound interest, the interest is added each year to the principal and for the following year the interest is calculated on their sum. For example, the compound interest on £1,000 at 10% pa for four years is calculated as follows:

Year	Principal (£)	Interest (£)	Total amount (£)
1	1,000	$\frac{10}{100} \times 1,000 = 100$	1,000 + 100 = 1,100
2	1,100	$\frac{10}{100} \times 1,100 = 110$	1,100 + 110 = 1,210
3	1,210	$\frac{10}{100} \times 1,210 = 121$	1,210 + 121 = 1,331
4	1,331	$\frac{10}{100} \times 1,331 = 133.1$	1,331 + 133.1 = 1,464.1

An alternative way of writing this is now shown:

Year	Principal (£)	Total amount (£)		
1	1,000	1,000(1 + 0.1)		= 1,100
2	1,000(1 + 0.1)	1,000(1 + 0.1)(1 + 0.1)	= 1,000(1 + 0.1)^2	= 1,210
3	1,000(1 + 0.1)^2	1,000(1 + 0.1)^2(1 + 0.1)	= 1,000(1 + 0.1)^3	= 1,331
4	1,000(1 + 0.1)^3	1,000(1 + 0.1)^3(1 + 0.1)	= 1,000(1 + 0.1)^4	= 1,464.1

So the amount (A) at the end of the nth year is given by:

$$A = P(1+r)^n$$

where 100r = rate % pa. So the amounts at the end of successive years form a geometrical progression with common ratio $(1 + r)$ ie, $P(1 + r)$, $P(1 + r)^2$, $P(1 + r)^3$ . . .

1.6   Compound interest examples

(a)   Calculate the compound interest on £624 at 4% pa for 10 years.

(b)   Find the sum of money which, if invested now at 5% pa compound interest, will be worth £10,000 in 10 years' time.

1.7   Solution

(a)   Using $A = P(1 + r)^n$ with   P = £624

r = 0.04

n = 10

then $A = £624 (1 + 0.04)^{10}$

$= £624 (1.04)^{10}$

$= £923.67$

So the compound interest   =   £(923.67 – 624)

=   £299.67

(b)   Using $A = P(1 + r)^n$ with   A = £10,000

r = 0.05

n = 10

then $£10,000 = P(1 + 0.05)^{10}$

$$P = \frac{£10,000}{(1.05)^{10}}$$

$P = £6,139.13$

So £6,139.13 is the necessary sum of money.

1.8   Activity

In how many years will £1,000 amount to £3,207 at 6% pa compound interest?

1.9   Activity solution

Using $A = P(1 + r)^n$ with $A = £3,207$

$P = £1,000$

$r = 0.06$

$3,207 = 1,000 \times (1 + 0.06)^n$

$\dfrac{3,207}{1,000} = (1.06)^n$

$3.207 = 1.06^n$

Taking logs of both sides gives $\log 3.207 = \log(1.06^n)$

$= n \log 1.06$

From tables or using a calculator $0.5060 = n \times 0.0253$

$n = \dfrac{0.5060}{0.0253}$

$n = 20$

1.10   Activity

Find the annual percentage rate at which £552 amounts to £896 in 11 years at compound interest.

1.11   Activity solution

Using $A = P(1 + r)^n$ with $A = £896$

$P = £552$

$n = 11$

$\therefore$ $896 = 552 \times (1 + r)^{11}$

$\therefore$ $\dfrac{896}{552} = (1 + r)^{11}$

$1.623 = (1 + r)^{11}$

$\therefore$ $\sqrt[11]{1.623}^{\,*} = 1 + r$

$1.045 = 1 + r$

$\therefore$ $r = 1.045 - 1$

$r = 0.045$

The rate of interest is $100 \times 0.045 = 4.5\%$

* Note

The eleventh root can easily be obtained from an electronic calculator if it has an x^y or $x^{\frac{1}{y}}$ key making use of the fact that $\sqrt[11]{x} = x^{\frac{1}{11}}$.

If your calculator has an $x^{\frac{1}{y}}$ key put y = 11.

If it only has an x^y key, put $y = \dfrac{1}{11}$ (= 0.090909)

1.12   Conclusion

Conclusion   Interest is not always calculated on an annual basis: it may be calculated daily, weekly, monthly, quarterly, half-yearly or at any other interval of time.

It is important that the rate of interest and the time are in compatible units.

For example, if the time is in months, then the rate of interest needs to be r% per month. If the time is in half-years, then the rate of interest must be r% per half-year.

The general compounding formula can be applied to situations other than money problems.

For example, it can be applied to population statistics, index numbers or rates of increase and decrease generally.

1.13   Comprehensive example

This is an example which can utilise the basic work already done on compound interest and applies the same basic formula to different problems.

(a)   Calculate the effective annual rate of interest of:

6% pa compounded monthly;

6¼% pa compounded quarterly.

Note: the effective annual rate of interest is called the Annual Percentage Rate ('APR').

(b)   In 19X4 the monthly average index of retail prices was 107, and in 19X14 it was 208. Both values are relative to 16 January 19X2 = 100.

Calculate in relation to the index for the period 19X4 to 19X14:

(i)   the annual compounded rate of change of the index of retail prices; and

(ii)   the annual compounded rate of change in the purchasing power of £1.

1.14   Solution

(a)   (i)   6% pa $= \dfrac{6}{12}\%$ $= \dfrac{1}{2}\%$ per month $(\dfrac{1}{2}\% = \dfrac{1/2}{100} = 0.005)$

Compounding this monthly gives an annual growth rate of:

$(1 + 0.005)^{12}$ =   1.0617

So the growth rate is 106.17% giving an effective rate of interest of 6.17%.

(ii)   6¼% pa = $\dfrac{6\frac{1}{4}}{4}$% =   1.5625% per quarter.

Compounding this quarterly gives an annual growth rate of:

$(1 + 0.015625)^4$ =   1.0640

So the growth rate is 106.40% giving an effective rate of interest of 6.40%.

(b)   19X4 Index =   107. 19X14 Index =   208

(16 January 19X2 Index = 100)

(i)   Let r   =   annual rate of change (increase) of the retail price index.

Over ten years the index has risen from 107 to 208.

$\therefore$ $107 \times (1 + r)^{10}$ =   208

$\therefore$ $(1 + r)^{10}$ = $\dfrac{208}{107}$ =   1.944

$\therefore$ $(1 + r)$ = $\sqrt[10]{1.944}$

$\therefore$ $1 + r$ =   1.069

$\therefore$ r =   0.069

So the annual rate of change in the index of retail prices is 6.9%.

(ii)   The purchasing power of £1 in 19X4 was $100p \times \dfrac{100}{107}$ =   93.5p

The purchasing power of £1 in 19X14 was $100p \times \dfrac{100}{208}$ =   48.1p

Let r = annual rate of change (decrease) in the purchasing power of the pound. Over ten years, the purchasing power has fallen from 93.5p to 48.1p.

$93.5 \times (1 - r)^{10}$ =   48.1

$\therefore (1 - r)^{10}$ = $\dfrac{48.1}{93.5}$ =   0.5144

$\therefore (1 - r)$ = $\sqrt[10]{0.5144}$

$\therefore 1 - r$ =   0.9356

$\therefore r$ =   0.0644

So the annual rate of change in the purchasing power of the pound is 6.44%.

If the formula is used with 1 + r instead of 1 – r all that happens is that r works out to be a negative value (ie, – 6.44%). The negative sign shows that it is a decrease in value.

1.15   Graphical representation

Consider £500 invested at 10% pa for 6 years at (a) simple interest and (b) compound interest.

(a) $I = \dfrac{10}{100} \times 500 = £50$ pa.

So the total amount at the end of the years 1 - 6 is:

Year	Principal and interest	Amount
1	500 + 50	£550
2	500 + 2 × 50	£600
3	500 + 3 × 50	£650
4	500 + 4 × 50	£700
5	500 + 5 × 50	£750
6	500 + 6 × 50	£800

(b)   Using $A = P(1 + r)^n$ to calculate the amount at the end of the nth year where n = 1, 2, 3, 4, 5, 6.

Year	Principal and interest	Amount
1	$500(1 + 0.1)$	550
2	$500(1 + 0.1)^2$	605
3	$500(1 + 0.1)^3$	665.5
4	$500(1 + 0.1)^4$	732.05
5	$500(1 + 0.1)^5$	805.26
6	$500(1 + 0.1)^6$	885.78

Showing these graphically gives the following:

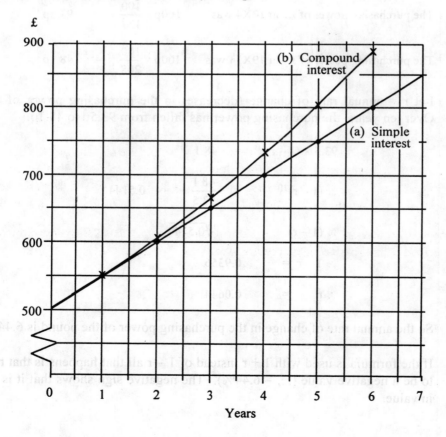

Notes on the graph

(a)   The simple interest is a straight line.

(b)   The compound interest graph is a curve.

(c)   At any point in time, after the end of the first year, the amount at compound interest is greater than that at simple interest.

(d)   The difference between these amounts becomes greater at later points in time.

2   TERMINAL VALUES

2.1   Comparison of projects

If we were to be given the choice between two projects X and Y, the expected profits of which over the next three years are:

    X   :   £200,000 pa
    Y   :   £210,000 pa

which would we prefer (assuming both require the same initial outlay)?

On the face of it, project Y would seem preferable since we can expect a larger profit, even though it is a fairly marginal difference. However, suppose that project X is operated on a cash basis (and hence profits equate to cash) whereas project Y is more of a long-term contract and although we choose to spread its profits over the three years, no cash is received until the end of the period. The cash flows would therefore be as follows:

Year	X £	Y £
1	200,000	-
2	200,000	-
3	200,000	630,000

Our decision now becomes less obvious. Certainly project Y will generate more cash, but project X will enable us to receive cash sooner.

Why do we consider this? The reason is that by selecting X we could be investing the cash as received and be earning interest, or if we were financed by borrowing we could use the receipts from project X to reduce our borrowings and hence save interest. Whichever way round it is there is a hidden cost attached to selecting project Y in that we would be losing interest that could have been earned/saved by selecting project X. Our decision will now depend on the rate of interest. Suppose we could receive 10% pa and all cash is received at the end of the relevant year then the effects of selecting X or Y would be as follows.

An approach which can be adopted is to compound interest on each cash flow individually. We can use the same method of compounding as previously:

Project X

			£
Year 1	$200,000 \times (1.1)^2$	=	242,000
Year 2	$200,000 \times 1.1$	=	220,000
Year 3	200,000	=	200,000
			£662,000

Project Y

			£
Year 3	630,000	=	£630,000

Here we have compounded each flow by adding on interest at 10% pa for the number of years remaining until the end of the projects, thus the year 1 cash flow of £200,000 earns two years interest and is thus worth £242,000 at the end of the project. We have compounded the flows to produce what is termed the **terminal value** of each flow. On this basis, project X is obviously the better choice. In conclusion, it would certainly seem that it is in any investor's interest to pay attention to the cash flows expected from an investment and to the timing of these cash flows rather than simply the level of profit.

2.2   Net terminal value

With the calculations just carried out we are in a position to choose between the two projects since they both require the same initial outlay. However, we have not as yet considered whether either of them is worthwhile. This will depend on the size of the initial outlay required to generate the terminal value of £662,000 which we could receive by selecting project X. If we end up with a deficit we would reject the project.

Suppose in this case the projects require an initial outlay of £450,000 at the beginning of year 1 (referred to as year 0). Clearly we cannot compare this outlay directly to the £662,000 generated since this is the return at the end of three years. At that time we will have lost three year's potential interest on the outlay of £450,000. To allow for this we need to calculate the terminal value of the initial outlay by adding three years' interest at 10%.

The full solution to the problem is then:

Year	Cash flows £		Compound factor	Terminal value £
0	(450,000)	×	$(1.1)^3$	(598,950)
1	200,000	×	$(1.1)^2$	242,000
2	200,000	×	(1.1)	220,000
3	200,000			200,000
				£63,050

Note the numbering of the years. The year column refers to the **end** of the various years. Thus the initial outlay occurs at the start of the project ie, the **end** of year 0 (which is the same as the beginning of year 1). The first cash flow is received at the **end** of year 1, and so on for the subsequent cash flows.

The net surplus in this example is £63,050 and is called the net terminal value (NTV) and since it is positive, indicating a surplus, the project is worthwhile and should be accepted. The positive net terminal value indicates that the cash and interest earned from the project exceeds the value of the initial outlay plus interest. Had it been negative, indicating a deficit, the project would have been rejected.

2.3   Example

Find the net terminal value of the following investment.

An initial outlay of £80,000, which will generate the following cash flows:

Year	Cash flow
1	30,000
2	-
3	80,000

The annual interest rate available for deposits is 6%.

2.4   Solution

The net terminal value calculations are:

Year	Cash flows £	Compound factor		Terminal value £
0	(80,000)	×	$(1.06)^3$	(95,281.28)
1	30,000	×	$(1.06)^2$	33,708.00
2	-		-	0.00
3	80,000			80,000
				18,426.72

so the project would be accepted.

2.5   Activity

An initial outlay of £100,000 will generate the following cash flows.

Year	Cash flow £
1	10,000
2	20,000
3	30,000
4	50,000

The annual interest rate available for deposits is 8%. Calculate the net terminal value.

2.6   Activity solution

The net terminal value calculations are:

Year	Cash flows £	Compound factor		Terminal value £
0	(100,000)	×	$(1.08)^4$	(136,048.90)
1	10,000	×	$(1.08)^3$	12,597.12
2	20,000	×	$(1.08)^2$	23,328.00
3	30,000	×	(1.08)	32,400.00
4	50,000			50,000.00
				(17,723.78)

3   PRESENT VALUES

3.1   Introduction

In the previous section we say that one way of allowing for interest on cash flows is to calculate the terminal values, that is the value at the end of a project. This approach is useful but it can be misleading at times eg, if a project is for six years and leads to a terminal value of £22,500, we shall not receive the £22,500 in full until six years' time.

A further problem arises if we wish to compare projects of different lengths. If one project lasts for two years and has a terminal value of £5,000, a second project lasts for four years and has a terminal value of £10,000, which would we choose? We cannot simply compare the terminal values as they stand. We could add interest to the £5,000 to see what it would be after four years and then make the comparison. However, this is a rather inefficient approach and a more common way of allowing for the interest is to look at what the cash flows would be now. These are called the **present values** of each cash flow, and are found by discounting each cash flow back to the start of the project.

3.2   Discounting

The calculation of compound interest and of the amount to which an invested sum would grow ie, compounding have already been described. Discounting is working the other way round, ie, a method of calculating the sum which, invested now at r% pa would yield £100 (say) after one year.

Let £V be the required sum of money to be invested now at r% and to grow to £100 in one year's time.

Then $100 = V(1 + r)$

$$\therefore V = \frac{100}{(1+r)}$$

£V is called the **present value** of £100, or £100 discounted for one year at the rate of r% pa.

If £100 is required in two years time then the sum £V which needs to be invested now is given by:

$$100 = V(1 + r)^2$$

$$\therefore V = \frac{100}{(1+r)^2}$$

If £100 is required in n years' time then

$$V = \frac{100}{(1+r)^n}$$

3.3   Present values

£V as shown in the previous formula is more usually called the **present value** of £A when invested at r% pa for n years.

$$V = \frac{A}{(1+r)^n}$$

Definition   The present value (V) of an amount A receivable in n years' time is thus defined as that amount that must be invested now at r% pa to accumulate to A at the expiry of n years.

3.4   Example

Calculate the present value of £2,000 at 10% pa for 1 year, 2 years, or 3 years.

1 year: $V = \dfrac{2,000}{(1+0.1)} = \dfrac{2,000}{1.1} = £1,818.18$

2 years: $V = \dfrac{2,000}{(1+0.1)^2} = \dfrac{2,000}{1.1^2} = £1,652.89$

3 years: $V = \dfrac{2,000}{(1+0.1)^3} = \dfrac{2,000}{1.1^3} = £1,502.63$

This means that £1,818.18 must be invested now to yield £2,000 in one year's time, £1,652.89 must be invested now to yield £2,000 in two years' time, etc.

3.5   The use of present value tables

Because discounting is so widely used in business problems, present value (PV) tables are available to shortcut the computations. In fact, with scientific calculators, it is as quick to calculate present values of single sums in the way shown in the section above. A PV table is included at the start of this text.

This table provides a value (the 'PV factor') for a range of years and discount rates. Thus, the PV factor is the answer to the sum:

$$\frac{1}{(1+r)^n}$$

where r is the discount rate

n is the number of years

In this table, the values are to three decimal places. This involves some rounding and loss of accuracy, but is adequate for most purposes.

Students should note the time scale:

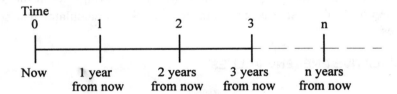

(the PV factor for time 0 is always 1, so this is not included in the table)

Below is an extract from the present value tables given at the front of the text.

At rate r After n years	1%	2%	3%	4%	5%	6%	7%	8%	9%	10%
1	0.990	0.980	0.971	0.962	0.952	0.943	0.935	0.926	0.917	0.909
2	0.980	0.961	0.943	0.925	0.907	0.890	0.873	0.857	0.842	0.826
3	0.971	0.942	0.915	0.889	0.864	0.840	0.816	0.794	0.772	0.751
4	0.961	0.924	0.888	0.855	0.823	0.792	0.763	0.735	0.708	0.683
5	0.951	0.906	0.863	0.822	0.784	0.747	0.713	0.681	0.650	0.621
6	0.942	0.888	0.837	0.790	0.746	0.705	0.666	0.630	0.596	0.564
7	0.933	0.871	0.813	0.760	0.711	0.665	0.623	0.583	0.547	0.513
8	0.923	0.853	0.789	0.731	0.677	0.627	0.582	0.540	0.502	0.467
9	0.941	0.837	0.766	0.703	0.645	0.592	0.544	0.500	0.460	0.424
10	0.905	0.820	0.744	0.676	0.614	0.558	0.508	0.463	0.422	0.386

If we are trying to find the present value of say, £60,000 receivable in 5 years time at a rate of interest, discount rate, cost of capital (all terms which effectively mean the same when doing this type of question) of 7%, using the tables, we perform the following steps.

Step 1   Look in the column headed 'After n years' for 5.

Step 2   Look at the row headed 'At rate r' for the rate of interest 7%.

Step 3   Where the row for 5 years intersects with the column for 7% in the bulk of the table, is the relevant present value factor. In this case it is 0.713.

Step 4   Multiply £60,000 by 0.713 = £42,780. Thus, £42,780 is the present value of £60,000 receivable in five years at 7%. In other words £42,780 is the amount which, if invested now at 7%, will give £60,000 after five years.

Step 4   Multiply £60,000 by 0.713 = £42,780. Thus, £42,780 is the present value of £60,000 receivable in five years at 7%. In other words £42,780 is the amount which, if invested now at 7%, will give £60,000 after five years.

3.6   Example

Calculate the present value of the given cash flows using a 5% discount rate.

Time	Cash flow £	PV factor	PV £
0	(60,000)	1.000	(60,000)
1	(10,000)	0.952	(9,520)
2	15,000	0.907	13,605
3	20,000	0.864	17,280
4	20,000	0.823	16,460
5	20,000	0.784	15,680
6	20,000	0.746	14,920
	NPV		£8,425

Finally, it should be noted that some electronic calculators now directly calculate present values. Any reasonable scientific calculator, a useful tool in the exam, can calculate $(1+r)^{-n}$ quickly. If these are used in the examination, students should show all their workings, as in the above table, except that there will be no PV factors; it is important to state that a calculator has been used to obtain the present values.

4   ANNUITIES AND CUMULATIVE PRESENT VALUES

4.1   Annuities

Definition   An annuity is a series of equal annual receipts or payments extending over a specified number of years, or for the life of the annuitant (the person who purchases the annuity).

A ground rent is an example of an annuity, the holder of the freehold receiving an annual payment for the number of years specified in the lease.

Annuities and ground rent are constantly being bought and sold and the method of present values can be used to calculate a fair price for the transaction.

4.2   Example

Find the present value of an annuity of £300 for 10 years, reckoning compound interest at 4% pa, the first receipt being in one year's time.

The present value of the first receipt of £300 is:

$$P = \frac{£300}{(1+0.04)} = \frac{£300}{(1.04)}$$

The present value of the second receipt of £300 is:

$$P = \frac{£300}{(1+0.04)^2} = \frac{£300}{(1.04)^2}$$

... etc

The present value of the tenth receipt of £300 is:

$$P = \frac{£300}{(1+0.04)^{10}} = \frac{£300}{(1.04)^{10}}$$

So, the total present value (in £'s) is:

$$P = \frac{300}{1.04} + \frac{300}{(1.04)^2} + \frac{300}{(1.04)^3} + \ldots + \frac{300}{(1.04)^{10}}$$

These terms form a geometric progression with $a = \dfrac{300}{1.04}$, $r = \dfrac{1}{1.04}$ and $n = 10$

Using $S_n = \dfrac{a(1-r^n)}{1-r}$

$$= \frac{\frac{300}{1.04}\left(1-\left(\frac{1}{1.04}\right)^{10}\right)}{\left(1-\frac{1}{1.04}\right)}$$

$$= \frac{\frac{300}{1.04}(1-0.6756)}{\left(\frac{1.04-1}{1.04}\right)}$$

$$= \frac{300(0.3244)}{0.04}$$

$$= 2,433$$

So, the present value of the annuity is £2,433, ie, this is a fair price to pay for the annuity.

4.3   The use of cumulative present value tables

In the above example, P was defined as:

$$P = \frac{£300}{1.04} + \frac{£300}{(1.04)^2} + \frac{£300}{(1.04)^3} + \ldots + \frac{£300}{(1.04)^{10}}$$

Taking out the £300 as a common factor,

$$P = £300\left[\frac{1}{1.04} + \frac{1}{(1.04)^2} + \frac{1}{(1.04)^3} + \ldots + \frac{1}{(1.04)^{10}}\right]$$

The terms inside the square brackets are the cumulative present value of £1 for years one to ten, which can be found directly from the tables at the front of this text. From the table:

Cumulative PV of £1 for ten years at 4% pa = 8.111

Hence: P   =   £300 × 8.111

=   £2,433 (as before)

The cumulative present values of £1 are also called 'annuity factors' and are denoted by the symbol $a\,\overline{n}\,r$ where a stands for annuity, n = number of years and r = rate of interest.

Thus $a\,\overline{10}\,0.04 = 8.111$

4.5   Activity solution

The first income payment will be received at the end of five years from now and has a present value of

$$\frac{£5,000}{(1.06)^5}$$

The second payment has a present value of $\frac{£5,000}{(1.06)^6}$, etc.

The total PV of the ten payments will therefore be:

$$P \quad = \quad £5,000\left[\frac{1}{(1.06)^5} + \frac{1}{(1.06)^6} + \frac{1}{(1.06)^7} + ... + \frac{1}{(1.06)^{14}}\right]$$

The terms inside the square brackets can be regarded as the cumulative PV of £1 for the first fourteen years minus the cumulative PV of £1 for the **first four** years. It is worthwhile checking that years 5 to 14 inclusive correspond to years 1 to 14 less years 1 to 4. Thus:

$$P \quad = \quad £5,000 \times [9.295 - 3.465] \text{ (from the tables)}$$

$$= \quad £29,150$$

4.6   Present value and annuity factors compared

Note that the annuity factors are simply the cumulative present value factors, eg:

Year	10% discount factors from Present Value Tables
1	0.909
2	0.826
3	0.751
	2.486

$a\,\overline{_{3|}}\,0.10$ from Cumulative Present Value Table

$$= \quad 2.487$$

4.7   Perpetuities

Where an annuity is to be received indefinitely ie, for ever, this is known as a perpetuity, because the amount is receivable in perpetuity.

The present value of a perpetuity where:

the annual amount receivable	=	a
the discount rate	=	r

is given by $\boxed{PV = \dfrac{a}{r}}$

4.8   Example

An investment will yield future cash flows of £5,000 in perpetuity. What is the present value of this income stream at a discount rate of 20%?

4.9   Solution

Using the formula above

$$\text{Present value} \quad = \quad \frac{\text{Annual perpetuity}}{\text{Discount rate}}$$

$$= \quad \frac{5,000}{0.20}$$

$$= \quad £25,000$$

4.10   Activity

A project requires an initial outlay of £10,000 and will then generate £2,000 annually. Should the project be accepted at a discount rate of 16%?

4.11   Activity solution

$$\text{NPV of project} \quad = \quad \text{PV of initial outlay} + \text{PV of perpetual receipts}$$

$$= \quad (10,000) + \frac{2,000}{0.16}$$

$$= \quad (10,000) + 12,500$$

$$= \quad £2,500$$

The NPV is positive therefore the project should be accepted.

5   THE INTERNAL RATE OF RETURN

5.1   Introduction

An alternative technique for appraising projects is computing the internal rate of return (IRR) of the project.

Definition   The IRR is the discount rate that, when applied to the cash flows of a project, produces a net present value of zero.

Another way of looking at it is to consider it as the maximum/minimum rate of interest that one could afford to pay for funds raised to finance a project without making a loss.

5.2   Estimating the IRR of a project with even annual cash flows

The IRR of the following project is 6%.

Time	Cash flow £	6% discount factor	Present value £
0	(421,200)	1	(421,200)
1 - 5	100,000	4.212	421,200
			_____
			-
			_____

How was the IRR found?

Since the PV of the initial outflow is £421,200, the PV of the inflows must also be £421,200 in order to produce an NPV of zero; remember we are trying to find a discount rate to produce a zero NPV.

Since the even annual inflows are £100,000, the 5 year discount factor that must be applied to them therefore must be £421,200 ÷ £100,000 = 4.212. Using the cumulative present value table and looking along the 5 year row, the discount rate that gives a discount factor of 4.212 is **6%**. Hence 6% must be the IRR of the project.

5.3   Example

Find the IRR of the following cash flows:

An investment of £2,226,000 to produce £500,000 annually in arrears for five years.

5.4   Solution

$$\text{Five year cumulative factor} = \frac{£2,226,000}{£500,000} = 4.452$$

Using the cumulative present value tables, looking along the five year row shows the IRR to be = 4%.

5.5   Estimating the IRR of a project with uneven cash flows

With most project cash flows the IRR can only be estimated by trial and error ie, by computing NPV's at various discount rates until the discount rate is found which gives an NPV of zero.

Example

An investment opportunity is available which requires a single cash outlay of £850. Cash inflows of £388 will then arise at twelve month intervals for three years commencing in one year's time. Bank overdraft finance is available at 8% pa.

5.6   Solution

Year	Cash flow £	PV factor @ 8%	Present value £
1	388	0.926	359
2	388	0.857	333
3	388	0.794	308

Present value of future cash receipts	1,000
Less: Present value of initial outlay	(850)
Net present value	150

Our next estimate of the discount rate must be greater than 8% since the larger the discount rate, the lower the present value of future cash receipts. Initially, try 15%;

Year	Cash flow £	PV factor @ 15%	Present value £
0	(850)	1.000	(850)
1	388	0.870	338
2	388	0.756	293
3	388	0.658	255
Net present value			36

The NPV of 36 is lower than previously computed but still positive.

Therefore, increase the discount rate again to, say, 20%:

Year	Cash flow £	PV factor @ 20%	Present value £
0	(850)	1.000	(850)
1	388	0.833	323
2	388	0.694	269
3	388	0.579	225
Net present value			(33)

The IRR lies between 15% and 20%. A closer estimate can be found by linear interpolation.

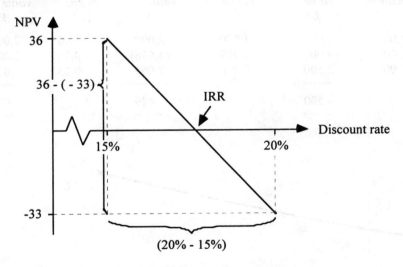

From the graph, and by similar triangles, it can be seen that:

$$\frac{IRR - 15\%}{36 - 0} = \frac{20\% - 15\%}{36 - (-33)}$$

$$IRR = 15\% + (5\% \times \frac{36}{69})$$

$$= 17.6\%$$

approx. $\underline{17\%}$

The formula for the IRR is

$$\text{IRR} = i_1 + \frac{\text{NPV}_1}{\text{NPV}_1 - \text{NPV}_2} (i_2 - i_1)$$

where NPV_1 is the NPV at a discount rate of i_1, and NPV_2 is the NPV at a discount rate of i_2.

5.7   Multiple rates of return

One of the problems of the IRR method is that projects may have either no IRR, one IRR, or more than one IRR. Situations leading to these conclusions are set out below.

5.8   Example

A project has the following cash flows:

Year	Cash flow £
0	2,000
1	(4,000)
2	2,500

Plot a graph of net present values against discount rate and from it deduce the IRR.

5.9   Solution

Year	Cash flow £	at 0% Discount factor	at 0% Present value £	at 10% Discount factor	at 10% Present value £	at 100% Discount factor	at 100% Present value £
0	2,000	1.00	2,000	1.000	2,000	1.00	2,000
1	(4,000)	1.00	(4,000)	0.909	(3,636)	0.50	(2,000)
2	2,500	1.00	2,500	0.826	2,065	0.25	625
			500		429		625

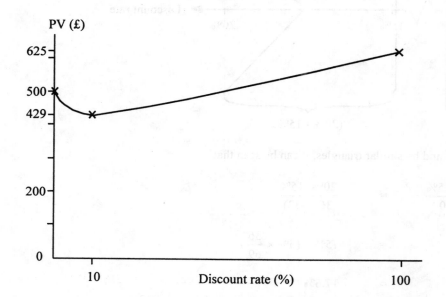

There is no discount rate at which the NPV is zero. The IRR does not exist.

5.10   Example

A project has the following cash flows:

Year 0: – £9,550   Year 1: + £18,769   Year 3: – £9,999

Plot a graph of the present values and from it deduce the IRR.

5.11   Solution

		Present value at (%)				
Year	Cash flow					
		5	10	20	30	50
	£	£	£	£	£	£
0	(9,550)	(9,550)	(9,550)	(9,550)	(9,550)	(9,550)
1	18,769	17,831	17,080	15,578	14,452	12,575
3	(9,999)	(8,599)	(7,499)	(5,799)	(4,599)	(3,000)
NPV		(780)	(318)	(31)	229	303	(25)

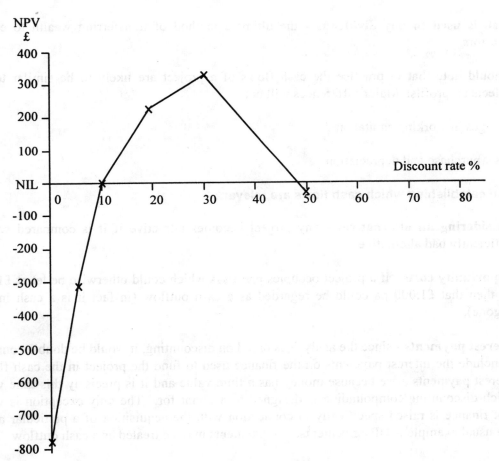

This graph shows that this project has two IRRs, at just over 10% and at around 48%.

Note on examination technique

It is important to know if multiple rates of return will occur. The rule is that if the cash flow has a substantial second reversal, then there may be two IRRs.

6   INVESTMENT ANALYSIS AND APPRAISAL

6.1   The approach to project appraisal

The method used in evaluating projects in this chapter will be based on the discounting techniques explained previously.

It should be noted that it is assumed that the normal situation is that the company is able to raise the finance it requires, and that the problem is the shortage of suitable investment opportunities. The alternative situation, **capital rationing,** is where there are inadequate funds to finance all the attractive investment opportunities. This is outside the syllabus.

6.2   Why discount cash flows rather than profits?

(a)   **Cash is what ultimately counts** - profits are only a guide to cash availability, they cannot actually be spent.

(b)   **Profit measurement is subjective** - which time period income or expenses are recorded in, and so on.

(c)   **Cash is used to pay dividends** - the ultimate method of transferring wealth to equity investors.

Students should note that in practice the cash flows of a project are likely to be similar to the project's effects on profits. Major differences will be:

(a)   Changes in working capital; and

(b)   Asset purchase and depreciation.

6.3   Problems in establishing which cash flows are relevant

(a)   **Considering all alternatives** - any project becomes attractive if it is compared with a sufficiently bad alternative.

(b)   **Opportunity costs** - if a project occupies premises which could otherwise be let at £1,000 pa, then that £1,000 pa could be regarded as a cash outflow (in fact it is a cash inflow forgone).

(c)   **Interest payments** - since the analysis is based on discounting, it would be double counting to include the interest payments on the finance used to fund the project in the cash flows. Interest payments arise because money has a time value and it is precisely this time value which discounting/compounding is designed to account for. The only exception is when debt finance is raised specifically in connection with the acquisition of a particular asset. The usual example is HP agreements. HP payments may be treated as a cash outflow.

(d)   **Taxation payments** - are a cash outflow when they are paid; savings in tax payments through capital allowances or tax losses may be treated as cash receipts at the point in time when they reduce a tax payment.

(e)   **Scrap or terminal proceeds** - where any equipment used in a project is scrapped, then the proceeds are a cash inflow.

6.4   Applying discounting in investment decisions

It is now possible to develop criteria for accepting or rejecting investment opportunities. Consider the situation where management can acquire funds at a known rate of interest and are considering whether to *accept or reject an investment project*. There are two main approaches:

(a)   *Internal rate of return approach* – is the IRR on the project greater than the borrowing rate? – if so, accept.

(b)   *Net present value (NPV) approach* – at the borrowing rate, is the present value of cash inflows less initial cash outflows (ie, the net present value) positive? – if so, accept.

In the type of decisions described above, both methods will normally lead to identical conclusions.

6.5   Activity

An initial investment of £2,000 in a project yields cash inflows of £500, £500, £600, £600 and £440 at twelve month intervals. There is no scrap value. Funds are available to finance the project at 12%.

You are required to decide whether the project is worthwhile, using:

(a)   Net present value approach.

(b)   Internal rate of return approach.

6.6   Activity solution

It is useful to set out the cash flows:

Years	0	1	2	3	4	5
	−£2,000	+£500	+£500	+£600	+£600	+£440

(a)   **Net present value approach**

Year	Cash flow £	PV factor @ 12%	Present value £
0	−2,000	1.000	−2,000
1	+500	0.893	+447
2	+500	0.797	+399
3	+600	0.712	+427
4	+600	0.636	+382
5	+440	0.567	+249
Net present value			−96

Since the net present value is negative, the project should be rejected.

(b)   **Internal rate of return approach**

Calculating IRR requires a trial and error approach. Since we have already calculated in (a) that NPV at 12% is negative, we must decrease the discount rate to bring the NPV towards zero – try 8%.

Year	Cash flow	Present value @ 12% (a)	PV factor @ 8%	Present value @ 8%
	£	£		£
0	−2,000	−2,000	1.000	−2,000
1	+500	+447	0.926	+463
2	+500	+399	0.857	+429
3	+600	+427	0.794	+476
4	+600	+382	0.735	+441
5	+440	+249	0.681	+300
Net present value		−96		+109

Thus, the IRR lies between 8% and 12%. We may estimate it by interpolation:

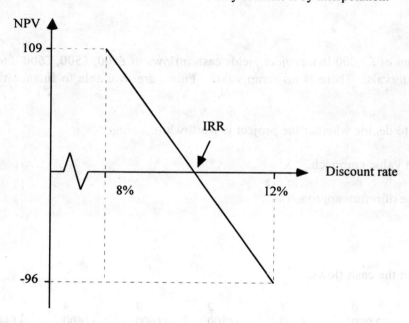

From the graph, and by similar triangles:

$$\frac{IRR - 8\%}{109 - 0} = \frac{12\% - 8\%}{109 - (-96)}$$

$$IRR = 8\% + (4\% \times \frac{109}{205})$$

$$= 10.13\%$$

approx.   10%

Conclusion

The project should be rejected because the IRR is less than the cost of borrowing, which is 12% ie, the same conclusion as in (a) above.

6.7   What net present value means

In the investment problem, the net present value at 12% was − £96. At 8%, it was + £109. Another way of expressing this, is as follows:

If the funds were borrowed at 12%, the investment proceeds would only be enough to repay principal and interest on £1,904 – the investor would be £96 out of pocket.

If funds were borrowed at 8%, the investment proceeds would be able to pay interest and principal on £2,109 – the investor would be £109 in pocket.

In other words, a positive net present value is an indication of the surplus funds available to the investor now as a result of accepting the project.

6.8   Relationship between IRR, NPV and the discount rate

Example

Using the data in the activity in 6.5, calculate additionally the NPV at 0%, 5% and 20%. Plot these, plus those already calculated, on a graph of net present values (Y axis) against discount rates (X axis).

Solution

Year	Cash flow (= PV @ 0%)	PV factor @ 5%	PV @ 5%	PV factor @ 20%	PV @ 20%
	£		£		£
0	−2,000	1.000	−2,000	1.000	−2,000
1	+500	0.952	+476	0.833	+417
2	+500	0.907	+454	0.694	+347
3	+600	0.864	+518	0.579	+347
4	+600	0.823	+494	0.482	+289
5	+440	0.784	+345	0.402	+177
NPV	+640		+287		−423

Graph of NPV against discount rate

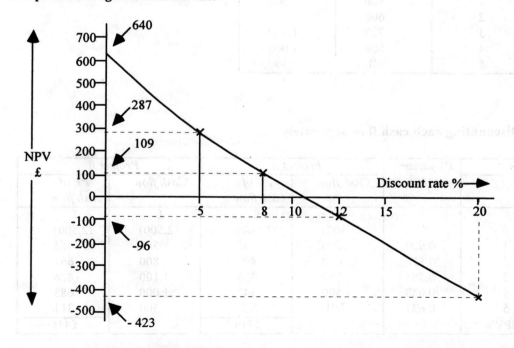

The graph shows that the higher the discount rate, the lower the NPV. Where the NPV is zero (ie, cuts the X axis), then we may read off the IRR.

Note that the 'curve' is nearly, but not quite, a straight line.

Thus, if we select a 'cut-off discount rate' (eg, the borrower's rate) of 12% on the NPV criterion, we see that the NPV is negative; on the IRR criterion the X axis is cut at a lower discount rate than 12%. Either way we reject the project.

7   OTHER APPROACHES

7.1   Absolute and relative cash flows

When deciding between two projects (known as **mutually exclusive projects**) two approaches are possible.

(a)   Discount the cash flows of each project separately and compare NPVs; or

(b)   Find the **differential** cash flow year by year, ie, the **difference** between the cash flows of the two projects. Then discount those differential cash flows.

Either approach will give us the same conclusion, although the second is only valid if you know that you **must** adopt one of the **two** projects.

7.2   Example

Two projects A and B, are under consideration. Either A or B, but not both, may be accepted. The relevant discount rate is 10%. You are required to recommend A or B by:

(a)   discounting each cash flow separately and
(b)   discounting relative (or differential) cash flows.

The cash flows are as follows:

Year	A	B
	£	£
0	(1,500)	(2,500)
1	500	500
2	600	800
3	700	1,100
4	500	1,000
5	NIL	500

Solution

(a)   **Discounting each cash flow separately**

Year	PV factor at 10%	Project A Cash flow	Project A PV of cash flow	Project B Cash flow	Project B PV of cash flow
		£	£	£	£
0	1.000	(1,500)	(1,500)	(2,500)	(2,500)
1	0.909	500	455	500	455
2	0.826	600	496	800	661
3	0.751	700	526	1,100	826
4	0.683	500	342	1,000	683
5	0.621	NIL	NIL	500	311
NPV's			£319		£436

Project B is preferred because its NPV exceeds that of A by £(436 − 319) = £117.

(b)   Discounting relative cash flows

Year	Project A	Project B	Relative cash flow B – A	PV factor at 10%	PV of relative cash flow
0	(1,500)	(2,500)	(1,000)	1.000	(1,000)
1	500	500	NIL	0.909	NIL
2	600	800	200	0.826	165
3	700	1,100	400	0.751	300
4	500	1,000	500	0.683	342
5	NIL	500	500	0.621	310
NPV of relative cash flow					£117

In other words, the net present value of the cash flows of project B are £117 more than those of project A. B is preferred. *Note:* the result is exactly the same in (a) and (b). This gives a useful shortcut to computation when comparing two projects.

(However, method (b), whilst indicating that B is better than A, does not indicate that either are worthwhile. B may simply be less bad than A.)

7.3   Cost benefit ratio

[Definition]   Variously known as the cost benefit ratio, profitability index, or simply NPV per £ initial outlay, the ratio is given by:

$$\frac{\text{NPV}}{\text{Initial outlay}}$$

7.4   Example

Compare two projects, A and B, using the cost benefit ratio at a discount rate of 20%.

Cash flows are as follows:

Year	A £	B £
0	(1,000)	(4,000)
1	500	2,000
2	800	2,800
3	500	1,500

7.5   Solution

Year	A PV cash flow @ 20% £	B PV cash flow @ 20% £
0	(1,000)	(4,000)
1	415	1,660
2	552	1,932
3	290	870
NPV	257	462
Profitability index	$\frac{257}{1,000} = 0.257$	$\frac{462}{4,000} = 0.1155$

Thus, whereas project B has the higher NPV, project A has the preferable ratio.

Validity of ratio

A comparison of NPV to initial outlay is only relevant when the funds available for investment are restricted – a capital rationing situation.

In all other situations, the ratio is irrelevant, and does not provide a valid decision base. Therefore, in the above example, B is to be preferred unless a capital rationing situation prevails.

7.6   Changing cost of funds

It has so far been implicitly assumed that the cost of capital is constant. However, if the cost of capital does change from year to year a net present value may still be computed.

Illustration

Interest rates are expected to be 10% pa throughout year 1 and 15% throughout year 2. Therefore, if £100 were invested at year 0 then by the end of the second year it would have grown to:

$$£100 \times 1.1 \times 1.15 = £126.50$$

Similarly, the present value of £100 receivable in two years' time is:

$$£100 \times \frac{1}{1.15} \times \frac{1}{1.1} = £79.05$$

Thus, where the cost of funds changes from year to year, the overall discount factor is found by taking the product of the discount factors for the prevailing interest rates for each year.

7.7   Activity

A project has the following cash flows:

>   Initial outlay £1,135
>
>   Annual receipts from year 1 to year 4 are £350

Interest rates (that is, cost of capital) are expected to be 10% pa until the end of the second year, and 5% pa thereafter. Is the project worth investing in?

7.8   Activity solution

Year	Cash flow £	Discount factor	Present value £
0	(1,135)	1.000	(1,135)
1	350	0.909	318
2	350	0.826	289
3	350	0.952 × 0.826 = 0.786	275
4	350	0.907 × 0.826 = 0.749	262
			9

The net present value of the project = £9, and the project should, therefore, be undertaken.

Note that whilst an IRR could have been computed (it is in fact approximately 9%), there is no way of using this figure. It is greater than the cost of funds for the latter part of the project's life, and less than the cost of funds for the first two years.

8   NPV v IRR

8.1   The choice between the NPV and IRR approaches

The two most common discounting methods of project appraisal are the net present value (NPV) and internal rate of return (IRR) approaches.

> **Definition**   Net present value is the sum of the project cash flows discounted at the company's cost of capital.

> **Definition**   Internal rate of return is the discount rate which, when applied to the project cash flows, gives an NPV of zero.

The use of the two approaches under different situations may be summarised as follows:

Type of decision	NPV criteria	IRR criteria
Accept/reject	Accept if NPV is positive	Accept if IRR exceeds cost of capital
Mutually exclusive	Accept project with highest NPV	Complex; see explanation below

Accept or reject decisions are those when there is a series of projects which must be considered separately. Each one may be accepted or rejected irrespective of the decisions regarding other projects. It has been shown earlier that there is no conflict between the two methods of investment appraisal in these circumstances.

Mutually exclusive decisions, on the other hand, are those where only one out of several alternatives can be accepted. An example would be where a choice must be made between several different manufacturing methods.

It is only in this latter type of decision that the choice between the two approaches matters.

8.2   Example

The Mutual Company has to decide between two projects, A and B, with the following cash flows:

	Project A £	Project B £
Year 0	−50,000	−75,000
Year 5	+80,000	+110,000
Absolute net cash flows	+30,000	+35,000

8.3   Solution

A graph of the present values of the two projects may be constructed by plotting a range of present values:

					Present values			
Year	Discounting @ 5%		Discounting @ 10%		Discounting @15%		Discounting @ 20%	
	A £	B £	A £	B £	A £	B £	A £	B £
0	−50,000	−75,000	−50,000	−75,000	−50,000	−75,000	−50,000	−75,000
5	+62,400	+85,800	+49,600	+68,200	+40,000	+55,000	+32,000	+44,000
NPV	+12,400	+10,800	−400	−6,800	−10,000	−20,000	−18,000	−31,000

Note: as the discount rate is raised, the NPV declines.

Graph of present values of two projects, A and B

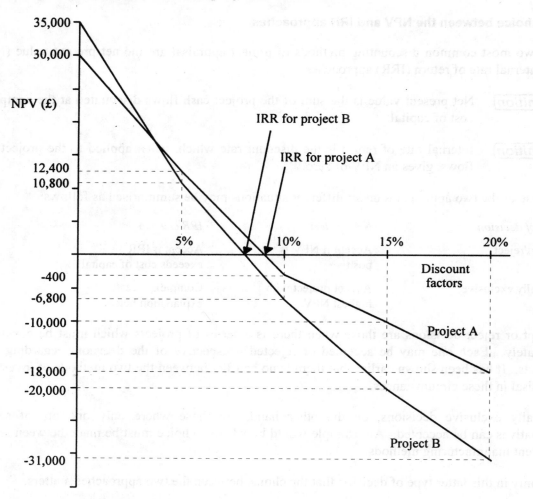

8.4   Conclusions drawn from the diagram

(a)   As the discount rate is increased, NPV of both projects declines.

(b)   The NPV of project B declines faster than that of project A, so that although initially it is more attractive, it soon becomes less attractive.

(c)   By definition, the internal rate of return is that discount rate where NPV is zero ie, where each curve cuts the x axis.

(d)   This point is determined by the relative size and timings of the cash inflows to the initial outflow for each individual project. Thus, for example, the IRR of project A would be unchanged if both inflows and outflows were multiplied by a factor of 10 ie, initial expenditure year 0 = £500,000, receipts year 5 = £800,000, IRR is unchanged at 9.5%.

(e)   Hence it follows that IRR gives no measure of the absolute return of the project, but only of *the size and timings of the cash inflows in relation to the cash outflows*.

(f)   For a measure of absolute return, NPV must be used.

8.5   NPV or IRR – dealing with the conflict

An accept or reject decision is one where each project may be accepted or rejected independently of what happens to other projects.

Selection is made as follows:

(a)   using IRR, accept the project if IRR is above the target discount rate;

(b)   using NPV, accept the project if NPV is positive at the target discount rate.

It is concluded that in accept and reject situations IRR and NPV lead to the same result.

In the case of mutually exclusive projects, the two methods will sometimes lead to different rankings.

Mutually exclusive projects means the situation where only one out of several alternative projects may be selected.

The conclusion reached is that *NPV based on discounting the return at the equity cost of capital always gives the correct ranking.* This is because NPV measures the absolute increase in wealth. IRR deals in relative returns and it must be remembered that a small percentage return on a large project is often preferable to a larger return on a smaller project.

8.6   Conclusions on IRR and NPV

The case may be summarised as follows:

NPV advantages

(a)   Always provides the correct ranking without recourse to IRR of differential cash flows.

(b)   Avoids the problem of nil, or multiple, rates of return.

(c)   Can cope when cost of funds changes from year to year.

(d)   Only practical method for multi-period capital rationing.

(e)   Directly measures the benefit to be received by investors as a result of investing in the project.

IRR advantages

(a)   Results, being expressed as a percentage, are more easily understood by business people.

(b)   As a rule of thumb, a premium can be added to the target discount rate in order to take account of the risk of the project. It is argued by some that this is simpler than computing a revised NPV at the new target rate.

(c)   It is argued that working in terms of IRR avoids (or at least defers) the need to compute the cost of capital. The cost of capital raised by bank loans is different from the cost of capital raised by issuing ordinary shares, thus there may be a range of target rates at any one time.

9   CHAPTER SUMMARY

This chapter has considered simple and compound interest. The principles of compound interest have then been used to discount future cash flows and thereby evaluate investment projects.

10   SELF TEST QUESTIONS

10.1   What is meant by simple interest? (1.1)

10.2   What is compound interest? (1.5)

10.3   What is the terminal value of a project? (2.1)

10.4   What are the major drawbacks of using net terminal values for project appraisal? (3.1)

10.5   Explain the meaning of 'present value'. (3.1)

10.6   What is an annuity? (4.1)

10.7   Explain the meaning of 'internal rate of return'. (5.1)

10.8   What is the method of estimating the IRR of a project with uneven cash flows? (5.5)

10.9   What is the cost-benefit ratio and when should it be used? (7.3, 7.5)

10.10   What are the accept or reject criteria when using the IRR and NPV methods of appraisal? (8.5)

11   EXAMINATION TYPE QUESTIONS

11.1   Cash flows for projects A and B

The cash flows for two projects are expected to be as follows:

Project A			Project B	
Time	Cash flow £'000		Time	Cash flow £'000
0	−25		0	−25
1	10		1	0
2	10		2	5
3	10		3	10
4	10		4	30

(a)   Use present value tables or first principles to compute the present values for each project at discount rates of 10%, 20%, 30% and 40%.

(b)   Plot the two sets of points on a single sheet of graph paper, and join the two sets of points to produce two smooth curves.

(c)   Use the graphs to read off the internal rate of return for the two projects.

(Total: 18 marks)

11.2   Oracle plc

Oracle plc invests in a new machine at the beginning of Year 1 which costs £15,000. It is hoped that the net cash flows over the next five years will correspond to those given in the table below:

Year	1	2	3	4	5
Net cash flow	£1,500	£2,750	£4,000	£5,700	£7,500

You are required:

(a)   (i)   to calculate the net present value assuming a 15% cost of capital;

(ii)   to calculate the net present value assuming a 10% cost of capital;

(iii)   to calculate the internal rate of return of the above project using the results of (i) and (ii).

(10 marks)

(b)   An alternative machine would cost £17,500 but would produce equal net cash flows of £5,500 over the next five years. What cost of capital would produce a break-even situation on the project?

(10 marks)

(Total: 20 marks)

12   ANSWERS TO EXAMINATION TYPE QUESTIONS

12.1   Cash flows for projects A and B

(a)

Project A

Cash flow	Time	Present values (£'000)			
£'000		10%	20%	30%	40%
(25)	0	(25.0)	(25.0)	(25.0)	(25.0)
10	1 – 4	31.7	25.9	21.7	18.5
Net present value		6.7	0.9	(3.3)	(6.5)

Project B

Cash flow	Time	Present values (£'000)			
£'000		10%	20%	30%	40%
(25)	0	(25.00)	(25.00)	(25.00)	(25.00)
0	1	0.00	0.00	0.00	0.00
5	2	4.15	3.45	2.95	2.55
10	3	7.50	5.80	4.60	3.60
30	4	20.40	14.40	10.50	7.80
Net present value		7.05	(1.35)	(6.95)	(11.05)

(b)

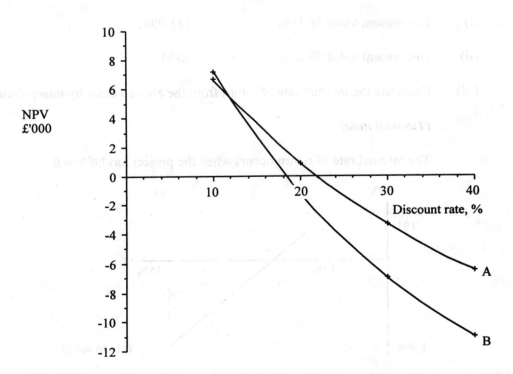

(c)   The internal rate of return is the point on the graph where the curve cuts the horizontal axis. For Project A this is approximately 22%, and for Project B approximately 18%.

To obtain these values, graph paper must be used.

Note: for practice students may wish to calculate the approximate IRR by interpolation:

$$IRR \approx A + \left(\frac{N_A}{N_A - N_B}\right)(B - A)$$

Project A (using 20% & 30%)   Project B (using 10% & 20%)

$20\% + (30\% - 20\%) \times \dfrac{0.9}{(0.9 - (3.3))}$ $10\% + (20\% - 10\%) \times \dfrac{7.05}{(7.05 - (1.35))}$

$20\% + 0.214 \times 10\%$ $10\% + 0.839 \times 10\%$

$= \ 22.1\%$ $= \ 18.4\%$

The differences are due to the fact that the interpolation method assumes a straight line relationship between NPV and discount rate and also because it is difficult to plot and read the graph accurately.

12.2   Oracle plc

(a)

Year	Cash flow £	Discount factor (15%)	Present value £	Discount factor (10%)	Present value £
0	(15,000)	1.000	(15,000)	1.000	(15,000)
1	1,500	0.870	1,305	0.909	1,364
2	2,750	0.756	2,079	0.826	2,272
3	4,000	0.658	2,632	0.751	3,004
4	5,700	0.572	3,260	0.683	3,893
5	7,500	0.497	3,728	0.621	4,658
			(1,996)		191

(i)   Net present value @ 15%   =   (£1,996)

(ii)   Net present value @ 10%   =   £191

(iii)   Calculate the internal rate of return from the above values by interpolation.

(Tutorial note:

The internal rate of return occurs when the project has NPV = 0.

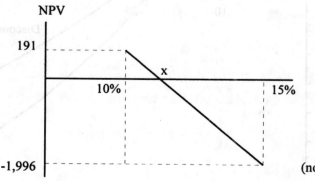

(not to scale)

Calculate by interpolation:

$$\frac{191}{x-10} = \frac{191+1,996}{15-10}$$

$$x - 10 = 5 \times \frac{191}{2,187}$$

$$x = 10.44$$

$$IRR = 10.4\%$$

(b)   At 15% the cumulative present value factor for five years is 3.352. The net present value for the project is given by (£17,500) + 3.352 × £5,500 ie, £936.

At 20% the cumulative present value factor for five years is 2.991. The net present value for the project is given by (£17,500) + 2.991 × £5,500 ie, (£1,050).

Calculate the internal rate of return from the above values by interpolation.

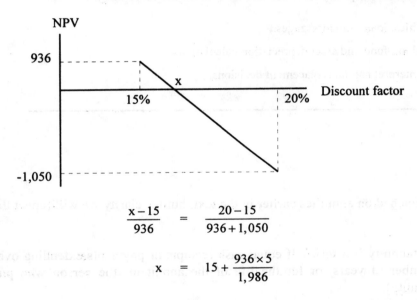

$$\frac{x-15}{936} = \frac{20-15}{936+1,050}$$

$$x = 15 + \frac{936 \times 5}{1,986}$$

$$x = 17.36$$

Break-even cost of capital   =   17.4%

(Tutorial note:

One formula for calculating IRR by interpolation is:

$$\text{Lower rate} + \left(\begin{array}{c} \text{Higher} \\ \text{rate} \end{array} - \begin{array}{c} \text{Lower} \\ \text{rate} \end{array} \right) \times \frac{\text{NPV at lower rate}}{\text{NPV lower} - \text{NPV higher}}$$

but it is important that students understand the derivation as shown above.

When calculating the IRR by interpolation it is best always to have one positive NPV and one negative NPV.*)*

9 ANNUITIES, LOANS AND MORTGAGES

INTRODUCTION & LEARNING OBJECTIVES

Syllabus area 7c. Calculation and appraisal of annuities, loans and mortgages. (Ability required 3).

Depreciation and capital replacement. (Ability required 3).

The use of spreadsheets for these methods. (Ability required 1).

When you have studied this chapter you should be able to do the following:

- Calculate annuities, loans and mortgages.
- Understand sinking fund and asset depreciation calculations.
- Calculate and interpret capital replacement decisions.

1 ANNUITIES

1.1 Introduction

We have already touched on annuities earlier in the text, but for clarity we will repeat the definition here.

Definition An annuity is a series of equal cash receipts or payments extending over a specific number of years, or for the life of the annuitant (the person who purchases the annuity).

Annuities were mentioned earlier as a way of introducing cumulative present value tables, otherwise known as annuity tables. In this section we shall consider the types of questions which could be asked on the subject of annuities. These basically fall into two groups.

(a) If I have a certain sum of money now to purchase an annuity commencing in n years and continuing at r%, what would the annuity be?

This is a practical question which many people will eventually have to ask themselves on reaching retirement when perhaps part of their pension will be given as a lump sum and they wish to know how much income this will generate.

(b) How much do I need to invest now at r% in order to obtain an annuity of £x per annum commencing in n years time for m years?

The easiest way to demonstrate how to compute these types of questions is by examples.

1.2   Examples

(a)   **Example**

What annuity would I be able to purchase commencing now and continuing for 10 years at 5% rate of interest if I have £20,000 to invest?

Solution

Let the amount of each receipt = £A.

The first annuity is received at the end of the first year.

£20,000 = Present value of annuity receipts

$$= A\left(\frac{1}{1.05} + \frac{1}{1.05^2} + \frac{1}{1.05^3} \cdots \frac{1}{1.05^{10}}\right)$$

$$= A \times 7.722 \text{ (from cumulative PV table)}$$

$$\therefore A = \frac{20,000}{7.722}$$

$$= £2,590$$

(b)   **Example**

What annuity would I be able to purchase if I invested £15,000 now at 8% and I wish the annuity to commence in 5 years time and run for 10 years?

Solution

The first income payment will be received at the end of five years from now and has a present value of

$$\frac{£A}{(1.08)^5}$$

The second payment has a present value of $\dfrac{£A}{(1.08)^6}$ etc.

Hence, the total PV of the 10 payments will therefore be:

$$£15,000 = A\left(\frac{1}{1.08^5} + \frac{1}{1.08^6} \cdots + \frac{1}{1.08^{14}}\right)$$

The terms inside the brackets can be regarded as the cumulative PV of £1 for the first fourteen years minus the cumulative PV of £1 for the **first four** years. Thus:

$$£15,000 = A(8.244 - 3.312) \text{ from the tables}$$

$$\therefore A = \frac{15,000}{4.932}$$

$$= £3,041$$

(c)   **Example**

What annuity, to be received indefinitely, would I be able to purchase if I invested £25,000 now at 4%, the first payment being received at the end of the year?

Solution

The formula to be used here is the one for a perpetuity since the amount is receivable in perpetuity.

If you recall, the formula for a perpetuity is

$$PV = \frac{a}{r} \quad \text{where} \quad a = \text{the annual amount receivable}$$
$$r = \text{the discount rate}$$

Thus,   £25,000 $= \dfrac{a}{0.04}$

$$\therefore \quad a = £25,000 \times 0.04$$

$$= \mathbf{£1,000}$$

1.3   Activity

How much do I need to invest now at 5% in order to obtain an annuity of £12,000 a year for 10 years, starting in 4 years time?

1.4   Activity solution

$$PV = 12,000\left(\frac{1}{1.05^4} + \frac{1}{1.05^5} \cdots \frac{1}{1.05^{13}}\right)$$

From the tables $= 12,000(9.394 - 2.723)$

(See example 2 above if you are unsure of these figures.)

$$= 12,000 \times 6.671$$

$$= £80,052$$

The amount to be invested must be **£80,052**.

2   MORTGAGES

2.1   Definition

Definition   The term mortgage can be used to mean a debt which is repaid by regular instalments. Such repayments consist partly of interest and partly repayment of some of the loan. The amount of each instalment remains constant, but as the amount of the outstanding debt decreases, the proportion of the instalment which goes to paying the interest decreases, and the proportion which goes to paying off the outstanding debt increases.

From the point of view of the lender (mortgagee) it is equivalent to an annuity. He invests a lump sum in the borrower (mortgager) and receives a regular income in return.

2.2 Examples

(a) Example

To find the annual repayment on a building society mortgage of £40,000 over five years at 12% pa.

Solution

This is equivalent to an annual income derived from an investment of £40,000.

Let the amount of each repayment = £A.

The first repayment is made at the end of the first year, the second at the end of the second year, and so on, so that:

$$£40,000 = \text{Present value of all repayments}$$

$$= A\left[\frac{1}{1.12^1} + \frac{1}{1.12^2} + \frac{1}{1.12^3} + \frac{1}{1.12^4} + \frac{1}{1.12^5}\right]$$

$$= A \times 3.605 \text{ (from cumulative PV table)}$$

$$\therefore A = \frac{40,000}{3.605}$$

$$= £11,096$$

The correctness of the result can be demonstrated by following through each transaction:

Year	Debt b/f	Interest	Debt & interest	Repaid	Debt c/f
	£	£	£	£	£
1	40,000	4,800	44,800	11,096	33,704
2	33,704	4,044	37,748	11,096	26,652
3	26,652	3,198	29,850	11,096	18,754
4	18,754	2,250	21,004	11,096	9,908
5	9,908	1,189	11,097	11,096	1

Thus the debt has been cleared by the end of the fifth year. The small residue of £1 is due to the use of tables which only run to 3 decimal places and rounding errors in the calculations. You could rework the calculations using the formula for the sum of a geometric progression to find the cumulative discount factor as 3.6048.

(b) Example

A man wishes to set up a company and needs to obtain finance of £30,000.

Find where appropriate the annual payment in each of the following situations:

(i) He takes out an immediate mortgage of £30,000 repayable in six equal annual instalments, the first payment to be made one year after receiving the mortgage. The rate of interest is a constant 15% per annum.

(ii)   The man takes out an identical mortgage as in part (i) but, due to unforeseen circumstances, is unable to pay the third instalment. It is decided that the man should rearrange payments so that he completes the repayment at the end of six years as originally agreed, by making three equal annual payments commencing when the fourth instalment is due. The rate of interest remains at 15%.

Solution

(i)   Let x = the annual payment.

We require the present value of an annuity factor for six years at 15% pa (ie, $a\overline{6}|0.15$).

$$3.784x \quad = \quad 30,000$$

$$x \quad = \quad \frac{30,000}{3.784}$$

$$= \quad £7,928$$

(ii)

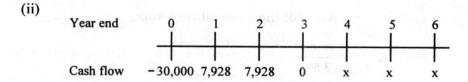

Year end	0	1	2	3	4	5	6
Cash flow	−30,000	7,928	7,928	0	x	x	x

The balance outstanding at the end of year 3 is the future value of £30,000 for three years, less the future value of the repayments of £7,928.

$$\text{Balance at end of 3rd year} \quad = \quad (30,000 \times 1.15^3) - (7,928 \times 1.15^2) - (7,928 \times 1.15)$$

$$= \quad 45,626 - 10,485 - 9,117$$

$$= \quad £26,024$$

This sum must now be paid by a three year annuity of £x.

We require the present value of an annuity factor for three years at 15% pa.

$$2.283x \quad = \quad 26,024$$

$$x \quad = \quad \frac{26,024}{2.283}$$

$$= \quad £11,399$$

2.3   Activity

What is the annual repayment on a mortgage of £50,000 over eight years at 9% pa.?

2.4 Activity solution

Let annual repayment be A.

Present value of 8 repayments of A at 9%   =   £50,000.

$$A \times 5.535 \quad = \quad £50,000$$

$$\therefore A \quad = \quad £9,033$$

Note: as the calculations in 2.2 show, there is no point in stating results to the nearest penny since the tables do not allow for that accuracy.

3 LOANS

3.1 Introduction

In the previous section we looked at mortgages which are a special type of loan. In this section we shall look at general loan type questions.

Earlier in the text we covered all the relevant basic discounting and compounding formulae, in this section we shall use one new formula which is only a derivation of the basic formulae.

This section will give examples of the main types of questions which are asked and indicate the way in which they should be answered.

3.2 Examples

(a)   **Calculation of total interest payments**

Short-term Loans plc charges borrowers 2.25% compound interest per calendar month. Mr Big borrowed £800 on 1 December 19X8 and settled his account on 30 November 19X9. Calculate the amount Mr Big was required to pay to clear his account.

Solution

Step 1   Calculate the time period.

From 1 December 19X8 to 30 November 19X9 is 12 months.

Step 2   Use the compound interest law.

$$A \quad = \quad P(1 + r)^n$$

Hence $A \quad = \quad 800(1 + 0.0225)^{12}$

$$= \quad \mathbf{£1,044.84}$$

(b)   **Calculation of rate of interest when terminal value and principal known**

In repayment of a loan of £1,250, for five years a borrower paid £1,925.

Calculate the rate of compound interest the borrower was charged.

Solution

Using the compound interest law:

$$A = P(1 + r)^n$$

$$1,925 = 1,250(1 + r)^5$$

$$\therefore (1 + r)^5 = \frac{1,925}{1,250} = 1.54$$

$$(1 + r) = \sqrt[5]{1.54} = 1.09$$

$$\therefore r = 0.09$$

$$= 9\%$$

(c) **Calculating the amount of an outstanding debt**

If £5,000 is borrowed at 18% annual compound interest and annual repayments of £1,200 are made, what will be the amount outstanding after 4 years?

Solution

There are several ways of approaching this question, two are rather long winded, the third uses a formula.

Method 1

Year	Opening Balance £	Interest @ 18% £	Repayment £	Closing Balance £
1	5,000	900	1,200	4,700
2	4,700	846	1,200	4,346
3	4,346	782	1,200	3,928
4	3,928	707	1,200	3,435

The answer is therefore £3,425.

Method 2

Year	Balance	£
1	$5,000(1.18) - 1,200$	= 4,700
2	$5,000(1.18)^2 - 1,200(1.18) - 1,200$	= 4,346
3	$5,000(1.18)^3 - 1,200(1.18)^2 - 1,200(1.18) - 1,200$	= 3,928
4	$5,000(1.18)^4 - 1,200(1.18)^3 - 1,200(1.18)^2 - 1,200(1.18) - 1,200$	= 3,435

As you can see, these calculations can become very tedious.

Method 3 - using an extension to the basic compounding formula

Let   A   =   sum outstanding after n years

      P   =   initial loan

      a   =   annual repayment

      r   =   rate of interest

Then the formula is:

$$A = \left(P - \frac{a}{r}\right)(1+r)^n + \frac{a}{r}$$

$$= \left(5{,}000 - \frac{1{,}200}{0.18}\right)(1+0.18)^4 + \frac{1{,}200}{0.18}$$

$$= (5{,}000 - 6{,}667)1.94 + 6{,}667$$

$$= -3{,}234 + 6{,}667$$

$$= \textbf{£3,433} \text{ (difference due to rounding)}$$

3.3   Activity

Find the outstanding debt after 10 years if £800 is borrowed at an annual compound interest rate of 5% and annual repayments of £90 are made at the end of each year.

3.4   Activity solution

Using the formula

$$A = \left(P - \frac{a}{r}\right)(1+r)^n + \frac{a}{r}$$

$$A = \left(800 - \frac{90}{0.05}\right)(1+0.05)^{10} + \frac{90}{0.05}$$

$$= (800 - 1{,}800)(1.05)^{10} + 1{,}800$$

$$= -1{,}630 + 1{,}800$$

$$= \textbf{£170}$$

The outstanding debt is £170.

4   SINKING FUND

4.1   Definition

Definition   A sinking fund is obtained by investing an amount at regular intervals to provide capital for future projects.

4.2   Example

£2,000 is invested at the end of each year for five years at 8% compound interest. What is the accumulated amount at the end of five years?

Solution

The first contribution to the fund will earn interest for four years, the second contribution for three years and so on. Summarising in a table:

Instalment	Amount (£)	Duration (yrs)	Accumulated amount (£)
1	2,000	4	$2,000 (1 + 0.08)^4$
2	2,000	3	$2,000 (1 + 0.08)^3$
3	2,000	2	$2,000 (1 + 0.08)^2$
4	2,000	1	$2,000 (1 + 0.08)^1$
5	2,000	0	2,000

The total amount in the fund at the end of the period is the sum of the values in the final column. Thus, taking these from the bottom upwards:

$$\text{Total} = 2,000 + 2,000(1 + 0.08) + 2,000(1 + 0.08)^2 + 2,000(1 + 0.08)^3 + 2,000 (1 + 0.08)^4$$

This is a geometric progression with a = 2,000, R = 1.08, n = 5.

The formula for the sum of a GP is $\dfrac{a(R^n - 1)}{R - 1}$ (R is the common ratio of the GP)

$$= \frac{2,000 \times (1.08^5 - 1)}{1.08 - 1}$$

$$= £11,733$$

From the second line of the calculation, it will be seen that the formula for the total would be:

$$\text{Total} = \frac{a\left[(1 + R)^n - 1\right]}{R}$$

where R is rate of interest = 0.08

However, you are strongly advised to perform the calculation by first principles rather than by use of a formula.

If the instalments are paid into the fund at the start of each year instead of the end, the first term will become $2,000 (1.08)^5$ and the last, $2,000(1.08)$. Each term is therefore increased by a factor 1.08, so that the total would then be £11,733 × 1.08 = £12,672.

The formula becomes:

$$\text{Total} = \frac{a(1 + R)[(1 + R)^n - 1]}{R}$$

But, remember, you should be able to do this without relying on the formula.

4.3 Activity

Joe, saving to pay for his daughter's wedding in five years' time intends to save £400 each year in a building society account which will earn interest at 9% (effective rate).

How much will he have by then?

4.4 Activity solution

The question is ambiguous as to whether the final instalment will be saved immediately prior to the wedding or twelve months in advance.

Therefore, we may assume that the former is the case. If faced with such uncertainty in the exam, read the question again to check that the information is missing then STATE your assumption clearly. In total there will be six instalments and the amount saved will be:

$$S = \frac{a(r^n - 1)}{r - 1} \quad \text{where} \quad a = £400,$$

$$r = 1.09,$$

$$n = 6$$

$$= \frac{£400 \times (1.09^6 - 1)}{1.09 - 1}$$

$$= £3,009$$

4.5 Activity

Charlotte, an ambitious young student accountant, has put her name down on the waiting list for a Morgan Plus 8 sports car. The delivery time is seven years and she expects the price to be £35,000 at that time.

How much does she need to invest annually in a savings account earning 11% pa in order to be able to buy the car outright at that time?

4.6 Activity solution

Rearranging the previous formula we have:

$$a = \frac{S_n(r - 1)}{(r^n - 1)} \quad \text{where} \quad S_n = £35,000$$

$$n = 8$$

$$r = 1.11$$

$$a = \frac{£35,000 \times 0.11}{(1.11^8 - 1)}$$

$$= £2,951$$

5 DEPRECIATION

5.1 Definition

> **Definition** Depreciation is an accounting technique whereby the cost of a capital asset is spread over a number of accounting periods as a charge against profits of each of the periods.

There are several methods of calculating depreciation, but the one we shall consider here is the reducing balance method as it is the only common one which uses compounding techniques.

5.2 Compound depreciation

If a machine costs £1,000 and depreciates in value by 10% per annum on written down value, its value in successive years is shown in the following table (all values in £).

Year	Amount of depreciation			Depreciated value		
0				1,000		
1	10% of 1,000	=	100	1,000 – 100	=	900
2	10% of 900	=	90	900 – 90	=	810
3	10% of 810	=	81	810 – 81	=	729
4	10% of 729	=	72.90	729 – 72.90	=	656.10

etc.

This is known as the **reducing balance** method of depreciation, as distinct from 'straight line' depreciation, which is depreciation by the same amount each year on cost (rather than on written down value.)

Compound depreciation is similar to compound interest except that instead of adding interest, we subtract depreciation. The law is therefore:

$$D = P(1 - r)^n \qquad \text{where}$$

D = the depreciated value

P = the initial value

r = rate of depreciation

n = number of periods

5.3 Activity

A new machine costs £5,000 and is depreciated by 8% per annum. What is the book value of the new machine when it is five years old?

5.4 Activity solution

P = £5,000

r = 8% = $\dfrac{8}{100}$ = 0.08

n = 5

$$
\begin{aligned}
D &= P(1-r)^n \\
&= £5,000 \times (1-0.08)^5 \\
&= £5,000 \times 0.6591 \\
&= £3,295
\end{aligned}
$$

5.5 Activity

A new machine costs £8,000 and has a useful life of ten years, after which it can be sold as scrap for £100. Calculate the annual rate of compound depreciation.

5.6 Activity solution

$$
\begin{aligned}
D &= £100 \\
P &= £8,000 \\
n &= 10
\end{aligned}
$$

$$
\text{So} \quad 100 = 8,000(1-r)^{10}
$$

$$
(1-r)^{10} = \frac{100}{8,000} = 0.0125
$$

$$
(1-r) = \sqrt[10]{0.0125}
$$

$$
= 0.6452
$$

$$
r = 1 - 0.6452
$$

$$
= 0.3548 \text{ or } 35.48\%
$$

6 REPLACEMENT THEORY

6.1 The nature of replacement problems

The replacement problem is concerned with the decision to replace existing operating assets. The main questions to be evaluated are:

(a) When should the existing equipment be replaced?

(b) How should the replacement be financed?

We have already covered the second of these two questions when discussing loans and sinking funds. Any of these methods of finance can be used to fund the replacement of an asset. What we shall be concentrating on in this section is the optimum time when an asset should be replaced.

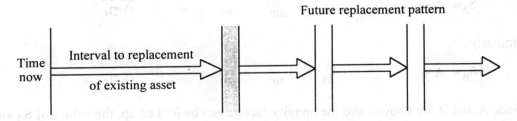

It is difficult to determine the replacement policy of the existing asset in isolation, because that decision will be dependent on the cost of the future replacement pattern.

This section is concerned with developing a systematic approach to replacement analysis.

6.2   Factors in replacement decisions

(a)   *Capital cost of new equipment* – the higher cost of equipment will have to be balanced against known or possible technical improvements.

(b)   *Operating costs* – operating costs will be expected to increase as the machinery deteriorates over time. This is referred to as *operating inferiority*, and is the result of:

   (i)   increased repair and maintenance costs;
   (ii)   loss of production due to down-time resulting from (i);
   (iii) lower quality and quantity of output.

(c)   *Resale value* – the extent to which old equipment can be traded in for new.

(d)   Taxation and investment incentives.

(e)   *Inflation* – both the general price level change, and relative movements in the prices of inputs and outputs.

6.3   The time-scale problem

A special feature of replacement problems is to compare alternatives with different time-scales. The act of deciding alternative replacement lives, in itself, means comparing costs of different time periods.

If the choice is between replacing an item of machinery every two or every three years, it would be meaningless to simply compare the NPV of the two costs.

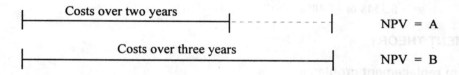

Almost certainly A < B. However, this does not take account of the cost of providing an asset for the third year. A method of calculating the equivalent annual cost is required.

This is provided by annuity factors. Remember that the present value of the cash flow of S per annum for *n* years, when discounted at rate *r*, is given by:

$$S \times A_{\overline{n}|r} \qquad\qquad \text{where } A_{\overline{n}|r} \text{ is the annuity factor}$$

In the problem described above, the present value is known, but not the amount S. In the above example over two years:

$$S_A \times A_{\overline{2}|r} = A \qquad \text{or} \qquad S_A = \frac{A}{A_{\overline{2}|r}}$$

Similarly:

$$S_B \times A_{\overline{3}|r} = B \qquad \text{or} \qquad S_B = \frac{B}{A_{\overline{3}|r}}$$

Since A and B are known, and the annuity factors can be looked up, the values of S_A and S_B can be calculated.

S_A and S_B are, therefore, the annual amounts which have the same NPV as A and B ie, they are *equivalent annual amounts*.

6.4   Example

A decision has to be made on replacement policy for vans. A van costs £12,000 and the following additional information applies:

		Maintenance costs	
Interval between replacement (years)	Trade in allowance	Age at year end	Maintenance cost paid at year end
	£		£
1	9,000	Year of replacement	Nil
2	7,500	1	2,000
3	7,000	2	3,000

Calculate the optimal replacement policy at a cost of capital of 15%. There are no maintenance costs in the year of replacement. Ignore taxation and inflation.

6.5   Solution

It is assumed that a brand new van is owned at the beginning of the cycle, and therefore must be owned at the end of the cycle.

Equivalent annual amount

The costs incurred over a single cycle are computed and the EAA is found as follows:

Year	Discount factor	One year cycle Cash flow £	PV £	Two year cycle Cash flow £	PV £	Three year cycle Cash flow £	PV £
1	0.870	3,000	2,610	2,000	1,740	2,000	1,740
2	0.756	-	-	4,500	3,402	3,000	2,268
3	0.658	-	-	-	-	5,000	3,290
PV			2,610		5,142		7,298
Annuity factor			0.870		1.626		2.283

Equivalent annual cost $\dfrac{2,610}{0.870} = 3,000$ $\dfrac{5,142}{1.626} = 3,162$ $\dfrac{7,298}{2.283} = 3,197$

It is concluded that annual replacement has the lowest annual cost and is the policy to be adopted.

6.6   Activity

Use the equivalent annual amount method to determine when to replace a machine costing £30,000 which has a maximum life of three years. The maintenance and operating costs and resale values are as follows:

Year:	1	2	3
Operating and maintenance costs (£):	8,000	8,500	9,000
Resale value (£):	20,000	12,000	8,000

Assume cost of capital is 12% pa.

6.7   Activity solution

Year	Discount factor	One year cycle		Two year cycle		Three year cycle	
		Cash flow £'000	PV £'000	Cash flow £'000	PV £'000	Cash flow £'000	PV £'000
1	0.893	8.0	7.144	8.0	7.144	8.0	7.144
		10.0	8.930				
2	0.797			8.5	6.775	8.5	6.775
				18.0	14.346		
3	0.712					9.0	6.408
						22.0	15.664
PV			16.074		28.265		35.991
Annuity factor			0.893		1.690		2.402
Equivalent annual cost			£18,000		£16,725		£14,984

We conclude that the machine should be replaced every three years.

6.8   Incorporation of deterioration and obsolescence

In many situations, as the machine ages, a predictable gap, or operating inferiority, between it and new machines, emerges. As the machine ages, the annual cost of operating inferiority becomes greater. On the other hand, the capital cost declines as an annual cost with machine age. The optimal replacement policy will be the minimum cost combination.

6.9   Example

The capital cost of an item of new equipment is £5,000. It has no value once installed except from continued use, and it has a maximum life of seven years. However, every year of use there is a cost of operating inferiority (made up of maintenance costs and production losses) which increases at £500 pa. This cost may be treated as a cash outflow occurring annually starting two years after installation.

Calculate the optimal replacement interval. The cost of capital is 10%. Ignore taxation, incentives and inflation.

6.10   Solution

The data above must be tabulated to calculate the two cost elements for each alternative replacement cycle up to seven years:

Year	(1) Cost of operating inferiority for year £	(2) PV of operating inferiority @ 10% £	(3) Cumulative PV of operating inferiority £	(4) Annuity factor for year @ 10%	(5) Operating inferiority [(3)÷(4)] £	(6) Equivalent annual cost for life Capital cost [£5,000÷(4)] £	(7) Total [(5)+(6)] £
1	-	-	-	0.909	-	5,501	5,501
2	500	413	413	1.736	238	2,880	3,118
3	1,000	751	1,164	2.487	468	2,010	2,478
4	1,500	1,025	2,189	3.170	691	1,577	2,268
5	2,000	1,242	3,431	3.791	905	1,319	2,224
6	2,500	1,410	4,841	4.355	1,112	1,148	2,260
7	3,000	1,539	6,380	4.868	1,311	1,027	2,338

This analysis can be presented graphically:

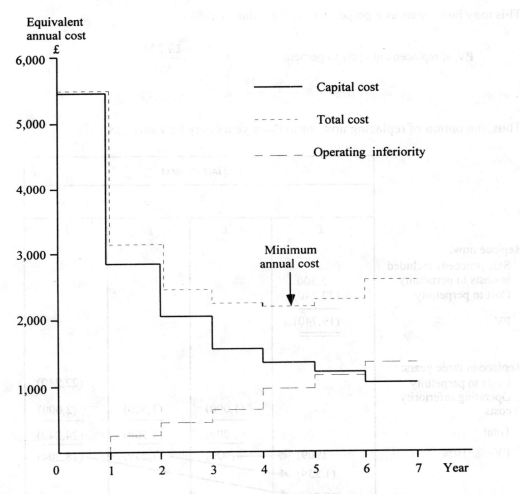

The cost is minimised with a five year (year 0 to year 5) replacement policy.

Technical note

The calculation of the equivalent annual cost differs from that used in the previous example. Here, we are assuming that the new equipment is purchased in year 0, and, therefore, an outlay of £5,000 occurs at that time. As a result, there is an equivalent annual cost for a one year replacement interval of £5,000 ÷ 0.909 ≃ £5,500. This, being greater than the cost of £5,000, may seem odd, but it is just a consequence of the above assumption. Alternatively it could have been assumed that the new equipment is purchased at the end of the replacement interval, as was the case in the previous example.   However, the assumption adopted makes no difference to the ultimate replacement decision – it is essential though to consider costs over an entire cycle.

6.11   One-off replacement decisions

In addition to the long-term replacement problem, there are also one-off replacement decisions.

Using the data above, the company has currently installed and been running a two year old machine. It has received a one-off offer of £2,500 for the machine, if it sells now.

Should it accept the offer, or wait until the normal replacement date?

6.12   Solution

This is an exercise in differential costing.   It is known from the calculations above that the equivalent annual cost from the next replacement is £2,224:

This may be viewed as a perpetuity with a value at 10% of:

$$\text{PV of replacement cycle to perpetuity} \quad = \quad \frac{£2,224}{0.1}$$

$$= \quad £22,240$$

Thus, the option of replacing now, or in three years may be viewed as:

	Time (years)			
	2	3	4	5
	£	£	£	£
Replace now:				
Sale proceeds included in costs to perpetuity	2,500			
Cost to perpetuity	(22,240)			
PV	(19,740)			
Replace in three years:				
Costs to perpetuity				(22,240)
Operating inferiority costs	-	(1,000)	(1,500)	(2,000)
Total		(1,000)	(1,500)	(24,240)
PV @ 10%	(909)	(909)	(1,239)	(18,204)
	(1,239)			
	(18,204)			
	(20,352)			

It is concluded that the optimal solution is immediate replacement.

Since we are taking the new equipment to have been purchased in year 0, the costs to perpetuity will include the initial £5,000 capital cost. If, however, we had taken the new equipment as having been purchased at the end of the replacement interval, the costs to perpetuity would have been £17,240 and excluded the initial £5,000 capital cost, incurred in years 2 or 5.

Note on examination technique: in this solution only the options of replacement now or in three years (the normal replacement date) were considered, because of the terms of the question. However, given a more open-ended question, all replacement options starting with a two year-old machine would have to be considered; there is no reason to suppose that the optimal replacement pattern in the future applies to the machine already owned which is, in effect, free.

7   USING COMPUTER PACKAGES

7.1   Introduction

It is commonly accepted that there are two types of computer package available which may be used to assist in solving operational problems. These are

(a)   general purpose packages (such as spreadsheets); and

(b)   specialist packages which are designed to meet specified requirements.

There are many parts of the Management Science Applications syllabus which may be related to the use of computer packages. The following paragraph describes spreadsheets in this context.

7.2   Spreadsheets and discounted cashflow

Discounted cashflow techniques involve the discounting of future cashflows to establish whether a particular project is likely to provide a return in excess of the return required. This is a mathematical exercise once the cashflows have been predicted and is thus ideally suited to the use of a spreadsheet.

Most spreadsheet packages have such a function already included so that the user does not need to determine their own formula for such calculations.

The following screen shows how such calculations would be made:

	A	B	C	D	E	F
1			PROJECT APPRAISAL			
2	TIME	CASHFLOW				
3	0	(100)		(100)		
4	1	30		27		
5	2	40		36		
6	3	50		45		
7	4	10		9		
8						
9						
10						
11						
12						

It is assumed that the expected cashflows are entered in column B, rows 3-7 and that cell B9 contains a formula to discount these cashflows at a particular discount rate and show the resulting net present value. By inserting a similar formula but with a different discount rate in cell B11 the sensitivity of the solution to a change in the discount rate may be determined.

The cashflows in column D are based on those in column B with the inflows being 90% of those originally expected. Such a calculation may be effected automatically by a simple formula and may be applied to all of the inflows (as shown) or to them individually or in sub-groups. By discounting the revised values (in cells D9 and D11) the sensitivity of the project to changes in cashflows can be shown.

7.3   Activity

Use a computer spreadsheet to determine the discounted value of the above cashflows using discount rates of 10% in row 9 and 15% in row 11.

7.4   Activity solution

B9 = 4.8   D9 = (5.68)

B11 = (4.8)   D11 = (14.32)

8   CHAPTER SUMMARY

In this chapter we looked at the more practical applications of compounding and discounting techniques.

9   SELF TEST QUESTIONS

9.1   What are two typical annuity type questions that might be asked in an examination? (1.1)

9.2   Define a mortgage. (2.1)

9.3   What formula can be used to find the outstanding amount of a debt? (3.2)

9.4   What is a sinking fund? (4.1)

9.5   What formula can be used in sinking fund calculations? (4.2)

9.6   What is the difference between straight line depreciation and reducing balance depreciation? (5.2)

9.7   What formula can be used in reducing balance depreciation calculations? (5.2)

10   EXAMINATION TYPE QUESTIONS

10.1   Buying a machine

The managing director of a small manufacturing company is considering buying a piece of machinery which costs £15,000.

Required:

If the machine is to be purchased by taking a five-year loan at 9% per annum which will be paid off in five equal annual instalments, calculate the size of each instalment to the nearest £.

(Total: 5 marks)

10.2   £50,000 mortgage

A £50,000 mortgage is arranged now for 15 years at a rate of interest of 10%. Interest is compounded on the balance outstanding at the end of each year. The loan is to be repaid by 15 annual instalments, the first being due after the end of one complete year.

You are required

(a)   to find the gross annual instalments:

   (i)   using CIMA tables;

   (4 marks)

   (ii)   using any other method but without using CIMA tables;

   (6 marks)

(b)   to find the amount outstanding after two complete years, using either solution to (a) above;

   (6 marks)

(c)   if the rate of interest changes to 13% after two complete years, to find the revised annual instalments.

   (4 marks)

Note: the sum, S, of a geometric progression of n terms, with first term A and common ratio R is given by:

$$S = A(R^n - 1)/(R - 1)$$

   (Total: 20 marks)
   (CIMA May 89)

11   ANSWERS TO EXAMINATION TYPE QUESTIONS

11.1   Buying a machine

To determine the size of the instalment uses cumulative present value tables.

Let a = annual instalment.

Thus,

£15,000	=	a × annuity factor of five years at 9%
	=	a × 3.890 (from tables)
∴ a	=	$\dfrac{15,000}{3.890}$
	=	£3,856

Each instalment is **£3,856**.

11.2   £50,000 mortgage

(a)   (i)   Using the cumulative present value tables:

15 years, rate of interest = 10%

Factor = 7.606

∴ $PV = 7.606 \times E$ where E = annual repayment

∴ $E = \dfrac{50,000}{7.606} = £6,574$ per annum

(ii)

Year end	Cash flow	10% Discount factor	Discounted cash flows
0	(50,000)	1	(50,000)
1	E	1.1^{-1}	0.9091E
2	E	1.1^{-2}	0.8264E
3	E	1.1^{-3}	0.7513E
.	.	.	
.	.	.	
.	.	.	
15	E	1.1^{-15}	0.2394E
			0

The mortgage will be repaid when the sum of the present values of the equal annual instalments equals the debt.

This is the sum of a GP

The first term $= 0.9091E = A$

The common ratio is $\dfrac{1}{1.1} = 0.9091 = R$

There are 15 terms $\therefore N = 15$

The sum $= £50,000 = S$

Using $S = A (R^N - 1)/(R - 1)$

$$50,000 = 0.9091E (0.9091^{15} - 1)/(0.9091 - 1)$$

$$\therefore \quad 50,000 = \frac{0.9091E \times (-0.7606)}{-0.0909} = 7.6068E$$

$$E = \frac{50,000}{7.6068} = £6,573 \text{ per annum}$$

(to the nearest £, difference due to rounding).

(b)

	Amount o/s	+	Interest 10%			-	Repayment	=	Amount o/s
Year 1	50,000	+	5,000	=	55,000	-	6,573	=	48,427
Year 2	48,427	+	4,842.70	=	53,269.70	-	6,573	=	£46,696.70

At the end of year 2 **£46,696.70** will be outstanding.

(c)   £46,696.70 will be outstanding after two years. There are 13 more instalments to meet, now at 13% pa using the cumulative present value tables:

13 years, 13% pa interest

Factor = 6.122

Then $46,696.70 = 6.122E$ where $E =$ new annual repayment

=> $E = \dfrac{46,696.70}{6.122} = $ **£7,628** per annum.

10 DECISION TREES

INTRODUCTION & LEARNING OBJECTIVES

Syllabus area 7d. Simple decision trees; drawing tree diagrams and identification of optimal decisions using expected values. (Ability required 3).

When you have studied this chapter you should be able to do the following:

- Explain what a decision is.
- Explain the difference between decisions made under conditions of (i) certainty and (ii) uncertainty.
- Explain the use of expected values as a decision criterion.
- Explain the use of decision trees.
- Evaluate decision alternatives using decision trees and expected values.

1 DECISION ANALYSIS - SINGLE DECISIONS

1.1 What is a decision?

[Definition] A decision is a choice between two or more alternatives.

1.2 Certainty or uncertainty?

Decisions may be taken under conditions of certainty eg,

I have received an offer to sell my car for £5,000. Should I accept the offer?

The decision has a simple yes/no choice which can be evaluated:

Accept - receive £5,000 and have no car.

Reject - keep a car but do not receive £5,000.

Alternatively the decision may involve:

(a) keeping the car;

(b) **trying** to sell it privately for £5,000;

(c) **trying** to sell it at auction for £4,800.

Clearly the outcome of (b) and (c) is uncertain, the car may not be sold at all, and if it is sold the proceeds may not be for the sums suggested.

1.3   Decisions made under uncertainty

Most decisions which a company's management has to make can be described as **decisions made under uncertainty**. The essential features of making a decision under uncertain conditions are:

(a)   the decision-maker is faced with a choice between several alternative courses of action;

(b)   each course of action may have several possible outcomes, dependent on a number of uncertain factors ie, even when a decision has been made the outcome is by no means certain;

(c)   which choice is made will depend upon the criteria used by the decision-maker in judging between the outcomes of the possible courses of action.

1.4   Expected values

In order to have a **rational** basis for decision-making it is necessary to have some estimate of the probabilities of the various outcomes and then to use them in a decision criterion. One such criterion is the **maximisation of expected value**.

The expected value $\bar{x}$ of a particular action is defined as the **sum of the values of the possible outcomes, each multiplied by their respective probabilities** (it is analogous to the arithmetic mean) $\bar{x} = \sum px$

1.5   Example

Using the following data, apply the criteria of **maximisation of expected value** to decide the best course of action for the company, assuming the following probabilities:

P (low demand)	0.1
P (medium demand)	0.6
P (high demand)	0.3
	——
	1.0

A company has three new products A, B and C, of which it can introduce only one. The level of demand for **each** course of action might be low, medium or high. If the company decides to introduce product A, the net income that would result from the levels of demand possible are estimated at £20, £40 and £50 respectively. Similarly, if product B is chosen, net income is estimated at £80, £70 and – £10, and for product C, £10, £100 and £40, respectively.

The expected value of the decision to introduce product A is given by the following summation:

$$0.1 \times £20 + 0.6 \times £40 + 0.3 \times £50 \ = \ £41$$

(ie, on 10% of all occasions demand will be low and net income £20, on 60% of all occasions demand will be medium and net income £40 and on 30% of all occasions demand will be high and net income £50. Thus, on average, net income will be the weighted average of all three net incomes, weighted by their respective probabilities.)

The expected value of all the products may be calculated by a table:

Table of expected values

State of the world (demand)	Prob of state of the world	A Income £	A Income × Prob £	B Income £	B Income × Prob £	C Income £	C Income × Prob £
Low	0.1	20	2	80	8	10	1
Medium	0.6	40	24	70	42	100	60
High	0.3	50	15	(10)	(3)	40	12
Total	1.0		£41		£47		£73

Thus, if the criterion is to maximise the expected value, it means that the product with the highest expected value will be chosen, in this case product C.

1.6 Applicability of expected values

The criterion of expected value is only valid where the decision being made is either:

(a) one that is repeated regularly over a period of time; or

(b) a **one-off** decision, but where its size is fairly small in relation to the total assets of the firm and it is one of many, in terms of the sums of money involved, that face the firm over a period of time.

In other words, the **law of averages** will apply in the long run, but clearly the result of any single action must, by definition, be one of the specified outcomes. Thus, while the expected value of introducing product C is £73, each actual outcome will result in either £10, £100 or £40 net income, and it is only if a whole series of product introductions were involved that the **average** over a period of time would approach £73, so long as the expected value criterion was applied consistently to all the decisions.

Therefore, it is quite acceptable to adopt the expected value as the decision-making criterion for the company in the example, so long as it has several other products and the same sort of marketing decision arises fairly regularly.

To illustrate the distinction being made, consider a man insuring his house against fire damage for a year. Suppose the house is worth £50,000 and the probability of the house being burnt down is 0.0001 (the only other outcome being that the house is not burnt down with a probability of 0.9999). The man would be quite prepared to pay, say, £15.00 pa to insure his house even though the expected value if he did not (or expected cost in this case) is only $0.0001 \times £50,000 + 0.9999 \times 0 = £5.00$. The man cannot afford to pay £50,000 out more than once in his lifetime and therefore cannot afford to **play the averages** by using expected value as his decision criterion (if so he would refuse to pay a premium greater than £5.00). However, to the insurance company, £50,000 is not a large sum, most of their transactions being for similar or greater amounts and therefore expected value would be appropriate as a decision criterion for them. In fact, the expected value of the insurance company's decision to insure the house at £15.00 pa is:

$$0.0001 \times (-£49,985) + 0.9999 \times £15$$

or $\quad -£4.9985 + £14.9985 \quad = \quad £10$

and any positive expected value would, in theory, have made it worth their while to insure.

1.7   Activity

If the three possible outcomes of a decision are profits of £10, £50 and £80 with probabilities of 0.3, 0.3 and 0.4 respectively, what is the expected profit?

1.8   Activity solution

Expected profit = 0.3 × £10 + 0.3 × £50 + 0.4 × £80   =   £50

2   DECISION ANALYSIS – MULTIPLE DECISIONS

2.1   Decision trees

So far only a single decision has had to be made. However, many managerial problems consist of a rather long, drawn-out structure involving a whole sequence of actions and outcomes. Where a number of decisions have to be made sequentially the complexity of the decision-making process increases considerably. By using **decision trees**, however, highly complex problems can be broken down into a series of simpler ones while providing, at the same time, opportunity for the decision-maker to obtain specialist advice in relation to each stage of his problem.

A **decision tree** is a way of applying the expected value criterion to situations where a number of decisions are made sequentially.

It is so called because the decision alternatives are represented as **branches** in a **tree** diagram.

2.2   Decision points and random outcome points

Example

A retailer must decide whether to sell a product loose or packaged. In either case, the product may sell, or not sell.

The decision facing the retailer can be represented by a tree diagram:

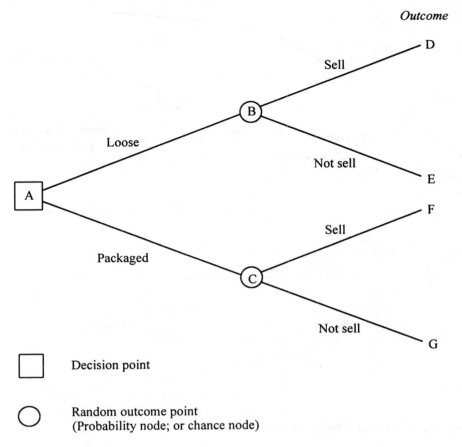

Outcome

◻ Decision point

◯ Random outcome point
(Probability node; or chance node)

As you can see, in a decision tree there are two types of events (points where a branch occurs).

- **Decision points**, signified by a ◻ in the tree. At this point the decision or branch taken can be chosen by the decision-maker. In this example the decision point is ▣A where the decision-maker can choose whether to sell the product loose or packaged.

- **Random outcome points**, signified by a ◯. At this point the branch taken is completely outside the control of the decision-maker. In the example above, the random outcome points are at Ⓑ and Ⓒ; the retailer has no control over which branch is followed from this point, the product will either sell or it won't.

2.3   Activity

Using the data given below, draw a decision tree and mark clearly on the tree the decision points and the random outcome points.

Mr A is a microcomputer retailer who has recently bought a large consignment of popular micros, of which he knows some will be faulty. He has to decide whether or not to inspect every micro of this type prior to sale. If he does do the inspection, there is still a chance that he will not pick up the fault in the faulty micros. However, if Mr A sells a faulty micro it is equally likely that either the customer will return it for repair or will have it repaired elsewhere and discontinue trading with him.

2.4   Activity solution

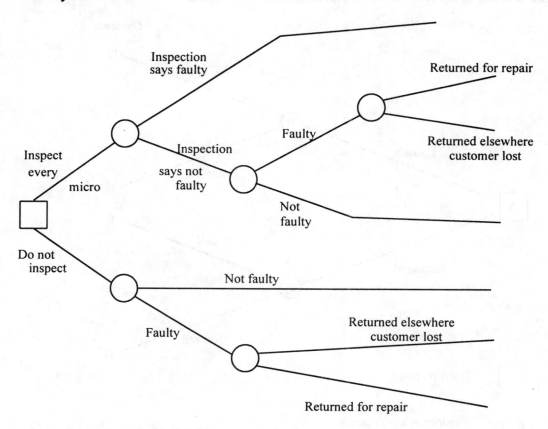

2.5   Expected values and the roll back method

Now return to the previous example about packaging or selling a product loose. The profitability of selling packaged products is £10, loose products £15. The loss through not selling is £5 in either case. The probability of the product being sold is 0.7 for packaged products, 0.5 for loose products.

You are required to evaluate the expected values of each decision alternative.

Step 1   Add all the relevant information ie, probabilities and profits and losses, to the decision tree ending at the right hand side of the tree with a column for outcomes.

Step 2   Evaluate the decision tree by working back from right to left towards the first decision under consideration. In this example it is decision point (A). At each random outcome point calculate the EV of revenue, cost, profit or whatever type of pay off the question gives.

Step 3   Block off all other routes from the decision point (sometimes called a decision **fork**) with a double parallel line '//'. (This is important when trees have several decision forks.)

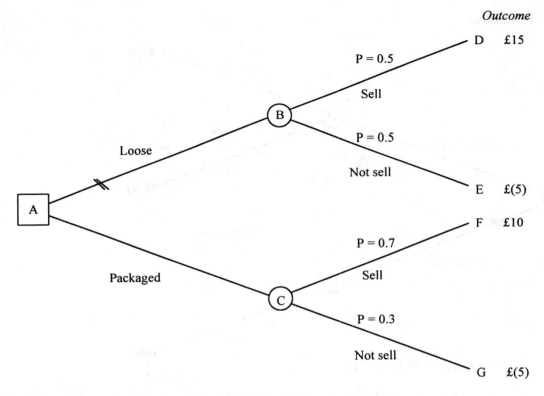

The diagram is evaluated as follows (using obvious notation):

$$EV_B = (0.5 \times EV_D) + (0.5 \times EV_E)$$
$$= (0.5 \times £15) + (0.5 \times (-£5))$$
$$= £5$$

$$EV_C = (0.7 \times EV_F) + (0.3 \times EV_G)$$
$$= (0.7 \times £10) + (0.3 \times (-£5))$$
$$= £5.5$$

∴ at decision point A the retailer will choose to go towards node C as this has the higher EV. The discarded routes are indicated by drawing two short parallel lines across that particular path.

Therefore, the decision to sell a packaged product has the higher expected value.

The method just described is known as the **rollback technique**.

Note: the expected values here (EV) are sometimes called expected monetary values (EMV). At point C the probability that the product will sell is 0.7, therefore the probability that it will not is 1 − 0.7 = 0.3. The total probability at any chance fork must be 1.00.

2.6   Activity

A company manufactures a single product which it may sell directly to the public or via a retailer. If it sells directly to the public the profit is £100; whereas via the retailer the profit is only £70.

The probability of the product being sold if the retailer is used is 0.8 whereas the use of direct selling techniques have a sale probability of 0.6. If a sale is not made the resulting losses are:

        direct selling method   £30

        retail method   £50

Advise the company which technique to use, illustrating your solution using a tree diagram.

2.7   Activity solution

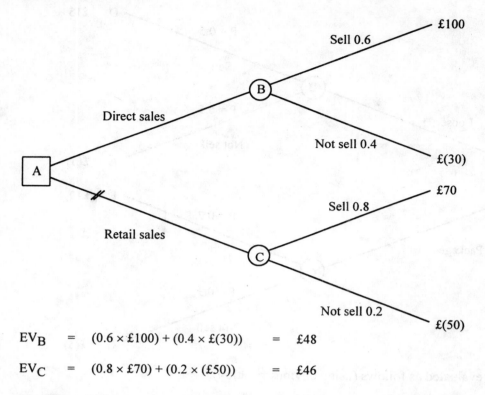

EV_B = $(0.6 \times £100) + (0.4 \times £(30))$ = £48

EV_C = $(0.8 \times £70) + (0.2 \times (£50))$ = £46

The direct sales route is recommended because it has the higher expected value.

2.8   Decision trees - a comprehensive example

The last problem could have been solved without a tree diagram, but the technique comes into its own in a more complex situation, as illustrated by the next example. If in doubt it is always safer to draw a tree.

Example

The manager of a newly formed specialist machinery manufacturing subsidiary has to decide whether to build a small plant or a large plant for manufacturing a new piece of machinery with an expected market life of ten years.

One of the major factors influencing his decision is the size of the market that the company can obtain for its product. He estimates that there is a 70% chance of a high level of demand and a 30% chance of a low level of demand if a large plant is built. However, if a small plant is originally constructed there is only a 50% chance of there being a high demand.

The level of demand will not change throughout the project's life.

If the company initially builds a large plant, it must live with it for the whole ten years, regardless of the market demand. If it builds a small plant, it also has the option, after two years, of expanding the plant but this expansion would cost more overall, when taken with the initial cost of building small, than starting by building a large plant.

Various pieces of information have been collected, or estimated by the management.

(a)   **Annual income estimates**

(i)   For a large plant with high demand annual earnings will be £1m. This applies whether the plant was originally constructed as 'large' or had to be extended.

(ii)   For a large plant with low market demand annual earnings will be £0.1m.

(iii)   For a small plant with low demand annual earnings will be £0.4m.

(iv)   For a small plant with high demand annual earnings will be £0.6m.

(c)   **Capital costs**

(i)   Initial cost of building a large plant   £3m
(ii)   Initial cost of building a small plant   £1.3m
(iii)   Additional cost of expanding a small plant   £2.6m

Using expected value as the decision criterion, advise the manager on what choice of plant to make.

Ignore the time value of money and taxation.

2.9   Solution

Step 1   The first stage in solving a problem of this nature, which involves more than one decision being made over a period of time, is to construct a decision tree to demonstrate the structure of the decisions which have to be made.

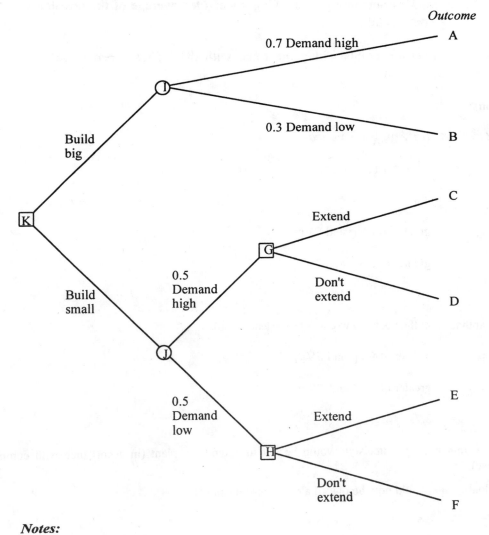

Outcome

0.7 Demand high — A

0.3 Demand low — B

Build big

Extend — C

Don't extend — D

0.5 Demand high

Build small

0.5 Demand low

Extend — E

Don't extend — F

Notes:

(a)   ☐   Decision point.

○   Random outcome point, probabilities given.

(b)   Each path represents a different series of events and eventual outcome. For example, outcome C is reached by originally building a small plant, finding that demand is high and subsequently extending the plant.

Step 2   It is now necessary to evaluate the monetary value of the outcomes. This is best achieved by tabulation, in order to avoid needless repetition.

			£m			
Outcome	A	B	C	D	E	F
Total revenue in years 1–2	2	0.2	1.2	1.2	0.8	0.8
Total revenue in years 3–10	8	0.8	8.0	4.8	0.8	3.2
Original cost	(3)	(3)	(1.3)	(1.3)	(1.3)	(1.3)
Cost of extension	–	–	(2.6)	–	(2.6)	–
Net income/(cost)	7	(2)	5.3	4.7	(2.3)	2.7

Step 3   Having found the outcomes the tree is worked through from right to left

•   at random outcome points taking a weighted average of the possible outcomes, and

•   at decision points taking the route with the higher expected value ('EV').

Thus:

EV_I = $0.7 \times EV_A + 0.3 \times EV_B$

      = $0.7 \times 7 + 0.3 \times (-2)$

      =   4.3

EV_G =   greater of EV_C and EV_D

      =   greater of 5.3 and 4.7

      =   5.3

∴   at that point the decision would be to extend the plant.

EV_H =   greater of EV_E and EV_F

      =   greater of –2.3 and 2.7

      =   2.7

∴   at that point the decision would be not to extend the plant (in accordance with common sense).

A double line would now be placed along lines GD and HE.

EV_J = $0.5 \times EV_G + 0.5 \times EV_H$

      = $0.5 \times 5.3 + 0.5 \times 2.7$

      =   4

$$EV_K \quad = \quad \text{greater of } EV_I \text{ and } EV_J$$

$$= \quad \text{greater of 4.3 and 4}$$

$$= \quad 4.3$$

∴ the decision should be to build a large plant immediately, since the expected value of doing so, £4.3m, is greater than that of building a small plant.

However, it should be noted that if this decision were to be taken there is a possibility of incurring losses of £2m. If the decision were taken instead to build the small plant, and extend it only if demand is high, the worst that can happen is that the firm makes net revenues of only £2.7m. It may well be, therefore, that this less risky option is preferred, notwithstanding the higher EV available through the other route. This shows that maximising EV is not necessarily the best strategy in all situations, but that the amount of risk is also a factor that must be taken into account.

2.10   Other decision criteria

Whilst expected value is the most commonly used measure of outcomes used to evaluate decisions made under conditions of uncertainty it is not the only technique.

Expected value takes an average position; other factors which influence the decisions are the risk attitudes of the decision maker - the pessimist would look to maximise the benefit from the worst possible outcome whereas the optimist would seek to maximise the benefit from the best possible outcome. This is outside the syllabus.

3   CHAPTER SUMMARY

This chapter has considered the nature of a decision and distinguished between decisions made under conditions of certainty and those made under conditions of uncertainty.

The technique of expected value and the use of decision trees has then been used to show how decisions made under conditions of uncertainty may be evaluated.

4   SELF TEST QUESTIONS

4.1   What is a decision? (1.1)

4.2   How do conditions of uncertainty differ from conditions of certainty? (1.2)

4.3   What is an expected value? (1.4)

4.4   The criterion of expected value is only valid under certain conditions. What are they? (1.6)

4.5   What is a decision tree? (2.1)

4.6   What is a decision point? (2.2)

4.7   What is a random outcome point? (2.2)

4.8   Describe the rollback technique. (2.5)

4.9   At what points on the tree are expected values calculated? (2.5)

4.10   What is the decision criterion for following one route compared to another? (2.5)

5   EXAMINATION TYPE QUESTIONS

5.1   Product launch

A company is considering launching a new product and has already carried out preliminary investigations both into the potential market and also into problems associated with the manufacture of the product.

It is estimated that the initial development work will cost £5,000 and it is believed that there is a 70% chance that it will be successful. If it is successful then further development work will be carried out at a cost (after discounting) of £20,000. The company feels that there is a 10% chance of failure at this stage. Providing that the development work is satisfactory, the product will be launched and the company considers that there would be a 25% chance of its being **very successful**, a 45% chance of being **successful** and a 30% chance of it being **disappointing**, where these terms are taken to mean that the net present value of profits earned from the launching date would be £60,000, £40,000 and £25,000 respectively.

You are required to find the expected value of this project.

5.2   Test marketing

A company has the opportunity of marketing a new package of computer games. It has two possible courses of action: to test market on a limited scale or to give up the project completely. A test market would cost £160,000 and current evidence suggests that consumer reaction is equally likely to be 'positive' or 'negative'. If the reaction to the test marketing were to be 'positive' the company could either market the computer games nationally or still give up the project completely. Research suggests that a national launch might result in the following sales:

Sales	Contribution £ m	Probability
High	1.20	0.25
Average	0.30	0.50
Low	−0.24	0.25

If the test marketing were to yield 'negative' results the company would give up the project. Giving up the project at any point would result in a contribution of £60,000 from the sale of copyright etc to another manufacturer. All contributions have been discounted to present values.

You are required

(a)   to draw a decision tree to represent this situation, including all relevant probabilities and financial values;

(8 marks)

(b)   to recommend a course of action for the company on the basis of expected values;

(8 marks)

(c)   to explain any limitations of this method of analysis.

(4 marks)

(Total: 20 marks)

6   ANSWERS TO EXAMINATION TYPE QUESTIONS

6.1   Product launch

The following tree shows cash flows and the various possible outcomes and their associated probabilities.

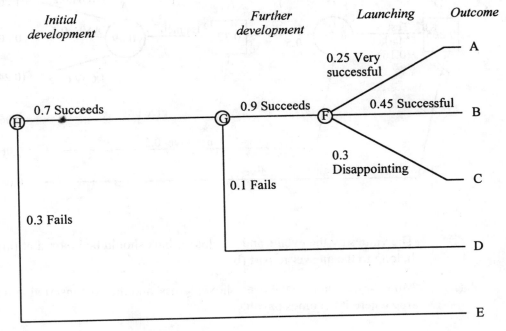

Note: that there are no decision points on this tree.

However, the tree is still evaluated in the usual way:

			£'000		
Outcome	*A*	*B*	*C*	*D*	*E*
Sales revenue	60	40	25	0	0
Initial development	(5)	(5)	(5)	(5)	(5)
Further development	(20)	(20)	(20)	(20)	(0)
Net revenue	35	15	0	(25)	(5)

$$EV_F = 0.25 \times EV_A + 0.45 \times EV_B + 0.3 \times EV_C$$

$$= 0.25 \times 35 + 0.45 \times 15 + 0.3 \times 0$$

$$= 15.5$$

$$EV_G = 0.9 \times EV_F + 0.1 \times EV_D$$

$$= 0.9 \times 15.5 + 0.1 \times (-25)$$

$$= 11.45$$

$$EV_H = 0.7 \times EV_G + 0.3 \times EV_E$$

$$= 0.7 \times 11.45 + 0.3 \times (-5)$$

$$= 6.515$$

Expected value of this project is £6,515. (Strictly speaking this is an expected net present value.)

6.2   Test marketing

(a)

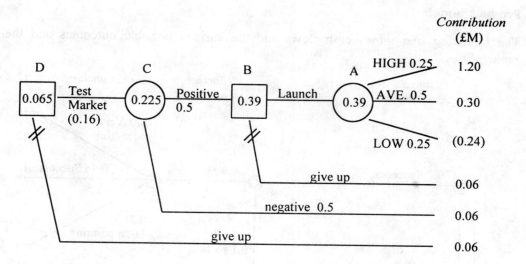

Notes:

(i)   The values by the events and the double bars should be ignored at this stage as they belong to the answer to part (b).

(ii)   Monetary amounts have been shown 'gross' and the cost inserted at that point in the tree where it becomes payable.

(b)   The tree is evaluated as follows, in £m

At A,   EMV = $(0.25 \times 1.2) + (0.5 \times 0.3) - (0.25 \times 0.24)$

                 =   0.39

At B,   EMV for 'launch'   =   0.39
                EMV for 'give up'   =   0.06
                ∴ choose 'launch' and insert its EMV by the decision point and block off the other branch.

At C   EMV = $(0.5 \times 0.39) + (0.5 \times 0.06)$

                 =   0.225

At D,   EMV of 'test market'   = $0.225 - 0.16$

                                        =   0.065

                EMV of 'give up'   =   0.06
                ∴ choose 'test market' and block off the other branch.

The optimum strategy is to test the market and if it proves positive, to carry out the national launch. The net EMV of this policy is £0.065m or £65,000.

Notes:

(i)   In the evaluation, do **not** eliminate probability branches as the decision maker has no control over which branch is taken.

(ii)   The optimum strategy must state which branch is to be taken at **each** decision point.

(c)   Possible limitations of the method are:

(i)   There is difficulty in estimating the relevant cash flows and their probabilities.

(ii)   In practice there are likely to be a whole range of possible outcomes at each stage, rather than the two or three shown in this example.

(iii)   The EMV may not be the best criterion. A possible reason for this is that being an average, the EMV assumes that losses are permissible as well as gains, provided they have a relatively low probability. In practice, management may not be prepared to gamble on making a loss which might ruin the firm.

11 LINEAR PROGRAMMING

INTRODUCTION & LEARNING OBJECTIVES

Syllabus area 7d. Linear programming: graphical solution for two-variable problems; formulation and interpretation (only) of two-plus-variable models. (Ability required 2).

When you have studied this chapter you should be able to do the following:

- Identify scarce resources within a decision problem.

- Recognise when linear programming is required to solve the problem.

- Formulate a two-variable problem.

- Solve a two variable problem using graphical linear programming.

- Formulate and interpret a problem with more than two variables.

---

1 SCARCE RESOURCES

1.1 What is a scarce resource?

Definition | Economics defines a scarce resource as a good or service which is in short supply. This definition is modified in the context of decision-making to a resource which is in short supply and which, because of this shortage, limits the ability of an organisation to provide greater numbers of products or service facilities.

1.2 Decision-making objectives

These are really organisational objectives which are many and varied; however, in order to evaluate a decision mathematically one single objective is assumed, that of profit maximisation.

Other factors may then be considered before a final decision is taken, but this is part of the management process after the profit maximising solution has been found.

2 SINGLE SCARCE RESOURCE PROBLEMS

2.1 Identifying the scarce resource

In any situation it can be argued that all of the resources required are scarce. What is important is to identify the key resource(s) which limit the ability of the organisation to produce an infinite quantity of goods or services.

2.2 Example

X Ltd makes a single product which requires £5 of materials and 2 hours labour. There are only 80 hours labour available each week and the maximum amount of material available each week is £500.

2.3 **Solution**

It can be said that the supply of both labour hours and materials are limited and that therefore they are both scarce resources. However, there is more to this problem than meets the eye. The maximum production within these constraints can be shown to be:

Materials:	£500/£5	=	100 units
Labour hours:	80 hours/2 hours	=	40 units

Thus the shortage of labour hours is the significant factor - the scarcity of the materials does not limit production.

In the context of the decision in this example the materials are not a scarce resource.

2.4 **Multiple product situations**

When more than one product or service is provided from the same pool of resources, profit is maximised by making the best use of the resources available.

2.5 **Example**

Z Ltd makes two products which both use the same type of materials and grades of labour, but in different quantities as shown by the table below:

	Product A	Product B
Labour hours/unit	3	4
Material/unit	£20	£15

During each week the maximum number of labour hours available is limited to 600; and the value of material available is limited to £6,000.

Each unit of product A made and sold earns Z Ltd £5 and product B earns £6 per unit. The demand for these products is unlimited.

Advise Z Ltd which product they should make.

2.6 **Solution**

Step 1 Determine the scarce resource.

Step 2 Calculate each product's benefit per unit of the scarce resource consumed by its manufacture.

Each resource restricts production as follows:

Labour hours	600/3	=	200 units of A; or
	600/4	=	150 units of B
Materials	£6,000/£20	=	300 units of A; or
	£6,000/£15	=	400 units of B

It can be seen that whichever product is chosen the production is limited by the shortage of labour hours, thus this is the limiting factor or scarce resource. (Again this is not an easy point to notice and the method used later will overcome the problem of identifying resources that are not limiting.)

Benefit per hour

Product A benefit per labour hour

$\qquad$ =   £5/3 hours   =   £1.66 per hour

Product B benefit per labour hour

$\qquad$ =   £6/4 hours   =   £1.50 per hour

Thus Z Ltd maximises its earnings by making and selling product A.

2.7   Conclusion

Where there is only one 'real' scarce resource the method above can be used to solve the problem, however where there are two or more resources in short supply which limit the organisation's activities, (for example if materials had been limited to £3,000 per week in the example above), then **linear programming** is required to find the solution.

2.8   Activity

A Ltd makes two products, X and Y. Both products use the same machine and the same raw material which are limited to 200 hours and £500 per week respectively. Individual product details are as follows:

	Product X	Product Y
Machine hours/unit	5	2.5
Materials/unit	£10	£5
Benefit/unit	£20	£15

Identify the limiting factor.

2.9   Activity solution

Production is restricted as follows:

Machine hours	200/5	=	40 units of X; or
	200/2.5	=	80 units of Y
Materials	£500/£10	=	50 units of X; or
	£500/£5	=	100 units of Y

Therefore machine hours is the limiting factor since X's and Y's production are most severely limited by machine hours.

2.10   Activity

Using the data of the activity above recommend which product A Ltd should make and sell (assuming that demand is unlimited).

2.11   Activity solution

Benefit per machine hour:

Product X	£20/5 hours	=	£4/hour
Product Y	£15/2.5 hours	=	£6/hour

Product Y should be made.

3   LINEAR PROGRAMMING (INEQUALITIES AND CONSTRAINTS)

3.1   Introduction

Linear programming is one of the most important post-war developments in **operations research**. It is in fact the most widely used of a group of mathematical programming techniques.

Linear programming can be thought of as a method of balancing many factors (eg, distance, time, production capacity) to obtain a predetermined objective (eg, minimum cost). Some of the factors are variable, while others are fixed.

In order to apply linear programming there must be, as its title suggests, a linear relationship between the factors. For example, the cost of shipping 5 extra units should be 5 times the cost of shipping one extra unit.

3.2   Field of application of linear programming

(a)   Mixing problems

A product is composed of several ingredients, and what is required is the least costly mix of the ingredients that will give a product of predetermined specification.

(b)   Job assignment problems

A number of jobs or products must be handled by various people and/or machines, and the least costly arrangement of assignments is required.

(c)   Capacity allocation problems

Limited capacity is allocated to products so as to yield maximum profits.

(d)   Production scheduling

An uneven sales demand is met by a production schedule over a period of time, with given penalties for storage, overtime, and short-time working.

(e)   Transportation problems

Various suppliers (or one company with several plants) throughout the country make the same products, which must be shipped to many outlets that are also widely distributed. This may involve different transportation costs and varying manufacturing costs. Linear programming can determine the best way to ship; it denotes which plant shall service any particular outlet. It can also evaluate whether it pays to open a new plant.

(f)   Purchasing

Multiple and complex bids can be evaluated, in order to ensure that the orders placed with suppliers comply with the lowest cost arrangement.

(g)   Investment problems

The results of alternative capital investments can be evaluated when finance is in short supply.

(h)   **Location problems**

Linear programming can help to select an optimum plant or warehouse location where a wide choice is possible.

3.3   Method of linear programming

Linear programming reduces the kind of problems outlined above to a series of linear expressions and then uses those expressions to discover the best solution to achieve a given objective. The student should appreciate that not all situations can be reduced to a linear form. Nevertheless, a surprising number of problems can be solved using this relatively straightforward technique.

3.4   Stages in linear programming – graphical method

Step 1   Define the unknowns ie, the variables (that need to be determined).

Step 2   Formulate the constraints ie, the limitations that must be placed on the variables.

Step 3   Graph the constraints.

Step 4   Define the objective function (that needs to be maximised or minimised).

Step 5   Manipulate the objective function to find the optimal feasible solution.

We will now look at each of these steps in more detail by working through a comprehensive example

3.5   Step 1 - defining the unknowns

Hebrus Ltd manufactures summer-houses and garden sheds. Each product passes through a cutting process and an assembly process. One summer-house, which makes a contribution of £50, takes six hours cutting time and four hours assembly time; while one shed makes a contribution of £40, takes three hours cutting time and eight hours assembly time. There is a maximum of thirty-six cutting hours available each week and forty-eight assembly hours.

The variables that need to be determined in this example are the number of summer-houses and garden sheds to be produced each week.

Let x =   number of summer-houses produced each week;

and y =   number of garden sheds produced each week.

3.6   Example

Alfred Ltd is preparing its plan for the coming month. It manufactures two products, the flaktrap and the saptrap. Details are as follows.

	Product		Price/wage rate
	Flaktrap	*Saptrap*	
Amount/unit:			
Selling price (£)	125	165	
Raw material (kg)	6	4	£5/kg
Labour hours:			
Skilled	10	10	£3/hour
Semi-skilled	5	25	£3/hour

The company's variable overhead rate is £1/labour hour (for both skilled and semi-skilled labour). The supply of skilled labour is limited to 2,000 hours/month and the supply of semi-skilled labour is limited to 2,500 hours/month. At the selling prices indicated, maximum demand for flaktraps is expected to be 150 units/month and the maximum demand for saptraps is expected to be 80 units/month. The directors of Alfred believe that demand for each product could be increased by advertising.

You are required to define the decision variables.

3.7   Example solution

The variables are:

1.   The quantity of Flaktraps to produce per month.

2.   The quantity of Saptraps to produce per month.

> Let x   =   number of Flaktraps produced per month.
>
> Let y   =   number of Saptraps produced per month.

3.8   Step 2 - define the constraints

As we saw earlier in the chapter most resources are limited to a certain degree which usually puts some limitation on what can be achieved. When formulating a linear programming problem those limitations are included as a set of conditions which any solution to the problem must satisfy and they are referred to as **constraints**.

The constraints (limitations) in our Hebrus example are the amounts of cutting and assembly time available.

If   1 summer-house requires 6 hours cutting time,
       x summer-houses require $6x$ hours cutting time.

If   1 shed requires 3 hours cutting time,
        y sheds require $3y$ hours cutting time.

Hence total cutting time required = 6x + 3y hours

Similarly, if 1 summer-house and 1 shed require 4 and 8 hours assembly time respectively, the total assembly time for x summer-houses and y sheds will be $4x + 8y$.

The conventional way of setting out the constraints is to place the units utilised on the left, and those available on the right; the inequality sign is the link.

Constraint		*Utilised*		*Available*
cutting time	(i)	6x + 3y	≤	36
assembly time	(ii)	4x + 8y	≤	48

In addition, two other logical constraints must be stated, ie,

x   ≥   0
y   ≥   0

These simply state that negative amounts of garden sheds or summer-houses cannot be made.

3.9   Activity

Using the information in the previous activity (Alfred Ltd), formulate the constraints.

3.10   Activity solution

Skilled labour	10x	+	10y	≤	2,000
Semi-skilled labour	5x	+	25y	≤	2,500
Flaktrap demand	x			≤	150
Saptrap demand			y	≤	80
Non-negative constraints }	x			≥	0
			y	≥	0

3.11   Step 3 - define the objective function

[Definition]   The objective function is a quantified statement of what is trying to be achieved, for instance the minimisation of costs or maximisation of profit. The objective function is always expressed in terms of the unknown variables (defined in Step 1). In the Hebrus example, these are x and y. Hence, continuing this example:

The objective is to maximise contribution C, given by:

$$C = 50x + 40y$$

The company undoubtedly wishes to maximise profit, however, given the usual assumptions of linear programming (stated later), this is achieved by maximising contribution. Take care that the coefficients of x and y (ie, 50 and 40 respectively) represent the amount by which contribution (and hence profit) increases per unit of each item produced and sold.

3.12   Graphing a straight line

This section is for those students who have not done any basic mathematics for a while. This is a revision section on graphing a straight line, a technique which is required for evaluating linear programming problems.

[Step 1]   We must have a linear relationship between two measurements, in other words if we know the value for x we can work out the value for y.

Examples	y	=	3x + 1
	y	=	2x + 42 etc.

Note:

1.   To recognise a **linear** relationship the equation must have only 'x' not 'x' to the power of anything eg, x^2.

2.   A straight line has two characteristics.

   (i)   A slope or gradient - which measures the 'steepness' of the line.

   (ii)   A point at which it cuts the y axis - called the intercept.

$$y = slope \times x + intercept$$

eg, $$y = 2x + 3$$

∴ the gradient is 2 and the point at which the line cuts the y axis is 3.

Step 2   To draw a straight line graph we only need to know two points which can then be joined.

Consider the following two equations.

(i) $y = 2x + 3$

(ii) $y = 2x - 2$

In order to draw the graphs of these equations it is necessary to decide on two values for x and then to calculate the corresponding values for y. Let us use x = 0 and 3. These calculations are best displayed in tabular form.

	x	0	3
1.	$y = 2x + 3$	3	9
2.	$y = 2x - 2$	-2	4

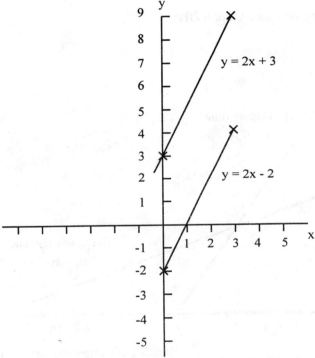

Note: the lines are parallel because the equations have the same gradient of 2.

3.13   Step 4 - graph the constraints

Having revised how to plot a straight line on a graph, we can now move on to graphing the constraints which are simply linear equations of the type we have just looked at.

In order to plot the constraints it is normally best to compute the intercepts of the equalities on the horizontal and vertical axes. Thus, x and y are each set equal to zero in turn and the value of y and x computed in these circumstances.

Returning to the Hebrus example.

For the equation   6x + 3y = 36 - cutting time constraint

when x = 0, $y = \dfrac{36}{3} = 12$

when y = 0, $x = \dfrac{36}{6} = 6$

For the equation   4x + 8y = 48 - assembly time constraint

when x = 0, $y = \dfrac{48}{8} = 6$

when y = 0, $x = \dfrac{48}{4} = 12$

The constraints can now be represented graphically:

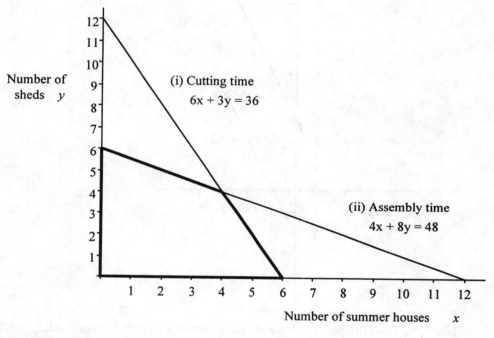

3.14   The feasible region

Having inserted the straight lines in the graph, we are then ready to work out what is called the **feasible region**.

If you recall each line inserted on the graph represents a constraint. In the Hebrus example, there can only be 36 hours of cutting time and no more and only 48 hours of assembly time and no more. Therefore the area on the graph **above** these lines is 'out of bounds' or more technically 'not feasible'. The area below these lines is therefore called the feasible region; it is possible for total cutting time and total assembly time to be any of these values up to and on the constraint line **but not above**.

Hence, the feasible region for Hebrus is as shown below.

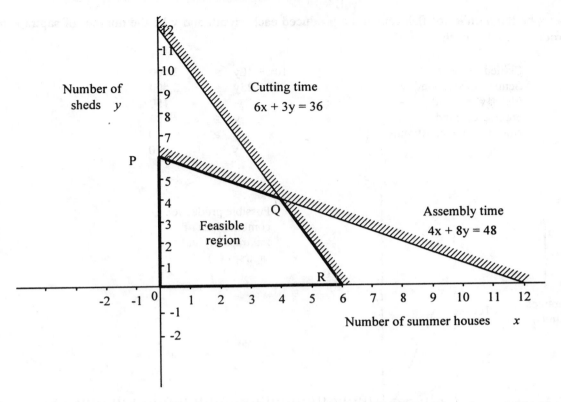

The area OPQR which is outlined in bold represents all feasible solutions ie, combinations of the two products which are achievable given the constraints. It is therefore called the **feasible region**.

To recognise that feasible solutions are, as in this case all **below** the constraint lines, it is normal practice to hatch **above** the line indicating that anything above is outside the feasible region. Some questions can be minimising problems eg, the objective function will be to minimise costs subject to minimum output levels. The constraints will be minimum output levels, therefore the feasible region will be on or above the line and will be hatched under the line ‌‌.

3.15   Example

Using the Alfred Ltd example again **you are required** to define the constraints, plot them on a graph and indicate on the graph the feasible region.

Alfred Ltd is preparing its plan for the coming month. It manufactures two products, the flaktrap and the saptrap. Details are as follows.

	Product		Price/wage rate
	Flaktrap	*Saptrap*	
Amount/unit:			
Selling price (£)	125	165	
Raw material (kg)	6	4	£5/kg
Labour hours:			
Skilled	10	10	£3/hour
Semi-skilled	5	25	£3/hour

The company's variable overhead rate is £1/labour hour (for both skilled and semi-skilled labour). The supply of skilled labour is limited to 2,000 hours/month and the supply of semi-skilled labour is limited to 2,500 hours/month. At the selling prices indicated, maximum demand for flaktraps is expected to be 150 units/month and the maximum demand for saptraps is expected to be 80 units/month. The directors of Alfred believe that demand for each product could be increased by advertising.

3.16   Example solution

Let x be the number of flaktraps to be produced each month and y be the number of saptraps to be produced each month.

Skilled labour	:	$10x + 10y$	$\leq$	2,000
Semi-skilled labour	:	$5x + 25y$	$\leq$	2,500
Flaktrap demand	:	x	$\leq$	150
Saptrap demand	:	$y \leq$		80
Non-negative constraints	:	x	$\geq$	0
	:	$y \geq$		0

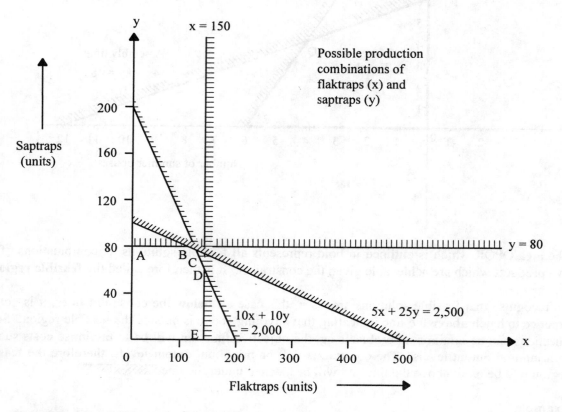

Possible production combinations of flaktraps (x) and saptraps (y)

This give a feasibility region of OABCDE.

3.17   Step 5 - manipulate the objective function

Having found the feasible region the problem now is to find the optimal solution within this feasible region.

There are two approaches to this final stage:

(a)   by inspection it is clear that the maximum contribution will lie on one of the corners of the feasible region. In the Hebrus example the corners are P, Q, R (it could lie on the line PQ or the line QR) – the optimal solution can be reached simply by calculating the contributions at each; or

(b)   by drawing an **iso-contribution** line (an objective function for a particular value of C), which is a line where all points represent an equal contribution. This is the recommended approach, particularly for more complex problems.

Using the Hebrus example, consider a contribution of £200. This would give the contribution line $50x + 40y = 200$ and could be achieved by producing four summer-houses, or five sheds, or any combination on a straight line between the two.

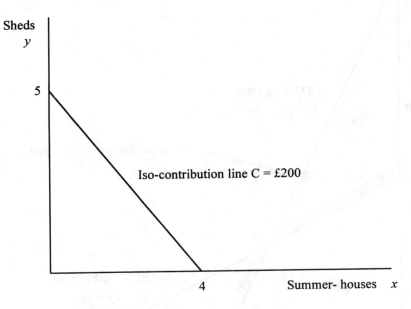

Another iso-contribution line could be drawn at £240, ie, $50x + 40y = 240$:

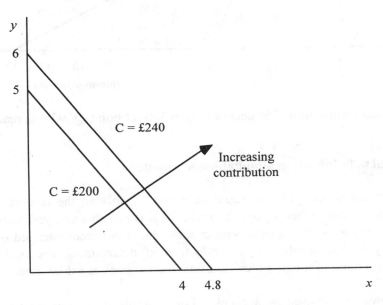

Clearly, iso-contribution lines move to and from the origin in parallel; the arrow indicates increasing contribution. The object is to get on the highest contribution line within (just touching) the binding constraints.

The point is found by drawing an example of an iso-contribution line on the diagram (any convenient value of C will do), and then placing a ruler against it. Then, by moving the ruler away from the origin (in the case of a maximisation problem) or towards the origin (in the case of a minimising problem) but keeping it parallel to the iso-contribution line, the last corner of the feasible solution space which is met represents the optimum solution.

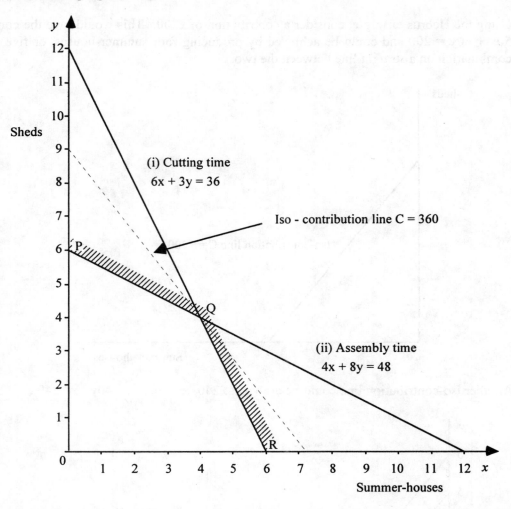

The highest available iso-contribution line occurs at $C = 360$, at point Q, where, reading from the graph, $x = 4$ and $y = 4$.

3.18   Evaluating the optimal solution using simultaneous equations

You may consider that the whole process would be easier by solving the constraints as sets of simultaneous equations and not bothering with a graph. This is possible and you may get the right answer, but such a technique should be used with caution and is not recommended until you have determined graphically which constraints are effective in determining the optimal solution. Furthermore if the question asks for a graphical solution, then a graph **must** be used.

The technique can however, be used as a check. For example using the Hebrus example the optimal solution can be checked by solving the two simultaneous equations for the two constraint boundaries.

Point Q is the intersection of the lines:

Constraint

$$6x + 3y \;\; = \;\; 36 \qquad \text{(i)}$$
$$4x + 8y \;\; = \;\; 48 \qquad \text{(ii)}$$

$3 \times$ (ii) $- 2 \times$ (i) gives

$$18y \;\; = \;\; 72$$
$$y \;\; = \;\; 4$$

Substituting into (i)

$$x \;\; = \;\; 4$$

Thus, the maximum contribution is obtained when four summer-houses and four sheds per week are produced, and the maximum contribution is 4 × £50 + 4 × £40 = £360.

3.19   Limitations to linear programming

There are a number of limitations to this technique.

- Single value estimates are used for the uncertain variables.

- Linear relationships must exist.

- Only suitable when there is one clearly defined objective function.

- When there are a number of variables, it becomes too complex to solve manually and a computer is required.

- It is assumed that the variables are completely divisible.

- It is assumed that the situation remains static in all other respects.

3.20   Activity

J Farms Ltd can buy two types of fertiliser which contain the following **percentage** of chemicals:

	Nitrates	Phosphates	Potash
Type X	18	5	2
Type Y	3	2	5

For a certain crop the following minimum quantities (kg) are required:

Nitrates	100	Phosphates	50	Potash	40

Type X costs £10 per kg and type Y costs £5 per kg. J Farms Ltd currently buys 1,000 kg of each type and wishes to minimise its expenditure on fertilisers.

You are required

(a)   to write down the objective function and the constraints for J Farms Ltd;

(6 marks)

(b)   to draw a graph to illustrate all the constraints (equations/inequalities), shading the feasible region;

(8 marks)

(c)   to recommend the quantity of each type of fertiliser which should be bought and the cost of these amounts;

(2 marks)

(d)   to find the saving J Farms Ltd can make by switching from its current policy to your recommendation;

(2 marks)

(e)   to state briefly any limitations of using this approach to problem-solving in practice.

(2 marks)

(Total: 20 marks)
(CIMA Nov 87)

3.21   Activity solution

(a)   *(Tutorial note:* The chemicals are given in percentage terms which are converted to decimals.*)*

Let x = number of kg of X,   cost =   10x
Let y = number of kg of Y,   cost =   5y

Total cost: z = 10x + 5y, the objective function which has to be minimised.

The constraints exist on the chemical composition of the fertilisers:

Nitrates:	$0.18x + 0.03y$	$\geq$ 100	1
Phosphates:	$0.05x + 0.02y$	$\geq$ 50	2
Potash:	$0.02x + 0.05y$	$\geq$ 40	3

Logic: $x \geq 0, \ y \geq 0$

(b)   In this example, all the points where the lines cut the axes are required, so that the easiest way to draw the constraints is to calculate these points.

$$0.18x + 0.03y = 100 \qquad x = 0 \quad \therefore \quad y = \frac{100}{0.03} \quad = \quad 3{,}333.3$$

$$y = 0 \quad \therefore \quad x = \frac{100}{0.18} \quad = \quad 555.5$$

$$0.05x + 0.02y = 50 \qquad x = 0 \quad \therefore \quad y = \frac{50}{0.02} \quad = \quad 2{,}500$$

$$y = 0 \quad \therefore \quad x = \frac{50}{0.05} \quad = \quad 1{,}000$$

$$0.02x + 0.05y = 40 \qquad x = 0 \quad \therefore \quad y = \frac{40}{0.05} \quad = \quad 800$$

$$y = 0 \quad \therefore \quad x = \frac{40}{0.02} \quad = \quad 2{,}000$$

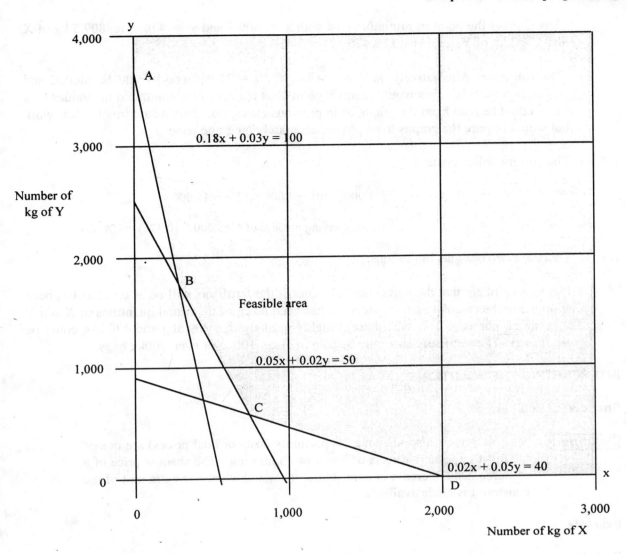

(c)   Considering the vertices of the feasible area.

A: $x = 0$ $y = 3,333.3$ $z = 10x + 5y$
$$z = 10(0) + 5(3,333.3) = £16,666.5$$

B: Solving $(0.18x + 0.03y = 100) \times 2$ $0.36x + 0.06y$ = 200
      and $(0.05x + 0.02y = 50) \times 3$ $0.15x + 0.06y$ = 150
                                        $\therefore\ 0.21x$ = 50
                                        $\therefore\ x$ = 238.1
                                        replacing gives y = 1,904.8

$$z = 10(238.1) + 5(1,904.8)$$
$$= £11,905$$

C: Solving $(0.05x + 0.02y = 50) \times 5$ $0.25x + 0.1y$ = 250
      and $(0.02x + 0.05y = 40) \times 2$ $0.04x + 0.1y$ = 80
                                        $\therefore\ 0.21x$ = 170
                                        $\therefore\ x$ = 809.5
                                        replacing gives y = 476.2

$$z = 10(809.5) + 5(476.2)$$

$$= £10,476$$

D: $x = 2,000$ $y = 0$ $z = 10(2,000) + 5(0) = £20,000$

Thus C gives the point of minimum cost with x = 809.5 and y = 476.2, ie, 809.5 kg of X and 476.2 kg of Y, total cost £10,476.

(Tutorial note: Alternatively, an iso-cost line for z = 20,000 (say) could be plotted and moved downwards. This would identify point C as the optimum point, and the values of x and y could be read from the graph, as in previous examples. This would involve less work but would require the graphs to be plotted accurately on graph paper.*)*

(d)   The current policy costs:

$$1,000 \ (£10) \ + 1,000 \ (£5) \ = \ £15,000$$

so the saving made is of £(15,000 – 10,476) = £4,524

(e)   There are two obvious limitations:

It is very unlikely that the percentage contents of the fertilisers will be as exact as has been assumed in the calculations. No account has been taken of the actual quantities of X and Y that can be purchased. It would seem highly unlikely that 809.5kg and 476.2kg could be purchased. The fertilisers may only be sold in 50kg, 100kg or even 500kg bags.

4   INTERPRETING THE SOLUTION

4.1   Shadow (or dual) prices

Definition	Shadow prices (also known as opportunity costs or dual prices) are one of the most important aspects of linear programming. The shadow price of a resource is the increase in contribution obtained when one extra unit of the constraint is made available.

4.2   Example

Refer back to the earlier example concerning Hebrus Ltd.

Suppose one extra hour was available for the cutting process each week.

By how much would contribution (and profit) be increased?

The extra hour would alter the constraints to:

Cutting   (i) $6x + 3y \ \le \ 37$; and

Assembly   (ii) $4x + 8y \ \le \ 48$;

To solve simultaneously multiply (ii) by 1.5.

(iii) $6x + 12y \ \le \ 72$

Solving as before:

Subtracting (i) from (iii) gives

$9y = 35$

and thus $y = 3\frac{8}{9}$

Inserting this value in (i) gives

$$6x + (3 \times 3\tfrac{8}{9}) = 37$$

$$6x + 11\tfrac{6}{9} = 37$$

$$6x = 25\tfrac{3}{9}$$

$$x = 4\tfrac{2}{9}$$

$$\begin{array}{lll} & & £ \\ C = (£50 \times 4\tfrac{2}{9}) + (£40 \times 3\tfrac{8}{9}) & = & 366\tfrac{2}{3} \\ \text{Original contribution} & & 360 \\ \hline \text{Increase} & & 6\tfrac{2}{3} \end{array}$$

Thus, £$6\tfrac{2}{3}$ is the shadow price of one hour in the cutting process.

Note: There is a great potential for rounding errors when finding dual prices. The problem has been avoided here by working in fractions. If decimals are used retain several decimal places.

Similarly the shadow price of assembly time may be found by keeping the cutting time constraint unchanged, but relaxing the assembly constraint by one unit so that it becomes:

Assembly $4x + 8y \leq 49$ (ii)

Whilst (i) remains as:

Cutting $6x + 3y \leq 36$ (i)

Solving as before:

$$3 \times \text{(ii)} - 2 \times \text{(i)} \implies 18y = 75$$

$$y = 4.16667 \qquad \text{(Keep this value in the memory of your calculator.)}$$

Substituting into (i) gives $x = 3.91667$

$$\begin{array}{ll} & £ \\ \text{Contribution } C = (£50 \times 3.91667) + (£40 \times 4.16667) = & 362.5 \\ \text{Original contribution} = & 360.0 \\ \hline \text{Increase} & 2.5 \end{array}$$

Thus, the shadow price of one hour of assembly time = £2.5.

(Note: in view of these calculations it is important that no attempt is made to simplify the original constraints by cancelling, otherwise you will not be able to calculate correct values for the shadow prices.*)*

4.3   Tabular approach

An alternative method of arriving at the shadow price is to set out the two critical constraints (cutting and assembly) as a table:

Column		(1)		(2)		
Cutting	Cu	$6x$	$+$	$3y$	$= 36$	(i)
Assembly	As	$4x$	$+$	$8y$	$= 48$	(ii)
Contribution	$=$	$50x$	$+$	$40y$		

The shadow prices are found by solving the **columns** (1) and (2), replacing x and y with the constraint symbols Cu and As.

Column	(1)	(2)
replace x and y with Cu	6 Cu	3 Cu
replace x and y with As	4 As	8 As
Contribution	50	40

Turning these into equations:

$$6Cu + 4As = 50 \quad (1)$$

$$3Cu + 8As = 40 \quad (2)$$

Solve simultaneously

Multiply (1) by 2:
$$12Cu + 8As = 100 \quad (3)$$

Subtract (2) from (3):

$$9Cu = 60$$

$$Cu = \frac{60}{9} = £6\tfrac{2}{3} \quad \text{(the same solution as above for shadow price)}$$

Substituting in (2) gives: As $=$ £2.5.

These shadow prices represent the amount of contribution forgone by **not** having one extra hour available in each department.

4.4   Activity

Using the following data, calculate the shadow prices of respectively one hour of machine time and one hour of finishing time.

(i) $20x + 25y \leq 500$ (machining time)

(ii) $40x + 25y \leq 800$ (finishing time)

$C = 80x + 75y$ (contribution)

Solution: $x = 15$, $y = 8$

Use the constraint alteration (incremental) method for machining time and the table method for finishing time.

4.5   Activity solution

Machining time - the constraints become:

(i) $20x + 25y \leq 501$

(ii) $40x + 25y \leq 800$

Subtracting (i) from (ii) gives

$$20x = 299$$

and thus $x = 14.95$

Inserting into (i) gives

$$(20 \times 14.95) + 25y = 501$$

$$25y = 202$$

$$y = 8.08$$

Original contribution:

	£
$(15 \times £80) + (8 \times £75)$	= 1,800

Amended contribution

$(14.95 \times £80) + (8.08 \times £75)$	= 1,802

Increased contribution   2

The shadow price per machine hour is £2.

Finishing time:

| Machining | M | $20x + 25y = 500$ |
| Finishing | F | $40x + 25y = 800$ |

| Contribution | $80x + 75y$ |

becomes:

(i) $20M + 40F = 80$

(ii) $25M + 25F = 75$

Multiply (i) by 1.25 gives

(iii) $25M + 50F = 100$

Subtracting (ii) from (iii) gives

$$25F = 25$$

$$F = 1$$

Thus the dual price per hour of finishing time is £1.

4.6   Usefulness of shadow prices - conclusion

Shadow prices have the following relevance:

(a)   The shadow price is the extra profit that may be earned by relaxing by one unit each of the constraints.

(b)   It therefore represents the maximum **premium** which the firm should be willing to pay for one extra unit of each constraint.

(c)   Since shadow prices indicate the effect of a one unit change in each of the constraints, they provide a measure of the sensitivity of the result (but see later).

The shadow price for any constraint which is not binding at the optimum solution is zero. In the above example suppose production of summer-houses and sheds was also limited by the amount of painting time available – each product took 4 hours to paint and only 40 hours a week were available.

Since the optimum plan involved production of 4 sheds and 4 summer-houses the painting time would only be 32 hours a week – consequently it would make no difference to the optimum solution if painting time availability either increased to 41 hours or decreased to 39. Under these circumstances the dual price of painting time is zero.

However, if the painting time was reduced to only 32 hours this too would become a binding constraint, and a reduction by one further hour, to 31 may affect the optimum solution. It should be noted that shadow prices are valid for only a small range of changes before, eventually, they become non-binding or make different resources critical. The shadow price of a non-binding resource is zero.

4.7   Slack

Slack is the amount by which a resource is under utilised. It will occur when the optimum point does not fall on the given resource line.

In the above example, the optimum point Q lies on both the cutting and assembly time lines therefore both resources are fully utilised. This can be checked from the constraint inequalities.

When $x = 4$, $y = 4$,

Cutting time:	available = 36,	utilised	=	$6x + 3y$
			=	$6 \times 4 + 3 \times 4$
			=	36

Assembly time:	available = 48,	utilised	=	$4x + 8y$
			=	$4 \times 4 + 8 \times 4$
			=	48

hence all available time in both departments is utilised.

If, however, the optimum had been at P ($x = 0$, $y = 6$) then, because P does not lie on the cutting time line, there would be slack cutting time.

Cutting time utilised   = $6 \times 0 + 3 \times 6$ =   18

Slack   = $36 - 18$
         =   18 hours

Slack is important because unused resources can be put to another use - eg, hired out to another manufacture.

5   SENSITIVITY ANALYSIS

5.1   Introduction

Having calculated the shadow prices of each of the constraints these can then be used to ascertain how sensitive the results are. For instance, what would happen to the optimal solution if the following questions were asked?

1.   What if the contribution from product X were £1 higher than expected?

2.   What if the sales price of produce Y was reduced by 15%?

3.   What would happen if we had ten or more quantities of a scarce resource?

This type of 'what if' questioning is known as sensitivity analysis.

5.2   Example

Returning once again to the Hebrus example.

Suppose the contributions from summer-houses and sheds turned out to be slightly different from £50 and £40 respectively, perhaps due to an error in estimating costs.

Would the optimal solution change?

This question is best answered by looking again at the graphical solution:

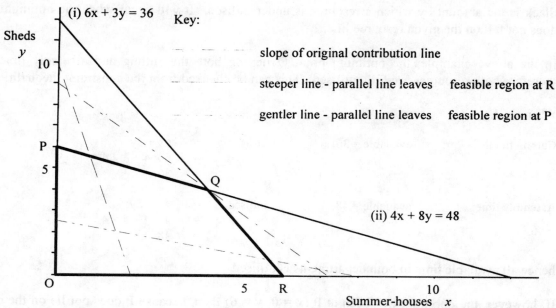

As the contribution line is moved further from the origin, point Q will be the last point of the feasible region which it touches, unless the slope of the contribution line alters considerably. If the slope was steeper than that of the line 6x + 3y = 36, point R would be the last point to be touched and so would represent the revised optimum solution. Conversely, if the slope was gentler than that of the line 4x + 8y = 48, point P would be the last point to be touched.

These slopes (or gradients) may be expressed mathematically.

(a)   **Cutting constraint line**

6x + 3y = 36

This may be rewritten, in standard form, 3y = 36 – 6x or y = 12 – 2x

This is of the form y = a + bx where a represents the intercept of the line with the y axis and b represents the gradient.

Thus, in the case of the cutting constraint line, the gradient is –2.

(b)   **Assembly constraint line**

4x + 8y = 48

$8y \quad = \quad 48 - 4x$

$y \quad = \quad 6 - \frac{1}{2} x$

The gradient is therefore $- \dfrac{1}{2}$

(c)   **Contribution line**

In general terms   C = px + qy, where   p =   contribution from a summer-house
                              and   q =   contribution from a shed

Re-arranging: $qy = C - px$

$$y = \frac{C}{q} - \frac{px}{q}$$

The gradient is $\therefore \dfrac{-p}{q}$ (The coefficient of x ÷ the coefficient of y.)

It was stated above that the optimal solution would not alter provided that the gradient of the contribution line lay between the gradients of the constraint lines.

$\therefore$ Optimal solution will not alter provided that:

$\dfrac{-p}{q}$ lies between -2 and $-\frac{1}{2}$

In other words, $\dfrac{p}{q}$ must lie between 2 and $\frac{1}{2}$

Initially p was £50. If this does not alter, q may vary so that $50/q$ lies between 2 and $\frac{1}{2}$. Therefore, q can vary between 25 and 100.

Similarly, q was initially £40 and if this does not alter, p may vary so that $p/40$ lies between 2 and $\frac{1}{2}$. Therefore p can vary between 80 and 20.

The optimal product mix is, therefore, remarkably insensitive to changes in the original data. Note, however, that the above contribution ranges are valid only if the contributions of the two products are varied independently. For instance, if contribution from a summer-house falls to the extreme value of £20, the optimal solution will change if contribution from a shed simultaneously rises above £40, since p/q will then be less than $\frac{1}{2}$.

Note also that if the unit contribution alters, so will the shadow prices calculated earlier. This will also be the case if the optimal solution lies at the intersection of different lines of constraint.

5.3   Activity

Given the following machine time constraint calculate the gradient of the line.

$20x + 25y = 500$

5.4   Activity solution

Rearranging gives: $25y = 500 - 20x$

Dividing by 25 gives: $y = 20 - 0.8x$

The gradient is therefore -0.8.

5.5   Activity

Given the answer to the previous activity and the following finishing time constraint calculate the range of contribution gradients which will not cause the optimal solution to alter.

$40x + 25y = 800$

5.6   Activity solution

Re-arranging gives: $25y = 800 - 40x$

Dividing by 25 gives: $y = 32 - 1.6x$

The gradient is therefore -1.6.

The gradient of the objective function $= \dfrac{p}{q} = \dfrac{-\text{ contribution from X}}{\text{contribution from Y}}$

which must lie between -0.8 and -1.6

Thus $\dfrac{p}{q}$ must lie between 0.8 and 1.6 for the optimal solution not to alter.

6   PROBLEMS INVOLVING MORE THAN TWO VARIABLES

6.1   Introduction

The above examples involved only two variables. When three or more variables are involved, it is usually impossible to solve the problem graphically and the best method of solution is the simplex method. Although simplex is outside the syllabus, the **formulation** of problems involving more than two variables and interpretation of the results is within the syllabus.

6.2   Simplex method - introduction

The simplex method is an algorithm developed in the 1960s for solving linear programming problems.

In the two-variable problem considered in the last section, it was seen that the optimum solution was to be found at a corner of the feasible region. This is still true in the multi-variable problem, even though one cannot draw a region with corners in more than two dimensions. The technique of the simplex method is to move from corner to corner of the feasible region, calculating the value of the objective function at each successive corner, and ensuring that each move is to a corner which gives a higher profit than the one before.

The simplex method, which readily lends itself to computer solution, is invaluable in problems with three or more variables which cannot be solved graphically and which would be inordinately time-consuming to solve by any clerical method other than simplex. For simplicity, however, it will be demonstrated on a two-variable problem, even though in such a case it offers little or no advantage over the methods already discussed and indeed may be thought to be somewhat more complicated. One advantage, however, is that shadow prices emerge automatically as part of the solution.

It is not necessary from an examination point of view to know how to **find** the solution using simplex. However, to aid your understanding of how to interpret a simplex tableau, the method is explained below. The method will be demonstrated on the problem solved in the last section. This is repeated here for ease of reference.

Example

Hebrus Ltd manufactures summer houses and garden sheds. Each product passes through a cutting process and an assembly process. One summer house, which makes a contribution of £50, takes 6 hours cutting time and 4 hours assembly time, while one shed, which makes a contribution of £40, takes 3 hours cutting time and 8 hours assembly time. There is a maximum of 36 cutting hours available each week and 48 assembly hours.

Solution

Let x =   number of summer houses produced per week
and y =   number of sheds produced per week,

the objective is to maximise contribution, £C, where

$$C \quad = \quad 50x + 40y$$

subject to:

$$6x + 3y \quad \leq \quad 36$$
$$4x + 8y \quad \leq \quad 48$$
$$(x \geq 0) \quad \text{non-negative constraint}$$
$$(y \geq 0) \quad \text{non-negative constraint}$$

6.3   Slack variables

Inequalities are difficult to deal with algebraically and for the simplex method must be converted into equations. If an unknown quantity z say, is less than 36, then another quantity can be added to z to make it equal to 36. Similarly, if $z \geq 36$, then another quantity can be subtracted from z to make it equal to 36. The variable which is added or subtracted is called a *slack variable*.

As both inequalities in the Hebrus model are '$\leq$', the slack variables are added. Denoting these by S_1 and S_2, we get:

$$6x + 3y + S_1 \quad = \quad 36$$
$$4x + 8y + S_2 \quad = \quad 48$$

S_1 represents the amount by which the utilised cutting time ($6x + 3y$) falls short of the available cutting time (36) and therefore is the amount of unused cutting time. Similarly, S_2 is the amount of unused assembly time.

6.4   The initial simplex tableau

The constraint equations and objective function are first set out so that the variables are aligned in columns. This necessitates re-arranging the objective function to bring the x and y terms to the left-hand side, giving:

$$6x \; + \; 3y + S_1 = 36$$
$$4x \; + \; 8y + S_2 = 48$$
$$C - 50x \; - \; 40y \qquad = 0$$

The coefficients of each term are then tabulated, putting zeros in the blank spaces.

C is placed in a separate column called the basic variable or basis column. The other entries in this column are the slack variables associated with each constraint, S_1 for the first constraint and S_2 for the second constraint.

Basic variable	x	y	S_1	S_2	Solution
S_1	6	3	1	0	36
S_2	4	8	0	1	48
C	-50	-40	0	0	0

Note that the non-negativity constraints are not included. The simplex method implicitly assumes that all variables are greater than or equal to zero.

6.5   Interpretation of initial tableau

The basic variable column is not essential, but it makes the interpretation of the simplex tableau much easier. It contains those variables whose values are listed in the solution column. Reading across the rows from the basic variable column to the solution column,

$$S_1 = 36$$
$$S_2 = 48$$
$$C = 0$$

This means that if all the variable time is slack ie, no work is being done, then the contribution will be zero. If no work is being done, x and y both $= 0$. This is readily inferred from the tableau; any variables not listed in the basic variable column always have a value of zero.

The initial tableau therefore represents the feasible but trivial solution, that if no items are produced, there will be no contribution.

(Note: the basic variables can be identified from those columns having one cell, and one only, equal to 1, and all the other cells in that column equal to zero. The position of the 1 gives the row to which the basic variable relates. Thus, in the above tableau, the S_1 column has a 1 in the first row and all other values in this column are zero. Hence S_1 is the basic variable for the row in which the 1 occurs ie, row 1.)

6.6   The simplex algorithm

This section may be omitted. It is not required for the final examination but is inserted for those students who are interested to see how the final tableau is obtained.

The simplex process is an iterative one, that is, the optimum solution is approached in a series of repetitive stages called *iterations*, each iteration giving a solution nearer to the optimum. For an iterative process, it is necessary to start with a feasible solution, however trivial it may be, and work to improve it. The algorithm (ie, the set of rules) for performing the iterations is given below, the first iteration using the initial simplex tableau.

(1)   Select the column containing the largest negative value in the objective function row (the pivotal or key column).

(2)   Divide each value in the solution column by the corresponding value in the pivotal column. This should be done for each row. Any constraint with a negative value in the pivotal column should be ignored at this stage.

(3)   Select the row which has the lowest result from the calculations in instruction (b) (the pivotal or key row).

(4)   Encircle the value at the intersection of the pivotal row and pivotal column (the pivotal value or pivot element).

(5)   Formulate a new tableau as follows:

(i)   All column headings are unchanged.

(ii)   Replace the basic variable in the pivotal row by that at the head of the pivotal column. All other basic variables remain as before.

(iii)   Each new value in the pivotal row equals the old value divided by the pivotal value.

(iv)   Put all other values in the pivotal column equal to zero.

(v)   For *all* other values, use the 'rectangle' rule ie:

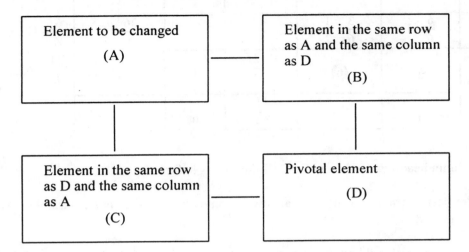

New value of A equals old value of A minus $\dfrac{B \times C}{D}$

(6)   Test the new tableau for optimality. It will be the optimum if all the values in the objective function row are positive or zero.

(7)   If not optimum, repeat from instruction 1, operating on the new tableau, and iterate until the optimum tableau is obtained.

Applying these rules to the initial tableau of the Hebrus problem:

Basic variable	x	y	S1	S2	Solution	Calculations
S1	⑥	3	1	0	36 ←	$\dfrac{36}{6} = 6$ ←
S2	4	8	0	1	48	$\dfrac{48}{4} = 12$
C	−50	−40	0	0	0	

Rule 1: The largest negative value in the objective function row is −50, in the *x* column. This is therefore the pivotal column, indicated by ↑.

Rule 2: The calculations are shown in the calculations column.

Rule 3: The lowest result in the calculation column is 6, in the first row. This is therefore the pivotal row, indicated by ←.

Rule 4: The value at the intersection of the pivotal row and pivotal column is 6, which is encircled.

Rule 5: The new tableau is as follows:

Basic variable	x	y	S1	S2	Solution	Calculations
x	$\frac{6}{6}=1$	$\frac{3}{6}=\frac{1}{2}$	$\frac{1}{6}$	0	$\frac{36}{6}=6$	$\frac{6}{\frac{1}{2}}=12$
S2	0	⑥	$-\frac{2}{3}$	1	24 ←	$\frac{24}{6}=4$ ←
C	0	-15	$8\frac{1}{3}$	0	300	

(i)   Column headings (BV, x, y, S_1, S_2, Solution) as before.

(ii)   The basic variable in the pivotal row becomes x, the other basic variables (S_2 , C) being unchanged.

(iii)   All values in the old pivotal row are divided by 6. The results have been left in fractions to show the method.

(iv)   The other values in the x column (ie, those in the second and third rows) are put equal to zero.

(v)   The rectangle rule applies to all the remaining cells. Four typical values are calculated below.

row 2, column y,

$A = 8, B = 4, C = 3, D = 6$, hence:

$$\begin{aligned} \text{new value} \quad &= \quad 8 - \frac{4 \times 3}{6} \\ &= \quad 8 - 2 \\ &= \quad 6 \end{aligned}$$

row 2, column S_1 ,

$A = 0, B = 4, C = 1, D = 6$, hence:

$$\begin{aligned} \text{new value} \quad &= \quad 0 - \frac{4 \times 1}{6} \\ &= \quad -\frac{2}{3} \end{aligned}$$

row 3, column y,

$A = -40, B = -50, C = 3, D = 6$, hence:

$$\begin{aligned} \text{new value} \quad &= \quad -40 - \left(\frac{-50 \times 3}{6} \right) \\ &= \quad -40 + 25 \\ &= \quad -15 \end{aligned}$$

row 3, solution column,

A = 0, B = –50, C = 36, D = 6, hence:

$$\text{new value} \quad = \quad 0 - \left(\frac{-50 \times 36}{6} \right)$$

$$= \quad 0 + 300$$

$$= \quad 300$$

Rule 6: There is still a negative value in the objective function row (– 15 in column *y*), hence the tableau is not optimum.

Rule 7: The operations must be repeated on the new tableau, starting with rule 1. The pivotal element will be in row 2, column *y*. The result of the second iteration is:

Basic variable	x	y	S1	S2	Solution
x	1	0	$\frac{2}{9}$	$-\frac{1}{12}$	4
y	0	1	$-\frac{1}{9}$	$\frac{1}{6}$	4
C	0	0	$6\frac{2}{3}$	$\frac{15}{6}$	360

Notes:

(i)   The results have been left mostly as fractions to make the method more transparent. In practice, use a calculator and express the results in decimals.

(ii)   Care must be taken when subtracting negative values. For example:

row 1, column S_1 ,

$A = \frac{1}{6}, B = \frac{1}{2}, C = -\frac{2}{3}, D = 6$, hence:

$$\text{new value} \quad = \quad \frac{1}{6} - \left(\frac{\frac{1}{2} \times -\frac{2}{3}}{6} \right)$$

$$= \quad \frac{1}{6} - \left(-\frac{1}{18} \right)$$

$$= \quad \frac{1}{6} + \frac{1}{18}$$

$$= \quad \frac{2}{9}$$

Testing for optimality, all the values in the objective function row are now positive or zero, hence the optimum has been reached.

6.7   Interpretation of final tableau

Reading from the basic variable column to the solution column, maximum value of $C = 360$, achieved when:

$$
\begin{aligned}
x &= 4 \\
y &= 4 \\
S_1 &= 0 \\
S_2 &= 0
\end{aligned}
$$

The last two variables are zero because they do not appear in the basic variable column. Zero solutions are often as important as non-zero solutions and should be stated.

The final conclusions must always be stated in terms of the original problem ie:

Produce 4 summer-houses and 4 sheds per week. This uses all the cutting and assembly time, and gives the maximum contribution of £360 per week.

6.8   Shadow prices in the final tableau

The values in the objective function row of the final tableau are the shadow prices for cutting and assembly times which were derived earlier (any discrepancy is due to rounding errors). The other values in these columns show how the shadow costs are made up. Taking for example, the S_1 column, S_1 is the slack variable for cutting time. Hence if one extra hour of cutting time could be made available, it would increase the contribution by £ $6\frac{2}{3}$. This would be made up of additional production of x of $\frac{2}{9}$ units and reduced production of y of $\frac{1}{9}$ units. Substituting these values into the contribution equation, the extra contribution would be:

$$
£\left(50\left(\frac{2}{9}\right) + 40\left(-\frac{1}{9}\right)\right) = \frac{100}{9} - \frac{40}{9} = \frac{60}{9} = £6\frac{2}{3}
$$

This assumes that x and y can have fractional values, which is not true in this particular example. This is one of the limitations of the simplex method.

There is a limit to the extra contribution that could be achieved by extra cutting hours being made available, because y cannot be reduced below zero. The present optimum has 4 units of y. If each extra hour of cutting time reduces this by $\frac{1}{9}$, then the number of extra cutting hours to reduce y to zero would be $4/(1/9) = 36$ hours. Any increase in cutting hours above 36 would not increase the contribution, but result in slack or idle time in the cutting department unless available assembly hours were also increased.

6.9   Example

Three products, X, Y and Z are processed in three departments, 1, 2 and 3. The number of hours required in each department per unit of product is given in the table below, together with the maximum number of hours available in each department, and the contribution per unit of product.

The simplex method has been used to produce the final tableau also given below. Set up the linear programming model to maximise the total contribution and fully interpret the final tableau.

Dept.	Hours/unit of product			Maximum hours available
	X	Y	Z	
1	2	5	1	40
2	1	1	1	10
3	3	1	1	20
Unit contribution (£)	9	12	4	

Third tableau

Basic variable	x	y	z	S_1	S_2	S_3	Solution
y	0	1	−0.33	0.33	−0.67	0	6.67
x	1	0	1.33	−0.33	1.67	0	3.33
S_3	0	0	− 2.67	0.67	−4.33	1	3.33
C	0	0	4	1	7	0	110

As all the values in the bottom row are now ≥ 0, this is the final tableau.

6.10   Example solution

The algebraic model is:

Let x =   no. of units of product X produced
         y =   no. of units of product Y produced
         z =   no. of units of product Z produced
         C =   total contribution in £

Objective function, to be maximised:
$$C = 9x + 12y + 4z$$

Constraints:

Dept 1:	2x	+ 5y	+ z	$\leq$	40
Dept 2:	x	+ y	+ z	$\leq$	10
Dept 3:	3x	+ y	+ z	$\leq$	20

Rearranging and adding slack variables S_1, S_2, S_3:

$$2x + 5y + z + S_1 \qquad\qquad = 40$$
$$x + y + z \qquad + S_2 \qquad = 10$$
$$3x + y + z \qquad\qquad + S_3 = 20$$
$$C - 9x - 12y - 4z \qquad\qquad\qquad = 0$$

Interpretation of final tableau

Variables

The maximum value of $C = 110$, obtained when $y = 6.67$, $x = 3.33$, $S_3 = 3.33$ and all other variables $(z, S_1, S_2) = 0$.

This means that the maximum contribution is £110, obtained when production is 3.33 units of X, 6.67 units of Y and no units of Z. This uses all available time in departments 1 and 2, but leaves 3.33 hours spare time in department 3.

Shadow prices

Department 1:

The shadow price is £1. Each additional hour in this department will increase the contribution by £1. This would be effected by an increase in y of 0.33, a decrease in x of 0.33 and an increase in S_3 of 0.67.

The extra amount of time to reduce x to zero

$$= \frac{3.33}{0.33}$$

$$= 10 \text{ hours}$$

Hence time in department 1 should not be increased by more than 10 hours.

Department 2:

The shadow price is £7. Each additional hour in this department will increase the contribution by £7. This would be effected by a decrease in y of 0.67, an increase in x of 1.67 and a decrease in S_3 of 4.33.

The extra time to reduce S_3 to zero

$$= \frac{3.33}{4.33}$$

$$= 0.77 \text{ hours}$$

The extra time to reduce y to zero

$$= \frac{6.67}{0.67}$$

$$= 10 \text{ hours}$$

Taking the lower of these two values, the time in department 2 should not be increased by more than 0.77 hours.

Product Z

The shadow price is £4. This means that if management ignores the recommendation to make no product Z, each unit of Z produced will decrease the contribution by £4.

It should be noted that whereas increasing resources increases contribution, increasing a non-profitable product will decrease contribution. The effect is opposite to that of increasing resources. Hence the values in column z show that for each unit of Z produced, y will *increase* by 0.33, x will *decrease* by 1.33 and S_3 *increase* by 2.67. As x is at present 3.33, and cannot be reduced below zero, the maximum amount by which z could be increased is 3.33/1.33 = 2.5 units. This would reduce the total contribution by 2.5 × 4 = £10.

7   CHAPTER SUMMARY

This chapter has considered decision problems where activity is limited by the existence of one or more scarce resources.

The distinction between one or more scarce resource problems has been illustrated and solved, two and more than two variable problems have also been shown and the former solved using graphical linear programming techniques.

8   SELF TEST QUESTIONS

8.1   What is a scarce resource? (1.1)

8.2   What is linear programming? (3.1)

8.3   List some common applications of linear programming. (3.2)

8.4   What is the feasible region? (3.14)

8.5   What is an iso-contribution line? (3.17)

8.6   What are the limitations of linear programming? (3.19)

8.7   What is a shadow price? (4.1)

8.8   What is slack in the context of linear programming? (4.7)

8.9   What is the importance of sensitivity analysis in the context of linear programming? (5.1)

8.10   What method can be used for solving problems with more than two variables? (6.2)

9   EXAMINATION TYPE QUESTIONS

9.1   Flintstones

The Flintstones are involved in the manufacture of two products, Chip and Dale. Due to an industrial dispute, which is expected to go on for some time, material B, which is required in the production of Dale, is expected to be limited to 300 units per week. Material A, required for both products, is freely available.

Flintstones are experiencing labour shortages and it is expected that only 800 hours of unskilled labour and 1,000 hours of skilled labour will be available in any week, in the short run.

Due to a transport problem, the Flintstones will be able to import only 400 Dinos into the country each week. This item is required in the manufacture of both Chip and Dale.

It is the company's policy to limit the production of Dale to not more than three times the production of Chip.

The following information is available:

	Chip £	Dale £
Material B (2 units for Dale only)	–	10
Material A	15	10
Labour – unskilled £3 per hour	12	15
– skilled £5 per hour	50	20
Dinos (£10 each)	20	20
Total cost	97	75
Selling price	127	100

Fixed costs each week amount to £3,000.

You are required to calculate the optimal plan for Flintstones together with the weekly profit which may be earned.

9.2   Electronic component mix

In a machine shop a company manufactures two types of electronic component, X and Y, on which it aims to maximise the contribution to profit. The company wishes to know the ideal combination of X and Y to make. All the electronic components are produced in three main stages: Assembly, Inspection and Packing.

In Assembly each *X* takes 1 hour and each *Y* takes 2 hours.

Inspection takes 7.5 minutes for each *X* and 30 minutes for each *Y*, on the average, which includes the time required for any faults to be rectified.

In total there are 600 hours available for assembly and 100 hours for inspection each week. At all stages both components can be processed at the same time.

At the final stage the components require careful packing prior to delivery. Each *X* takes 3 minutes and each *Y* takes 20 minutes on average to pack properly. There is a total of 60 packing hours available each week.

The contribution on *X* is £10 per unit and on *Y* is £15 per unit. For engineering reasons not more than 500 of *X* can be made each week. All production can be sold.

You are required

(a)   to state the objective function in mathematical terms;

(2 marks)

(b)   to state the constraints as equations/inequalities;

(5 marks)

(c)   to graph these constraints on a suitable diagram, shading the feasible region;

(8 marks)

(d)   to advise the company on the optimal product mix and contribution.

(5 marks)
(Total: 20 marks)
(CIMA Nov 89)

10   ANSWERS TO EXAMINATION TYPE QUESTIONS

10.1   Flintstones

From the tabulated information given, per week:

No. of hours unskilled labour per Chip	$= \dfrac{12}{3} =$	4 hours
No. of hours unskilled labour per Dale	$= \dfrac{15}{3} =$	5 hours
No. of hours skilled labour per Chip	$= \dfrac{50}{5} =$	10 hours
No. of hours skilled labour per Dale	$= \dfrac{20}{5} =$	4 hours
No. of Dinos per Chip	$= \dfrac{20}{10} =$	2
No. of Dinos per Dale	$= \dfrac{20}{10} =$	2
Contribution per Chip	$= £(127 - 97) =$	£30
Contribution per Dale	$= £(100 - 75) =$	£25

As each Dale requires 2 units of B, and only 300 units of B are available, this limits the number of Dales to 150.

There is no constraint on the amount of material A.

Fixed costs will be the same, whatever mix of Chip and Dale is produced, hence they can be ignored for the purpose of obtaining the optimum product mix, but must be included in the calculation of profit.

Let C =   number of Chips produced per week.
Let D =   number of Dales produced per week.
Let Z =   total contributions per week.

The objective function then is to maximise contribution to fixed overheads, ie,

$$\text{Maximise:} \quad Z \;=\; 30C + 25D$$

						Constraint Number	
Subject to:	$4C$	$+$	$5D$	$\leq$	800	(1)	Unskilled labour
	$10C$	$+$	$4D$	$\leq$	$1{,}000$	(2)	Skilled labour
	$2C$	$+$	$2D$	$\leq$	400	(3)	Dinos
			D	$\leq$	$3C$	(4)	Production policy
			$2D$	$\leq$	300	(5)	Material B
			C, D	$\geq$	0		

Note that there is a constraint which appears confusing at first, that of company policy with regard to the production of Chips and Dales. However, it can be dealt with simply by taking the expression of the policy, as expressed in words, and turning it into symbols, thus:

The production of Dales is to be not more than (ie, less than or equal to) three times the production of Chips.

$$D \qquad \leq \quad 3C$$

$$\text{or} \qquad -3C + D \quad \leq \quad 0$$

For graph see below. The feasibility region is CBAO (outlined in bold).

The solution is at the intersection of constraints (1) and (2), the two labour constraints. The solution can be found by solving (1) and (2) simultaneously.

$$
\begin{aligned}
4C + 5D &= 800 & (1)\\
10C + 4D &= 1{,}000 & (2)
\end{aligned}
$$

$$5 \times (2) - 4 \times (1) \text{ gives} \quad 34C = 1{,}800$$

$$C = 52.94 \;\simeq\; 53$$

$$D = 117.65 \;\simeq\; 118$$

$$\text{Contribution} \;=\; 30C + 25D \;=\; £30 \times 53 + £25 \times 118 \;=\; \underline{£4{,}540}$$

$$\text{Thus, profit} \;=\; £4{,}540 - £3{,}000 \;=\; \underline{£1{,}540 \text{ per week}}$$

Note: the non-integer solutions have been rounded up. Strictly speaking this puts the optimal solution outside the feasible region (52 and 117 might be more appropriate). The values of C and D have been rounded since, in any one week it is difficult to sell 117.65 Dales. However the Flintstones might consider making on average 117.65 Dales per week.

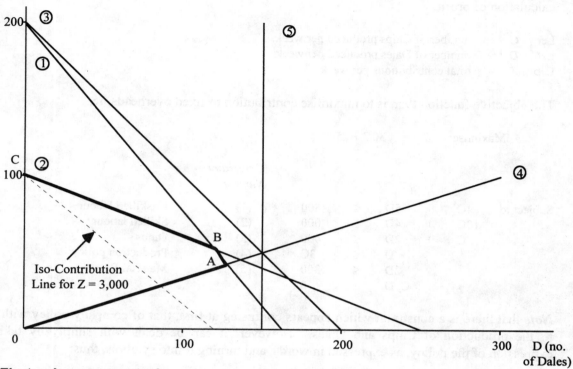

10.2   Electronic component mix

(a)   Let number of X components   = x
       Let number of Y components   = y
       Let contribution   =   £C
       Objective function: this is the total contribution, given by
$$C = 10x + 15y$$
       which is to be maximised.

(b)   **Constraints:**

   (i)   Assembly time:

$$x + 2y \leq 600$$

   (ii)   Inspection:

$$\frac{7.5}{60}x + \frac{30}{60}y \leq 100$$

       Multiply through by 8 to clear fractions:

$$x + 4y \leq 800$$

   (iii)   Package time:

$$\frac{3}{60}x + \frac{20}{60}y \leq 60$$

Multiply through by 60 to clear fractions:

$3x + 20y \leq 3,600$

(iv)   Engineering limitation on X

$x \leq 500$

(v)   Non-negativity

$x \geq 0$
$y \geq 0$

(c)   **Calculations for graph**

(i) $x + 2y = 600$
When $x = 0$, $y = 300$
When $y = 0$, $x = 600$

(ii) $x + 4y = 800$
When $x = 0$, $y = 200$
When $y = 0$, $x = 800$

(iii) $3x + 20y = 3,600$
When $x = 0$, $y = 180$
When $y = 0$, $x = 1,200$

The x scale must go to 1,200 and the y scale to 300

Iso-contribution line:

Let $C = 1,500$, giving $10x + 15y = 1,500$
When $x = 0$, $y = 100$
When $y = 0$, $x = 150$

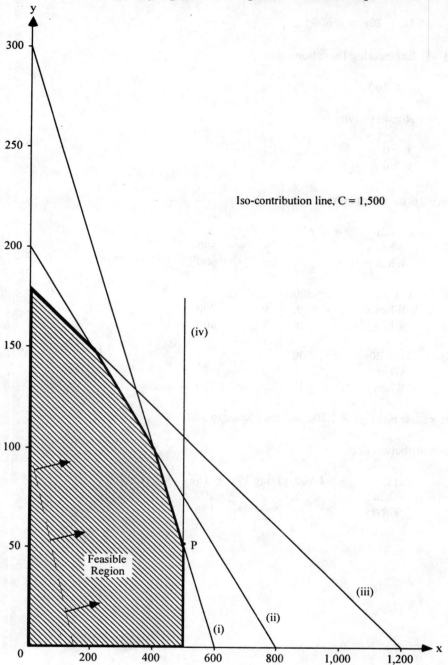

Linear programme for production of components X & Y

(d)   Moving the iso-contribution line away from the origin, keeping the same slope, the last point of the feasibility region to be reached is P, where $x = 500$, $y = 50$.

Hence for maximum contribution, produce 500 X and 50 Y per week,

Contribution   = $10 \times 500 + 15 \times 50$ (£)
              =   £5,750 per week

12 SIMULATION

INTRODUCTION & LEARNING OBJECTIVES

Syllabus area 7d. Simulation; application of simple probability distributions and random numbers to problems of budgeting, queues, stocks, accidents etc. (Ability required 3).

The use of the computer in these techniques. (Ability required 1).

When you have studied this chapter you should be able to do the following:

- Know the steps in setting up a simulation.

- Be able to analyse and simulate a complex situation.

- Appreciate the use of computers in the techniques of linear programming and simulation.

---

1 SIMULATION

1.1 Introduction

[Definition] A **simulation** model can be defined as a model which imitates real-life conditions.

Earlier in this text we looked at simple mathematical models which were designed to handle a specific situation. Simple models cannot, however, handle complicated mathematical relationships, they simply cannot represent the problem in a realistic way. For instance, using linear programming all the relationships between the variables are assumed to be linear ie, if output doubles, costs double. Obviously in real life this is not the case. In such cases simulation can be used.

Simulation can be used to solve a variety of problems, such as queuing, component replacement, stock control and even corporate financial models.

1.2 Disadvantages of simulation

(a) A simulation run uses only a sample of test data. It is necessary therefore, to carry out further runs before the results are sufficiently accurate. Statistical techniques can be applied to the results to estimate their accuracy.

(b) Since simulation involves the application of test data to a *model*, it is inevitably a lengthy process, and will usually necessitate the use of a computer.

(c)   Simulation is not an optimisation technique. Whereas other techniques (such as linear programming) determine the optimal solution, simulation only indicates the likely results of taking a particular decision. It is necessary for the decision-maker to evaluate the results according to pre-determined criteria, and to compare the results of different decisions in an attempt to identify the optimal solution. However, by carrying out a large number of simulations with varying values of the inputs, an optimum can sometimes be found. For example, by simulating a stock control system with different re-order levels and quantities, the optimum values can be found, but it is a very lengthy process, only feasible with the use of a computer.

1.3   Advantages of simulation

(a)   Where the application of analytical techniques would be unsuitable, for instance for strategical planning models, simulation provides a method of at least providing information if not solving problems. It is also more suitable where the user wishes to study a range of possible combinations of variables and the different outcomes that may occur.

(b)   Simplifying assumptions, necessary in both simulation and mathematical models, are not usually so great in the former. This means that more variables can be included providing a more realistic model.

(c)   Some decision-makers place more reliance on simulation methods even where analytical methods are appropriate. This is particularly true where the amount of uncertain variables is large so that EV calculations would give a false view of possible variations in outcomes.

(d)   Simulation can provide an insight into how the system behaves before reaching equilibrium. For example, simulation of a queuing system will show how the system can vary from start-up, whereas queuing formulae will only give the steady state results.

1.4   Planning a simulation

Step 1   Analyse the problem, determining what decisions are involved and by what criteria the results are to be measured.

Step 2   Data about the problem must be collected to assist in formulating and testing the model.

Step 3   The model must be formulated and exhaustively tested with the collected data to ensure that it is valid. Testing may indicate areas in which the model has been over-simplified, or conversely where simplifications can be made.

Step 4   The parameters of the variables must be estimated from collected data and assessed for interdependence of variables.

Step 5   The hypotheses to be tested are determined.

Step 6   The simulation run is now carried out, using random data determined by the parameters of the variables. The simulation can be undertaken manually or by computer: in the latter case there is the additional step of writing and testing the computer program.

1.5   Example

The techniques of carrying out a simulation can best be shown by means of a simple illustration.

A company has several identical machines in a production department, each containing three bearings which are liable to fail due to wear. The company has in the past replaced bearings when they failed, but, because of the high cost of idle time, the company wishes to consider a preventive maintenance policy. Two alternative criteria have been selected:

(a)   If one bearing fails, replace all three:

(b)   If one bearing fails, replace it and any other bearing which has been in use for 1,700 hours or more.

The following data is available:

(a)   To replace one bearing costs £30;

(b)   To replace two bearings costs £40;

(c)   To replace three bearings costs £50;

(d)   A survey of 150 bearings produced the following performance records:

Life in hours	1,050 – 1,349	1,350 – 1,649	1,650 – 1,949	1,950 – 2,249	Total
No. of bearings	18	60	54	18	150
% of bearings	12	40	36	12	100

(e)   random number table – 2 digit:

58	79	15	11	92
22	46	02	73	34
81	87	24	17	60

1.6   Solution

The model used is a simple one, where the life of a bearing is determined by the use of random numbers. We use the random numbers 00 to 99 and allocate to each number a life in proportion to class frequencies as follows:

Random numbers 00 to 11   indicate a life between 1,050 and 1,349 (twelve random numbers corresponding to 12% of the bearings).

Random numbers 12 to 51   indicate a life between 1,350 and 1,649 (forty random numbers corresponding to 40% of the bearings), etc.

Specific lives are then allocated to each number by spreading the numbers equally amongst the class, as indicated by the diagram:

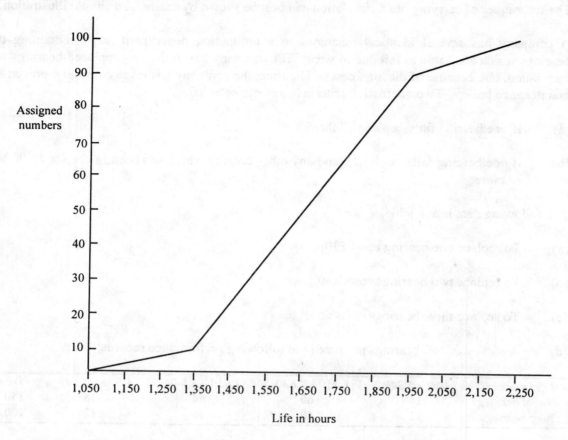

Random numbers are then chosen, in order, from a random number table and the results of each policy evaluated on a work table.

(a)   Replace all bearings when one fails

Using the random number table given in (e) in the question:

		Bearing number					Time of failure	Cumulative cost	Cost per hour of operation
		1		2		3			
Time	RN	Life	RN	Life	RN	Life			£
									£
0	58	1,700	79	1,875	15	1,380	1,380	50	$\frac{50}{1,380}$
1,380	11	1,050	92	2,050	22	1,425	2,430	100	$\frac{100}{2,430}$

Picking the first three random numbers (58, 79, 15) and reading from the graph gives bearing lives of 1,700, 1,875 and 1,380. Thus, after 1,380 hours one bearing fails and, under this policy, they are all replaced at a cost of £50. At this stage the cost per hour of operation is £50 ÷ 1,380. Three more random numbers are chosen and the process repeated, giving a cost per hour of operation of £100 ÷ 2,430.

The process is continually repeated until the cost per hour of operation settles to a more or less constant value, this situation being called the *steady state situation*.

The alternative policy is then evaluated.

(b)   Replace all bearings older than 1,700 hours when one fails

		Bearing number 1			2 RN	Life	Age	Life left	3 RN	Life	Age	Life left	Time of failure	Cost of replacement	Cumulative cost	Cost/hr of operation
Time	RN	Life	Age	Life left	RN	Life	Age	Life left	RN	Life	Age	Life left		£	£	£
0	58	1,700	1,380	320	79	1,875	1,380	495	15	1,380	1,380	F	1,380	30	30	$\frac{30}{1,380}$
1,380		320	1,700	F		495	1,700	R	11	1,050	320	730	1,700	40	70	$\frac{70}{1,700}$
1,700	92	2,050			22	1,425						730	2,430	30	100	$\frac{100}{2,430}$

F denotes failure,
R denotes replacement.

As before, bearing no. 3 fails after 1,380 hours and is replaced. The other bearings aged less than 1,700 hours are not replaced. The cost is £30 and the cost per hour of operation is £30/1,380. After a further 320 hours, bearing no. 1, which has a life of 1,700 hours, fails and is replaced. Bearing no. 2 is also replaced, being 1,700 hours old, whereas bearing no. 3 is now only 320 hours old. The cost of replacement is £40 and the cost per hour of operation is £70/1,700. This process is repeated until the steady state situation is reached.

The criterion for choosing the policy would be to minimise the cost per hour of operation, so the two steady state costs are compared and the policy with the smallest cost is chosen.

A slightly simpler but less accurate approach would be to assume that all life values occur at the mid-point of each group ie, 1,200, 1,500, 1,800 and 2,100 hours. Thus random numbers from 00 to 11 would all return a life of 1,200 hours, those from 12 to 51 all return a life of 1,500 hours, etc. This method is used in the next example.

1.7   Probabilistic and deterministic simulation

In the above example, the life of a bearing was not known for certain, but the probability distribution was estimated. This was a case of probabilistic simulation, sometimes referred to as *Monte Carlo* simulation.

Much simpler examples occur when variables are known eg, if the economic order quantity for stock is determined by simulation when weekly demand is known with certainty. This is deterministic simulation.

1.8   Queue simulation

The following data gives the distributions of inter-arrival times (ie, time interval between successive arrivals) and lengths of service for a server system with one service point:

Inter-arrival time (minutes)		Probability
0 and less than	2	0.28
2 and less than	4	0.35
4 and less than	6	0.27
6 and less than	8	0.10
		1.00

Service length (minutes)		Probability
0 and less than	2	0.20
2 and less than	4	0.55
4 and less than	6	0.25
		———
		1.00

It is required to simulate the flow of customers through the system and obtain data on the time spent in the queue and length of queue.

Method

Step 1 Assume that all items in a group have the value of the interval centre so that the inter-arrival times are 1, 3, 5 and 7 minutes and the service times 1, 3 and 5 minutes, respectively.

Step 2 Allocate two digit numbers to each group in proportion to the probability.

Step 3 Draw up a suitable simulation table.

Step 4 Select inter-arrival times and lengths of service by random numbers from a table of random numbers or other source.

Step 5 Follow each customer through the system recording the required information.

It may be assumed that the arrival of the first customer initiates the system, so that the time of arrival for this customer is zero.

Allocation of digits

Inter-arrival time (minutes)	Probability	Digit allocation
1	0.28	00-27
3	0.35	28-62
5	0.27	63-89
7	0.10	90-99

The first 28 numbers (00 to 27) are allocated to an inter-arrival time of 1 minute, the next 35 numbers (28 – 62) are allocated to an inter-arrival time of 3 minutes, and so on.

Similarly, for lengths of service:

Length of service (minutes)	Probability	Digit allocation
1	0.20	00-19
3	0.55	20-74
5	0.25	75-99

Simulation table (random numbers as given)

Customer no.	Ran. no. arrival	Arrival interval	Time of arrival	Time service begins	Ran. no., service	Length of service	Time service ends	Time in queue	No. in queue after arrival	Cum. average time in queue
(1)	(2)	(3)	(4)	(5)	(6)	(7)	(8)	(9)	(10)	(11)
1	-	-	0	0	16	1	1	0	0	0
2	03	1	1	1	22	3	4	0	0	0
3	47	3	4	4	77	5	9	0	0	0
4	43	3	7	9	94	5	14	2	1	0.5
5	23	1	8	14	39	3	17	6	2	1.6
6	86	5	13	17	49	3	20	4	2	2.0
7	36	3	16	20	54	3	23	4	2	2.3
8	02	1	17	23	85	5	28	6	2	2.8
9	26	1	18	28	70	3	31	10	3	3.6
10	92	7	25	31	46	3	34	6	2	3.8
etc.										

Explanation of table

Customer 1 initiates the system, so arrives at time 0. He can go straight to the service point, so service starts at time 0. The random number for length of service is 16. Reference to the digit allocation shows that this corresponds to a length of service of 1 minute. Service will therefore be completed at 1 minute after zero and he will leave the system. There was no queue.

Following through a later customer as a typical example, customer 6 has a random number for arrival interval of 86. Reference to the digit allocation table gives an arrival interval of 5 minutes. He therefore arrived 5 minutes after the previous customer, so his time of arrival was $8 + 5 = 13$ minutes. He cannot start to be served until the previous customer has finished, which is at time 17 minutes after zero. He must therefore queue for $17 - 13 = 4$ minutes. When he arrived, customer 4 was still being served (his service did not finish until 14 minutes), customer 5 was forming a queue so customer 6 will be the second in the queue. A random number of 49 for his service time gives a length of 3 minutes, so he left the system at $17 + 3 = 20$ minutes after zero.

The cumulative average time spent in the queue is the sum of all the values in column 9 divided by the number of customers. Thus, the cumulative average time in the queue up to and including customer 6 is $(2 + 6 + 4)/6 = 2.0$.

When to stop the simulation

It will be found that, provided the system is a stable one, the cumulative average in column 11 eventually settles down to a steady value. When this is so, the random effects of the initial phase of the system have been removed and the simulation can be stopped. In practice, this may take several thousand simulations.

Advantages of the simulation method

The above method makes no assumption about the nature of the distributions, as is necessary for applying queuing formulae. The mathematics is extremely simple, but it does require many simulations, which are only practicable on a computer. It also gives an indication of what can happen in the initial stages of the system whereas queuing formulae only give the queuing situation once the system has settled down to a steady state.

1.9 Simulation and the Poisson distribution

The Poisson distribution (named after the French mathematician who invented it) is a probability distribution used to model **discrete** variable, ie, those that can only take integer values.

An example would be the number of cars passing a particular point in a road per minute. It could be 0, 1, 2, 3, etc in a particular minute but could not be 2.7 cars or any other non-integer. So while the normal distribution is often used to model continuous variables, the Poisson distribution is often used to model discrete variables.

Example

Seismograph records over a number of years indicate that in a particular place the average number of earthquakes (over a given strength) is two a year.

Calculate the probability that in the next year there will be

(a)   zero earthquakes
(b)   at least three earthquakes.

Solution

The CIMA book of mathematical tables contains a set of tables (Table 9) which enables Poisson probabilities to be read directly from the table. All you need is a value for m, the expected number of occurrences.

We have m = 2, so look to the column of probabilities headed m = 2.0. We can read off the probabilities directly:

p (0 earthquakes next year)	=	0.1353
p (1 earthquake next year)	=	0.2707
p (2 earthquakes next year)	=	0.2707
p (3 earthquakes next year)	=	0.1804

To answer the questions that were set:

(a)   p (zero earthquakes next year)   =   0.1353

(b)   p (at least 3 earthquakes next year)
$$
\begin{aligned}
&= p(3) + p(4) + \ldots\ldots\ldots \\
&= 1 - [p(0) + p(1) + p(2)] \\
&= 1 - 0.1353 - 0.2707 - 0.2707 \\
&= 0.3233.
\end{aligned}
$$

1.10   Activity

Accident records show that, on average, three people die in road accidents in a certain county each week. Estimate the probability that during the coming week exactly four people will die in road accidents.

1.11   Activity solution

m = 3

From tables, p(4) = 0.1680

So the probability that four people will die next week in road accidents is 0.168.

1.12   Mean and variance of a Poisson distribution

You would not be asked to prove this relationship, but you should be aware of the fact that m, the expected value or mean of a Poisson distribution, is also the variance of the distribution.

Example

Consider the Poisson probability distribution with m = 0.5.

Number of items x	Probability p	xp	$p(x - \bar{x})^2$
0	0.6065	0	0.1516
1	0.3033	0.3033	0.0758
2	0.0758	0.1516	0.1706
3	0.0126	0.0378	0.0787
4	0.0016	0.0064	0.0196
5	0.0002	0.0010	0.0041
		0.5001	0.5004

Allowing for roundings we see that:

$$\text{Mean } \bar{x} = \Sigma xp = 0.5 = m$$

$$\text{Variance } s^2 = \Sigma p(x - \bar{x})^2 = 0.5 = m$$

1.13   Using the Poisson distribution in a simulation exercise

In a simulation exercise the Poisson distribution can be used to generate the input into the model. For example if a queue simulation was being carried out and it was known that the average time interval between successive arrivals was 1.5 minutes, a probability distribution of inter-arrival times could be read straight off the Poisson tables with m = 1.5 to be:

Inter-arrival time (minutes)	Probability (rounded to 2 dp)
0	0.22
1	0.33
2	0.25
3	0.13
4	0.05
5	0.01
6	0.01
	1.00

Random numbers could then be allocated to the inter-arrival times in the usual way as described earlier, and the simulation carried out.

2   SPECIALIST PACKAGES AND PROJECT PLANNING/CONTROL

2.1   Introduction

Project planning commences with the preparation of a list of possible actions and their likely outcomes which are commonly expressed in the form of a decision tree. This is then evaluated and the optimal course of action chosen. The difficulty of solving such situations manually is that the answer obtained is dependent on a number of uncertain variables. To evaluate the effect of a change in these variables manually would be very time consuming, yet it is necessary if the project is to be properly evaluated.

This problem is similar to that in the earlier paragraph - what is needed is an efficient way of determining the sensitivity of the solution to a change in the variables.

In order to this a specialist package is required, this will be able to draw the decision tree based on the original data and evaluate it, and then manipulate each of the values in turn and redraw and evaluate the decision tree based on the new values. To do this the relevant data must be entered first, namely:

(a)   the actions which may be taken;
(b)   the costs of those actions;
(c)   the possible outcomes of those actions;
(d)   the value of those possible outcomes; and
(e)   the likelihood of those outcomes occurring.

These must be entered for each action point and linkages between outcomes and subsequent action points must also be specified.

Once the decision as to which course of action is to be taken has been made it is then necessary to identify its critical path and the resources it requires. This forms the main part of planning and controlling the project in an operational sense.

Again this may be done by hand but an alternative is to use a specialist computer package which may be able to cope more easily with modifications to the original plan. The project will need to be divided into a series of tasks, and estimates made of the resources required, including the time to complete the task. These details must be entered into the package together with the task sequence necessary to complete the project and any requirements concerning the commencement of a task, for example:

> 'Task 2 cannot start until Task 1 is completed, but Task 3 is not dependent on the completion of Tasks 1 or 2, Task 4 cannot start until Tasks 1, 2 and 3 are completed.'

Different packages contain different ways of entering such information, so no attempt will be made here to give a specific method. Needless to say, this is essential information if an accurate network is to be produced and evaluated. Where such packages have clear advantages over non-computerised methods is that:

(a)   a Gantt chart may also be produced from the same data input showing the allocation of resources to the project; and

(b)   an alteration of the data on one or more of the tasks can be dealt with and a revised network/Gantt chart drawn automatically.

Some of these packages also allow actual data to be entered for each task, thus allowing comparisons to be made with plans. This would be important, for example, if the duration of an early task differs from that expected and affects later tasks to the extent that they are on the critical path.

Illustration

The following screen shows the input of a typical network package

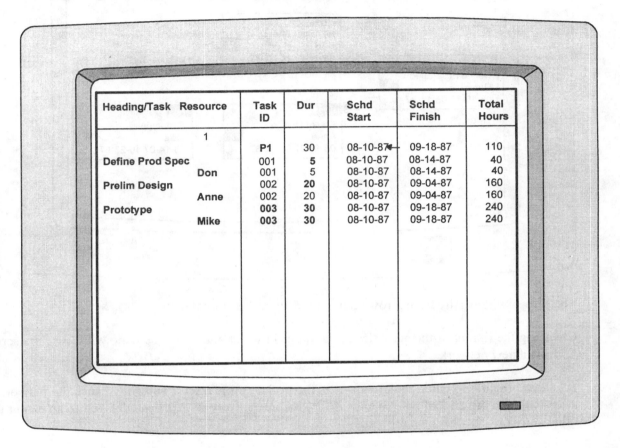

Heading/Task Resource	Task ID	Dur	Schd Start	Schd Finish	Total Hours
1					
	P1	30	08-10-87	09-18-87	110
Define Prod Spec	001	5	08-10-87	08-14-87	40
Don	001	5	08-10-87	08-14-87	40
Prelim Design	002	20	08-10-87	09-04-87	160
Anne	002	20	08-10-87	09-04-87	160
Prototype	003	30	08-10-87	09-18-87	240
Mike	003	30	08-10-87	09-18-87	240

Three people (Don, Anne and Mike) are going to perform three activities (001, 002 and 003) which will take a given number of days (5, 20 and 30 respectively). The scheduled start time is entered. The package will calculate the finish time.

The package will now have an input screen for determining the order in which the activities must be done (eg, 001 must precede 002 etc). The output screen will then look typically as follows:

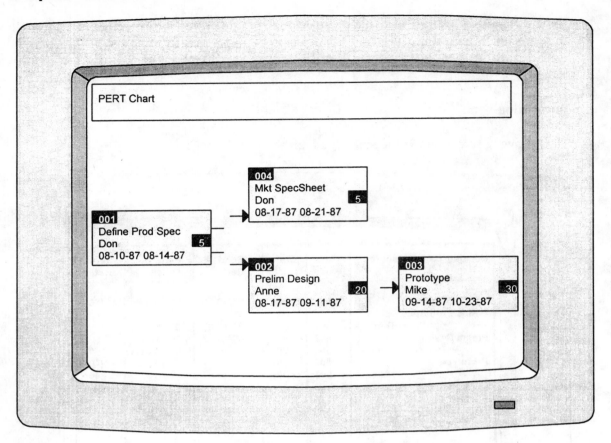

The screen will usually have arrow coding to identify the critical path.

Changing the timing of the activities or the order in which they must be done will cause the screen to show a new network.

It is also possible to enter actual values as the project progresses. This may cause the network to alter and even the critical path to alter if for example an activity has been delayed to an extent that other activities now become critical.

The value of this is clearly inestimable as it enables management to control the project precisely, adjusting the resource inputs to reflect changing conditions.

3   CHAPTER SUMMARY

This chapter described the modelling of real-life decision-making situations using simulation. The technique is not difficult but needs considerable practice in order to be confident in handling such questions.

4   SELF TEST QUESTIONS

4.1   State three advantages and three disadvantages of simulation. (1.2, 1.3)

4.2   What are the steps in planning a simulation? (1.4)

4.3

Demand:	0 - 2	3 - 5	6 - 8
Probability:	0.2	0.5	0.3

What range of random numbers would you allocate to the 3 - 5 range, assume you start allocating from random digit 0? (1.6)

4.4   What type of simulation is the Monte Carlo method? (1.7)

5   EXAMINATION TYPE QUESTIONS

5.1   AB Travel Agency

The AB Travel Agency deals with numerous personal callers each day and prides itself on its level of service. The time to deal with each caller depends on the client's requirements which range from, say, a request for a brochure to booking a round-the-world cruise. If clients have to wait more than 10 minutes for attention it is AB's policy for the manager to see them personally and to give them a £5 holiday voucher.

Observations have shown that the time taken to deal with clients and their arrival patterns follow the distributions below:

Time to deal with clients

Minutes	*Probability*
2	0.05
4	0.10
6	0.15
10	0.30
14	0.25
20	0.10
30	0.05
	1.00

Time between arrivals

Minutes	*Probability*
1	0.2
8	0.4
15	0.3
25	0.1
	1.00

You are required:

(a)   to describe how you would simulate the operation of the Travel Agency based on the use of Random Number Tables;

(5 marks)

(b)   to simulate the arrival and serving of 12 clients and show the number of customers who receive a voucher (use line 1 of the Random Numbers below to derive the arrival pattern and Line 2 for the serving times);

Random Numbers

Line 1	03	47	43	73	86	36	96	47	36	61	46	98
Line 2	63	71	62	33	26	16	80	45	60	11	14	10

(9 marks)

(c)   to calculate the weekly cost of vouchers, assuming the proportion receiving vouchers derived from (b) applies throughout a week of 50 opening hours.

(3 marks)

(Total: 17 marks)

5.2   Inventory control

A large garage, open for 50 weeks each year, is examining its inventory policy in relation to one type of tyre it stocks. Weekly demand for the tyre is distributed according to the following table.

Weekly demand	Probability
20	0.1
30	0.6
40	0.3

The garage uses a reorder level of 100 for this tyre and the lead time is fixed at three weeks.

The simple EOQ formula has shown that the optimum order quantity for this tyre is 160.

(a)   Use the random digits below to simulate the inventory operation for a period of 10 weeks in order to estimate the total weekly stockholding costs of this garage. Start with an initial stock of 150, use the order quantity found in (b) and assume that the cost of being out of stock is £0.25 per tyre. State any further assumptions made and explain how the demand data is generated.

Random digits: 6 9 1 4 7 1 8 9 3 0

(8 marks)

(b)   Explain how this simulation method might be used to determine the optimum order quantity and reorder level.

(2 marks)
(Total: 10 marks)

6   ANSWERS TO EXAMINATION TYPE QUESTIONS

6.1   AB Travel Agency

(a)   The operation of the system is studied first to find the procedure for dealing with clients and to obtain the probability distributions of arrivals and services.

The operation is then simulated by following each simulated client through the system, selecting time of arrival and length of service with probability proportional to size. This is achieved by allocating to each probability group a range of two digit numbers, the range being proportional to the probability of the group. Random number tables are then used to select the arrival interval and service time for each client. The times of arrival, length of wait and length of service for each client is recorded on a simulation pro-forma. If the waiting time is longer than 10 minutes this is recorded.

In practice a running average of waiting or service time would be recorded. When this settles down to a steady state, the simulation is finished. This may take many simulations to achieve and is best done on a computer.

(b)   Allocation of sampling digits:

Service times			Arrival times		
Service time (minutes)	Probability	Digit allocation	Arrival (minutes)	Probability	Digit allocation
2	0.05	00 – 04	1	0.2	00 – 19
4	0.10	05 – 14	8	0.4	20 – 59
6	0.15	15 – 29	15	0.3	60 – 89
10	0.30	30 – 59	25	0.1	90 – 99
14	0.25	60 – 84			
20	0.10	85 – 94			
30	0.05	95 – 99			

Simulation table

Client No.	R number arrival	Arrival interval	Arrival time	Start of service	R number service	Length of service	Depart-ure time	Time in queue	See manager
1	03	1	1	1	63	14	15	0	
2	47	8	9	15	71	14	29	6	√
3	43	8	17	29	62	14	43	12	√
4	73	15	32	43	33	10	53	11	
5	86	15	47	53	26	6	59	6	
6	36	8	55	59	16	6	65	4	
7	96	25	80	80	80	14	94	0	
8	47	8	88	94	45	10	104	6	
9	36	8	96	104	60	14	118	8	
10	61	15	111	118	11	4	122	7	
11	46	8	119	122	14	4	126	3	
12	98	25	144	144	10	4	148	0	

(Tutorial notes:

(i)   Two equally correct variants are possible.

    (A)   The system could be initiated by the first arrival who would therefore arrive at time zero. The random numbers would then be used to determine the arrival times of subsequent clients.

    (B)   As the arrival interval probabilities are only given to one significant figure, one digit numbers could have been used for this distribution.

These would give different results for the twelve simulations, although in the long run simulation they would make no difference.

(ii)   Time of start of service is whichever time is the greater of arrival time and time of departure of the previous client.

(iii)   It has been assumed that those clients who see the manager are still in the system and are therefore allocated their service time. If the manager takes them out of the system and allows the assistant to deal with the next client, the service time of those who see the manager would be zero.*)

(c)   In 148 minutes operation, two clients have seen the manager.

Hence the number seeing the manager in 50 hours $= \dfrac{2}{148} \times 50 \times 60$

$= 40.54$

Cost @ £5 $= 40.54 \times £5$

$= £202.7$

Tutorial note: an alternative method is to take $\frac{2}{12}$ ths of the number of clients who arrive in 50 hours. This is calculated as follows:

Time	Probability	Time × Probability
1	0.2	0.2
8	0.4	3.2
15	0.3	4.5
25	0.1	2.5

Average arrival interval in minutes =   10.4

Number of customers in 50 hours $= \dfrac{50 \times 60}{10.4}$

$\dfrac{2}{12}$ th of these see the manager $= \dfrac{2}{12} \times \dfrac{50 \times 60}{10.4}$

$= 48.08$

Cost @ £5 $= 48.08 \times £5$

$= £240.4$

The difference between the results from the two methods is due to short run random errors. In the long run, the results would agree.

6.2   Inventory control

(a)   **Allocation of digits**

Demand	Probability	Digit allocation
20	0.1	0
30	0.6	1 - 6
40	0.3	7 - 9

Simulation table

Week	Opening stock	Random no.	Demand	Delivery	Closing stock	Stock outs	S/O costs	Re-order ?	Re-order cost	Holding cost	Total cost
1	150	6	30	-	120	-	-	-	-	4.05	4.05
2	120	9	40	-	80	-	-	Yes	12	3.00	15.00
3	80	1	30	-	50	-	-	-	-	1.95	1.95
4	50	4	30	-	20	-	-	-	-	1.05	1.05
5	20	7	40	160	140	20	5	-	-	0.30	5.30
6	140	1	30	-	110	-	-	-	-	3.75	3.75
7	110	8	40	-	70	-	-	Yes	12	2.70	14.70
8	70	9	40	-	30	-	-	-	-	1.50	1.50
9	30	3	30	-	0	-	-	-	-	0.45	0.45
10	0	0	20	160	140	20	5	-	-	0	5.00
											52.75

$$\text{Average weekly cost} = \frac{52.75}{10} = £5.275$$

(Tutorial notes

(i)   The weekly holding cost per item $= \dfrac{\text{Annual holding cost}}{50}$

$$= \frac{£1.5}{50}$$

$$= £0.03$$

The total weekly holding cost is calculated on the average stock during the week. Thus for week one,

Average stock $= \dfrac{150 - 120}{2} = 135$

Holding cost $= 135 \times £0.03 = £4.05$

(ii)   On week 5 the opening stock was 20. The demand was 40, resulting in 20 stock outs. These 20 must be deducted from the 160 delivered at the end of the week, so that the closing stock is 140.

The stock-out cost $= £20 \times 0.25 = £5.00)$

Assumptions

(i)   Re-orders are made at the end of the week in which the stock falls to 100. Deliveries are therefore at the end of the third week on.

(ii)   The holding cost per item per week is $\frac{1}{50}$th of the annual cost. The weekly holding cost is calculated on the average stock during the week.

(iii)   Unfulfilled demands due to stock-out can be deferred until new stock is received, but each stock-out incurs the full weekly stock-out cost of £0.25.

Generation of demand data

The digits 0 to 9 are allocated to each demand in proportion to the probabilities ie, one digit to the first group, 6 digits to the second and 3 digits to the third.

Each week a random digit is taken from those given in the question and in whichever group this falls in the digit allocation, the corresponding demand is taken. Thus the first random number is 6. This falls in the digit group 1 to 6, which corresponds to a demand of 30, and so on.

(b)   By carrying out simulations with different re-order quantities and different re-order levels, calculating the average weekly cost in each case, the order quantity and level that gives the lowest average cost could be found.

13 FORECASTING AND REGRESSION

INTRODUCTION & LEARNING OBJECTIVES

Syllabus area 7e. Cost, demand and sales forecasting; qualitative methods. (Ability required 2).

Applications of least squares linear regression. (Ability required 3).

When you have studied this chapter you should be able to do the following:

- Describe different intuitive forecasting methods for qualitative issues.
- Calculate a regression line using the method of least squares.
- Calculate and interpret the correlation coefficient r.
- Interpret the meaning of the $100r^2$ coefficient.
- Determine a rank correlation coefficient.

---

1 FORECASTING METHODOLOGY

1.1 Projection

Projection is merely the extension of historical data into the future. Various techniques can be applied – such as regression analysis or exponential smoothing on the one hand, or putting a ruler across a graph on the other.

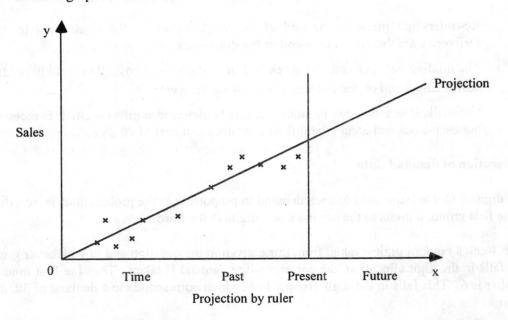

Projection by ruler

The student should note that such a method is very crude – your own ruler projection may vary from that illustrated on the graph. Other techniques are considered later.

Projections may give a good estimate of future results where a very stable situation is being considered, or where the situation is not affected by outside factors. It does not, however, anticipate changes in market conditions.

1.2   Prediction

Where outside factors are known to influence the situation in question, models can be built to take these external factors into account. This is known as *prediction*.

The difference between projection and prediction can best be illustrated by an example.

Building society example

For the past three months the net inflow of funds into a building society has been maintained at a static level of £30,000 per month. The projection for the next month's net inflow would be £30,000 based on past performance. However, if the base rate had just increased by 1%, and the building society is slow to adjust its interest rates accordingly, people may transfer their funds to investments now offering higher interest rates. The prediction of next month's net inflow would be less than £30,000, say £25,000.

1.3   Forecasting

Forecasting is more sophisticated than prediction. As well as considering known effects of changes in other situations, the forecaster brings his judgement to bear on the situation. To consider the example above, the forecaster may know that the government wishes to push interest rates even higher, and he would forecast gloomier results, a net inflow of only £20,000.

Forecasting does not remove risk and uncertainties, but it assists planning. A company would prefer to eliminate uncertainties entirely, but where this is not possible, forecasting can reduce the risks involved.

1.4   Designing a system

To decide upon its long-term policy and plan, a company will need to forecast results, such as sales. A system of forecasting will be designed, having regard to the following items:

(a) *Data*. Any forecast will take into consideration results which have been obtained in the past. No situation is static and the most up-to-date results are the most relevant to the forecasting model.

(b) *Models*. The forecaster must try to make a model which will fit the situation under review. He will need to plot graphs of past results to look for patterns, trends, seasonal fluctuations and other cycles which might appear from past results, which must be reflected in the model.

(c) *Smoothing*. As indicated above, the most recent data is the most relevant, and the system must have some way of including the new data. However, the model must be stable, and not react too violently to 'hiccups' in the data. This is known as smoothing, and techniques used include exponential smoothing and moving averages.

(d) *Forecasting*. The projections of the model must then be evaluated in the light of any outside factors or changed conditions.

(e)   *Errors*. Any forecast is, at best, a close approximation of an actual result, and the forecaster will want to make allowances for errors. Statistical theory can be applied to errors in forecasting by assuming that errors came from a normal distribution with a mean of zero. This enables the forecaster to calculate the tolerances on the forecast.

2   COST PREDICTION

2.1   Introduction

The use of the analysis described above rests on being able to forecast the costs associated with a given level of activity. Such data is not available from traditional cost analysis, and alternative approaches must be used. In this process historical information provides valuable guidance, but it must be recognised that the environment is not static, and what was relevant in the past may not be relevant in the future.

In all approaches to cost prediction the assumption is made that the accountant's model of cost behaviour is valid, and therefore the relation between costs, y, and activity, x, is of the form:

$$y = a + bx$$

$$\text{where: } \begin{aligned} y &= \text{total costs} \\ x &= \text{activity} \\ a &= \text{fixed costs} \\ b &= \text{unit variable (or marginal) cost} \end{aligned}$$

The various approaches are considered below, followed by the possibility of making less restrictive assumptions about cost behaviour.

2.2   The engineering approach

This approach is based on building up a complete specification of all inputs (eg, materials, labour, overheads) required to produce given levels of output. This approach is therefore based on the technical specification, which is then costed out using expected input prices.

This approach works reasonably well in a single product or start-up situation – indeed in the latter it may be the only feasible approach. However, it is difficult to apply in a multi-product situation, especially where there are joint costs, or the exact output mix is not known.

2.3   The account analysis approach

Rather than using the technical information, this approach uses the information contained in the ledger accounts. These are analysed and categorised as either fixed or variable (or semi-fixed or semi-variable). Thus, for example, material purchase accounts would represent variable costs, office salaries a fixed cost. Since the ledger accounts are not designed for use in this way, some reorganisation and reclassification of accounts may be required.

Students should note that this is the approach implicit in many examination questions.

The problems with this approach are several:

(a)   Inspection does not always indicate the true nature of costs. For example, today factory wages would normally be a fixed cost, with only overtime and/or bonuses as the variable element.

(b)   Accounts are by their nature summaries, and often contain transactions of different categories.

(c)   It rests on historical information with the problems noted above.

2.4   Scatter diagrams

Information about two variables that are considered to be related in some way can be plotted on a scatter diagram, each axis representing one variable. For example, the amount of rainfall and the crop yield per acre could be plotted against each other, or the level of advertising expenditure and sales revenue of a product.

It is important, however, to decide which variable can be used to predict the other – ie, which is the *independent* and which the *dependent variable*. In many cases it is quite clear eg, the amount of rainfall obviously causes a particular crop yield, and not vice-versa. Here, rainfall is the independent variable and crop yield the dependent variable (ie, yield depends on the amount of rainfall). Some relationships have classic 'chicken and egg' characteristics; for example, advertising and sales revenue. Whether a given level of advertising causes a particular level of sales or whether a particular level of sales provokes a certain level of advertising is not quite so clear. In fact, advertising tends to *directly* affect sales levels whereas sales only have an indirect influence on decisions about advertising expenditure and therefore sales tends to be regarded as the dependent variable and advertising expenditure the independent variable.

The independent variable is usually marked along the horizontal (x) axis and the dependent variable along the vertical (y) axis.

Students are advised to think in terms of the x-axis being the cause, and the y-axis the effect.

The values of the two variables are plotted together so that the diagram consists of a number of points. The way in which these are scattered or dispersed indicates if any link is likely to exist between the variables.

For example:

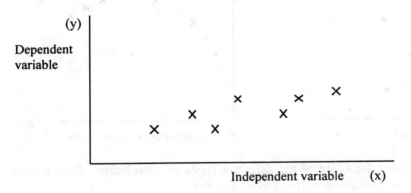

One advantage of a scatter diagram is that it is possible to see quite easily if the points indicate that a relationship exists between the variables ie, to see if any correlation exists between them.

It is not possible to measure the degree of correlation from a scatter diagram. However, as will be seen later, there are methods of calculating a numerical value for this.

Examples of scatter diagrams

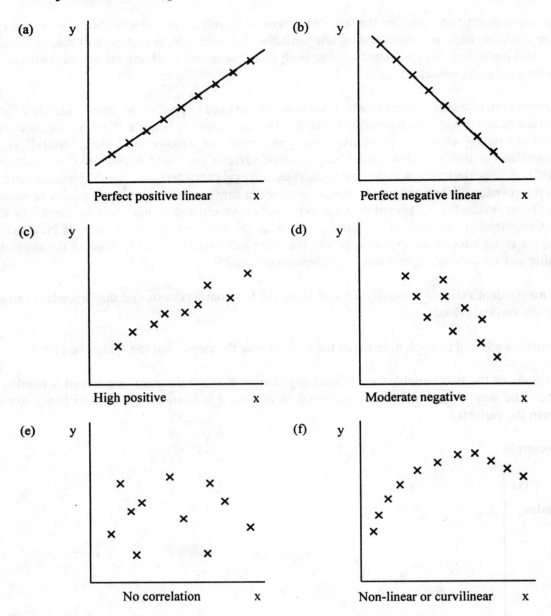

These six scatter diagrams illustrate some of the different types of correlation. Scatter graphs of non-linear correlation can assume many different types of curve.

If the points lie exactly on a straight line, then the correlation is said to be perfect linear correlation. In practice this rarely occurs and it is more usual for the points to be scattered in a band, the narrower the band the higher the degree of correlation.

Positive correlation exists where the values of the variables increase together. Negative correlation exists where one variable increases as the other decreases in value.

Thus, considering the six diagrams:

(a)   This is an example of perfect positive linear correlation since the points lie exactly on a straight line and as '*x*' increases so '*y*' increases.

(b)   This is an example of perfect negative linear correlation since the points again lie on a straight line, but as the *x* values increase so the *y* values decrease.

(c)   In this diagram, the points lie in a narrow band rather than on a straight line, but x and y still tend to increase together, therefore a high degree of positive correlation is evident.

(d)   This time the points lie in a much wider band and, as x increases, y tends to decrease, so this is an example of low negative correlation where, because of the wider spread of the points than those in (c), the correlation is only moderate.

(e)   When the points are scattered all over the diagram, as in this case, then little or no correlation exists between the two variables.

(f)   Here the points lie on an obvious curve. There is a relationship between x and y, but it is not a straight line relationship.

2.5   Regression

When the points on a scatter diagram tend to lie in a narrow band, there is a strong correlation between the variables. This band may be curved or straight. For example:

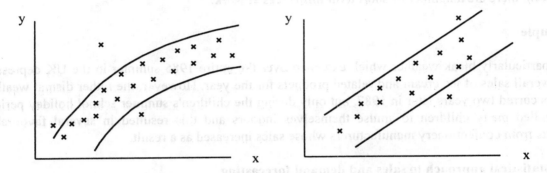

When the band is straight the correlation is linear and the relationship between the variables can be expressed in terms of the equation of a straight line.

2.6   Line of best fit

To obtain a description of the relationship between two variables in the form of an equation in order to forecast values, it is necessary to fit a straight line through the points on the scatter diagram which best represents all of the plotted points. There are several ways of accomplishing this.

One method is simply to fit a line 'by eye' which appears to suit all the points plotted. This method has the disadvantage that if there is a large amount of scatter no two people's lines will coincide and it is, therefore, only suitable where the amount of scatter is small.

The method of least squares regression is the most mathematically correct method of fitting a straight line to a set of data. This is a very important topic and we shall look at it in detail later in the chapter.

2.7   The uses of cost forecasts

(a)   **Budgeting**

Without being able to forecast costs, firms would be unable to implement any budgetary control system. All budgets are based on forecasted figures, even if these figures are based on intuition (see qualitative methods later in the chapter). Obviously, the more accurate the forecasts, the more accurate and useful will be the budgets and hence the control on costs.

(b)   **Setting of standards**

If an organisation uses standard costing as a control method, it will need to be able to set the standards as accurately as possible taking into account management philosophy of standard setting ie, low but obtainable, or high as an incentive. Such costs included in the standard will all be forecast figures.

3   DEMAND AND SALES FORECASTING

3.1   Short and long term fluctuations

The measures of an economic activity will fluctuate due to short and long term factors. For example the fluctuations in sales demand experienced by a company are due to short term causes, mainly seasonal variations and business cycle influences; and long term trends relating to growth, and the effects of government policy. For instance although demand for hand-held ice cream may be rising year into year, during each particular year it will show a pronounced peak during the summer months and a very pronounced trough for the rest of the year. Although seasonal influences can be foreseen, there are a number of short term influences at work.

Example

The particularly bleak weather which extended over the entire 1985 summer in the UK depressed the overall sales of ice cream and related products for the year. However, the rather dismal weather that occurred two years later in 1987, but only during the children's summer school holiday period, compelled many children to amuse themselves indoors and this resulted in several favourable reports from confectionery manufacturers whose sales increased as a result.

The statistical approach to sales and demand forecasting

The statistical approach to sales and demand forecasting is concerned with the projection of **time series**. A variety of methods is available including:

- moving averages
- exponential smoothing
- correlation analysis
- regression analysis.

Where there are numerous short and long term factors at work, forecasting becomes very difficult. If the series of data being analysed is very regular, some simple procedure such as **exponential smoothing** may be sufficient. On the other hand, more complex patterns may require techniques of **regression analysis**, **risk analysis** and **multiple regression**. By using relatively simple mathematics, it may be possible to calculate to a *'level of confidence'* the volume of demand, etc. Trend analysis is a particularly useful tool for companies who have to forecast demand which is influenced by seasonal fluctuations, or where demand is strongly influenced by the business cycle.

The important quantitative techniques involved will be dealt with later in this chapter and the ones following.

4   INTUITIVE FORECASTING METHODS

4.1   The concept

All forecasting techniques involve judgement. For example, statistical techniques require judgements about the amount of past data that is relevant, and how this data should be weighted, while causal models involve judgements about what are the critical variables in the situation. In both cases, judgements have to be made regarding the reliability of the data, the stability of the relationships between the variables over time, and the accuracy of the predictions. Therefore what distinguishes intuitive (or qualitative techniques as they are sometimes called) is the relative emphasis they place on judgement, and the value of such techniques lies not in their statistical sophistication but in the method of systemising expert knowledge. Intuitive forecasting techniques include the use of *think tanks, Delphi methods, scenario planning, brain-storming, derived demand analysis, and social and political forecasting.*

4.2   Think tanks

A think tank comprises a group of experts who are encouraged, in a relatively unstructured atmosphere, to speculate about future developments in particular areas and to identify possible courses of action. The essential features of a think tank are: the relative independence of its members, enabling unpopular, unacceptable or novel ideas to be broached; the relative absence of positional authority in the group, which enables free discussion and argument to take place; and the group nature of the activity which not only makes possible the sharing of knowledge and views, but also encourages a consensus view or preferred **'scenario'**. Think tanks are used by large organisations, including government, and may cross the line between forecasting and planning. However, the organisations that directly employ, or fund them, are careful to emphasise that their think-tank proposals do not necessarily constitute company or government policy.

Think tanks are useful in generating ideas and assessing their feasibility, as well as providing an opportunity to test out reaction to ideas prior to organisational commitment.

4.3   Delphi method

This forecasting technique is named after the Oracle of Apollo at Delphi, renowned for somewhat ambiguous predictions. The method was pioneered at the Rand Corporation in 1950 to assess the timing and likelihood of new technology, and it since has gained considerable recognition as a valuable planning tool with a great variety of applications. Delphi seeks to avoid the group pressures to conformity that are inherent in the *'think tank'* method. It does this by **individually, systematically** and **sequentially** interrogating a panel of experts. Members do not meet, and questioning is conducted by formal questionnaires. A central authority evaluates the responses and feeds these back to the experts who are then interrogated in a new round of questions. After several such rounds, the result, generally, is that widely differing opinions increasingly adapt themselves to one another. The system is based on the premise that knowledge and ideas possessed by some but not all of the experts can be identified and **shared** and this forms the basis for subsequent interrogations.

Example of how **Delphi** works:

Step 1   A **'staff team'** in collaboration with management develop an initial questionnaire.

Step 2   The questionnaire is sent to **'respondents'** who have been carefully selected to participate because of their direct or related interest and experience or knowledge of the issue at hand.

Step 3   The **'staff team'** receives responses which are analysed and collated.

Step 4   The **'staff team'** prepares a summary of the responses of the first questionnaire, and designs a second questionnaire based on the summary. The second questionnaire is then sent to respondents.

Step 5   The respondents independently reappraise their earlier responses taking into account the informed opinion of the other experts, the views of whom they now know. They complete and return the questionnaire.

Step 6   This **'back and forth'** procedure continues as many times as might be required depending on the magnitude of the issue, the dispersal of the responses and the time available for evaluation.

The Delphi method offers a significant advantage over other predictive procedures; because of the anonymity, distortions in forecasting, which may easily occur as a result of the forecasting experts' personal interests, are avoided, or at least reduced. It also promises a way off the horns of a dilemma: the greatest competence is all too often associated with the strongest personal interest, so objective forecasting cannot necessarily be expected from an authoritative and sometimes self-styled 'leading' expert. The main problem with the Delphi method is the inverse of that of the **'think tank'**. In the absence of group pressures there is the possibility of generating as many scenarios as there are experts. In both cases, however, the crucial decision is the selection of the experts.

4.4   Scenario planning

In its most simplest form a scenario might be developed by a specialist writing a detailed account of his or her opinions and views about a particular issue eg, 'The fiscal strategy of a coalition UK government influenced by a minority Liberal balance'. The scenario is then subjected to critical examination, discussion and amendment until the management are satisfied that it represents a constructive dissertation from which decisions can be influenced.

4.5   Brainstorming

Brainstorming is a method of generating ideas. There are different approaches but a popular one is for a number of people (no fewer than six, no more than fifteen) drawn from all levels of management and expertise to meet and propose answers to an initial **single** question posed by the session leader. For instance, they may be asked 'How can we improve product A ?' Each person proposes something, no matter how absurd. No one is allowed to criticise or ridicule another person's idea. One idea provokes another, and so on. All ideas are listed and none rejected at this initial stage. Rationality is not particularly important, but what is essential is that a wide range of ideas emerge and in the ensuing spoken answers for these to be picked up, developed, combined and reshaped. Only after the session are ideas evaluated and screened against rational criteria for practicability. An enlargement on this is for an idea proposed and seen to be promising when matched against criteria, to be subjected to a brainstorming session in which the question 'How might the idea fail ?' is asked.

Brainstorming provides a forum for the interchange of ideas without erecting the normal cultural, behavioural and psychological barriers which so often inhibit the expression of ideas.

4.6   Derived demand analysis

Derived demand exists for a commodity, component or good because of its contribution to the manufacture of another product. For example, the demand for chrome, copper and rubber which are used in the manufacture of many different products, including cars, are derived demands. The forecasting technique involves analysing some aspects of economic activity so that the level of other aspects can be deduced and projected. The principle is simple, but the practice is complex and costly. Take the example of chrome matched with car manufacture. In order to forecast the demand for cars (thus chrome) the forecaster will be faced with the mammoth task of analysing an enormous number of influences and correlated factors. Due to its cost and complexity the technique has a very restricted use.

4.7   Social and political forecasting

(a)   **Delphi**

The Delphi method described above can also be used to forecast social and political trends.

(b)   **Cross-impact analysis and scenarios**

These techniques have particular application in situations where trend analysis and mathematical quantification is difficult. They are used to make technological, social and political forecasts. First, segmental views of the future are built up - for instance a social forecast, an economic forecast, a technological forecast, a financial forecast etc. Then an event in one of the forecasts is taken and a *cross-impact analysis* carried out. For instance, if *wave power* became a reality in 1999 (an event which might be contained in the technological forecast) what effect would this have on social conditions? This can be looked at in probability terms - will such an event happening increase or decrease the probability of other events happening?

Scenarios take the process further: instead of taking segmental views of the future an attempt is made to forecast a complete picture containing events which are consistent with each other. Since it is almost impossible to come up with the **right** scenario three or more forecasts should be made so that the company can assess what action it would have to take in each of the conceivable situations. If a computerised mathematical model of the company is available this can be used to assess the effect of each of the possible scenarios.

(c)   **Probability-diffusion matrix**

An assessment is made of the probability of certain events happening within a given timescale, and of the diffusion of these events - ie, if they happen, how much of the population will they affect? An illustration is given below.

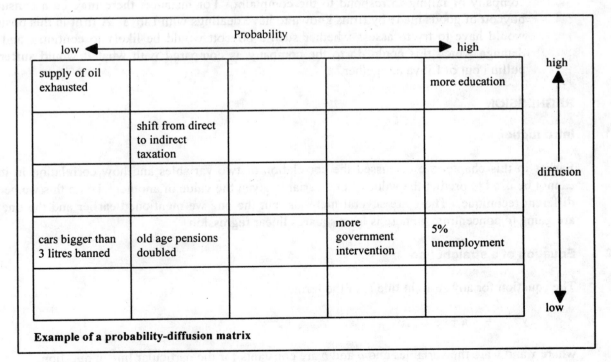

Example of a probability-diffusion matrix

(d)   **Values profile**

This is an attempt to assess the shift of values over a period of time. Two extremes are placed at opposite ends of a scale and an assessment is made as to where the current position lies between those two extremes and what the position will be in *n* years time. Again, this is described by a short illustration.

Key: 1989 | 2000

Stable families				Widespread divorce and single-parent families
Private enterprise				Nationalisation
Private health care				National health service
Religion				Atheism
Saving				Spending

Example of a value profile

(e)   **Social pressures analysis**

A list is made of common complaints against the performance of the company (or industry in general). An attempt is made to assess the effect which changing trends will have on the complaint - eg, will technological progress give rise to more complaint or will it lessen complaint? Further, one must assess the number of people affected and the impact on the company of failing to respond to the complaint. For instance, there may be a consumer boycott of goods made by firms known to have dealings with Libya. A firm in this position would have to try to assess whether such a boycott would be likely to continue, and the damage which this could do to the company as compared with what it would suffer by pulling out of Libya altogether.

5   REGRESSION

5.1   Introduction

Earlier in this chapter we discussed the correlation of two variables and how correlation in itself cannot be used to predict the value of one variable given the value of another. To do this we need a different technique. There are several methods, but the one we mentioned earlier and the one we are going to concentrate on here is least squares linear regression.

5.2   Equation of a straight line

The equation for any straight line is of the form:

$$y = a + bx$$

where *x* and *y* are the variables and *a* and *b* are constants for the particular line in question.

a is called the **intercept** on the y-axis and measures the point at which the line will cut the y-axis.

b is called the **gradient** of the line and measures its degree of slope.

a and *b* can take any value, including zero, and may be positive or negative.

In order to locate any particular line, it is therefore necessary to determine the values of *a* and *b* for that line.

5.3   Parameters of a regression line by inspection

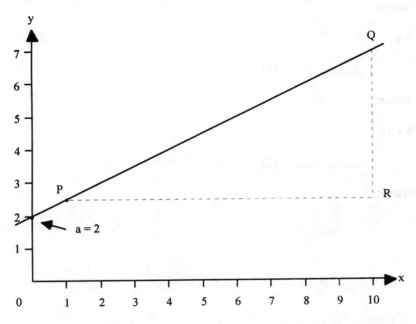

The diagram shows a line which has been fitted to a scatter graph by eye. The points of the scatter graph have been omitted for clarity. It is required to find the values of *a* and *b* for this line in the general equation $y = a + bx$.

Method

a is the intercept on the y-axis, ie, the value of *y* at which the line cuts the y-axis. Hence $a = 2$.

To find the slope, *b*, take any two points (*P* and *Q*) on the line.

The further apart *P* and *Q* are, the more accurate will be the result.

Draw horizontal and vertical lines through *P* and *Q* to meet at *R*.

The length of PR **as measured on the x-scale**   =   9 units

The length of RQ **as measured on the y-axis**   =   4.5 units

The slope $= \dfrac{RQ}{PR} = \dfrac{4.5}{9} = 0.5$, hence $b = 0.5$

The equation is therefore:

$$y \quad = \quad 2 + 0.5x$$

Note: that for this method, no part of the x-scale can be omitted, otherwise the vertical axis is not the true y-axis and the intercept will not be correct.

An alternative method which can be used if part of the x-scale needs to be omitted is to read off from the graph the values of x and y at P and Q, substitute these values into the general equation and solve the resulting simultaneous equations for a and b.

$$y = a + bx$$

at P, $x = 1$, $y = 2.5$, hence:

$$2.5 = a + b \times 1$$

ie, $a + b = 2.5$ ....   (1)

at Q, $x = 10$, $y = 7$,   hence:

$$7 = a + b \times 10$$

ie, $a + 10b = 7$ ....   (2)

Subtract (1) from (2) to eliminate a:

$$a + 10b = 7$$

$$\underline{a + b = 2.5}$$

$$9b = 4.5$$

$$b = \frac{4.5}{9} = 0.5$$

Substitute in (1) to find a:

$$a + 0.5 = 2.5$$

$$a = 2.5 - 0.5$$

$$\therefore \qquad a = 2.0$$

Hence $a = 2.0$ and $b = 0.5$ as before.

5.4   Least squares linear regression

The method of least squares regression is the most mathematically acceptable method of fitting a line to a set of data.

It is possible to calculate two different regression lines for a set of data, depending on whether the horizontal deviations or the vertical deviations of the points from the line are considered. It is the sum of the **squares** of these deviations which is minimised; this overcomes problems that might arise because some deviations would be positive and some negative, depending on whether the point was above or below the line. It is not necessary to go into the theory of this method any more deeply at this level.

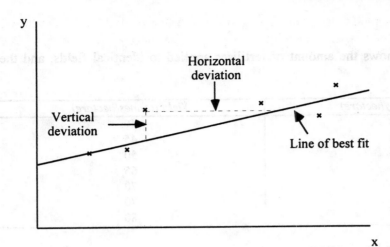

The regression line of *y* on *x* must be used when an estimate of *y* is required for a given value of *x*. This line minimises the sum of the squares of the vertical distances of the points from the line. The regression line of *x* on *y* must be used when an estimate of *x* is required for a known value of *y*. This line minimises the sum of the squares of the horizontal distances of the points from the line.

The scatter diagram has the following appearance when the regression lines are graphed:

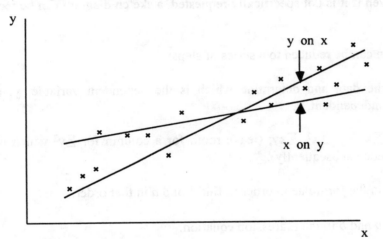

The two lines will intersect at the point $(\bar{x}, \bar{y})$, ie, the mean of the *x*-values and the mean of the *y*-values.

5.5 The regression line of y on x

Assuming that the equation of the regression line of *y* on *x* is:

$$y = a + bx$$

it is necessary to calculate the values of *a* and *b* so that the equation can be completely determined.

The following formulae may be used; a knowledge of their derivation is not necessary. They do not need to be memorised since they are supplied in the exams.

$$a = \bar{y} - b\bar{x} = \frac{\sum y}{n} - \frac{b\sum x}{n}$$

$$b = \frac{n\sum xy - \sum x \sum y}{n\sum x^2 - (\sum x)^2}$$

n is the number of pairs of *x*, *y* values, ie, the number of points on the scatter graph.

The value of *b* must be calculated first as it is needed to calculate *a*.

5.6   Example

The following table shows the amount of fertiliser applied to identical fields, and their resulting yields:

Fertiliser (kg/hectare)	Yield (tonnes/hectare)
100	40
200	45
300	50
400	65
500	70
600	70
700	80

Calculate the regression line for y on x.

5.7   Solution

Notes on the calculation

(a)   A scatter diagram is always a useful aid in answering questions on correlation and regression. Even if it is not specifically requested, a sketch diagram can be included as part of a solution.

(b)   The calculation can be reduced to a series of steps:

Step 1   Tabulate the data and determine which is the dependent variable, y, and which the independent, x.

Step 2   Calculate Σx, Σy, Σx^2, Σxy; (leave room for a column for Σy^2 which may well be needed subsequently).

Step 3   Substitute in the formulae in order to find b and a in that order.

Step 4   Substitute a and b in the regression equation.

The calculation is set out as follows, where x is the amount of fertiliser in units of **hundreds** of kg/hectare and y is the yield in tonnes/hectare.

x	y	xy	x^2
1	40	40	1
2	45	90	4
3	50	150	9
4	65	260	16
5	70	350	25
6	70	420	36
7	80	560	49
28	420	1,870	140

$n = 7$

$$b = \frac{n\Sigma xy - \Sigma x \Sigma y}{n\Sigma x^2 - (\Sigma x)^2}$$

(Try to avoid rounding at this stage since, although n Σxy and $\Sigma x \Sigma y$ are large, their difference is much smaller.)

$$= \frac{(7 \times 1{,}870) - (28 \times 420)}{(7 \times 140) - (28 \times 28)}$$

$$= \frac{13{,}090 - 11{,}760}{980 - 784}$$

$$= \frac{1{,}330}{196}$$

$$= 6.79$$

(Ensure you make a note of this fraction in your workings. It may help later.)

$$a = \frac{\sum y}{n} - \frac{b \sum x}{n}$$

$$= \frac{420}{7} - 6.79 \times \frac{28}{7}$$

$$= 60 - 27.16$$

$$= 32.84$$

∴   the regression line for *y* on *x* is:

$$y = 32.84 + 6.79x \qquad \text{(x in hundreds of kg per hectare,}$$
$$\text{y in tonnes per hectare)}$$

(Always specify what *x* and *y* are very carefully.)

This line would be used to estimate the yield corresponding to a given amount of fertiliser. If, say, 250 kg/hectare of fertiliser is available, it is possible to predict the expected yield by using the regression line and replacing *x* with 2.5:

$$y = 32.84 + 6.79 \times 2.5$$

$$= 32.84 + 16.975$$

$$= 49.815$$

∴ y = 50 tonnes/hectare (rounding to whole numbers in line with original data)

5.8   The regression line of x on y

If asked to find a line of best fit the calculations just shown are what is required. This second regression line is less likely to be needed in the exam, but it may be requested, and it gives some insight into correlation.

The method of finding the regression line is the same as for the regression line of *y* on *x*, but with *x* and *y* interchanged. Thus the equation is:

$$x = a' + b'y$$

where $\quad a' = \bar{x} - b'\bar{y} \qquad = \frac{\sum x}{n} - \frac{b' \sum y}{n}$

$$b' = \frac{n \sum xy - \sum x \sum y}{n \sum y^2 - (\sum y)^2}$$

To calculate the equation for the data of the previous section, $\sum y^2$ is required.

$$y^2$$

1,600
2,025
2,500
4,225
4,900
4,900
6,400
_____

26,550
_____

$$b' = \frac{n\sum xy - \sum x \sum y}{n\sum y^2 - (\sum y)^2}$$

$$= \frac{1,330}{7 \times 26,550 - (420)^2} \quad \text{(1,330 comes from the previous calculation)}$$

$$= \frac{1,330}{9,450}$$

$$= 0.141$$

$$a' = \frac{\sum x}{n} - \frac{b'\sum y}{n}$$

$$= \frac{28}{7} - \frac{0.141 \times 420}{7}$$

$$= -4.46$$

$\therefore$ The regression line of x on y is:

$$x = -4.46 + 0.141y$$

This equation would be used to estimate the amount of fertiliser that had resulted in a given yield. Eg, if the yield was 60 tonnes/hectare, the estimated amount of fertiliser would be given by:

$$x = -4.46 + 0.141 \times 60$$

$$= 4.0 \quad \text{(hundreds of kg/hectare)}$$

$\therefore$ 400 kg/hectare of fertiliser would have been used to give a yield of 60 tonnes/hectare.

5.9   Activity

If $\sum x = 560$, $\sum y = 85$, $\sum x^2 = 62,500$, $\sum xy = 14,200$ and $n = 12$, find the regression line of y on x (the line of best fit).

5.10   Activity solution

Equation of line is: $y = a + bx$

$$b = \frac{12 \times 14,200 - 560 \times 85}{12 \times 62,500 - 560 \times 560} = \frac{122,800}{436,400} = 0.281$$

$$a = \frac{85}{12} - 0.281 \times \frac{560}{12} = -6.03$$

Regression line is: $y = -6.03 + 0.281x$

5.11   Regression and correlation

The angle between the two regression lines y on x and x on y decreases as the correlation between the variables increases.

In the case of perfect correlation the angle between the lines is zero, ie, the two lines coincide and become one.

At the other extreme, the angle between the lines becomes 90^0 when there is no correlation between the variables. In this case one line is parallel to the x-axis and the other parallel to the y-axis.

Measures of correlation are discussed later in this chapter.

5.12   Interpolation and extrapolation

As has been shown, regression lines can be used to calculate intermediate values of variables, ie, values within the known range. This is known as **interpolation** and it is one of the main uses of regression lines.

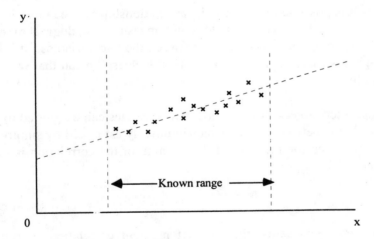

It is also possible to extend regression lines beyond the range of values used in their calculation. It is then possible to calculate values of the variables that are outside the limits of the original data, this is known as **extrapolation**.

The problem with extrapolation is that it assumes that the relationship already calculated is still valid. This may or may not be so.

For example, if the fertiliser was increased outside the given range there would come a point where it had an adverse effect on the yield. The seed might actually be damaged by too much fertiliser.

The resultant diagram could be of this form:

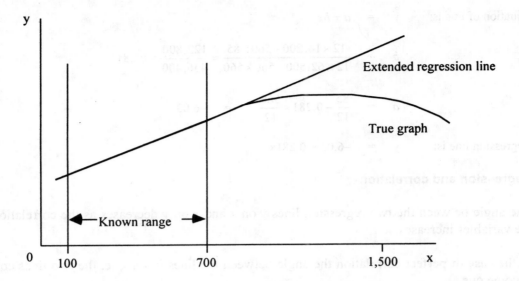

Therefore the yield from using 1,500 kg/hectare of fertiliser as estimated from the regression line may be very different from that actually achieved in practice.

Generally speaking, extrapolation must be treated with caution, since once outside the range of known values other factors may influence the situation, and the relationship which has been approximated as linear over a limited range may not be linear outside that range. Nevertheless, extrapolation of a time series is a valuable and widely used technique for forecasting.

6   CORRELATION

6.1   Introduction

Through regression analysis it is possible to derive a linear relationship between two variables and hence estimate unknown values. However, this does not measure the **degree of correlation** between the variables, ie, how strong the connection is between the two variables. It is possible to find a line of best fit through any assortment of data points; this doesn't mean that we are justified in using the equation of that line.

Earlier in the chapter we discussed **correlation** and how two variables can be plotted together on a scatter diagram and the correlation between the variables intuitively estimated by simply looking at the diagram. However a more scientific measure of the strength of the correlation is available by calculating the correlation coefficient.

6.2   Correlation coefficient

Pearson's correlation coefficient, also called the 'product moment correlation coefficient', r, is defined as:

$$ r = \frac{n\sum xy - \sum x \sum y}{\sqrt{(n\sum x^2 - (\sum x)^2)(n\sum y^2 - (\sum y)^2)}} $$

where x and y represent pairs of data for two variables x and y, and n is the number of pairs of data used in the analysis.

This formula does not have to be memorised, since it is also supplied in the exam, but practice is needed at applying it to data and interpreting the result.

6.3   Example

Fertiliser (kg/hectare)	Yield (tonnes/hectare)
100	40
200	45
300	50
400	65
500	70
600	70
700	80

The totals required are:

$\Sigma x = 28$, $\Sigma y = 420$, $\Sigma xy = 1,870$, $\Sigma x^2 = 140$, $\Sigma y^2 = 26,550$, $n = 7$

Thus

$$r = \frac{(7 \times 1,870) - (28 \times 420)}{\sqrt{((7 \times 140) - (28 \times 28))((7 \times 26,550) - (420 \times 420))}}$$

$$= \frac{13,090 - 11,760}{\sqrt{(980 - 784)(185,850 - 176,400)}}$$

$$= \frac{1,330}{\sqrt{(196 \times 9,450)}}$$

$$= 0.98$$

(If you look at your calculations for b and b' you will notice that you've already found the terms in this section.)

6.4   Interpretation of coefficient of correlation

Having calculated the value of r, it is necessary to interpret this result. Does $r = 0.98$ mean that there is high correlation, low correlation or no correlation?

r varies between +1 and −1 where:

$\quad r = +1$ means perfect positive linear correlation;

$\quad r = 0$ means no correlation; and

$\quad r = -1$ means perfect negative linear correlation.

So in this case the value of 0.98 indicates a high degree of positive correlation between the variables.

In general, the closer that r is to +1 (or − 1) the higher the degree of correlation. This will usually be confirmed by the scatter diagram where the points will lie in a narrow band for such values.

It must be realised that r only measures the amount of linear correlation, ie, the tendency to a straight line relationship. It is quite possible to have strong non-linear correlation and yet have a value of r close to zero. This is one reason why it is important in practice to draw the scatter graph first.

The more data points the farther r may be from 1 and still indicate good correlation. If there are few data points, as here, we would wish to see r very close to 1 (clearly if there were only 2 points they will lie exactly on the line of best fit).

6.5   Coefficient of determination

The coefficient of determination is the square of the coefficient of correlation, and so is denoted by r^2. The advantage of knowing the coefficient of determination is that it is a measure of how much of the variation in the dependent variable is 'explained' by the variation of the independent variable. The variation not accounted for by variations in the independent variable will be due to random fluctuations, or to other specific factors which have not been identified in considering the two-variable problem.

In the example on fertiliser and yield, r had a value of 0.98 and so $r^2 = 0.96$ and $100r^2 = 96\%$.

Thus, variations in the amount of fertiliser applied account for 96% of the variation in the yield obtained.

This is an important measure because of the effect of squaring 'r'. A correlation coefficient of 0.7 appears not too significantly different from one of 0.5. However r^2 is 49% in the former case and 25% in the latter. In other words, the correlation is almost twice as strong since 49% is almost twice the size of 25%.

6.6   Activity

If $r = 0.42$, how much of the variation in the dependent variable is explained by the variation of the independent variable?

6.7   Activity solution

If $r = 0.42$, then $r^2 = 0.1764$, so about 17.6% of the variation is explained by variations in the independent variable (poor correlation).

6.8   Spurious correlation

Students should be aware of the big danger involved in correlation analysis. Two variables, when compared, may show a high degree of correlation but they may still have no direct connection. Such correlation is termed **spurious** or **nonsense** correlation and unless two variables can reasonably be assumed to have some direct connection the correlation coefficient found will be meaningless, however high it may be.

The following are examples of variables between which there is high but spurious correlation:

(a)   Salaries of school teachers and consumption of alcohol.

(b)   Number of television licences and the number of admissions to mental hospitals.

Such examples clearly have no direct **causal** relationship. However, there may be some other variable which is a causal factor common to both of the original variables. For example, the general rise in living standards and real incomes is responsible both for the increase in teachers' salaries and for the increase in the consumption of alcohol.

7   RANK CORRELATION

7.1   Introduction

For Pearson's correlation coefficient, x and y must both be quantifiable as numerical values. It is possible, however, to consider correlation between attributes which cannot be quantified numerically, such as artistic ability, skill, intelligence, beauty, etc.

Provided the items or people can be ranked, that is, placed in order of merit, ability, magnitude or any other relevant order, a correlation coefficient can still be obtained.

One method is to use Spearman's rank correlation coefficient (*R*).

$$R = 1 - \frac{6\sum d^2}{n(n^2 - 1)}$$

where   *d*   =   difference between ranks in each attribute

   n   =   number of items or people ranked

7.2   Example

To investigate whether correlation exists between ability in writing plays and ability in English, a group of 10 playwrights were set a test in English and also had the quality of their plays assessed by a panel of experts, who ranked them in order of merit.

The following results were obtained:

Candidate	A	B	C	D	E	F	G	H	I	J
Mark in English (%)	60	75	40	62	64	71	58	50	83	45
Rank in play writing	5	3	8	6	4	2	9	7	1	10

(Rank 1 is the best play and 10 the worst)

Is there any evidence of correlation?

7.3   Discussion

The quality of a play is not something that can be quantified, but plays can be placed in order of merit. As far as English is concerned, it is true that the examination mark could be used to quantify ability, but an examination does not really measure ability, it merely enables candidates to be compared and ranked. In any case, for Pearson's correlation coefficient to be used, both attributes would need to be quantified. This is clearly a case where ranking methods must be used.

7.4   Solution

First, the candidates must be ranked in English on the same basis as the rank for play writing, that is, the best (83%) is given a rank of 1, down to the worst (40%) with a rank of 10.

Candidate	A	B	C	D	E	F	G	H	I	J
Rank in English	6	2	10	5	4	3	7	8	1	9

The calculation can now be set out as follows:

Candidate	Rank in English	Rank in Play	Difference d	d^2
A	6	5	1	1
B	2	3	−1	1
C	10	8	2	4
D	5	6	−1	1
E	4	4	0	0
F	3	2	1	1
G	7	9	−2	4
H	8	7	1	1
I	1	1	0	0
J	9	10	−1	1
			$\sum d = 0$	$\sum d^2 = 14$

($\sum d$ is not used, but serves as a check on your arithmetic.)

$$n = \text{number of candidates} = 10$$

$$\therefore R = 1 - \frac{6 \times 14}{10 \times (10^2 - 1)}$$

$$= 1 - \frac{84}{990}$$

$$= 0.92$$

7.5   Interpretation of R

Perfect positive correlation occurs when the ranks in both attributes are identical; the best in one is best in the other, etc.

Perfect negative correlation occurs when the ranks are in reverse order, ie, the best in one attribute is worst in the other, and so on.

If there is no tendency to either of these extremes, there is no correlation.

R behaves in the same way as r, ie,

For perfect positive correlation,	$R = +1$
For perfect negative correlation,	$R = -1$
For no correlation,	$R \simeq 0$

A value of $R = 0.92$ would therefore appear to indicate a high degree of positive correlation, showing that ability in English does tend to go with ability in play writing.

7.6   The problem of tied ranks

If two or more candidates have equal ranks (ie, they tie), errors may be introduced. A few ties can be tolerated provided they are treated correctly. Candidates who tie should be given the arithmetic mean of the ranks they would have had if they had not been quite equal. For example, if the marks in English had been:

Candidate	A	B	C	D	E	F	G	H	I	J
Mark in English (%)	83	70	70	65	60	52	52	52	50	45

Candidates B and C would have had ranks 2 and 3 if they had not been equal. They are both given a rank of $(2 + 3)/2 = 2.5$. Candidate D must follow on from 3 with a rank of 4. Candidates F, G and H would have had ranks of 6, 7 and 8 if they had not been equal. They are therefore given a rank of $(6 + 7 + 8)/3 = 7$. Candidate I must follow on from 8 with a rank of 9. Hence the ranks would be:

$$1, 2.5, 2.5, 4, 5, 7, 7, 7, 9, 10$$

7.7   Ranking of numerical data

Numerical data suitable for calculation of Pearson's correlation coefficient (r), can always be ranked in order of magnitude. Some of the information will be lost, and therefore Spearman's correlation coefficient will not give such an accurate result. However, it is much easier to calculate, and can be used as a quick method if only an approximate indication of the degree of correlation is required. If Spearman's coefficient indicates no correlation then Pearson's coefficient will give the same result, but if Spearman's coefficient indicates correlation, Pearson's coefficient may not confirm this if the correlation is weak.

7.8   Activity

Calculate a rank correlation coefficient for the fertiliser data given below.

Fertiliser (kg/hectare)	Yield (tonnes/hectare)
100	40
200	45
300	50
400	65
500	70
600	70
700	80

7.9   Activity solution

(Ranking 1, 2, 3 ... etc. is in order of increasing magnitude.)

Fertiliser x	Rank of x	Yield y	Rank of y	Difference in ranks d	d^2
100	1	40	1	0	0
200	2	45	2	0	0
300	3	50	3	0	0
400	4	65	4	0	0
500	5	70	5½	– ½	¼
600	6	70	5½	½	¼
700	7	80	7	0	0
				0	½

$$\therefore \ R \ = \ 1 - \frac{6 \times \frac{1}{2}}{7(7^2 - 1)}$$

$$= \ 1 - 0.0089$$

$$= \ 0.9911$$

The rank correlation coefficient shows almost perfect positive correlation, whereas Pearson's coefficient (0.98) indicates high but not so nearly perfect correlation. The latter is the more accurate conclusion.

8   THE USE OF CORRELATION AND REGRESSION IN FORECASTING

8.1   Introduction

So far we have looked at the technicalities of correlation and regression and how to interpret the results of such calculations. What we have not done is to make the link between these techniques and forecasting, bearing in mind forecasting is the part of the syllabus that this and the following chapter is all about.

Thus what we are establishing here is:

Step 1   Is there a causal relationship between two variables? (Correlation)

↓

If yes

↓

Step 2   Deduce the coefficient 'a' and 'b' in order to establish a line of best fit in the form y = a + bx. (Regression)

↓

Step 3   Use the equation to forecast the value of an unknown variable given that the value of the other variable can be ascertained for the period for which the forecast is to be made. (Forecasting)

Example

If there is a correlation between the demand for sun roofs in a given year and the sales of new cars on the previous year, then this year's car sales could be used to predict sun roof demand for next year.

9   CHAPTER SUMMARY

This chapter has been concerned with forecasting - both quantitative and qualitative methods. The three quantitative methods described were:

(a)   Scatter diagrams.
(b)   Regression analysis.
(c)   Correlation coefficients.

A number of formulae have been used; these must be well practised so that calculations can be made quickly and accurately. We shall go on to look at more quantitative forecasting techniques in the next chapter.

10   SELF TEST QUESTIONS

10.1   Name two methods of smoothing data. (1.4)

10.2   What is a scatter diagram? (2.4)

10.3   What is a 'line of best fit'? (2.6)

10.4   What is the Delphi method of intuitive forecasting? (4.3)

10.5   What is the equation of a straight line? (5.2)

10.6   What is the difference between interpolation and extrapolation? (5.12)

10.7   What is Pearson's correlation coefficient? (6.2)

10.8   What values does r take if there is perfect positive linear correlation and perfect negative linear correlation? (6.4)

10.9   What is the coefficient of determination and why is it important? (6.5)

10.10   What is spurious correlation? (6.8)

11   EXAMINATION TYPE QUESTIONS

11.1   Racing car powers and speeds

The following figures show the power to the nearest kilowatt and the top speeds to the nearest mile per hour, of twelve racing cars:

Power (kw)	70	63	72	60	66	70	74	65	62	67	65	68
Top speed (mph)	155	150	180	135	156	168	178	160	132	145	139	152

(a)   Plot the information on a scatter diagram, showing top speed as the dependent variable.

(b)   Calculate the line of regression of y on x.

(c)   Estimate the top speed of a car with a power rating of 71 kw.

(d)   From the calculations carried out so far, is it possible to estimate the power rating of a car which has a top speed of 175 mph? Give reasons.

(e)   What would be the problems involved in estimating a top speed for a car with a power rating of 95 kw?

11.2   D & E Ltd

D & E Ltd produces brakes for the motor industry. Its management accountant is investigating the relationship between electricity costs and volume of production. The following data for the last ten quarters has been derived, the cost figures having been adjusted (ie, deflated) to take into account price changes.

Quarter	1	2	3	4	5	6	7	8	9	10
Production, X, ('000 units)	30	20	10	60	40	25	13	50	44	28
Electricity costs, Y, (£'000)	10	11	6	18	13	10	10	20	17	15

(Source: Internal company records of D & E Ltd.)

$$\sum X^2 = 12{,}614, \qquad \sum Y^2 = 1{,}864, \qquad \sum XY = 4{,}728$$

You are required

(a)   to draw a scatter diagram of the data on squared paper;

(4 marks)

(b)   to find the least squares regression line for electricity costs on production and explain this result;

(8 marks)

(c)   to predict the electricity costs of D & E Ltd for the next two quarters (time periods 11 and 12) in which production is planned to be 15,000 and 55,000 standard units respectively;

(4 marks)

(d)   to assess the likely reliability of these forecasts.

(4 marks)

(Total: 20 marks)

12   ANSWERS TO EXAMINATION TYPE QUESTIONS

12.1   Racing car powers and speeds

(a)   Since top speed is the dependent variable it is plotted on the vertical y-axis. Power is therefore plotted on the x-axis.

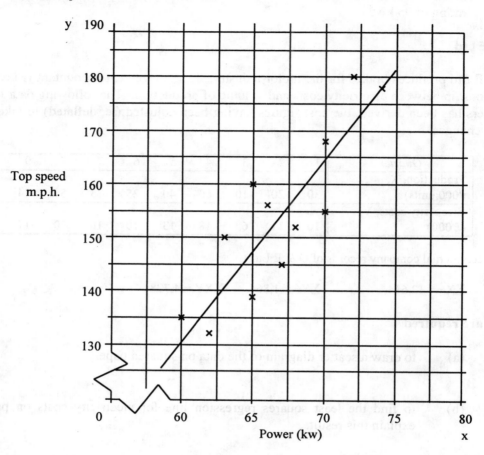

(b)

| Power (kw) | Top speed (mph) | | |
x	y	xy	x^2
70	155	10,850	4,900
63	150	9,450	3,969
72	180	12,960	5,184
60	135	8,100	3,600
66	156	10,296	4,356
70	168	11,760	4,900
74	178	13,172	5,476
65	160	10,400	4,225
62	132	8,184	3,844
67	145	9,715	4,489
65	139	9,035	4,225
68	152	10,336	4,624
$\sum x = 802$	$\sum y = 1,850$	$\sum xy = 124,258$	$\sum x^2 = 53,792$

$$y = a + bx$$

Using $\quad b = \dfrac{n\sum xy - \sum x \sum y}{n\sum x^2 - (\sum x)^2}, \quad$ and $\quad a = \dfrac{\sum y}{n} - \dfrac{b\sum x}{n}$

$$b = \frac{(12 \times 124{,}258) - (802 \times 1{,}850)}{(12 \times 53{,}792) - (802 \times 802)}$$

$$= \frac{1{,}491{,}096 \quad 1{,}483{,}700}{645{,}504 - 643{,}204}$$

$$= \frac{7{,}396}{2{,}300}$$

$$\therefore \quad b = 3.22 \ (3 \text{ s.f.})$$

$$a = \frac{1{,}850}{12} - 3.22 \times \frac{802}{12}$$

$$= 154.2 - 215.2$$

$$\therefore \quad a = -61.0$$

So the regression line is: $y = -61.0 + 3.22x$

(c) If power rating is 71 kw then replacing $x = 71$ in equation gives:

$$y = -61.0 + 3.22 \times 71$$

$$= -61.0 + 228.62$$

$$\therefore \quad y = 168 \text{ mph (to nearest whole number)}$$

(d) Strictly speaking, it is not possible to estimate power rating for a given top speed without working out the line of regression of x on y, which has not yet been done.

(e) As soon as a regression line is used to predict values of y for given values of x outside the observed range, there is an immediate risk of error which continues to increase the further away one goes from the observed values.

There is no reason why a particular relationship should remain linear for higher (or lower) values of the variables (in fact the reverse is often more likely as saturation point is reached).

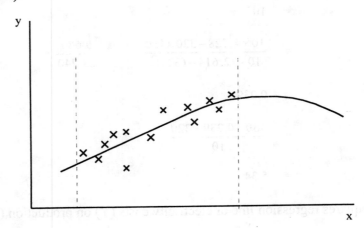

Thus, since 95 kw is a power rating well outside the present observed range, it would be unreliable to extrapolate in order to obtain an estimate of top speed for that rating.

12.2   D & E Ltd

(a)   **Scatter graph of electricity cost against production**

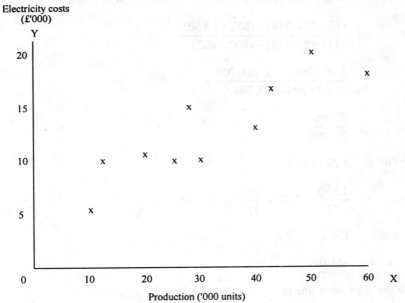

Notes:

(i)   Choose the scales so that the graph fits the graph paper.

(ii)   Do not attempt to draw a line through the scatter graph unless the question requires it.

(iii)   Label the axes and state the units.

(b)   The regression line of Y on X is Y = a + bX where

$$b = \frac{n\sum XY - \sum X \sum Y}{n\sum X^2 - (\sum X)^2} \quad \text{and} \quad a = \frac{\sum Y - b\sum X}{n}$$

$$\sum X = 320$$

$$\sum Y = 130$$

$$n = 10$$

$$b = \frac{10 \times 4,728 - 320 \times 130}{10 \times 12,614 - (320)^2} = \frac{5,680}{23,740}$$

$$= 0.239$$

$$a = \frac{130 - 0.239 \times 320}{10}$$

$$= 5.34$$

The least squares regression line of electricity costs (Y) on production (X) is therefore

$$Y = 5.34 + 0.239X$$

where Y is in £'000 and X in '000 units.

Explanation

Assuming there is an approximately linear relationship between production and electricity costs, which is shown to be reasonable by the scatter graph, the electricity costs are made up of two parts, a fixed cost (independent of the volume of production) of £5,340 and a variable cost per unit of production of £239 per 1,000 units (or 23.9p per unit).

(c)   For quarter 11, X = 15, hence

$$Y = 5.34 + 0.239 \times 15$$
$$= 8.93$$

The predicted electricity cost for quarter 11 is therefore £8,930.

For quarter 12, X = 55, hence

$$Y = 5.34 + 0.239 \times 55$$
$$= 18.5$$

The predicted electricity cost for quarter 12 is therefore £18,500.

(d)   There are two main sources of error in the forecasts:

(i)   The assumed relationship between Y and X.

The scatter graph shows that there can be fairly wide variations in Y for a given X. Also the forecast assumes that the same conditions will prevail over the next two quarters as in the last ten quarters.

(ii)   The predicted production for quarters 11 and 12.

No indication is given as to how these planned production values were arrived at, so that it is not possible to assess how reliable they are. If they are based on extrapolation of a time series for production over the past ten quarters, they will be subject to the errors inherent in such extrapolations.

Provided conditions remain similar to the past ten quarters, it can be concluded that the forecasts would be fairly reliable but subject to some variation.

Note: methods for calculation of confidence limits for forecasts are available, but are outside the scope of this syllabus. At this level it is impossible to quantify the reliability, so that comments can only be in general terms, although a correlation coefficient would be worth calculating **if time allowed.**

14 FORECASTING AND TIME SERIES

INTRODUCTION & LEARNING OBJECTIVES

Syllabus area 7e. Cost, demand and sales forecasting; qualitative methods. (Ability required 2).

When you have studied this chapter you should be able to do the following:

- Explain the use of time series analysis.

- Distinguish between additive and multiplicative time series models.

- Identify and quantify cyclical variations in time series data.

1   TIME SERIES

1.1   Introduction

Time series is another forecasting method which was examinable earlier in your studies in Stage 1. However it is included again here as the syllabus guidance notes mention that students should be knowledgeable about **all** the different forecasting methods so that comparison between methods can be made and so that candidates can demonstrate an ability to select the most appropriate technique for a given situation.

1.2   Definition of terms

A time series is the name given to a set of observations taken at equal intervals of time, eg, daily, weekly, monthly, etc. The observations can be plotted against time to give an overall picture of what is happening. **The horizontal axis is always the time axis.**

Examples of time series are total annual exports, monthly unemployment figures, daily average temperatures, etc.

1.3   Example

The following data relates to the production (in tonnes) of floggels by the North West Engineering Co. These are the quarterly totals taken over four years from 19X2 to 19X5.

	1st Qtr	2nd Qtr	3rd Qtr	4th Qtr
19X2	91	90	94	93
19X3	98	99	97	95
19X4	107	102	106	110
19X5	123	131	128	130

This time series will now be graphed so that an overall picture can be gained of what is happening to the company's production figures.

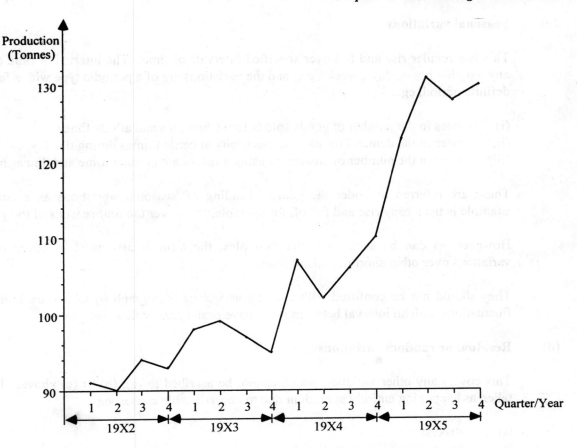

Note: that each point must be plotted at the **end** of the relevant quarter.

The graph shows clearly how the production of floggels has increased over the four-year time period. This is particularly true during the last year considered.

1.4   Variations in observations

A time series is influenced by a number of factors, the most important of these being:

(a)   **Long-term trends**

This is the way in which the graph of a time series appears to be moving over a long interval of time when the short-term fluctuations have been smoothed out. The rise or fall is due to factors which only change slowly, eg,

(i)   increase or decrease in population;
(ii)   technological improvements;
(iii)   competition from abroad.

(b)   **Cyclical variations**

This is the wave-like appearance of a time series graph when taken over a number of years. Generally, it is due to the influence of booms and slumps in industry. The period in time from one peak to the next is often approximately 5 to 7 years.

(c)   **Seasonal variations**

This is a regular rise and fall over specified intervals of time. The interval of time can be any length – hours, days, weeks, etc, and the variations are of a periodic type with a fairly definite period, eg:

(i)   rises in the number of goods sold before Christmas and at sale times;
(ii)   rises in the demand for gas and electricity at certain times during the day;
(iii)   rises in the number of customers using a restaurant at lunch-time and dinner time.

These are referred to under the general heading of 'seasonal' variations as a common example is the steady rise and fall of, for example, sales over the four seasons of the year.

However, as can be seen from the examples, the term is also used to cover regular variations over other short periods of time.

They should not be confused with cyclical variations (paragraph b) which are long-term fluctuations with an interval between successive peaks greater than one year.

(d)   **Residual or random variations**

This covers any other variation which cannot be ascribed to (a), (b) or (c) above. This is taken as happening entirely at random due to unpredictable causes, eg:

(i)   strikes;
(ii)   fires;
(iii)   sudden changes in taxes.

Not all time series will contain all four elements. For example, not all sales figures show seasonal variations.

1.5   A time series graph

The graph in the example covered the quarterly production of floggels over a four-year time period.

The long-term trend (a) and seasonal (quarterly) (c) were obvious from the graph. However, in order to be able to observe any cyclical variations it is usually necessary to have data covering a much wider time-span, say 10 – 15 years minimum.

The following graph shows the production (in tonnes) of widgets for each quarter of the 18 years from 19X1 to 19Y8.

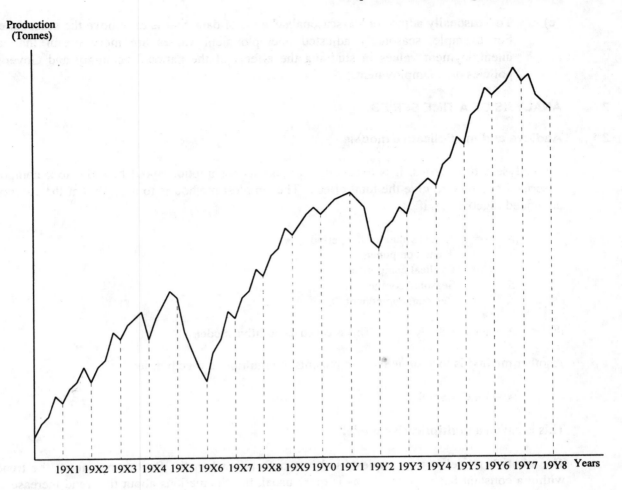

This time it is possible to detect:

(a)   The long-term trend – upwards in this case.

(b)   Cyclical variations – the wave like appearance of the graph shows that the cycle of production spans 6 years, ie, the distance in time between successive peaks (and successive troughs) is 6 years.

(c)   Seasonal variation – since these are quarterly production figures this is sometimes called **quarterly variation**. These are the small steps in each year which are evident on the first graph. They occur because some parts of the year are busier than others and the actual pattern will depend very much on the type of industry, eg, the building industry tends to be slack during the winter months because of the weather, whereas an engineering company may be quietest during the summer months due to holidays.

(d)   Residual variation – this is simply the difference between the actual figure and that predicted – taking into account trends, cyclical variations and seasonal variations. By its nature it cannot be fully explained.

1.6   Analysis of a time series

It is essential to be able to disentangle these various influences and measure each one separately. The main reasons for analysing a time series in this way are:

(a)   To be able to predict future values of the variable, ie, to make forecasts.

(b)   To attempt to control future events.

(c)   To 'seasonally adjust' or 'de-seasonalise' a set of data, that is to remove the seasonal effect. For example, seasonally adjusted unemployment values are more useful than actual unemployment values in studying the effects of the national economy and Government policies on unemployment.

2   ANALYSIS OF A TIME SERIES

2.1   Additive and multiplicative models

To analyse a time series, it is necessary to make an assumption about how the four components described combine to give the total effect. The simplest method is to assume that the components are added together, ie, if:

A   =   Actual value for the period
T   =   Trend component
C   =   Cyclical component
S   =   Seasonal component
R   =   Residual component

then $A = T + C + S + R$.   This is called an **additive model**.

Another method is to assume the components are multiplied together, ie:

$A = T \times C \times S \times R$

This is called a **multiplicative model**.

The additive model is the simplest, and is satisfactory when the fluctuations about the trend are within a constant band width. If, as is more usual, the fluctuations about the trend increase as the trend increases, the multiplicative model is more appropriate. Illustrated diagrammatically:

(a)   y

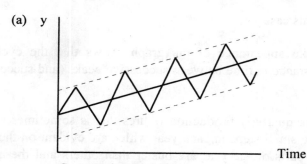

Constant band width.
Use additive model.

(b)   y

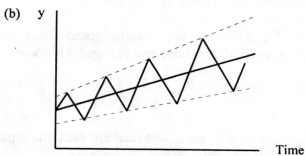

Band width proportional to trend.
Use multiplicative model.

2.2   Trend

The trend can be obtained by using regression analysis to obtain the line of best fit through the points on the graph, taking x as the year numbers (1, 2, 3.... etc) and y as the vertical variable. It is not necessary for the trend to be a straight line, as non-linear regression can be used, but for this method it is necessary to assume an appropriate mathematical form for the trend, such as parabola, hyperbola, exponential, etc. If the trend does not conform to any of these, the method cannot be used.

An alternative, which requires no assumption to be made about the nature of the curve, is to smooth out the fluctuations by moving averages.

The simplest way to explain the method is by means of an example.

2.3   Example

The following are the sales figures for Bloggs Brothers Engineering Ltd for the fourteen years from 19X1 to 19Y4.

Year	Sales (£'000)
19X1	491
19X2	519
19X3	407
19X4	452
19X5	607
19X6	681
19X7	764
19X8	696
19X9	751
19Y0	802
19Y1	970
19Y2	1,026
19Y3	903
19Y4	998

Using the method of moving averages the general trend of sales will be established.

2.4   Solution

Step 1   First, it is advisable to draw a graph of the time series so that an overall picture can be gained and the cyclical movements seen.

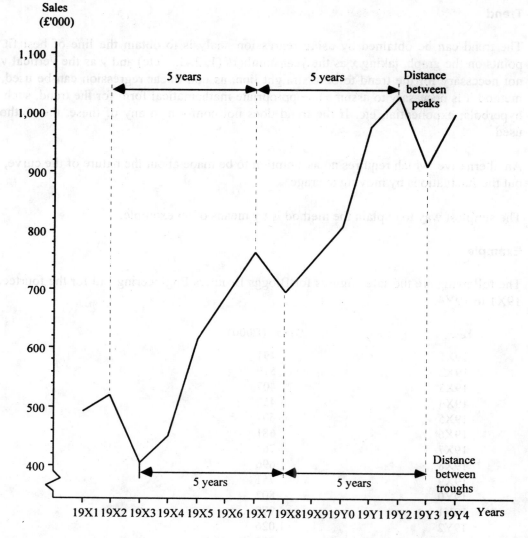

Sales
(£'000)

In order to calculate the trend figures it is necessary to establish the span of the cycle. From the graph it can easily be seen that the distance in time between successive peaks (and successive troughs) is 5 years; therefore a 5 point moving average must be calculated.

Step 2   A table of the following form is now drawn up:

Year	Sales (£'000)	5 yearly moving total	5 yearly moving average
19X1	491	-	-
19X2	519	-	-
19X3	407	2,476	495
19X4	452	2,666	533
19X5	607	2,911	582
19X6	681	3,200	640
19X7	764	3,499	700
19X8	696	3,694	739
19X9	751	3,983	797
19Y0	802	4,245	849
19Y1	970	4,452	890
19Y2	1,026	4,699	940
19Y3	903	-	-
19Y4	998	-	-

Notes on the calculation

(a)   As the name implies, the five yearly moving total is the sum of successive groups of 5 years' sales ie,

$$491 + 519 + 407 + 452 + 607 \quad = \quad 2,476$$

Then, advancing by one year:

$$519 + 407 + 452 + 607 + 681 \quad = \quad 2,666, \text{ etc.}$$

$$802 + 970 + 1,026 + 903 + 998 \quad = \quad 4,699$$

(b)   These moving totals are simply divided by 5 to give the moving averages, ie,

$$2,476 \div 5 \quad = \quad 495$$

$$2,666 \div 5 \quad = \quad 533$$

$$4,699 \div 5 \quad = \quad 940$$

(c)   Averages are always plotted in the middle of the time period, ie, 495 is the average of the figures for 19X1, 19X2, 19X3, 19X4 and 19X5 and so it is plotted at the end of 19X3, this being the mid-point of the time interval from the end of 19X1 to the end of 19X5. Similarly, 533 is plotted at the end of 19X4, and 940 is plotted at the end of 19Y2.

Step 3   The trend figures ie, the five yearly moving averages, can now be drawn onto the original graph alongside the raw data.

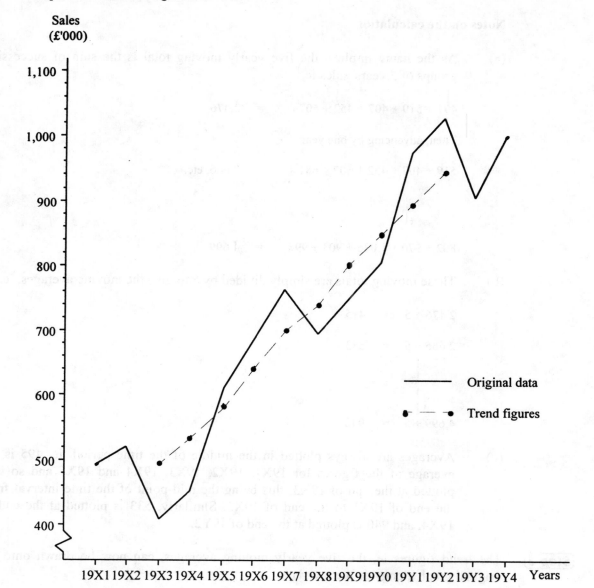

Sales
(£'000)

19X1 19X2 19X3 19X4 19X5 19X6 19X7 19X8 19X9 19Y0 19Y1 19Y2 19Y3 19Y4   Years

Original data

Trend figures

2.5   Cyclical variation

Having calculated the trend figures it is a simple matter to work out the cyclical variations.

For annual data, there cannot be a seasonal component. Hence, using the additive model,

$$A \quad = \quad T + C + R$$

Subtracting T from both sides,

$$A - T \quad = \quad C + R$$

So, by subtracting the trend values from the actual values, the combined cyclical and residual variation will be obtained.

If the multiplicative model is used, A must be divided by T,

$$A \quad = \quad T \times C \times R$$

$$\frac{A}{T} \quad = \quad C \times R$$

As before, this will be explained by way of an example.

2.6   Example

Using the same data, establish the cyclical variation, using the additive model.

2.7   Solution

Step 1   A table of the following type is drawn up:

Year	Period of moving averages	Sales (£'000) (A)	Trend figures (T)	Cyclical + Residual variation (A - T)
19X1	1	491	-	-
19X2	2	519	-	-
19X3	3	407	495	−88
19X4	4	452	533	−81
19X5	5	607	582	25
19X6	1	681	640	41
19X7	2	764	700	64
19X8	3	696	739	−43
19X9	4	751	797	−46
19Y0	5	802	849	−47
19Y1	1	970	890	80
19Y2	2	1,026	940	86
19Y3	3	903	−	−
19Y4	4	998	−	−

Notes on the calculation

The figures in the last column for the cyclical variation are just the differences between the actual sales and the trend figures, ie:

$$407 - 495 = -88$$
$$452 - 533 = -81$$
$$\vdots$$
$$1{,}026 - 940 = 86$$

The '+' and '−' signs are important since they show whether the actual figures are above or below the trend figures.

Step 2   To remove the residual component from $C + R$, another table must now be drawn up in order to establish the average cyclical variations.

	Period 1	Period 2	Period 3	Period 4	Period 5
Cyclical variation calculated above	− 41 80	− 64 86	−88 −43 −	−81 −46 −	25 −47 −
(i) Totals	121	150	−131	−127	−22
(ii) Average cyclical variation (= (i)/2)	60.5 ≈ 61	75	−65.5 ≈ −66	−63.5 ≈ −64	−11

The individual variations have been averaged out for each year of the cycle, ie,

$$\text{Year 1 of each cycle} = \frac{41+80}{2} = \frac{121}{2} = 60.5, \text{ rounded to 61;}$$

$$\text{Year 2 of each cycle} = \frac{64+86}{2} = \frac{150}{2} = 75$$

etc.

Step 3   One more step is necessary because the cyclical variation should total to zero, and $61 + 75 + (-66) + (-64) + (-11) = -5$.

The adjustment is made by dividing the excess (-5 in this case) by the number of years in the cycle (5 in this case) and subtracting the result from each of the cyclical variations.

Adjustment is $-5 \div 5 = -1$

Cyclical variations within each cycle are:

Year 1	$61 - (-1)$	$=$	$61 + 1$	$=$	62
Year 2	$75 - (-1)$	$=$	$75 + 1$	$=$	76
Year 3	$-66 - (-1)$	$=$	$-66 + 1$	$=$	-65
Year 4	$-64 - (-1)$	$=$	$-64 + 1$	$=$	-63
Year 5	$-11 - (-1)$	$=$	$-11 + 1$	$=$	-10

(and just as a check, the revised cyclical variations do total zero: $62 + 76 - 65 - 63 - 10 = 0$)

2.8   Seasonal variations

When figures are available for a considerable number of years, it is possible to establish the trend and the cyclical variations.

Usually, however, monthly or quarterly figures are only available for a few years, 3 or 4, say. In this case, it is possible to establish the trend by means of a moving average over an annual cycle by a method very similar to that used above. The span of the data is insufficient to find cyclical variations, but average seasonal variations can be found.

2.9   Example

The following table gives the takings (£000) of a shopkeeper in each quarter of 4 successive years.

Qtrs	1	2	3	4
19X1	13	22	58	23
19X2	16	28	61	25
19X3	17	29	61	26
19X4	18	30	65	29

Calculate the trend figures and quarterly variations, and draw a graph to show the overall trend and the original data.

2.10   Solution

Again the additive model will be used, but as the data is now over too short a time for any cyclical component to be apparent, the model becomes:

$$A = T + S + R$$

Step 1   It is necessary to draw up a table as follows:

1 Year & quarter	2 Takings (£'000) A	3 4 quarterly moving average	4 Centred value T	5 Quarterly + Residual variation S + R
1	13		-	-
2	22		-	-
19X1 3	58	29	30	28
4	23	30	31	-8
1	16	31	32	-16
2	28	32	33	-5
19X2 3	61	33	33	28
4	25	33	33	-8
1	17	33	33	-16
2	29	33	33	-4
19X3 3	61	33	34	27
4	26	34	34	-8
1	18	34	35	-17
2	30	35	36	-6
19X4 3	65	36	-	-
4	29		-	-

Notes on the calculation

Column 3

To smooth out quarterly fluctuations, it is necessary to calculate a 4-point moving average, since there are 4 quarters (or seasons) in a year.

ie, $\dfrac{13 + 22 + 58 + 23}{4} = \dfrac{116}{4} = 29$

then, advancing by one quarter:

$$\frac{22+58+23+16}{4} = \frac{119}{4} = 30 \quad \text{(rounding to nearest whole number)}$$

$$\frac{18+30+65+29}{4} = \frac{142}{4} = 36 \quad \text{(rounding to nearest whole number)}$$

29 is the average of the figures for the four quarters of 19X1 and so if plotted, would be at the mid-point of the interval from the end of the first quarter to the end of the fourth quarter, ie, half-way through the third quarter of 19X1.

Step 2   **Column 4**

To find A – T, it is essential that A and T both relate to the same point in time. The four-quarterly moving averages do not correspond with any of the A values, the first coming between the second and third A values and so on down. To overcome this, the moving averages are 'centred', ie, averaged in twos. The first centred average will coincide with the third A value and so on.

Note: that this is necessary because the cycle has an even number of values (4) per cycle. Where there is an odd number of values per cycle, as in the previous example, the moving averages themselves correspond in time with A values, and centring should not be done.

The centring is as follows:

$$\text{ie,} \quad \frac{29+30}{2} = 30 \quad \text{(rounding up)}$$

$$\frac{30+31}{2} = 31 \quad \text{(rounding up)}$$

$$\frac{35+36}{2} = 36 \quad \text{(rounding up)}$$

The first average now corresponds in time with the original value for the 3rd quarter, and so on.

These are the trend values.

Step 3   **Column 5**

A − T = S + R, hence the figures for the quarterly + residual variations are the differences between the actual figures and the centred values.

ie,   58 − 30   =   28
        23 − 31   =   −8
              |
              |
              |
              |
        30 − 36   =   −6

Step 4   In order to establish the quarterly variation another table must be drawn up (as in the earlier example), to remove the residual variation *R*.

	Quarter 1	Quarter 2	Quarter 3	Quarter 4
	−	−	28	−8
	−16	−5	28	−8
	−16	−4	27	−8
	−17	−6	−	−
Totals	−49	−15	83	−24
Seasonal variation	−16	−5	28	−8

The individual variations have been averaged out for each quarter of the cycle:

ie,   Quarter 1 $\dfrac{-16+(-16)+(-17)}{3}$ = $\dfrac{-49}{3}$ =   −16

        Quarter 2 $\dfrac{-5+(-4)+(-6)}{3}$ = $\dfrac{-15}{3}$ =   −5

Step 5   The quarterly variations should total to zero again, but −16 + (−5) + 28 + (−8) = −1. However, the adjustment would only be −1 ÷ 4, ie, −0.25 which means using a spurious accuracy of two decimal places. To avoid this one value only need be adjusted, choosing the greatest value as this will give the lowest relative adjustment error.

        1st   Quarter   =   −16
        2nd   Quarter   =   −5
        3rd   Quarter   =   28 + 1   =   29
        4th   Quarter   =   −8
                                                ——
                                                0
                                                ——

Step 6   Draw the graph

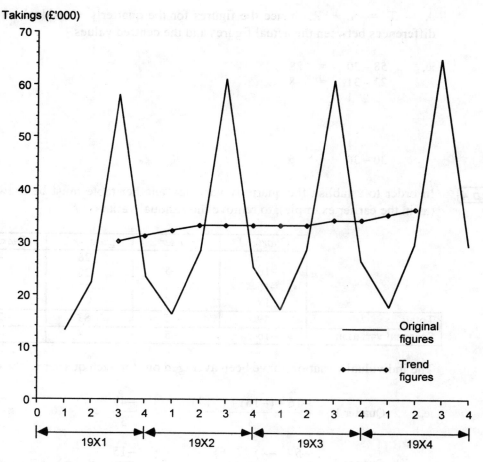

Step 7   **Comment**

As can be seen from the calculations and the graph, the takings show a slight upward trend and the seasonal (quarterly) variations are considerable.

2.11   Seasonally adjusted figures

A popular way of presenting a time series is to give the seasonally adjusted or de-seasonalised figures.

This is a very simple process once the seasonal variations are known.

For the additive model:

| Seasonally adjusted data | = | Original data | − | Seasonal variation | = | A − S |

For the multiplicative model:

| Seasonally adjusted data | = | Original data | ÷ | Seasonal indices | = | A ÷ S |

The main purpose in calculating seasonally adjusted figures is to remove the seasonal influence from the original data so that non-seasonal influences can be seen more clearly.

2.12   Example

The same shopkeeper found his takings for the four quarters of 19X5 were £19,000, £32,000, £65,000 and £30,000 respectively. Has the upward trend continued?

2.13   Solution

De-seasonalising the figures gives:

Seasonally adjusted figures (£'000)

Quarter 1	19 − (−16)	= 35
Quarter 2	32 − (−5)	= 37
Quarter 3	65 − 29	= 36
Quarter 4	30 − (−8)	= 38

So, as can be seen from comparing the seasonally adjusted figures with the trend figures calculated earlier, the takings are indeed still increasing, ie, there is an upward trend.

2.14   Example

Having mentioned a multiplicative model (or proportional model) this now needs illustrating.

The following data will be seasonally adjusted using 'seasonal indices.'

	Quarter			
	1	2	3	4
Sales (£'000)	59	50	61	92
Seasonal variation	−2%	−21%	−9%	+30%

If $A = T \times S \times R$, the de-seasonalised data is A/S.

A decrease of − 2% means a factor of 0.98. Similarly, an increase of 30% means a factor of 1.3. Hence the seasonal factors are   0.98,   0.79,   0.91,   1.30   respectively. The actual data, A, must be **divided** by these values to remove the seasonal effect. Hence:

A	*Seasonal factor (S)*	*Seasonally adjusted figure (= A/S)*
59	0.98	60
50	0.79	63
61	0.91	67
92	1.30	71

While actual sales are lowest in summer and highest in winter, the seasonally adjusted values show a fairly steady increase throughout the year.

2.15   Time series applied to forecasting models

It has been shown in the above sections how data can be de-seasonalised in order to identify the underlying trend. However, it is often the case that predictions are required to be made about the future, but taking into account seasonal factors.

This can be done in two ways:

(a)   by fitting a line of best fit (straight or curved) by eye (preferably through the trend found by moving averages); or

(b)   by using linear regression. This was considered earlier in the text.

The line is then extended to the right in order to estimate future trend values. This 'trend' value is then adjusted in order to take account of the seasonal factors.

Hence, the forecast = $T_e + S$,   where T_e = extrapolated trend.

Residual variations are by nature random and therefore unforecastable.

2.16   Example

Using the data from the shopkeeper predict the takings of the shop for the first and second quarters of 19X5.

2.17   Solution

Takings (£000)

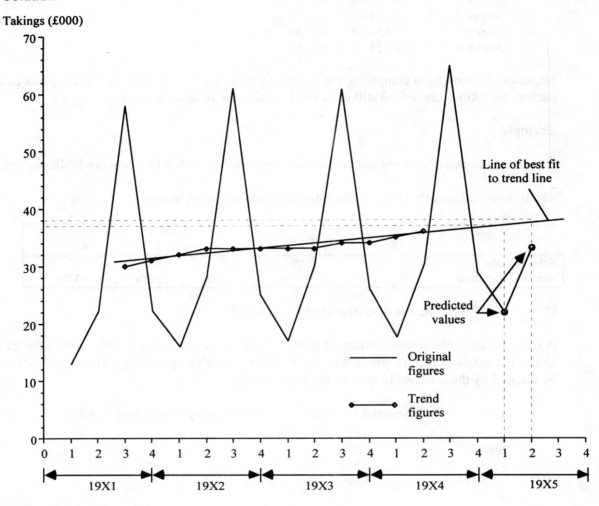

From the graph it can be seen that the trend line predicts values as follows:

Quarter in 19X5	(i) Trend value	(ii) Seasonal variation	(i) + (ii) Final prediction
1	37,000	−16,000	21,000
2	38,000	−5,000	33,000

The predicted values of £21,000 and £33,000 have been plotted on the graph.

For the multiplicative model, the extrapolated trend must be **multiplied** by the appropriate seasonal factor. Thus in the example in paragraph 2.14, if the predicted trend value for the first quarter of the following year was £65,000, the appropriate seasonal factor for this quarter being 0.98, the forecast of actual sales would be £65,000 × 0.98 = £64,000 (to the nearest £000).

2.18   Time series applied to forecasting models – alternative method

As we have seen in the previous chapter, an alternative method for making predictions is to use linear regression in order to establish the trend line in the first place (rather than using the method of moving averages), and then on the basis of this regression line it is possible to predict the figures for the underlying trend. These are then used to estimate seasonal variations and the extrapolated trend values are calculated from the regression equation.

3   CHAPTER SUMMARY

This was the second of the chapters looking at different forecasting techniques. Although time series methods were included at Stage 1, they are specifically mentioned in the syllabus guidance notes for this paper. A wise student would therefore look at this technique carefully!

4   SELF TEST QUESTIONS

4.1   What is a time series analysis? (1.2)

4.2   Which axis is always the time axis? (1.2)

4.3   What is a seasonal variation? (1.4)

4.4   What is the formula for an additive time series model? (2.1)

4.5   What does the method of moving averages try and achieve? (2.2)

5   EXAMINATION TYPE QUESTION

5.1   Daily visitors to a hotel

The number of daily visitors to a hotel, aggregated by quarter, is shown below for the last three years.

Year	Quarter 1	Quarter 2	Quarter 3	Quarter 4
19X6	-	-	-	88
19X7	90	120	200	28
19X8	22	60	164	16
19X9	10	80	192	-

The following additive model is assumed to apply:

Actual value = Trend + Seasonal variation + Residual (irregular) variation

You are required

(a)   to find the centred moving average trend;

(5 marks)

(b)   to find the average seasonal variation for each quarter;

(5 marks)

(c)   to plot the original data and the trend on the same time-series graph;

(5 marks)

(d)   to predict the number of daily visitors for the fourth quarter of 19X9, showing clearly how this is calculated, and state any assumptions underlying this answer.

(5 marks)

(Total: 20 marks)
(CIMA Nov 89)

6   ANSWER TO EXAMINATION TYPE QUESTION

6.1   Daily visitors to a hotel

(a)   Trend using centred moving average

Note: you are given considerable help in finding the trend using moving averages, you are told to find a centred moving average. Set out the original data on every other line, then the first 4 quarter moving average corresponds to a time period half way between the first two and the next two quarters. By finding an 8 quarter moving average a trend figure is found that can be compared with the original data. It is worth finding the seasonal variations for part (b) at the same time.

Year	Quarter	Visitors	4-quarter total	8-quarter total	Centred trend (8-quarter average)	Variations (visitors-trend)
19X6	4	88				
19X7	1	90				
			498			
	2	120		936	117	3
			438			
	3	200		808	101	99
			370			
	4	28		680	85	-57
			310			
19X8	1	22		584	73	-51
			274			
	2	60		536	67	-7
			262			
	3	164		512	64	100
			250			
	4	16		520	65	-49
			270			
19X9	1	10		568	71	-61
			298			
	2	80				
	3	192				

(b)   Average seasonal variations

Year/Quarter	1	2	3	4	Total
19X7		+3	+99	-57	
19X8	-51	-7	+100	-49	
19X9	-61				
Total	-112	-4	+199	-106	
Mean	-56	-2	+99.5	-53	-11.5
Adjusted mean	-53	+1	+102	-50	0.0

Note: the adjusted mean is the seasonal variations. The original mean variations add up to 11.5 so 3 is added to each of these figures, except Q3, to ensure that the total is zero.

(c)   Graph of time series

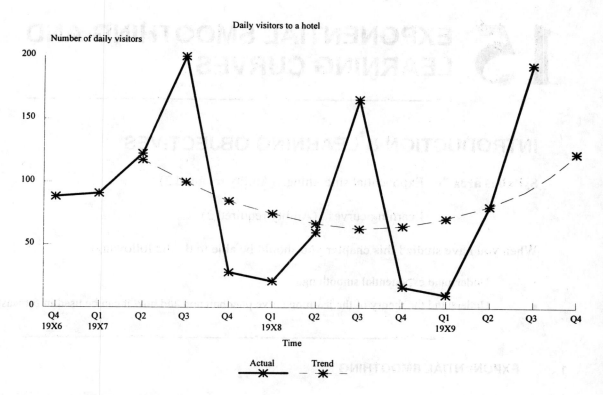

Daily visitors to a hotel

(d)   Forecast for quarter 4 in 19X9

The trend figure for quarter 4 in 19X9 is read from the graph as 120 visitors.

To this should be added the average seasonal variation for quarter 4 which, from (b), is –50.

This makes the best estimate for quarter 4 in 19X9.

120 – 50 = 70 visitors per day.

The assumptions include:

-        the additive model is more appropriate than the proportional model;
-        the random variations for the quarter will not be material; and
-        there are no unusual events that will make the quarter atypical.

15 EXPONENTIAL SMOOTHING AND LEARNING CURVES

INTRODUCTION & LEARNING OBJECTIVES

Syllabus area 7e. Exponential smoothing. (Ability required 2).

Learning curves. (Ability required 2).

When you have studied this chapter you should be able to do the following:

- Understand exponential smoothing.

- Understand the theory of the learning curve phenomenon and how it can be used in forecasting.

1 EXPONENTIAL SMOOTHING

1.1 Introduction

This is a method of forecasting applicable to regular short-term forecasts, such as monthly forecasts of demand for stock control purposes. It is an adaptive forecasting method ie, the latest information is used to 'adapt' the previous forecast to provide a new forecast.

New forecast = old forecast + a proportion of the forecasting error;

ie: New forecast = old forecast + A (latest observation − old forecast); (1)

or by re-arranging formula (1):

New forecast = A (latest observation) + (1 − A) (old forecast). (2)

It can be seen from the simple formulae that only the most recent data is needed, since only the previous forecast and the value of A (the smoothing constant) are required, together with the latest observation, as it becomes available, to update the forecast. A low value for the smoothing constant, say A = 0.1, is equivalent to a long period moving average, whilst a higher one, say A = 0.5, is equivalent to a shorter number of periods. Hence, for time series which change only slightly, a small value of A is appropriate, whereas, if a more sensitive method is needed, then larger values of A are more suitable.

'Exponential smoothing' is a shortened term for 'exponentially weighted moving average', which indicates that various weights are given to different observations. We have already used moving averages earlier in the text when establishing a trend. Simple moving averages are a special case of exponential smoothing in so far as **equal** weight is given to each of the observations. As can be seen in equation (2) above, the latest observation has a weight of A, and the weights of the other observations decrease by a factor of (1 − A) as they become older. Clearly, the older the observations the less weight attached. Equations (1) and (2) are a convenient and simple form of a weighted average of all previous observations, viz:

$$F_O = a_1D_1 + a_2D_2 + a_3D_3 + \ldots\ldots + a_kD_k + \ldots\ldots\ldots\ldots\ldots\ldots\ldots\ldots\ldots\ldots\ldots\ldots \quad (3)$$

where the subscript refers to the number of periods since the present:

F_O	is the forecast made now
D_i	is the observation i periods ago (ie, D_1 is the latest observation)
a_i	is the weight for an observation i periods old.

1.2   Forecast example

Given a first period's forecast of 127, compare the effect of using different values of the smoothing constant for the following data:

133, 118, 150, 132, 157, 132, 130, 139, 170, 132.

1.3   Solution

The forecast for the first period's demand was 127 and it turned out to be 133. Hence, for $A = 0.1$, the forecast of the second period's demand is given by equation (1):

$$F_O = F_1 + A (D_1 - F_1)$$

So $\quad F_O = 127 + 0.1 (133 - 127) = 127.6$

The forecast for the third period's demand is:

$$127.6 + 0.1 (118 - 127.6) = 126.6$$

A work table for $A = 0.1$ can be set up as follows:

Demands D	Forecast F₁	Error (D – F₁)	A × Error	New forecast F₀
133	127	6	0.6	127.6
118	127.6	-9.6	-0.96	126.6
150	126.6	23.4	2.34	128.9
132	128.9	3.1	0.31	129.2
157	129.2	27.8	2.78	132.0
132	132	0	0	132.0
130	132	-2.0	-0.2	131.8
139	131.8	7.2	0.72	132.5
170	132.5	37.5	3.75	136.3
132	136.3	-4.3	-0.43	135.9

1.4   Activity

Repeat the last example using $A = 0.5$ and compare the amount of smoothing that has been achieved.

1.5 Activity solution

Demands D	Forecast F_1	Error $(D - F_1)$	A × Error	New forecast F_0
133	127	6	3	130
118	130	-12	-6	124
150	124	26	13	137
132	137	-5	-2.5	134.5
157	134.5	22.5	11.25	145.75
132	145.75	-13.75	-6.88	138.87
130	138.87	-8.87	-4.44	134.43
139	134.43	4.57	2.28	136.71
170	136.71	33.29	16.64	153.35
132	153.35	-21.35	-10.68	142.67

The error terms are in general larger than using A equal to 0.10, hence the values have not been smoothed to the same extent.

1.6 Conclusion

It is important to appreciate that although the various methods which have been used to identify seasonal (and cyclical) factors and hence predict future values of a particular variable will give different results, it is often not possible to say that any one answer is more valid than another. All methods essentially assume that whatever has caused fluctuations and trends to occur in the past will continue similarly into the future. Clearly this is often not the case and therefore any value forecast by any of the methods should be treated with due caution.

2 THE LEARNING CURVE PHENOMENON

2.1 Introduction

Accountants tend to assume that, within the relevant range of activity, costs display linear characteristics so that the variable cost per unit and the total fixed cost remain unchanged and can be forecast given that the level of activity is known. This section considers the learning curve phenomenon where the linear assumption is dropped.

It is still a forecasting method, however, which can be used in the budgetary process to estimate direct and indirect labour costs.

2.2 The phenomenon stated and illustrated

It has been observed in some industries, particularly where skilled labour predominates, that as more of the same units are produced, there is a reduction in the time taken to manufacture them until the learning process is complete.

The learning curve phenomenon states that each time the number of units produced is **doubled**, the cumulative average time per unit is reduced by a **constant percentage**. If this constant reduction is 20%, this is referred to as an 80% learning curve, and a 10% reduction as a 90% learning curve. This is an important phenomenon which has been empirically observed. Note, the cumulative average time is the average time per unit for **all** units produced up to the present time, including right back to the very first unit made. The **doubling of output** is an important idea to grasp, remember if there is for instance a 60% learning curve, the cumulative average time per unit of output will fall to 60% of what it was before, every time output is doubled.

This will be illustrated by assuming that it has taken 400 direct labour hours to manufacture the first unit of a new product. As in the past for this business it is anticipated that a 75% learning curve will occur. A schedule can be drawn up with the following important headings and calculations:

(1) *Cumulative number* *of units*	*(2)* *Cumulative average* *time per unit*	*(1) × (2)* *Cumulative total* *hours*
1	400	400
2	300 (75% of 400)	600
4	225 (75% of 300)	900

The first two columns form the basis for the calculations as the cumulative total hours in the third column are obtained by multiplying together the figures in columns (1) and (2). As the output doubles the cumulative average time per unit is 75% of the previous figure.

Therefore, if one unit has been produced already taking 400 hours, the production of one more similar unit will only take (600 – 400), ie, 200 hours in the situation of a 75% learning curve. Once two units have been produced, and the learning process continues, the production of two more units will take only (900 – 600), ie, 300 hours. This represents 150 hours per unit.

2.3   Activity

Determine the cumulative total hours for 8 units and hence determine the total time to make the last four units.

2.4   Activity solution

Cumulative number *of units*	*Cumulative average* *time per unit*	*Cumulative total* *hours*
8	168.75 (75% of 225)	1,350

Therefore time for last 4 items = 1,350 – 900 = 450 hours.

2.5   Learning curve equation

The learning curve effect can be shown on a graph, or learning curve, either for unit times or for cumulative total times or costs.

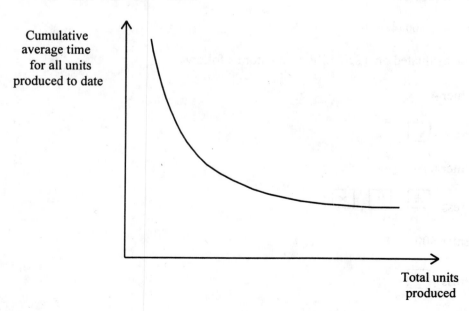

Cumulative
average time
for all units
produced to date

Total units
produced

As can be seen on the graph, eventually the curve becomes horizontal when many units have been produced, as the learning effect is lost and production time per unit becomes a constant.

The learning curve describing the cumulative average time per unit plotted against cumulative number of units can be represented by an equation of the form:

$$y = ax^{-b} \text{ or } y = \frac{a}{x^b}$$

where   y   =   cumulative average time per unit
        a   =   time for producing the first unit
        x   =   cumulative number of units
        b   =   index of learning ($0<b<1$)

The index of learning, $b = \dfrac{\text{logarithm of the inverse of the learning rate (in decimal form)}}{\text{logarithm of } 2}$

Therefore, for a 75% learning curve the index of learning is given by:

$$b = \frac{\log \frac{1}{0.75}}{\log 2}$$

$$= \frac{\log 1.333}{\log 2}$$

$$= \frac{0.1249}{0.3010}$$

$$= 0.415 = \text{index of learning for a 75\% learning curve}$$

The following is a calculational check using the figures in the previous illustration, where one unit had taken 400 hours and a cumulative of four units of production is assumed:

$$y = ax^{-b}$$

where   y   =   cumulative average time per unit
        a   =   400
        x   =   4
        b   =   0.415

$$y = 400 \, (4)^{-0.415}$$

This can be evaluated on a scientific calculator as follows:

(i)   Enter 4

(ii)   Press $\boxed{x^y}$

(iii)   Enter 0.415

(iv)   Press $\boxed{\pm}$, $\boxed{=}$, $\boxed{\times}$

(v)   Enter 400

(vi)   Press $\boxed{=}$

This gives y = 225.01 (2 dp)

(NB: on some calculators, the first $\boxed{=}$ may not be necessary.)

Therefore, the cumulative average time per unit when a total of four units is produced is 225 hours (as previously determined).

For a cumulative production of three units, one unit having been produced in 400 hours, the calculations would be as follows:

$$y = 400 (3)^{-0.415}$$
$$= 253.5 \text{ (the cumulative average time per unit)}$$

The cumulative total time for three units would be 760.5 hours (3 × 253.5).

2.6   Activity

If the learning curve rate is 85%, what is the value of b in the learning curve model $y = ax^{-b}$?

2.7   Activity solution

$$b = \frac{\log(1/0.85)}{\log 2} = \frac{\log 1.1765}{\log 2}$$

$$b = \frac{0.0706}{0.3010} = 0.234$$

2.8   Activity

In a certain company, a 60% learning curve is relevant. The first item of a new product took 50 hours to make. How long should the eighth item take?

2.9   Activity solution

$$y = ax^{-b}$$

$$b = \frac{\log \text{ of inverse learning rate}}{\log 2}$$

$$= \frac{\log \dfrac{1}{0.6}}{\log 2}$$

$$= \frac{\log 1.667}{\log 2}$$

$$= \frac{0.2219}{0.3010} = 0.737$$

$$\therefore \quad y = ax^{-0.737}$$

We first need to find how long the first seven items took to make.

Thus, when x = 7, a = 50

$$y = 50 \times 7^{-0.737}$$

$$= 11.92$$

∴ Total time for 7 units = 7 × 11.92   =   83.44 hours

Now we calculate the cumulative time for all 8 items.

x = 8, a = 50

$$y = 50 \times 8^{-0.737}$$

$$= 10.8$$

∴ Total time for 8 units = 8 × 10.8 = 86.4 hours

Time for the eighth item

Total time for all eight items	=	86.40 hours
Total time for first seven items	=	83.44
∴ Total time for eighth item	=	2.96 hours

2.10   Pricing example

The following worked example illustrates that the benefit of the learning curve relates to labour *and* labour-related costs, but *not* to the cost of materials.

A company wishes to determine the minimum price it should charge a customer for a special order. The customer has requested a quotation for ten machines; he might subsequently place an order for a further ten. Material costs are £30 per machine. It is estimated that the first batch of ten machines will take 100 hours to manufacture and an 80% learning curve is expected to apply. Labour plus variable overhead costs amount to £3 per hour. Setting-up costs are £1,000 regardless of the number of machines made.

(a)   What is the minimum price the company should quote for the initial order if there is no guarantee of further orders?

(b)   What is the minimum price for the follow-on order?

(c)   What would be the minimum price if both orders were placed together?

(d)   Having completed the initial orders for a total of twenty machines (price at the minimum levels recommended in (a) and (b)), the company thinks that there would be a ready market for this type of machine if it brought the unit selling price down to £45. At this price, what would be the profit on the first 140 'mass-production' models (ie, after the first twenty machines) assuming that marketing costs totalled £250?

Initial order

If there is no guarantee of a follow-up order, the setting-up costs must be recovered on the initial order. Costs are, therefore, as follows:

	£
Material (10 × £30)	300
Labour and variable overhead (100 × £3)	300
Setting-up cost	1,000
Total	1,600
Minimum price each	160

Follow-on order

The setting-up costs have been recovered on the initial order. Output is doubled; therefore, average time for each group of ten machines is reduced to

100 × 0.8 = 80 hours

ie, cumulative time for twenty machines = 160 hours

∴   Time for second group of ten   =   time for first 20 − time for first 10
=   160 − 100
=   60 hours

Costs are therefore

	£
Material	300
Labour and variable overhead	180
Total	480
Minimum price each	48

Both orders together

Total costs are:

	£
Material	600
Labour (160 hours)	480
Setting-up cost	1,000
Total	2,080
Minimum price each	104

This is, of course, the mean of the two previous prices: cumulative costs are the same but they are recorded evenly over twenty units instead of most of the cost being 'loaded' onto the first ten units.

The time spent on the first 140 mass production models is calculated as follows:

Working in units of 10 machines, $y = ax^{-b}$ where $a = 100$

$$b = \frac{\log\left(\frac{1}{0.8}\right)}{\log 2} \qquad = \quad 0.3219$$

Average time/unit for first 2 units (ie, first 20 machines)

	=	$100(2)^{-0.3219}$
	=	80 hours
Total time for first 2 units	=	80×2
	=	160 hours

Average time per unit for first 16 units (ie, first 160 machines)

	=	$100(16)^{-0.3219}$
	=	40.96 hours
Total time for first 16 units	=	40.96×16
	=	655.36 hours
Hence total time for units 3 to 16	(ie, the 140 mass-produced units)	
	=	(655.36 − 160) hours
	=	495.36 hours

Cost of first 140 mass-production models

	£
Material	4,200
Labour and variable overhead ($495.36 \times £3$)	1,486
Marketing	250
Total cost	5,936
Revenue	6,300
Profit	364

3   SELF TEST QUESTIONS

3.1   What is the term 'exponential smoothing' short for? (1.1)

3.2   What is the exponential smoothing equation for providing the new forecast? (1.1)

3.3   State the principle of a learning curve. (2.2)

3.4   If the cumulative average time per unit is reduced by a constant 20% every time cumulative output doubles, what is the learning curve which this refers to? (2.2)

3.5   What is the learning curve equation? (2.5)

4   EXAMINATION TYPE QUESTION

4.1   Learning curve for RS plc

RS plc manufactures domestic food mixers. It is investigating whether or not to accept a three-year contract to make a new model for sale through a supermarket chain. New machinery costing £50,000 would have to be bought at the start of the contract. The contract uses skilled labour which cannot be increased above that currently available and RS plc will receive a fixed price of £42 per mixer for all the mixers it can produce in the three-year period. The following estimates have been made:

Materials	£30 per mixer
Labour	£6 per hour
Cost of capital	15%

The factory manager knows from experience of similar machines that there will be a learning effect for labour. He estimates that this will take the form:

$$y = ax^{-0.3}$$

where   y   =   average labour hours per unit
        a   =   labour hours for first unit
        x   =   cumulative production

He estimates that the first mixer will take 10 hours to produce and that the fixed amount of labour available will enable 5,000 mixers to be produced in the first year. Fixed overheads of £25,000 will be payable each year.

Should the contract be accepted?

5   ANSWER TO EXAMINATION TYPE QUESTION

5.1   Learning curve for RS plc

$y = ax^{-0.3}$

For the first year

$$a \quad = \quad 10, x = 5,000,$$

hence, $y \quad = \quad 10 \times 5,000^{-0.3} \quad = \quad 0.7768$ hours

Total labour   =   Average per unit $\times$ No. of units

            = $0.7768 \times 5,000$

            =   3,884 hours

For the second year

x is unknown, but the means to calculate y is given, as the labour hours will be the same as in year 1.

Total labour hours for the two years   = $3,884 \times 3$

                                        =   7,768 hours

Let x = total production for 2 years.

Average labour hours per unit $= \dfrac{7{,}768}{x} = y$

Hence

$$\dfrac{7{,}768}{x} = 10x^{-0.3}$$

$$7{,}768 = 10x^{-0.3} \times x^{1}$$

$$= 10x^{0.7} \quad (x^{p} \times x^{q} = x^{p+q})$$

$$x^{0.7} = \dfrac{7.768}{10} = 776.8$$

$$\therefore \quad x = (776.8)^{1/0.7} = 13{,}459$$

(Tutorial note

To obtain the 0.7th root, use the $x^{1/y}$ function on your calculator, putting y = 0.7.

Hence the number of units in year 2   =   13,459 – 5,000

   =   8,459)

For the third year

Let x = cumulative production for all three years

Total labour hours for three years   =   3,884 × 3

   =   11,652

Average labour hours per unit   = $\dfrac{11{,}652}{x} = y$

Hence

$$\dfrac{11{,}652}{x} = 10x^{-0.3}$$

$$11{,}652 = 10x^{0.7}$$

$$x^{0.7} = 1{,}165.2$$

$$x = (1{,}165.2)^{1/0.7}$$

$$= 24{,}020$$

Hence the number of units produced in year 3   =   24,020 – 13,459

   =   10,561

Output (units)	Year 1 *5,000*	Year 2 *8,459*	Year 3 *10,561*
	£	£	£
Sales (output × £42)	210,000	355,278	443,562
Less costs:			
Labour (3,884 × £6)	23,304	23,304	23,304
Materials (output × £30)	150,000	253,770	316,830
Overheads	25,000	25,000	25,000
Total costs	198,304	302,074	365,134
Net cash flow	11,696	53,204	78,428
Present value at 15% pa	10,170	40,230	51,568

NPV   =   (10,170 + 40,230 + 51,568) − 50,000 (£)

      =   **£51,968**

The contract has a positive net present value so should be accepted.

16 MARKET DEMAND ANALYSIS

INTRODUCTION & LEARNING OBJECTIVES

Syllabus area 7f. Market demand analysis; use of price, income and cross-elasticities. (Ability required 3).

When you have studied this chapter you should be able to do the following:

- Know the definitions, formulae and meaning of price, income and cross elasticity of demand.

- Understand how to use elasticity to describe the shape of demand curves.

- Explain which factors affect the different types of elasticity, and the effect that each one has.

- Appreciate the practical uses of elasticity.

---

1 CALCULATING PRICE ELASTICITY OF DEMAND

1.1 The formulae for price elasticity of demand

Definition **Price elasticity of demand** is the degree of sensitivity of demand for a good to changes in price of that good.

One of the most important influences on demand is the price of the good in question. It is useful to be able to analyse in numerical terms the effect on demand of a change in price. We do this using price elasticity of demand (often shortened to 'elasticity of demand' or PED).

Price elasticity can be defined in a number of ways. One possible formula is:

$$PED = \frac{\text{Percentage change in quantity demanded}}{\text{Percentage change in price}}$$

1.2 Activity

If PED for a certain good currently equals -2, how will sales be affected if price rises by 10%?

1.3 Activity solution

Use the formula, PED = (percentage change in quantity demanded) ÷ (percentage change in price).

Here, -2 = (percentage change in quantity demanded) ÷ (+10%)

Therefore, percentage change in quantity demanded = $(-2) \times (+10\%) = -20\%$.

In other words, quantity will **fall** by 20%. Note the minus sign, which is important. The PED given in the question was negative and this fed through to give a negative change in quantity demanded; in other words, a **fall.** This accords with all your previous knowledge of this area: price rose, so demand fell.

1.4   An alternative formula

An alternative presentation of the formula is suitable for calculations involving a straight-line demand curve, and is illustrated below:

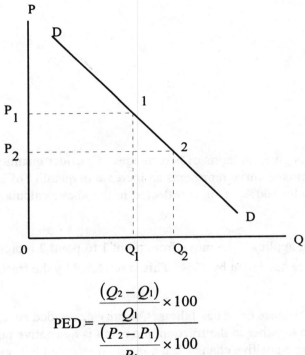

$$PED = \frac{\frac{(Q_2 - Q_1)}{Q_1} \times 100}{\frac{(P_2 - P_1)}{P_1} \times 100}$$

This equation calculates the elasticity at point 1 on the demand curve. The changes in quantity and price are expressed as a percentage of the quantity and price at point 1.

We will use an example to demonstrate how the equation works and how it relates to the first equation.

1.5   Example

A firm faces the following demand curve:

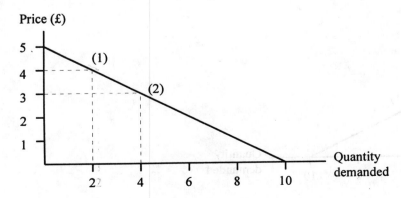

Figure 1

We want to work out the price elasticity of demand at point 1. The first step is to select any other point on the line to act as a reference point, point 2. Here we have chosen a point one step down the line from point 1, but on a straight-line demand curve any other point would give the same result.

The price and quantity at point 1 are P_1 and Q_1 respectively. So $P_1 = 4$ and $Q_1 = 2$. Similarly, price and quantity at point 2 are P_2 and Q_2 respectively. So $P_2 = 3$ and $Q_2 = 4$.

Applying the equation above:

$$\text{PED} = \frac{\dfrac{(4-2)}{2} \times 100}{\dfrac{(3-4)}{4} \times 100}$$

$$= \frac{\dfrac{2}{2} \times 100}{\dfrac{-1}{4} \times 100} = \frac{100}{-25} = -4.$$

So price elasticity of demand at point 1 is -4.

We can relate this to the formula which was given in terms of percentages. Consider quantity first. The move from point 1 to point 2 on the demand curve represents an increase in quantity of 2 units, from 2 to 4. In fact, quantity has gone up by 100%. This is reflected in the above calculation by the fraction $\frac{2}{2} = 1$ or 100%.

Moving on to the price, a similar reasoning applies. The move from point 1 to point 2 represents a **decrease** in price of £1, from £4 to £3. Price has fallen by 25%. This is reflected by the fraction $\frac{-1}{4}$ = -25%.

Again, note the minus sign, which is there because price has **fallen**. Quantity demanded **rose**, so its change is **positive**. When we bring the two together in the fraction, the result is a negative number. The same would happen if price rose, giving a positive change, but quantity demanded fell, giving a negative change. Since for most goods price and quantity demanded move in opposite directions, most goods will have a negative price elasticity of demand; often the minus sign will be omitted on the grounds that it can be assumed.

So the second equation is simply a different form of the first equation. They are both measuring the response of quantity demanded to a price change; and they both measure the changes in the variables in terms of percentages.

1.6   PED is different at each point

Figure 2 is a copy of Figure 1, but with a different point selected as point 1.

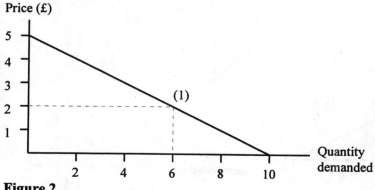

Figure 2

Calculate the price elasticity of demand at the new point 1.

1.7   Solution

Another point on the line must be chosen as a reference point. We have chosen point 2 as marked on Figure 3, but any other point should give the same result.

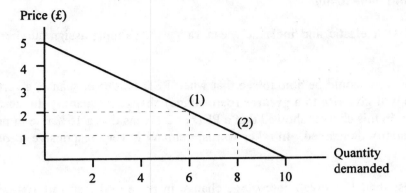

Figure 3

Using the second of the two formulae given in the previous section,

$$PED = \frac{Q_2 - Q_1}{Q_1} \bigg/ \frac{P_2 - P_1}{P_1}$$

$$= \frac{8 - 6}{6} \bigg/ \frac{1 - 2}{2} = \frac{2}{6} \bigg/ \frac{-1}{2} = \frac{1}{3} \times -2 = -\frac{2}{3}.$$

Price elasticity of demand at point 1 is 0.67 (ignoring the minus sign).

Note that this is different from the PED calculated in paragraph 1.5.

1.8   PED at different points on a straight line demand curve

This calculation, together with the one done in the previous section, demonstrates that PED is different at different points on a demand curve. The first PED we calculated was 4 and lay on the upper half of the line. The second one, 0.67, lay on the lower half. In fact, on a straight-line demand curve:

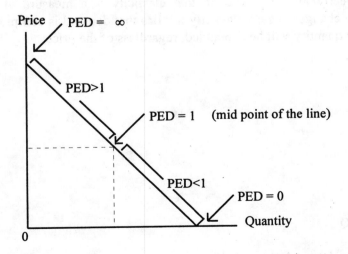

Figure 4

As shown in Figure 4, along the top half of the line, PED is greater than 1. We say that demand is **elastic**. Along the bottom half of the line, PED is less than 1 and we say that demand is **inelastic**. Exactly half-way along the line, PED =1; demand is of 'unitary elasticity'.

1.9   The meaning of elasticity and inelasticity

It is important to understand what 'elastic' and 'inelastic' mean, rather than simply assign numbers to price elasticity.

If you return to the formulae, you should be able to see that when PED is greater than 1, a certain (percentage) change in price will give rise to a **greater** (percentage) change in quantity demanded. For example, the first activity in this chapter showed that a PED of 2 means that a 10% rise in price will induce a 20% fall in quantity demanded. In other words, demand is very responsive to price changes.

Conversely, when PED is less than 1, a given percentage change in price will result in a **smaller** percentage change in demand, so demand is **not** responsive to price changes; and when PED equals 1, the percentage change in quantity demanded equals the percentage change in price.

> **Conclusion**   When PED>1, demand is relatively elastic and the quantity demanded is very responsive to price changes; when PED<1, demand is relatively inelastic and the quantity demanded is not very responsive to price changes.

Note that if demand is said to be inelastic, this does not mean that there will be no change in quantity demanded when the price changes, it means that the consequent demand change will be proportionately smaller than the price change. If demand does not change at all after a price change, demand is said to be perfectly inelastic, and this is a special case as will be seen below.

1.10   Unusual demand curves

There are three types of demand curve which merit special attention: those of zero elasticity, infinite elasticity and unitary elasticity. These are the only demand curves for which elasticity **is** the same at every point on the curve.

(a)   Zero elasticity

Such a curve is called 'perfectly inelastic'. Given that elasticity is a measure of the sensitivity of demand to price changes, a zero elasticity implies that demand is completely unaffected by price; the same quantity will be demanded, regardless of the price:

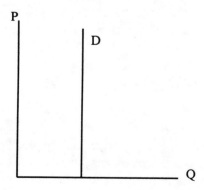

Figure 5   A perfectly inelastic demand curve

(b)   **Infinite elasticity**

Such a curve is called 'perfectly elastic'. A small change in price results in an infinitely large change in demand. So a minuscule rise in price will result in demand falling to zero; while a minuscule fall in price will cause demand to rise to infinity:

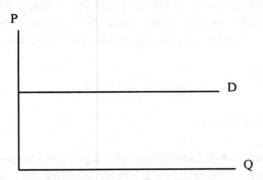

Figure 6 A perfectly elastic demand curve

(c)   **Unitary elasticity**

Such a curve has a PED of 1 at every point on the curve. It is a 'rectangular hyperbola'. The name comes from the fact that the area of any rectangle drawn touching the curve is the same:

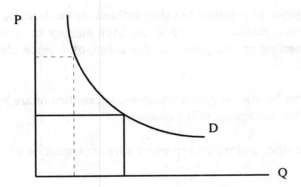

Figure 7 A demand curve of unitary elasticity

The two rectangles drawn in Figure 7 have the same area. In fact, the area of the rectangle is the revenue at that point on the demand curve (P × Q), so if a firm makes a good with **this** type of demand curve, total revenue will remain the same regardless of the price charged and the quantity sold. Each price reduction will be exactly matched by a rise in sales, so that total revenue will not change; and vice versa.

2   FACTORS AFFECTING PRICE ELASTICITY OF DEMAND

2.1   Positive PED

The earlier section pointed out that the PED for most goods is negative, as price and quantity demanded move in opposite directions. If a price rise caused a **rise** in quantity demanded, or vice versa, the good would have a positive PED (and an upward-sloping demand curve). Goods bought for the purpose of ostentation may have a positive PED, as will **Giffen goods**.

Giffen goods are sometimes called 'poor man's goods'. They are staple goods, which become inferior goods when they comprise the whole of a person's diet such as bread or potatoes; if their price rises, the poor may increase their consumption and forgo consumption of other goods. For example, suppose there are only two goods, meat and potatoes. Meat costs £4 per lb and potatoes cost 20 pence per lb. A family has a weekly income of £2 and at present buys 8lbs of potatoes per week, costing £1.60 and 0.1 lbs of meat, costing 40 pence. If the price of potatoes now goes up to, say, 24 pence per lb and the family continued to buy 8lbs per week, it would only have £2 − (8 × 0.24) = 8 pence left to spend on meat, which would not be worth doing. The family would have to reduce its consumption of potatoes so much in order to afford a suitable amount of meat that it could not survive. So it stops buying meat altogether, spending all its income on potatoes. The effect of the price rise is that consumption of potatoes **rises** from 8lbs per week to £2/0.24 = 8⅓ lbs.

2.2   The factors affecting PED

Price elasticity of demand is influenced by the following:

(a)   **The price of the product in relation to total spending** - if the price is low people may not notice a substantial relative increase. The price of a box of matches may double, but if matches are bought infrequently and the price is only a very small part of total spending, few people will notice the rise.

(b)   **The availability of substitutes** - if there are goods considered to be equivalent to the product, people will readily switch to these if the price rises. This is one reason why producers try to build up brand loyalty by advertising: 'Don't say brown, say Hovis' and 'Don't be vague, ask for Haig' are typical examples.

(c)   **The relative importance of price in relation to other influences on demand** - a range of influences such as taste, income, market size and so on have already been identified. If these other influences are exerting strong pressure, the effect of a price change can be masked.

Price elasticity of demand will therefore be low for goods which are necessities or are habit forming because these have few substitutes in the perception of the consumer.

Equally goods which have many substitutes and which represent a large proportion of a consumer's expenditure have an elastic demand.

Also note that the passage of time will have an effect on elasticity. If the price of petrol rises substantially, for example, demand will only respond a little in the short term, but eventually the cost will make it worthwhile for society to develop products which can be used instead of petrol.

Conclusion   Demand is more elastic in the long run than in the short run.

2.3   Activity

Before reading further, think about the extent to which demand for the following goods will fall following a moderate price rise:

* Petrol;
* Coffee;
* 'Aquafresh' toothpaste; and
* Matches.

This activity should help analyse which factors affect the magnitude of PED.

2.4   Activity solution

(a)   Petrol is seen as a necessity by most people with a car and has few substitutes. Therefore, if price rose a little (as it often does), the effect on demand is likely to be very small. In other words, demand for petrol is inelastic; it has a low PED.

(b)   Coffee is habit-forming and is therefore perceived as a necessity by those who depend on it and does not have (in their eyes) any substitutes. As for petrol, demand for coffee is probably inelastic.

(c)   'Aquafresh' toothpaste has many substitutes. If its price goes up, it is likely that quite a few customers will simply buy another brand and demand for Aquafresh will fall. Here, PED is high and demand is elastic.

(d)   Finally, matches make up a very small proportion of a consumer's expenditure, so if their price rises, it is unlikely to affect demand significantly. Demand is inelastic.

3   PRACTICAL USES OF PRICE ELASTICITY

3.1   PED and revenue

The unitary elasticity demand curve in Figure 7 introduced the idea that there is a connection between PED and revenue. For that curve, total revenue stayed the same regardless of the price charged.

When demand is elastic, total revenue rises as price falls. This is because the quantity demanded is very responsive to price changes. A fall in the price gives rise to a **more** than proportionate rise in the quantity demanded. The net effect is that revenue (= price × quantity) rises.

Conversely, when demand is inelastic, total revenue falls as price falls. Here a fall in price causes a **less** than proportionate rise in quantity demanded, the result being a net fall in total revenue.

Equally, when demand is elastic, total revenue falls when price rises; and when demand is inelastic, total revenue rises when price rises.

It would therefore be very useful to a producer to know whether he is at an elastic or inelastic part of his demand curve. This will enable him to predict the effect on revenue of raising or lowering his price.

3.2   Graphing the relationship between PED and revenue

The following schedule and graph shows the relationship between a demand curve, the total revenue curve and the price elasticity. The numbers have been kept very simple to illustrate the principles.

(a)   **The schedule**

Price £	Demand (units)	Total revenue £
10	1	10
9	2	18
8	3	24
7	4	28
6	5	30
5	6	30
4	7	28
3	8	24
2	9	18
1	10	10

(b)   The graph

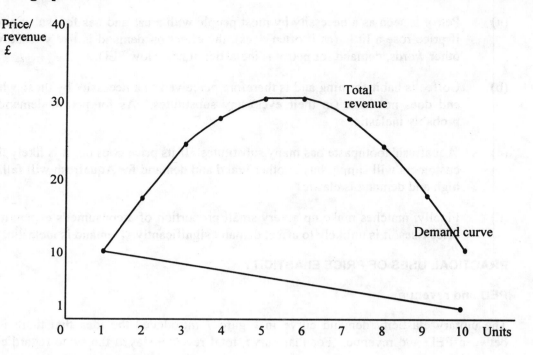

(c)   The price elasticity of demand

Calculate the PED at price £2, quantity 9 units by moving to price £3, quantity 8 units.

$$PED = \frac{9-8}{9} \div \frac{2-3}{2}$$

$$= \frac{1}{9} \div -\frac{1}{2} = -\frac{2}{9}$$

Now calculate the PED at price £9, quantity 2 units by moving to price £8, quantity 3 units.

$$PED = \frac{2-3}{2} \div \frac{9-8}{9}$$

$$= -\frac{1}{2} \div \frac{1}{9}$$

$$= -\frac{9}{2} = -4\frac{1}{2}$$

Notice that the PED is very elastic near the top of the demand curve, and inelastic near the bottom.

Notice also that if price is increased when demand is elastic (near the top of the curve) (ie, you move **up** the demand curve), total revenue will **fall**. If however price is increased when demand is inelastic (near the bottom of the curve) total revenue will increase.

4   INCOME ELASTICITY OF DEMAND

4.1   The formulae for income elasticity of demand

> **Definition**   Income elasticity of demand measures the sensitivity of demand for a good to changes in consumers' income.

The concept is just like price elasticity of demand, but this time we are concentrating on a different influence on demand, namely income. The acronym for income elasticity of demand is YED, the Y standing for income.

The formulae for income elasticity are analogous to those for price elasticity:

YED = (percentage change in quantity demanded) / (percentage change in income);

and

$$YED = \frac{(Q_2 - Q_1)}{Q_1} \bigg/ \frac{(Y_2 - Y_1)}{Y_1}$$, where the 'Y's represent changes in the level of income.

4.2   Activity

Draw a diagram showing the relationship between the quantity of colour televisions bought per week and national income. Show income along the vertical axis and quantity demanded along the horizontal axis. Predict whether the income elasticity of demand for colour televisions is positive or negative. Would your diagram and prediction change if the good in question were black and white televisions?

4.3   Activity solution

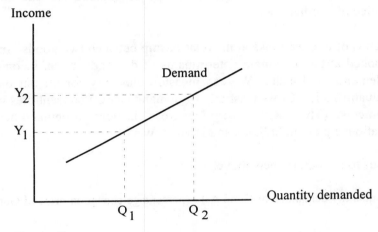

Figure 8

As consumers' income rises, they are likely to buy more colour televisions, so the demand curve will slope upwards (a rise in income from Y_1 to Y_2 induces a rise in quantity demanded from Q_1 to Q_2). Since income and quantity demanded move in the same direction, YED will be positive. Goods for which YED is positive are called **normal goods**.

The analysis would change if we were considering black and white televisions, which are generally considered to be inferior goods. People tend to prefer the more expensive colour televisions, so that when income rises and they can afford them, they will switch away from the black and white ones. Therefore the curve would be downward-sloping, as with the more familiar one which links quantity demanded with price. Similarly, YED will be negative.

4.4   Factors affecting income elasticity of demand

As we saw in the previous activity, YED can be positive or negative. If the good is generally considered to be inferior, as are black and white televisions, it will have a negative YED. Most goods are normal and will have a positive YED.

The size of YED depends on the current standard of living. For example, the western world has a high standard of living, so that when income expands, sales of consumer durables such as washing machines and cars will rise; sales of basic commodities (food etc) are unlikely to respond significantly to the rise in income. Thus in the UK, the YED of consumer durables is probably high, while that of basic commodities is likely to be low. On the other hand, Third World economies are likely to have the reverse pattern, as much of the population is unable to afford basic commodities at its current level of income.

4.5   Practical uses of income elasticity of demand

A producer may wish to know the income elasticity of demand for his product, as his plans for future production may depend on whether incomes are rising or falling. Alternatively, he could decide to switch to products which reflect changes in national income.

More importantly, a government must be able to predict its annual tax take. To the extent that taxes are levied on expenditure (such as VAT) the tax take from products with different income elasticities will respond differently to rises and falls in national income.

5   CROSS ELASTICITY OF DEMAND

5.1   The formulae for cross elasticity of demand

Definition   Cross elasticity of demand measures the sensitivity of demand for one good to changes in the price of another good.

The final type of elasticity which is of interest looks at the relationship between two goods. In your earlier studies you will have looked at the four main determinants of demand: price, income, the price of substitutes and complements, and taste. We can measure elasticity for all but the last determinant, since taste is not quantifiable. Cross elasticity of demand (XED) concentrates on the price of substitutes and complements. (There will be very low cross elasticity of demand between goods which have a tenuous relationship eg, light bulbs and lawn mowers.)

Again the formulae are analogous to the others seen above:

XED =   (percentage change in quantity demanded of Good A) / (percentage change in price of Good B); and

$$XED = \frac{(Q_{A2} - Q_{A1})}{Q_{A1}} \bigg/ \frac{(P_{B2} - P_{B1})}{P_{B1}}$$, where suffix A represents Good A and suffix B represents Good B.

5.2   Activity

The XED of butter with respect to margarine is +1.5. Suppose the price of margarine falls by 6%. What will happen to demand for butter?

5.3   Activity solution

Using the first of the two formulae,

XED =   (percentage change in quantity of butter demanded) / (percentage change in price of margarine).

Here   1.5 = (percentage change in quantity of butter demanded) / (-6%),

so percentage change in quantity of butter demanded = 1.5 × (-6%)

= – 9%.

Demand for butter will fall by 9%.

5.4   The sign of cross elasticity of demand

In the preceding activity, the XED between butter and margarine was positive. This is because butter and margarine are substitutes.   When the price of margarine **goes down**, demand for margarine rises and demand for butter **falls**. In other words, the price of margarine and demand for butter move in the same direction so XED is positive.

Conversely, the XED between complements is negative. Consider pens and ink. If the price of ink **fell**, demand for ink would rise. Ink and pens are complementary, so demand for pens is also likely to **rise**. The price of ink and demand for pens move in opposite directions, so the XED of complements is negative.

Conclusion	The XED of substitutes is positive, while that for complements is negative.

6   CHAPTER SUMMARY

Elasticity is a very powerful tool for describing different types of demand and supply curves and you will come across the concept many times in your studies.

The main points to remember are:

(a)   The formulae for all types of elasticity are based on that for price elasticity:

PED = (percentage change in quantity demanded) / (percentage change in price)

(b)   Elasticity measures the degree of responsiveness of demand (or supply) to changes in price, income or the price of other goods, as appropriate.

(c)   PED is almost always negative, so we usually ignore the minus sign.

(d)   If PED>1, demand is elastic and responsive to price changes. If PED<1, demand is inelastic and is not responsive to price changes.

7   SELF TEST QUESTIONS

7.1   Define price elasticity of demand and state its simple formula. (1.1)

7.2   Is price elasticity of demand positive or negative? (1.5)

7.3   If price elasticity of demand is −2 and price rises by 10%, by how much will quantity demanded fall? (1.9)

7.4   Draw a graph showing unitary elasticity of demand. What do you call this graph? (1.10)

7.5   What are Giffen goods? (2.1)

7.6   If a product is habit-forming, would you expect its demand to be relatively elastic or relatively inelastic? (2.4)

7.7   If demand for a product is relatively elastic and the price of that product rises, what will happen to the firm's total revenue? (3.1)

7.8   What is a normal good? (4.3)

7.9   Is the cross-elasticity of demand for complements positive or negative? (5.4)

8   EXAMINATION TYPE QUESTION

8.1   Elasticity of demand

(a)   A manufacturer expects to have revenue of £20,000 when he sells his product for £5. A fall in costs of production results in a new price of £4. His total revenue is now £30,000.

Calculate the price elasticity of demand over this price range.

(b)   Suppose that a further reduction in price to £3 brings revenue of £33,000.

What is the price elasticity over this price range? What conclusions can you draw from the answers you have given?

(c)   If revenue had not altered after the price change from £4 to £3, what then would be the price elasticity of demand?

(20 marks)

9   ANSWER TO EXAMINATION TYPE QUESTION

9.1   Elasticity of demand

Price elasticity of demand is measured by:

$$\frac{\%\ \text{change in quantity demanded}}{\%\ \text{change in price}}$$

A problem students encounter is how to measure the percentage change. If the change is taken as a percentage of the original cost, then a price change of £10 from £20 to £10 would give a percentage change of 50% whilst a change of £10 from £10 to £20 would give a percentage change of 100%. This would give a different coefficient of elasticity according to whether we were measuring the responsiveness of demand to an increase in price from £10 to £20 or a decrease in price from £20 to £10.

To avoid this problem, the change can be measured as a percentage of the average of the two prices in question.

Thus, for the example given:

(a)

Price £	Quantity demanded
5	$\frac{20,000}{5}$ = 4,000
4	$\frac{30,000}{4}$ = 7,500

Percentage change in price

$$= \frac{1}{4.5} \times 100$$

$$= 22.2\%$$

Percentage change in quantity

$$= \frac{3,500}{5,750} \times 100$$

$$= 60.9\%$$

Elasticity

$$= \frac{60.9}{22.2}$$

$$= 2.74$$

(b)

Price £	Quantity demanded
4	7,500
3	$\dfrac{33,000}{3}$ = 11,000

$$\text{Elasticity} = \dfrac{\dfrac{3,500}{9,250} \times 100}{\dfrac{1}{3.5} \times 100}$$

$$= \dfrac{37.8}{28.6}$$

$$= 1.32$$

Thus, although the same change in price (£1) gave the same increase in the units demanded (3,500), the elasticity has fallen. This is because at lower prices the same absolute change in price will give a higher percentage change than at higher prices, whilst, on the other hand, at higher levels of demand the same absolute change in demand gives a lower percentage change.

This illustrates the fact that elasticity can (and usually does) vary along a demand curve. It is also demonstrated by seeing that a fall in price from £5 to £4 gave additional revenue of £10,000 whilst a fall from £4 to £3 only gave additional revenue of £3,000. If price dropped a further £1 to £2 and the increase in quantity demanded was again 3,500, then revenue would actually fall, viz:

$$£2 \times 14,500 \quad = \quad \underline{£29,000}$$

Over this range elasticity is less than one ie, inelastic:

$$\dfrac{\dfrac{3,500}{12,750} \times 100}{\dfrac{1}{2.5} \times 100} \quad = \quad \dfrac{24.75}{40.0}$$

$$= \quad \underline{0.69}$$

(c) If revenue does not alter as a result of a price change the elasticity must equal one ie, the percentage change in quantity demanded must be the same as the percentage change in price. The usual calculation proves this, as follows:

Price £	Quantity demanded		
4	$\dfrac{30,000}{4}$	=	7,500
3	$\dfrac{30,000}{3}$	=	10,000

$$\text{Elasticity} = \frac{\dfrac{2,500}{8,750} \times 100}{\dfrac{1}{3.5} \times 100}$$

$$= \frac{28.57}{28.57}$$

$$= \underline{1}$$

(Note: in this type of question it is necessary to apply the formula for measuring elasticity of demand. Such questions will inevitably provide you with all the data which is required and it is thus necessary to use the data to determine the elasticity value. You should state whether or not the measurement is based upon the first price and quantity or the mid-point between the prices and quantities. Often the question will tell you the direction of price change; if it does not then you should state your assumptions.*)*

17 COSTS, REVENUE AND PROFITS

INTRODUCTION & LEARNING OBJECTIVES

Syllabus area 7f. Costs, production and profit analysis; characteristics of costs and production; economies of scale; economic efficiency. (Ability required 2).

When you have studied this chapter you should be able to do the following:

- Explain the difference between fixed, variable and marginal costs.

- Draw the shape of short run cost curves.

- Understand and explain total, average and marginal revenue.

- Define and understand the basic rule for profit maximisation.

- Understand the shape of the cost curves in the long run and the role of economies of scale.

---

1 THE SHORT RUN AND LONG RUN

Definition The short run is the period during which at least one factor of production remains fixed. In the long run, all factors are variable.

This needs a little explanation. Consider a manufacturing company which rents a factory on a five year lease. Other than the rent, all its costs are variable; they include raw materials and labour paid by the hour. Suppose the company signs its lease in 19X1. The firm has contracted to rent the factory until 19X6 and incurs the fixed cost of the rent. If it wants to reduce its output, for example, it cannot save rent by leasing a smaller factory. It will simply produce less in the factory which it has at present. After 19X6, if it still wants to reduce output, it has the option of not renewing the lease, but looking for a smaller, cheaper factory. In 19X1, when the lease is signed, the short run is the time period up to 19X6 and the long run is beyond 19X6.

If nothing changes for the next five years, the short run will get shorter and shorter and long run nearer and nearer. But in practice, firms do not have such simple production processes. There will be many factors of production which are fixed for varying lengths of time, which the firm must use until it can change them if it so wishes. In fact, firms are always operating in the short run, but planning in the long run.

Conclusion Firms operate in the short run and plan into the long run.

2 SHORT RUN COSTS

2.1 Introduction

Our aim in the next few sections is to build up a picture of how the average firm's costs behave. This section will concentrate on short-run costs. It will discuss average costs per unit, bearing in mind that these consist of average variable costs plus average fixed costs. It will also look at marginal costs.

2.2   Fixed costs and average fixed costs

Costs in the accountancy sense are the payments made by a firm in return for the inputs required for the production process. Some of these costs are **fixed**. This does not mean that they never change, it means that they do not vary in direct relation to changes in the level of output ie, changes in the amount of goods produced. Examples of this include the rent paid for the use of land or buildings, interest paid for the use of money, the **depreciation** (loss of value caused by the passage of time) of machines, salaries to managers and so on: in the short-term, these remain the same whatever the level of production or sales achieved by the firm.

Fixed costs can be illustrated as in the graph of Figure 1. Notice that they stay at £40 whether one or twelve units are being produced.

Figure 1

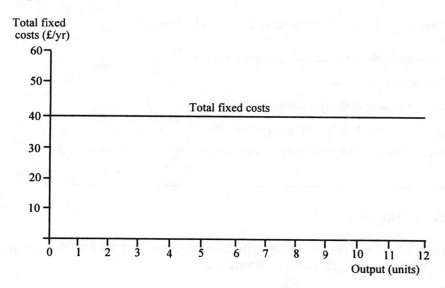

Average fixed cost is related to the number of units being produced. This must clearly fall as the number increases; if two units are produced, the average is £20 (£40 ÷ 2); if four are produced it is £10 (£40 ÷ 4). This is illustrated in Figure 2.

Figure 2

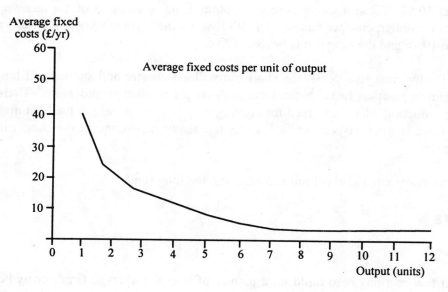

2.3 Total variable costs

If some costs do not change in direct relation to output in the short-term, some others do. Such costs include payments for materials used in producing goods, for fuel used in driving delivery vehicles, for postage and packing costs if goods are sent by mail, as well as some wages, where wage payments are based on **piece rates** (payment in accordance with the amount of work performed). Whilst accountants may wish to distinguish between fixed, semi-fixed and variable costs, it is sufficient at this stage to confine the division into fixed and variable.

If variable costs are constant ie, if they remain the same per unit produced, then total variable costs can be illustrated as in Figure 3. Here each unit has a variable cost of £8.

Figure 3

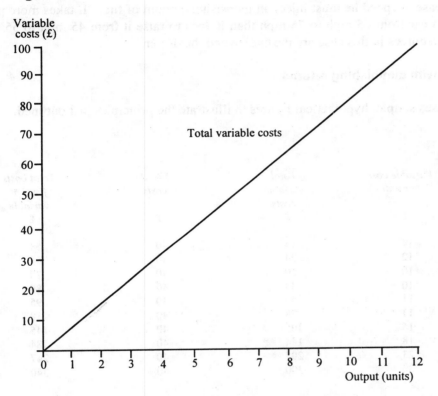

It is unlikely, however, that variable costs will be as regular as this. They are more likely to be subject to two influences. At low levels of output they may be constant or even fall on a unit basis; this is because firms are likely to get some benefit from such things as discounts from suppliers or find that other costs rise at less than the proportionate amount. As the firm continues to grow, however, it begins to experience what is usually referred to as **diminishing marginal returns.**

2.4 Diminishing marginal returns

The variations in output that result from applying more or less of a variable factor to a given quantity of a fixed factor are the subject of a famous economic hypothesis. Most frequently, it has been called the 'law of diminishing returns', but it has also been given other names, including the 'law of variable proportions'.

This hypothesis suggests that if a firm continues to add increasing inputs of factors (resources) when at least one factor is held constant (ie, this firm is operating in the short run), then the additional benefit gained from extra inputs will eventually start to fall. Thus, if a firm has one factory building and a set number of machines, continued recruitment of labour will at first produce more than proportional extra benefits, but, eventually, the benefits to be gained from each extra worker will start to fall. Remember that short-term positions are being considered and as some fixed costs are assumed then the input of some factors must be fixed. Therefore, the firm will experience diminishing marginal returns.

If the extra benefit from adding a fixed amount of an input starts to fall, then this is the same as suggesting that it will take more and more inputs to produce a steady increase in benefit. This can be demonstrated with a simple illustration from motoring: above a given speed, the extra speed to be gained from a steady increase in the injection of fuel will decline. If, therefore, the driver wishes to keep a steady increase in speed he must inject an increasing amount of fuel. It takes more petrol to raise the speed of a car from 65 mph to 75 mph than it does to raise it from 45 mph to 55 mph. The fixed factors or resources in this case are the engine and the driver.

2.5   Total variable costs with diminishing returns

The following table uses simple, hypothetical figures to illustrate the principles just outlined.

Table 1

Quantity units produced	Variable cost per unit	Total variable costs	Fixed costs	Total costs fixed + variable
	£	£	£	£
1	14	14	40	54
2	12	24	40	64
3	10	30	40	70
4	10	40	40	80
5	11	55	40	95
6	13	78	40	118
7	15	105	40	145
8	18	144	40	184
9	23	207	40	247
10	30	300	40	340

This table is illustrated in the graph of total costs (Figure 4). Notice how the gradual slope in the first stages of increasing production becomes rapidly steeper as diminishing returns begin to produce the increasing variable costs.

Figure 4

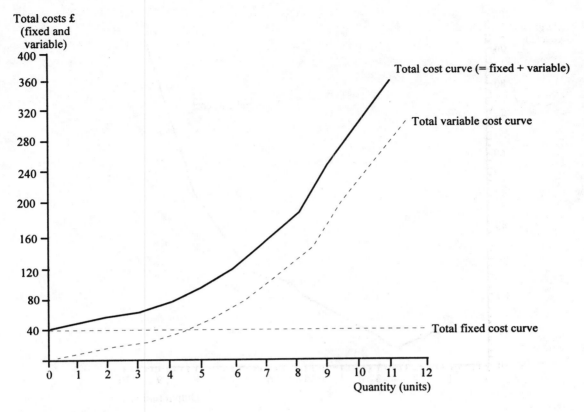

Total costs £
(fixed and
variable)

Total cost curve (= fixed + variable)

Total variable cost curve

Total fixed cost curve

Quantity (units)

2.6 Marginal costs

The following table takes the first and final column from the previous table to show the increase in quantity units and the total costs associated with each quantity level. The final column of the new table, however, shows the change in total costs as output changes from one unit level to the next. This is why it is shown between the two rows - it relates to a change in cost from one output level to the next. This change is known as the **marginal cost.** The marginal cost is thus the change in total cost as output changes. It is really the cost change related to a very small output change - usually considered to be one. Students with a knowledge of calculus will recognise this as dC/dQ where C = total cost and Q = quantity or output.

Table 2

Quantity units produced	Total costs £	Marginal costs £
1	54	
2	64	10
3	70	6
4	80	10
5	95	15
6	118	23
7	145	27
8	184	39
9	247	63
10	340	93

The marginal cost shown in the above table is illustrated in Figure 5. Notice that the marginal cost may be expected to fall at first and then to rise. This results from the suggestions concerning economies and diminishing returns to scale made earlier in the chapter.

Figure 5

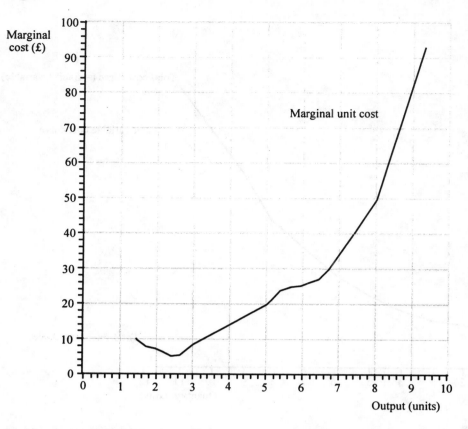

At this stage of study, situations may be considered where marginal cost is rising and the marginal cost curve is usually indicated by the J-shaped general curve of Figure 6.

Figure 6

The general shape of the normal short run marginal cost curve

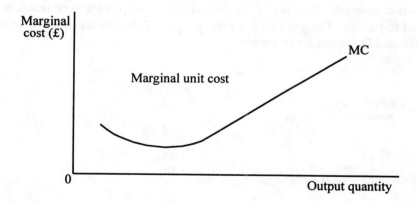

2.7 Average costs

The next table again uses the unit quantity column and total cost column of the earlier tables. This time, however, the final column is found by dividing the total cost by the number of units produced (ie, the second column by the first). This gives the average total cost, usually shortened to average cost.

Table 3

Quantity units	Total costs £	Average total costs £
1	54	54
2	64	32
3	70	23.3
4	80	20
5	95	19
6	118	19.7
7	145	20.7
8	184	23
9	247	27.4
10	340	34

Notice that in the early stages as the output (quantity) increases the average cost is falling. This is because fixed costs at £40 represent a high proportion of total costs (half or more up to 4 units). At this stage, the average fixed cost element is bringing the total average down very forcefully (see Figure 2). Then, as fixed costs decline in relative importance to the variable costs which, remember, are rising, the average cost curve also rises. This is illustrated in Figure 7.

Figure 7

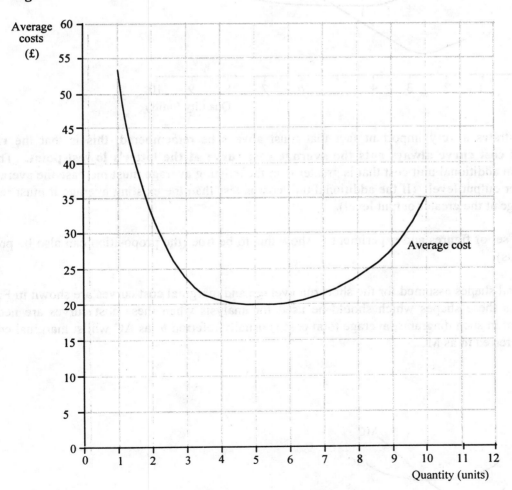

If the average total cost and the marginal cost curve are combined on the same graph ie, combine Figures 5 and 7, the graph of Figure 8 is produced.

Figure 8

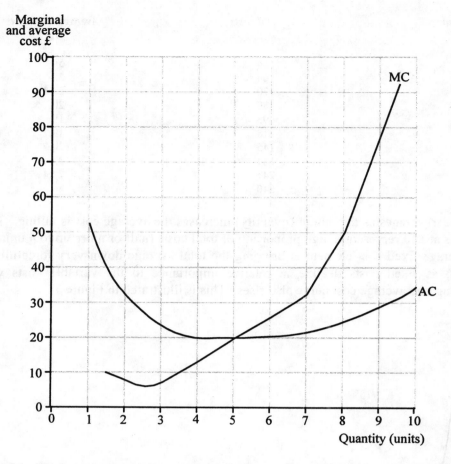

This illustrates a very important fact that must always be remembered: this is that the **rising marginal cost curve always cuts the average cost curve at the latter's lowest point.** This is because an additional unit cost that is greater than the existing average must increase the average at the greater output level. (If the additional unit cost is less than the existing average it must reduce the average at the greater output level).

Take any set of figures and experiment to show this to be true (the proposition can also be proved by calculus).

The general shapes assumed for the short run average and marginal cost curves are shown in Figure 9 and it is these shapes which should be used for analysis when these cost curves are needed. Notice that in such diagrams, average total cost is usually referred to as AC whilst marginal cost is usually referred to as MC.

Figure 9

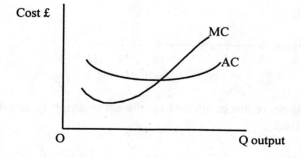

These, then, are the relationships usually assumed for the short run period. This period can be defined as that in which there is no pressure to increase capacity level beyond the range which can be achieved at the existing level of fixed costs. The actual time involved thus depends on the firm, on its desire to expand output, and on its success in this desire.

3   REVENUE

3.1   Introduction

The firm exists to convert inputs into outputs in the form of goods or services which it can sell to the public. So far, the costs of production (inputs) have been examined. The revenue or sales achieved by selling goods and/or services will now be considered.

3.2   Total revenue

Consider the simple case where the firm sells one product only and sells it at the same price however much it produces. Figure 10 shows the revenue that could be achieved at various levels of output at the constant price of £1 per unit. At 100 units (say, per week) total revenue would be £100, at 500 units per week it would be £500, 1,000 units £1,000 and so on.

Figure 10

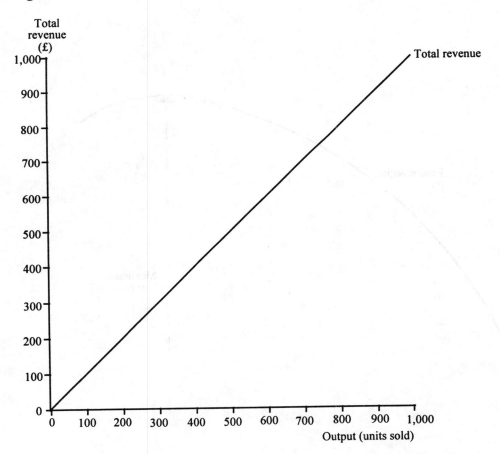

However, not all firms can sell all they produce at a constant price. It was suggested earlier that people were prepared to buy more as the price of a good fell. If the firm continued to increase its output it might find that it had to reduce price to be sure that it could sell all that it produced. Suppose a firm believes that it faces the following set of reactions from customers ie, that to sell the quantities shown in the table below it has to charge the prices indicated in the second column of the table.

Given the schedule, the possible total revenue that the firm can achieve can be found, simply by multiplying columns (1) and (2) to give the total revenue schedule of column (3).

Table 4

Output per week (1)	Price per unit (2) £	Total revenue (3) £
100	10	1,000
200	9.50	1,900
300	9	2,700
400	8.50	3,400
500	8	4,000
600	7.50	4,500
700	7	4,900
800	6.50	5,200
900	6	5,400
1,000	5.50	5,500
1,100	5	5,500
1,200	4.50	5,400

The possible total revenue at this range of prices is shown in the graph of Figure 11.

Figure 11

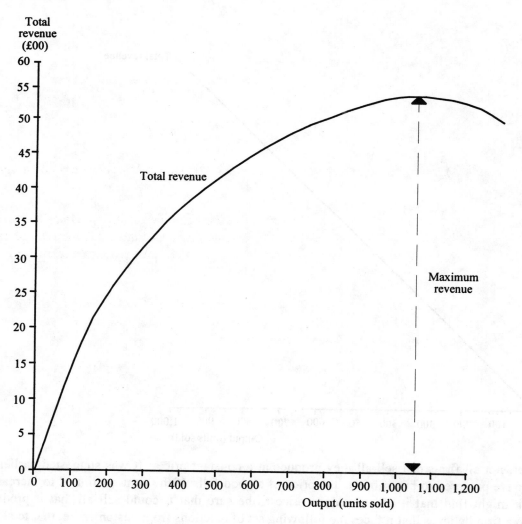

Notice that this total revenue curve slopes steeply at first, then rises less steeply until it reaches its peak at prices £5.50 - £5. Then, if the firm continues to reduce price and increase sales, the total revenue it achieves starts to decline. It declines further if it pushes sales beyond the amount shown.

Thus, if the firm has to reduce price in order to increase the quantity sold (ie, if it faces the normal downward sloping demand curve for its product) then there is likely to be one price where total revenue is at its maximum.

3.3   Average revenue

Average revenue is the **total revenue divided by the number of units of the product that are sold.** If all units are sold at the same price then the average revenue is, of course, the same as the price. If the firm can sell any output at the same price (the case illustrated in Figure 10 above) then the average revenue at any given range of prices and output levels will appear as in Figure 12.

Figure 12

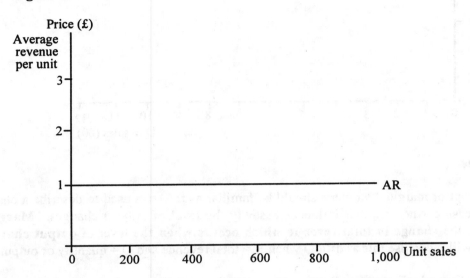

Such a firm can be said to be a **price-taker** ie, it accepts the prevailing price which its own output does not alter.

If, however, the firm does have to reduce price in order to increase the quantity it can sell ie, if it is in the position outlined in Table 4 used for the total revenue graph of Figure 11, then the price or average revenue curve or graph is as shown in Figure 13. This can be seen as the demand curve faced by the firm for its own product.

Such a firm is sometimes known as a **price-maker.** It can set **either** price **or** output, but it cannot control both. The shape of this average revenue (demand) curve depends on the decisions of buyers. The firm can try to influence it, but it cannot fully control it.

Figure 13

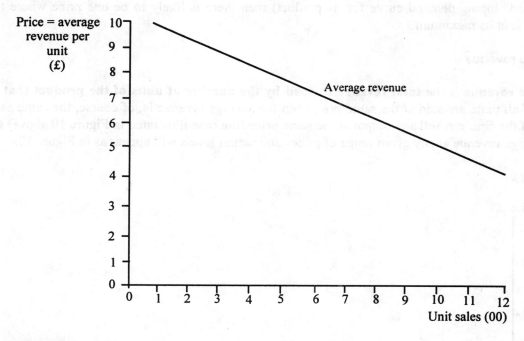

Price = average
revenue per
unit
(£)

Average revenue

Unit sales (00)

3.4   Marginal revenue

By now the concept of marginal amounts should be familiar as the term used to describe a change in some total measure when another influence (usually the level of output) changes. **Marginal revenue** is, then, the **change in total revenue which occurs when the level of output changes.** Mathematicians will recognise this as dR/dQ when R = total revenue and Q = quantity or output.

In the case of the firm which can sell all its production at the prevailing price, the total revenue will always change by the amount of the price per unit. In this case, therefore, the price or average revenue curve is the same as the marginal revenue curve. The marginal revenue is constant and is the same as the constant price.

In the second case, however, the marginal revenue clearly changes. Columns (1) and (3) of Table 4 can be reproduced and a further column added to show the marginal revenue (change in total revenue).

The new Table (5) is shown below and is the basis for the graph of Figure 14.

At the same time, it is useful now to continue the average revenue (price) schedule to cover the full range of prices down to £0.

Table 5

Output per week	Total revenue	Marginal revenue per unit
	£	£
100	1,000	9
200	1,900	8
300	2,700	7
400	3,400	6
500	4,000	5
600	4,500	4
700	4,900	3
800	5,200	2
900	5,400	1
1,000	5,500	0
1,100	5,500	-1
1,200	5,400	-2
1,300	5,200	-3
1,400	4,900	-4
1,500	4,500	-5
1,600	4,000	-6
1,700	3,400	-7
1,800	2,700	-8
1,900	1,900	-9
2,000	1,000	-10
2,100	0	

Note: marginal revenue = $\dfrac{\text{increase in revenue}}{\text{increase in units}}$

Figure 14 combines both the average revenue and the marginal revenue on the same graph.

Figure 14

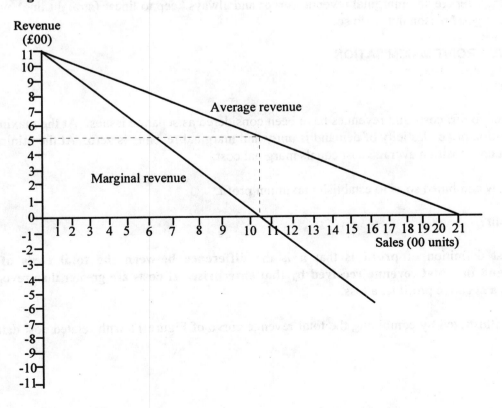

There are some important points which now arise from this and they apply to all downward sloping linear (straight line) revenue curves

(a)   The marginal revenue curve cuts the horizontal axis half-way between the point of intersection of the average revenue curve and the horizontal (quantity) axis, and the point of origin (O).

(b)   As output increases from zero to this half-way position, marginal revenue is positive, so that total revenue increases up to this point.

(c)   As output increases beyond this half-way point, marginal revenue is negative, so that total revenue falls when output rises beyond this point.

(d)   The point of maximum revenue is where the marginal revenue curve cuts the horizontal axis (ie, is zero). In this illustration this is the output level of 1,050 units per week sold at a price of £5.25 per unit to give the maximum total revenue of £5,512.50.

(e)   At the output level of 1,050 (price £5.25) price elasticity of demand is unity (1). At output levels below this (at higher prices), demand is elastic (greater than 1). At output levels higher than 1,050 (at lower prices), demand is price inelastic.

Consider again the total revenue curve of Figure 11 based on the same schedule of prices and output. It should be noted that the peak of the curve is at the output level of 1,050: here the marginal revenue changes from positive to negative as the slope of the total revenue curve rises to its peak and then falls. Finally, note that the marginal revenue slopes twice as steeply as the average revenue or price.

In the figures, price fell £0.50 for each 100 unit increase in output. As a result, the marginal revenue moved £1 for each 100 unit change in output. Always keep those relationships in mind when drawing average and marginal revenue curves and always keep to linear (straight line) curves unless there is good reason not to do so.

4   PROFIT AND PROFIT MAXIMISATION

4.1   Introduction

In the chapter so far, costs and revenues have been considered as separate issues. At the maximum revenue position price elasticity of demand is unity and marginal revenue is zero. At the minimum average unit cost position average cost equals marginal cost.

These are now combined so as to establish maximum profit.

4.2   What is profit?

The simplest definition of **profit** is that it is the **difference between the total costs of an enterprise and the total revenue received by that enterprise.** If costs are greater than revenue, then there is a negative profit ie, a loss.

This can be illustrated by combining the total revenue curve of Figure 11 with related cost data in Table 6.

Table 6

Output units per week	Unit variable cost £	Total variable cost £	Fixed cost £	Total cost £	Marginal cost per 100 units £
100	6	600	1,000	1,600	
200	5	1,000	1,000	2,000	400
300	4	1,200	1,000	2,200	200
400	3.50	1,400	1,000	2,400	200
500	3	1,500	1,000	2,500	100
600	3	1,800	1,000	2,800	300
700	3	2,100	1,000	3,100	300
800	3.50	2,800	1,000	3,800	700
900	4	3,600	1,000	4,600	800
1,000	4.50	4,500	1,000	5,500	900
1,100	5	5,500	1,000	6,500	1,000

Figure 15

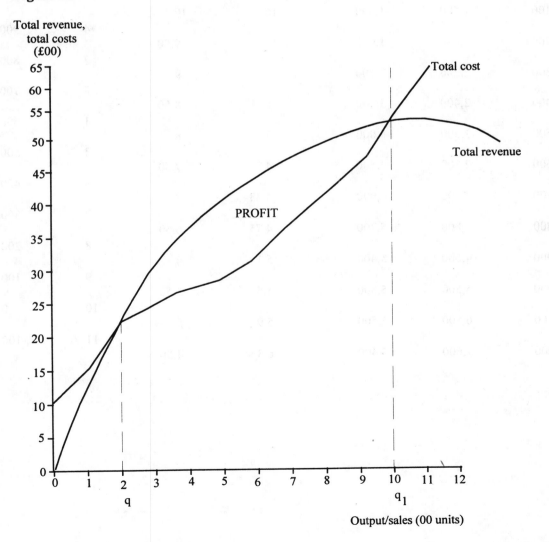

Output/sales (00 units)

Notes:

(a)   The firm makes a loss on output levels below Oq (a little over 200 units per week).

(b)   It continues to make a profit at output levels above Oq until output reaches Oq_1 units per week (1,000 units).

(c)   Above output level Oq_1 the firm again makes a loss which rapidly increases as diminishing returns affect variable and marginal costs. This is the level where additional fixed costs and productive capacity are evidently needed.

The profit area can be indicated in another way by using average costs and revenue. Below is a table of average costs and revenues, and marginal costs and revenues based on the same set of figures. These are illustrated in the graph of Figure 16.

Table 7

Quantity per week units	Total cost £	Total revenue £	Average cost £	Average revenue £	Marginal cost £	Marginal revenue per 100 units £
100	1,600	1,000	16	10		
					4	900
200	2,000	1,900	10	9.50		
					2	800
300	2,200	2,700	7.3	9		
					2	700
400	2,400	3,400	6	8.50		
					1	600
500	2,500	4,000	5	8		
					3	500
600	2,800	4,500	4.7	7.50		
					3	400
700	3,100	4,900	4.43	7		
					7	300
800	3,800	5,200	4.75	6.50		
					8	200
900	4,600	5,400	5.1	6		
					9	100
1,000	5,500	5,500	5.5	5.50		
					10	0
1,100	6,500	5,500	5.9	5		
					11	-100
1,200	7,600	5,400	6.3	4.50		

Figure 16

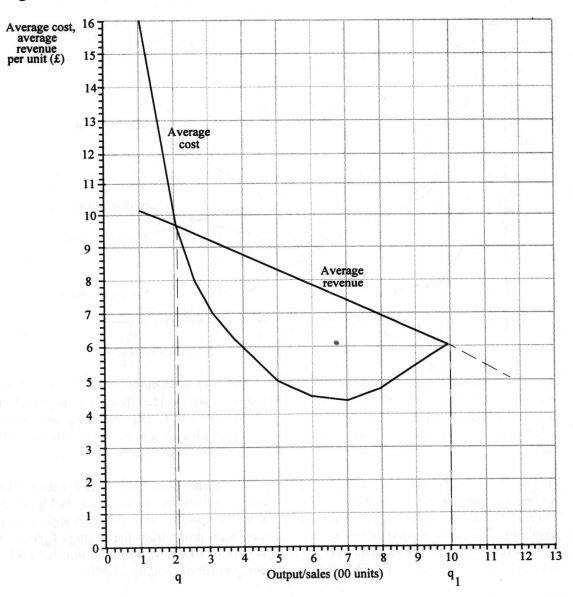

The same profit area may be seen from the average revenue curves as from the total revenue curves. These areas tell the quantity levels within which a profit can be made (Oq – Oq₁) but, in themselves, they do not tell which output level and price will give the best possible or **maximum profit.**

4.3   Profit maximising conditions

To find the best profit-making level from the above figure, the marginal revenue and marginal cost can be related. Now, assuming that the firm is operating in the area where marginal cost is rising and marginal revenue falling, then, if the firm finds that marginal cost is lower than marginal revenue it will pay it to increase output. To do so will bring in more revenue than it will pay in cost. This is because the change in revenue is more than the change in cost.

Figure 17 shows the average and marginal curves for both cost and revenue.

Figure 17

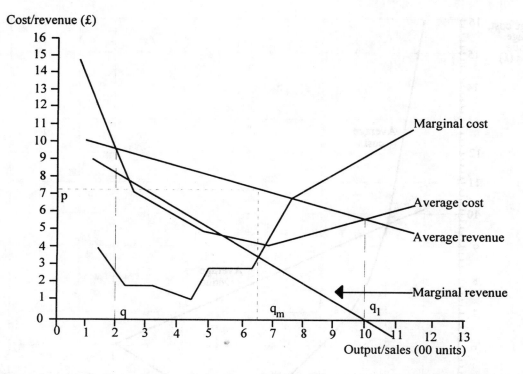

Cost/revenue (£)

Here the marginal cost curve cuts the marginal revenue curve at an output level just below 700 units and a price (average revenue) just above £7. If fractions are avoided, it can be suggested that the profit maximising output is 700 units per week sold at a price of £7 per unit. In general terms, this is Oq_m units at a price of Op. To produce more would bring in less revenue than the additional cost; to produce less would lose more revenue than would be saved in cost.

This solution can be checked by referring back to the table of total cost and revenue (Table 7). Adding a column to show total profit, being the difference between the total cost and total revenue, will reveal that, given the stages of the table, the highest profit figure (£1,800) appears at output level 700. The same answer is found by calculating total profit from the average figures. Given average revenue of £7 per unit and average cost per unit of £4.43 the profit per unit is £2.57 which, multiplied by the weekly output of 700, gives a weekly profit of roughly £1,800.

The best profit (**profit maximising**) output position is not altered if the firm faces a constant price for its goods at all possible ranges of output. Once again, the profit maximising output will be where marginal revenue is equal to the rising marginal cost. This is shown in the general diagram of Figure 18.

Figure 18

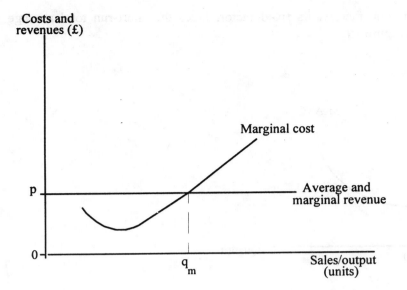

At output levels below Oq$_m$ it will pay the firm to increase production. At output levels above Oq$_m$ it will pay to cut back production. Again, the same argument holds good. Whenever the additional revenue to be gained from an extra unit of output is more than the extra cost, it will pay to produce more. Whenever the additional cost incurred by producing an extra unit of output is more than the revenue to be gained, it will pay to produce less. The same conclusion is again reached: that the **profit maximising output level is where marginal revenue is just equal to marginal cost.**

Remember, however, that this will only hold good if marginal cost is rising (or constant if marginal revenue is falling).

General profit maximising rule

At the maximum profit output/sales level
marginal cost = marginal revenue
and cuts marginal revenue from below

This can be deduced logically since all it really says is that output is increased until the extra cost of producing one extra unit (marginal cost) exactly equals the sale proceeds from the extra unit (marginal revenue).

5   LONG-RUN COSTS

5.1   Introduction

On a day-to-day basis, firms are operating in the short run. Certain factors of production are fixed and cannot be altered. Within the constraints imposed by those factors, the firm ensures that its profits are maximised. However, in the long run, by definition, all factors are variable, so the firm has far greater flexibility. It may be faced with constraints in its short run, day-to-day activities, but it can look ahead and plan long-run improvements which involve altering factors which are currently fixed.

5.2   From short-run to long-run average total cost

Suppose a firm which owns one factory, its fixed factor, faces the short-run total average cost (SRATC) structure given in Figure 19:

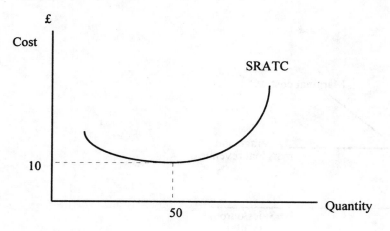

Figure 19

The minimum point of the curve occurs at 50 units, with a cost of £10 per unit. If the firm produces more or less than 50 units, its cost per unit will rise. In the short run, there is nothing the firm can do about this.

It may be that the firm wishes to make more than the quantity which will produce minimum costs, 100 units, say. As we have seen, in the short run it will have to accept the rise in the costs; but it can **plan** to avoid this rise in the long run. In the long run it can exactly replicate its current factory and operate two factories, each producing 50 units. It will then have a total of 100 units, all of which are produced at the minimum average total cost. This long-run option can be demonstrated graphically as in Figure 20:

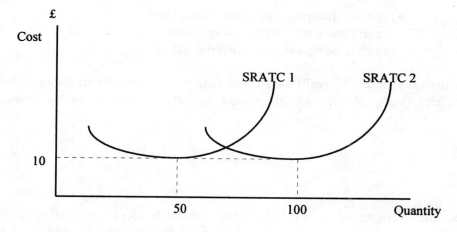

Figure 20

In fact, in the long run, the firm can make sure that it has exactly the right number of factories to produce all its output at minimum average cost (as long as the output is a multiple of 50 units):

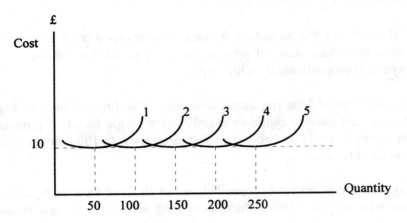

Figure 21   The numbers 1 to 5 indicate a series of short-run average total cost curves at different levels of output.

5.3   Long run average total cost with constant costs

We can generalise this to the average firm:

In the long run, firms can select the combination of factors of production which results in the minimum average total cost for their required level of production.

So the long-run average total cost curve in the above example (LRATC) is actually a straight line:

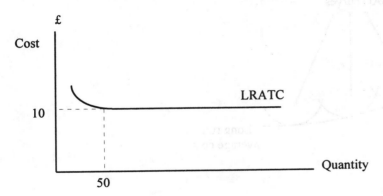

Figure 22

Notice that there is an initial downward slope, which reflects the fact that there are in practice what are referred to as indivisibilities. You cannot have a factory able to produce less than 50 units so that at output below 50 units you are producing on the initial cost curve which represents a fixed factor. Other than at very low levels of production, where the average total cost does fall, the long-run average cost is constant regardless of the quantity produced. Later in this chapter, it will be shown that not all LRATC curves look like this.

6   ECONOMIES OF SCALE

6.1   Introduction

Definition   **Economies of scale** are the reduction in long-term average total cost achievable when the whole scale of production is expanded, but not all factors are expanded proportionately with output.

The above is a rather simplistic view of long-run costs, however. The firm wishing to expand output from 50 to 100 units does not have to replicate exactly every single factor of production. The accounts department, for example, could probably cope just as easily with 100 units as with 50; the board of directors does not need to increase.

So the average total cost may well **fall** as output is expanded, as not all fixed factors of production need to be increased in line with output. This reduction in long-term average cost is due to economies of scale.

Note that economies of scale can occur only in the long run, as they are associated with the alteration of some or all of the firm's fixed factors.

Figure 23 shows long-run average total cost (LRATC) with economies of scale and therefore with decreasing costs:

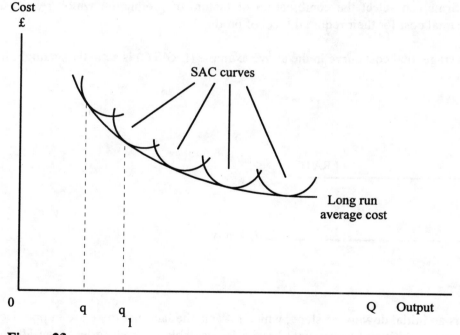

Figure 23

Note the succession of new short run average cost curves (SACs). These represent the new short run position created by a change in production capacity brought about by the steps in the fixed cost levels.

However, there is no guarantee that the firm can continue to obtain increasing benefits (returns) from increasing the size or scale of its operations. There may come a time when further savings are not possible and when the best that can be achieved is to avoid an upturn in the long run average cost curve. Average costs diminish, but then settle to a constant rate. In this position, the firm is achieving constant returns to scale The possibility is illustrated in Figure 24.

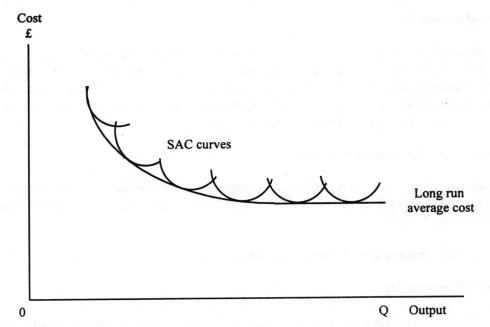

Figure 24

6.2   Categories of economies of scale

Economies of scale are often divided into categories as follows:

(a)   Internal economies

These are benefits which accrue to the individual firm, with no effect on other firms. They include:

- **Technical economies**

  Characteristics of the production process enable cost per unit to be reduced when output is expanded.   For example, expansion may make computerisation worthwhile, or may enable the firm to buy more sophisticated machinery.

- **Financial economies**

  It is generally accepted that larger firms can raise funds more easily and cheaply than small firms.

- **Trading economies**

  Some of the activities connected with trading can be carried out more efficiently by a large firm.   For example, advertising is more effective when it reaches a wide audience, such as television viewers. The cost per unit of advertising on television would be prohibitively high for a small firm, but far lower for a firm with a high output.

- **Managerial economies**

  Management costs can stay relatively static as output expands, since most of management's activities are not directly related to output. In addition, a large firm may be able to afford to hire specialist managers who perform better in that function than do staff with other skills who have to fulfil a management role as well.

(b)   **External economies**

Here advantages of an increased scale are obtained by all the firms in the industry or in the area. External economies occur often when an industry is heavily concentrated in one area and the local economy evolves around the industry. The region will supply the industry with a skilled labour force and specialist suppliers;   the industry may provide training facilities which benefit all the firms in the area.

6.3   Diseconomies of scale - problems of growth

Unlimited expansion of scale of output may not necessarily result in ever-decreasing costs per unit. There may be a point beyond which average costs begin to rise again, as the size of the business becomes uneconomic.

Diseconomies can be categorised in the same way as economies.

(a)   **Internal diseconomies**

These include increasing bureaucracy as the firm becomes more unwieldy, coupled with a loss of control as management becomes distanced from the shop floor. Communication is hampered, making it difficult for management to know what is happening and to ensure that their instructions are being carried out properly.

This distance may also affect labour relations, as workers cease to feel that they 'belong', and morale and motivation fall. Studies have shown that this is the atmosphere in which union-led strikes are encouraged, as workers are organised more easily. The existence of the union may also prevent changes in working practices which are needed to keep up with new technology.

As the firm increases in size, its managers may become complacent since it is less vulnerable to competition from other firms. This complacency leads to inefficiency which is sometimes termed 'x-inefficiency'.

(b)   **External diseconomies**

As the firm and the industry grows, it may be hampered by shortages of various types. It could be a shortage of raw materials, appropriately skilled labour, or even markets for their output. The firm or industry may have to start exporting in order to maintain sales.

Another problem could arise with government interference, particularly if the firm (and industry) appears to be abusing a monopolistic position.

The firm could attempt to avoid some of the problems caused by growth. For example, it could divide its operations into smaller units (a holding company with subsidiaries, perhaps), each of which is easier to run than the group as a whole. Employees could be made to feel more involved by operating employee share option schemes, or by including them in the decision-making activities of the firm.

6.4   The final LRATC curve

Conclusion   Long-run average total costs fall up to a given output level, due to economies of scale. They then start to rise, due to diseconomies of scale.

Figure 25 shows the final picture of long-run average total costs, with firstly decreasing and eventually increasing costs:

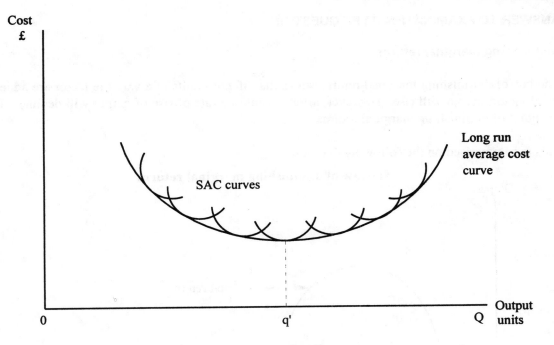

Figure 25

7 SELF TEST QUESTIONS

7.1   What is the difference between the short-run and the long-run? (1)

7.2   Distinguish between a fixed cost and a variable cost. (2.2, 2.3)

7.3   What happens to average fixed cost as output rises? (2.2)

7.4   State the law of diminishing returns. (2.4)

7.5   At what point of average cost is marginal cost equal to average cost? (2.7)

7.6   Define a price-taker and a price-maker. (3.3)

7.7   Define marginal revenue. (3.4)

7.8   If average revenue is falling will marginal revenue be more or less than average revenue? (3.4)

7.9   At what point of output will a firm maximise its profits? (4.3)

7.10   How far should a firm expand output? (4.3)

8 EXAMINATION TYPE QUESTION

8.1 Diminishing marginal returns

Explain the concept of diminishing returns.

(6 marks)

How might it be applicable in the following cases:

(a)   motor car production;

(4 marks)

(b)   wheat production;

(4 marks)

(c)   listening to lectures?

(4 marks)

(Total: 18 marks)

9   ANSWER TO EXAMINATION TYPE QUESTION

9.1   Diminishing marginal returns

The law of diminishing marginal returns states that, if extra units of a variable factor are added to a fixed factor, output will rise. However, after a point, the rate of rise of output will decline. This is the point of diminishing marginal returns.

This is summarised on the following diagram.

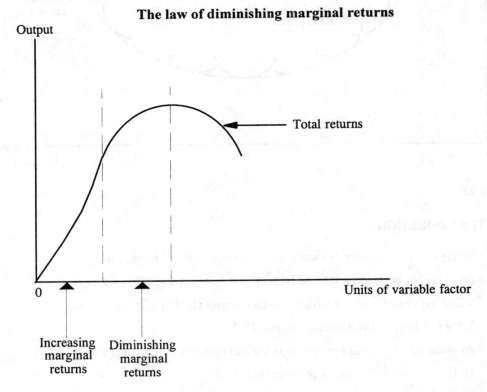

The law of diminishing marginal returns

Note that when marginal returns are increasing the slope of the line is increasing and where marginal returns are diminishing the slope of the line is decreasing even though total returns are increasing throughout.

(a)   In motor car production the fixed factor will be capital and the variable factor will be labour. Note that unit cost of production will fall as the capital equipment is used more intensively.

(b)   In wheat production the fixed factor will be land and the variable factor labour. In less developed economies the variable factor could be capital equipment and/or fertiliser as increasingly sophisticated production methods are adopted.

(c)   Listening to lectures may seem an unusual example but if you consider how effectively you can concentrate in the first ten minutes and compare it with the final ten minutes, you have quite a useful example of diminishing returns.

18 APPLICATIONS OF CALCULUS TO BUSINESS PROBLEMS

INTRODUCTION & LEARNING OBJECTIVES

Syllabus area 7f. Use of elementary calculus to optimise business functions. (Ability required 3).

Pricing policies in practice. (Ability required 2).

We start this chapter by studying the basic rules of differential calculus. We then examine how calculus techniques can be used in a business context, for example, to maximise revenue or profit.

When you have studied this chapter you should be able to do the following:

- Carry out calculations using the basic rules of differentiation.
- Distinguish between maximum and minimum points.
- Understand the situations when differentiation can be used.
- Apply these techniques to business situations.
- Understand how businesses price their products in practice.

---

1 AN INTRODUCTION TO BASIC DIFFERENTIAL CALCULUS

1.1 Gradients

Consider measuring a gradient eg, the gradient of a hill. This could be expressed as (say) 1 in 4.

Diagram of a 1 in 4 hill

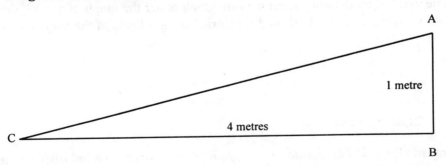

In other words, for each 1 metre rise it is necessary to travel 4 metres horizontally. Mathematically this would be expressed as a gradient of ¼.

The general equation of a gradient using the above triangle is $\dfrac{AB}{CB}$.

This is the mathematical definition of a gradient. In practice, hill gradients as sign-posted on the road may be measured differently. The mathematical gradient is also called the **slope** of the line CA.

Hence the gradient can also be defined as the increase in the vertical variable (y) per unit increase in the horizontal variable (x). This is called the **rate of change** of y with respect to x. For example, a graph of distance travelled (y) against time taken (x) at a constant speed would be a straight line. The gradient would be the distance travelled per unit time, which is the speed.

1.2   The gradient of a curve

The gradient of a curve varies continuously from one point on the curve to another, so we can only speak of the gradient of the curve at a given point. This is defined as follows:

The gradient of a curve at a point (T) is the gradient of the tangent to the curve at that point. (A tangent is a line that just touches the curve.)

Gradient of a curve at a given point (T)

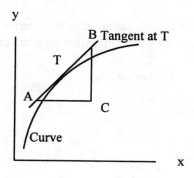

To measure the gradient, take any two points (A and B) on the tangent and draw horizontal and vertical lines through A and B respectively to meet at C. The gradient of the line AB is $\dfrac{CB}{AC}$. This is therefore the gradient of the curve at T.

At different points on the curve, the gradient will be different.

1.3   Calculation of the gradient of a curve at a given point

If the gradient of the curve $y = x^2$ is measured at any point on the curve, it will be found always to be twice the value of x at that point. At the point where x = 1, the gradient is 2, where x = 2, it is 4, and so on. This can be verified by drawing accurately on graph paper the graph of $y = x^2$, drawing tangents to it at the points where x =1, x =2, etc and measuring the gradients of the tangents.

Thus, in general,

if y   = x^2,

gradient   =   2x for any value of x.

The process of finding an algebraic expression for the gradient of a curve is called **differentiation**. The expression so found is called the **differential coefficient** or **derivative** of the curve and is denoted by the symbol $\dfrac{dy}{dx}$ (pronounced 'dee y by dee x').

Note: that this does not mean dy divided by dx, but is one composite symbol.

The above statement can therefore be rewritten as:

$$\text{if } y = x^2,$$

$$\frac{dy}{dx} = 2x.$$

Alternatively, it could be said that $2x$ is the derivative or differential coefficient of x^2.

The following derivatives can be obtained mathematically by methods which are beyond the scope of this course.

y	$\frac{dy}{dx}$	
x^2	$2x$	$(= 2x^1)$
x^3	$3x^2$	
x^4	$4x^3$	
x^5	$5x^4$	etc.

It will be seen that the derivatives follow a set pattern. The power of x becomes a coefficient and the new power has decreased by one unit. Hence in general,

$$\text{if } y = x^n,$$

$$\frac{dy}{dx} = nx^{n-1}$$

This is true for all values of n, including negative and fractional values.

1.4   Example

Write down the derivatives of:

(a) x^7

(b) x^{-7}

(c) $x^{3.3}$

(d) $x^{\frac{1}{2}}$

1.5   Solutions

(a) $7x^6$

(b) $-7x^{-8}$ (because $-7 - 1 = -8$)

(c) $3.3x^{2.3}$

(d) $\frac{1}{2}x^{-\frac{1}{2}}$

1.6   Activity

Write down the derivatives of:

(a) x^{10}

(b) x^{-13}

(c) $x^{\frac{1}{4}}$

(d) $x^{4.7}$

1.7   Activity solution

   (a) $10x^9$

   (b) $-13x^{-14}$

   (c) $\frac{1}{4}x^{-\frac{3}{4}}$

   (d) $4.7x^{3.7}$

1.8   Differentiating when the coefficient of x is not unity

   In all the previous equations, the coefficient of x was unity. Consider the following equation $y = 2x^3$. Here the coefficient of x^3 is 2. Differentiating this poses no new problems; the power of x multiplies the coefficient and the power is reduced by 1.

   $\therefore \qquad \frac{dy}{dx} = 3(2x^2) = 6x^2$.

1.9   Example

   Differentiate each of the following:

   (a) x^5 $5x^4$

   (b) $6x^5$ $30x^4$

   (c) $\frac{x^6}{3}$ $\frac{6x^5}{3}$ $2x^5$

   (d) $x^{1.5}$ $1.5x^{.5}$

   (e) $\sqrt{x}$ xx

1.10   Solutions

   (a) $5x^4$

   (b) $30x^4$

   (c) $2x^5$

   (d) $1.5x^{0.5} = 1.5\sqrt{x}$

   (e) $\dfrac{1}{2\sqrt{x}}$

            (Put $\sqrt{x} = x^{\frac{1}{2}}$, which on differentiation gives $\frac{1}{2}x^{-\frac{1}{2}} = \frac{1}{2} \times \frac{1}{x^{\frac{1}{2}}} = \frac{1}{2x^{\frac{1}{2}}}$)

1.11   Activity

   (a)   Calculate the gradient of the curve $y = 3x^3$ at the points where $x = \frac{1}{2}$ and $x = -\frac{1}{2}$.

   (b)   At which point on the curve $y = 4x^2$ is the gradient equal to:

            (i)   10

            (ii) -2

1.12   Activity solution

(a) $\dfrac{dy}{dx} = 3 \times 3x^{3-1} = 9x^2$

when   x = ½,   gradient = $9 \times (½)^2 = 2.25$

x = −½,   gradient = $9 \times (-½)^2 = 2.25$

(b) $\dfrac{dy}{dx} = 2 \times 4x^{2-1} = 8x$

(i)   if   gradient = 10

then   8x = 10

∴   x = $\dfrac{10}{8}$ = 1.25

Hence x = 1.25, y = 6.25

(ii)   if   gradient = −2

then   8x = −2

∴   x = $\dfrac{-2}{8}$ = −¼

Hence, the point is x = −¼, y = ¼

1.13   Differentiation of a constant

A constant may also appear in an expression which needs to be differentiated.

A constant can be made into a function of x by multiplying it by x^0, since $x^0 = 1$ whatever the value of x.

Hence, to differentiate y = 50 (say):

y = 50

= $50x^0$

$\dfrac{dy}{dx}$ = $50 \times 0 \times x^{-1}$ using the above rule.

= 0 since any expression with a factor 0 is equal to 0.

It will be seen that the same result would be obtained whatever the value of the constant, hence when a constant is differentiated, it disappears (ie, becomes zero). This becomes obvious when it is remembered that a constant does not change and therefore has no rate of change. The line y = 50 is a horizontal line of zero slope.

1.14   Example

If   y = $5x^4 - 20$, find $\dfrac{dy}{dx}$.

1.15 **Solution**

$$\frac{dy}{dx} = 20x^3$$

2 DIFFERENTIATION OF SUMS AND DIFFERENCES

2.1 **Introduction**

If a function comprises the sum of several terms and each contains the same variable, then each term is differentiated individually.

2.2 **Example**

Costs are related to production by the equation:

$$y = 4x^3 + 2x^2 + 6x + 40$$

$$12x^2 + 4x + 6$$

where y = costs and x = production level. What is the rate of change in the costs for each value of x?

2.3 **Solution**

The general rule is applied to each term in the above equation:

$$\therefore \quad \frac{dy}{dx} = 4 \times 3x^{(3-1)} + 2 \times 2x^{(2-1)} + 6x^{(1-1)} + 0$$

$$= 12x^2 + 4x + 6 \qquad (\textit{Note:} \text{ that } x^{(1-1)} = x^0 = 1)$$

2.4 **Differentiation of differences**

A similar rule applies to differentiation of differences: each term is differentiated individually, the arithmetic signs remain the same as in the original equation.

2.5 **Example**

Differentiate the following cost function with respect to x:

$$y = 4x^3 - 2x^2 + 6x - 40$$

2.6 **Solution**

$$\frac{dy}{dx} = 4 \times 3x^{(3-1)} - 2 \times 2x^{(2-1)} + 6x^{(1-1)}$$

$$= 12x^2 - 4x + 6$$

3 DIFFERENTIATION OF PRODUCTS

3.1 **The rule**

Where y = uv, and where both u and v are functions of x, the general formula for differentiating is as follows:

$$\frac{dy}{dx} = u\frac{dv}{dx} + v\frac{du}{dx}$$

This formula does not need to be proved mathematically.

3.2   Example

Differentiate with respect to x the following function:

$$y = x^2 (x + 3)$$

3.3   Solution

The function is a product function,

let   u   = x^2,   then $\dfrac{du}{dx}$ =   2x

let   v   =   x + 3,   then $\dfrac{dv}{dx}$ =   1

Using the general formula:

$$\dfrac{d(uv)}{dx} \quad = \quad u\dfrac{dv}{dx} + v\dfrac{du}{dx}$$

$$= \quad x^2 \times 1 + (x + 3) \times 2x$$

$$= \quad x^2 + 2x^2 + 6x$$

$$= \quad 3x^2 + 6x$$

4   GRADIENTS AND STATIONARY POINTS

4.1   Positive and negative gradients

Having developed the techniques for finding the gradient of a function at any point, it is necessary to establish a rule to identify when the gradient is positive or negative.

Consider the relationship $y = x^2$

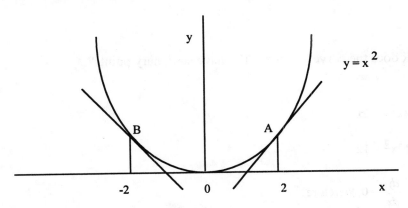

It is first necessary to establish whether the gradients at points A and B, arbitrarily selected, are positive or negative.

These are given by the gradient at any point on the graph ie, the derivative. Since $y = x^2$, then $\dfrac{dy}{dx} =$ 2x.

At point A, x = 2

∴ the gradient at A = 2 × 2 = 4.

As the result of substituting the value of x into the equation of the gradient is positive, the gradient is positive at point A (the line slopes upwards).

At point B, x = –2

Substituting this into the equation for the gradient,

Gradient at B = 2 × (–2) = –4.

This shows that the gradient is negative (the line slopes downwards).

To establish positive or negative gradients:

Step 1   Find the equation for the derivative of the function.

Step 2   Substitute the value of the point at which the gradient is required into the equation.

Step 3   If the result is positive, gradient is positive.
If the result is negative, gradient is negative.

4.2   Stationary points

It can be seen from the above calculation that between the points x = –2 and x = 2, the gradient moves from – 4 to + 4.

Therefore at one intervening point the gradient will equal zero. The point at which the gradient equals zero is called a **stationary point**. In this instance it represents a minimum. To find the stationary point for the function $y = x^2$, find the derivative and equate that to zero.

In this example $\dfrac{dy}{dx}$ =   2x

put   2x   =   0

giving   x   =   0

Therefore at the point where x = 0, the gradient is zero. The stationary point of $y = x^2$ is therefore at x = 0, y = 0. (*Note:* A point needs two co-ordinates.) The value of x that gives the minimum value of y is zero.

4.3   Example

At what values of x does the curve $y = 4x^3 - 12x$ have stationary points?

4.4   Solution

$$y \quad = \quad 4x^3 - 12x$$

$$\frac{dy}{dx} \quad = \quad 12x^2 - 12$$

For stationary points, $\dfrac{dy}{dx} = 0$, therefore

$$12x^2 - 12 \quad = \quad 0$$

$$12x^2 \qquad = \quad 12$$

$$x^2 \qquad = \quad 1$$

$$\therefore \quad x \qquad = \quad +1 \text{ or } -1$$

Stationary points are where x = ±1

5   MAXIMUM AND MINIMUM POINTS

5.1   Functions with both maximum and minimum points

Consider the function $y = x^3 - 12x + 12$

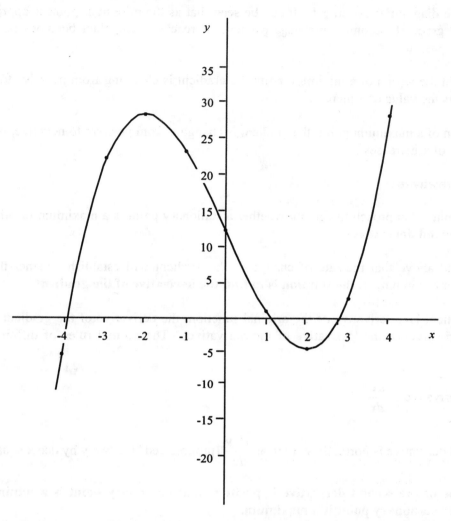

The function has two points at which the gradient is zero ie, has both a maximum and a minimum point.

First find the value for x at which the maximum or minimum occurs.

Step 1   Find derivative

$$y = x^3 - 12x + 12$$

$$\frac{dy}{dx} = 3x^2 - 12$$

Step 2   Equate derivative to zero

$$3x^2 - 12 = 0$$

$$3x^2 = 12$$

$$x^2 = \frac{12}{3} = 4$$

$$x = \sqrt{4} = +2 \text{ or } -2$$

The maximum and minimum points occur at x = +2 and x = –2. At this stage, however, there is no means of distinguishing between maximum and minimum.

5.2   Distinguishing between maximum and minimum points

Consider the diagram above in 5.1. It can be seen that as the minimum point is approached from the left the gradient becomes less negative until it reaches zero, then becomes positive as the minimum is passed.

Therefore, in the region of a minimum point the gradient is changing from negative to positive, ie, increasing as the value of x increases.

In the region of a maximum point, the gradient is changing from positive to negative, ie, decreasing as the value of x increases.

5.3   Second derivatives

The mathematical approach to finding whether a stationary point is a maximum or minimum is by means of **second derivatives**.

It was stated above that the rate of change of the gradient will establish whether the point is a maximum or minimum, ie, **the solution is to find the derivative of the gradient**.

As the gradient is a derivative of the original function, the derivative of the gradient is called the 'second derivative' or the 'derivative of the derivative'. The normal rules of differentiation will apply.

The first derivative is $\dfrac{dy}{dx}$

The second derivative is normally written as $\dfrac{d^2y}{dx^2}$ (pronounced 'dee two y by dee x squared')

If the value of the second derivative is positive, that stationary point is a minimum; if it is negative the stationary point is a maximum.

Sometimes, the first and second derivative are both equal to zero. When this happens the point on the graph is neither a minimum nor a maximum point, but is referred to as a 'point of inflexion'.

5.4   Calculating the second derivative

The second derivative may easily be calculated by treating the solution to the first derivative as a function in its own right. Thus if

$$y \quad = \quad 6x^3$$

$$\frac{dy}{dx} \quad = \quad 18x^2 \qquad \text{(first derivative), and}$$

$$\frac{d^2y}{dx^2} \quad = \quad 36x \qquad \text{(second derivative)}$$

5.5   The procedure to calculate maxima and minima

The problem of finding maxima and minima may be broken down to a five stage process:

Step 1   Differentiate to obtain the first derivative.

Step 2   Equate this to zero to find the stationary point(s).

Step 3   Differentiate the first derivative to obtain the second derivative.

Step 4   Substitute the values of x at the stationary point(s) in the second derivative.

Step 5   If the result is positive, the point is a minimum.

If the result is negative, the point is a maximum.

5.6   Example

For the function

$$y = x^3 - 27x + 12$$

find the maximum and minimum points.

5.7   Solution

Step 1   Find the first derivative.

$$y = x^3 - 27x + 12$$

$$\frac{dy}{dx} = 3x^2 - 27$$

Step 2   Equate to zero.

$$3x^2 - 27 = 0$$

$$x^2 = 9$$

$$x = \sqrt{9}$$

$$= \pm 3 \quad \text{(remember there are two square roots to any positive number: positive and negative)}$$

Step 3   Find the second derivative.

$$\frac{dy}{dx} = 3x^2 - 27$$

Differentiation of $3x^2$ gives 6x and of 27 gives zero.

$$\text{Hence } \frac{d^2y}{dx^2} = 6x - 0$$

$$= 6x$$

Step 4   Substitute the values of the stationary points.

$$\text{At} \quad x = +3, \quad \frac{d^2y}{dx^2} = 6 \times (+3) = +18 \quad \text{positive}$$

$$x = -3, \quad \frac{d^2y}{dx^2} = 6 \times (-3) = -18 \quad \text{negative}$$

Step 5   Since x = +3 is positive,   this gives a minimum value of y.

Since x = −3 is negative,   this gives a maximum value of y.

The value of y at the maximum
therefore is $-(3)^3 - 27 \times (-3) + 12$ (substituting for x in y)

$$= -27 + 81 + 12$$

$$= 66$$

This occurs when x = −3

The value of y at the minimum is $(3)^3 - 27 \times (3) + 12$ (substituting for x in y)

$$= +27 - 81 + 12$$

$$= -42$$

This occurs when x = +3.

6   APPLICATION OF DIFFERENTIATION - FINDING MINIMA

6.1   Introduction

At this stage the student should have mastered the basic techniques of differential calculus. However, examination questions are usually related to business situations. Students frequently find the transition difficult. The following example is designed to create familiarity with these types of problem.

6.2   Problem

The price per thousand units of a manufactured product, £p, and the number of products in thousands of units on the market each month, q, are related by the formula:

$$p = 4{,}000 + \frac{36{,}000}{q^2}$$

(a)   Plot the graph of p against q in the range $1 \le q \le 6$.

(b)   Find the expression for $\dfrac{dR}{dq}$ where £R is the monthly revenue, and calculate how many products on the market each month will yield the least revenue. What is the minimum revenue? (Revenue = Price × Quantity sold)

6.3   Solution

(a)

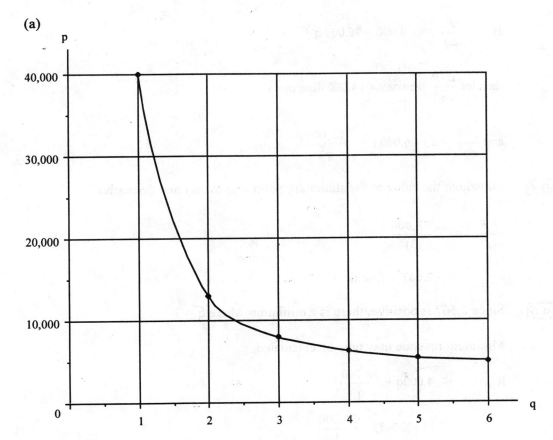

(b) $R = pq = \left(4,000 + \dfrac{36,000}{q^2}\right)q$

$\quad\quad\quad = 4,000q + \dfrac{36,000}{q}$ or $= 4,000q + 36,000q^{-1}$

Applying the procedure in 5.5:

Step 1   Find the first derivative:

$\quad\quad R = 4,000q + 36,000q^{-1}$

$\quad\quad \dfrac{dR}{dq} = 4,000 + [36,000 \times (-1) \times q^{-2}]$

$\quad$ Thus $\dfrac{dR}{dq} = 4,000 - \dfrac{36,000}{q^2}$

Step 2   Equate to zero

$\quad 4,000 - \dfrac{36,000}{q^2} = 0$

$\quad q^2 = 9$

$\quad q = \pm 3$

but for this particular problem, –3 is nonsensical and may be disregarded as a negative quantity cannot be produced.

Step 3 Calculate second derivative

If $\quad \dfrac{dR}{dq} \quad = \quad 4{,}000 - 36{,}000\, q^{-2}$

then for $\dfrac{d^2 R}{dq^2}$ the constant 4,000 disappears

and $\dfrac{d^2 R}{dq^2} = 2 \times 36{,}000 q^{-3} = \dfrac{72{,}000}{q^3}$

Step 4 Substitute the value of the stationary point into the second derivative

$$\dfrac{d^2 R}{dq^2} \quad = \quad \dfrac{72{,}000}{(3)^3}$$

$$= \quad 2{,}667 \quad \text{(positive)}$$

Step 5 Since 2,667 is positive, there is a minimum where $q = 3$

Minimum revenue may now be calculated,

$$R \quad = \quad 4{,}000q + \dfrac{36{,}000}{q}$$

$$= \quad (4{,}000 \times 3) + \dfrac{36{,}000}{3}$$

$$= \quad 24{,}000$$

It is concluded that minimum revenue is earned with 3,000 units on the market (q was in thousands), this minimum revenue is £24,000.

Note: Differentiation assumes that the variables are continuous whereas the number of units sold will be a discrete whole number. However, as q is in thousands, it can be treated approximately as a continuous variable with very little error.

7 APPLICATION OF DIFFERENTIATION - MAXIMISING PROFITS

7.1 Introduction

A typical problem concerns maximising profits when given functions for total revenue and total costs. There are two ways of doing this:

(a) Equating marginal revenue and marginal cost; and
(b) Maximising the function (total revenue - total cost)

Marginal cost can be defined as the gradient of the total cost curve and marginal revenue can be defined as the gradient of the total revenue curve when both are expressed in terms of the quantity of goods. Thus:

Marginal cost $\quad = \quad \dfrac{dC_T}{dq} \quad$ where C_T is total cost of producing a quantity q.

Marginal revenue $\quad = \quad \dfrac{dR_T}{dq} \quad$ where R_T is total revenue from selling a quantity q.

It is usually the case that where the quantity produced is the same as that sold (ie, there is no stock piling), then the maximum profit is obtained when marginal cost = marginal revenue.

7.2   Example

For one type of product it has been established that:

| Total cost in £s | (C_T) | = | $120q + 5,000$ | (£) |
| Total revenue in £s | (R_T) | = | $400q - 2q^2$ | (£) |

where q = quantity produced and sold.

Find the quantity that will maximise profit and the maximum profit.

7.3   Solution

(a)   Using marginal revenue = marginal cost.

(i)   Find quantity that will maximise profit.

$$\text{Marginal cost} \quad = \quad \frac{dC_T}{dq} \quad = \quad 120$$

$$\text{Marginal revenue} \quad = \quad \frac{dR_T}{dq} \quad = \quad 400 - 4q$$

For maximum profit, marginal cost = marginal revenue, ie,

$$120 \quad = \quad 400 - 4q$$

$$\therefore q \quad = \quad 70$$

(ii)   Find maximum profit

$$\text{Profit} \quad = \quad \text{Revenue} - \text{cost}$$

$$= \quad (400q - 2q^2) - (120q + 5,000)$$

Substituting $q = 70$,

$$\text{Maximum profit} \quad = \quad (400 \times 70 - 2 \times 70^2) - (120 \times 70 + 5,000)$$

$$= \quad (28,000 - 9,800) - (8,400 + 5,000)$$

$$= \quad £4,800$$

(b)   Using: profit = total revenue − total cost

$$\text{Profit } (\pi) \quad = \quad (400q - 2q^2) \quad - \quad (120q + 5,000)$$

$$\text{Differentiating} \quad \frac{d\pi}{dq} \quad = \quad 400 - 4q - \quad 120$$

$$= \quad 280 - 4q$$

Find stationary points

$$280 - 4q = \quad 0$$

$$4q = \quad 280$$

$$q = \quad 70$$

This is as before and the profit can then be found in the same way.

8   FURTHER MINIMISING APPLICATIONS

8.1   Introduction

Revenue is maximised at the top of the total revenue curve, where marginal revenue is zero ie,

$$\frac{dTR}{dQ} \quad = \quad 0$$

By differentiating the total revenue function with respect to quantity, the output level in units at this point may be found, and by substituting for Q in the revenue function a value for total revenue is determined. This is a maximum.

8.2   Example

The demand function for widgets is given by $P = £(120 - x)$ where $£P$ = unit price and x = quantity sold. Calculate the maximum revenue that can be achieved by the sale of widgets and the required level of production.

8.3   Solution

Step 1   Determine the total revenue function

Total revenue (TR)   =   Price (P) × Quantity sold (x)

TR   = $(120 - x) \times x$

= $120x - x^2$

Step 2   Differentiate with respect to x:

$$\frac{dTR}{dx} \quad = \quad 120 - 2x = 0 \text{ at a turning point}$$

∴ $120 = 2x$

∴ $x = 60$ This is the level of production which will generate maximum revenue.

To check it's a maximum

$$\frac{d^2TR}{dx^2} = -2 \text{ negative} \therefore \text{ maximum}$$

Step 3   Substitute the calculated value of x into the TR function.

TR   = $120x - x^2$

= $120 \times 60 - 60^2$

= $7,200 - 3,600$

∴ Maximum revenue   =   **£3,600**

8.4 Activity

The demand function for a product is given by $p = x^2 - 24x + 117$, where x units is the quantity demanded and £p the price per unit.

You are required:

(a)   to write down an expression for the total revenue for x units of production.

(b)   to use the methods of differential calculus to establish the number of units of production and the price at which total revenue will be maximised.

8.5 Activity solution

(a)   In order to establish the total revenue function, it is necessary to understand that total revenue is price multiplied by quantity.

$$\text{Thus TR} = \text{p.x}$$

$$\text{Substitute for p} = (x^2 - 24x + 117) \text{ to give}$$

$$\text{TR} = x(x^2 - 24x + 117)$$

Multiply out:

$$\text{TR} = x^3 - 24x^2 + 117x$$

(b)   To establish the number of units that will maximise the total revenue, first form dTR/dx and then solve dTR/dx = 0 to locate all maximum and minimum points. To establish the maximum, form d^2TR/dx^2 and find the value of x that gives $d^2TR/dx^2 < 0$.

$$\text{Thus, given} \quad \text{TR} = x^3 - 24x^2 + 117x$$
$$\text{dTR/dx} = 3x^2 - 48x + 117$$

Now dTR/dx = 0 when $3x^2 - 48x + 117 = 0$ or $x^2 - 16x + 39 = 0$
(solve by factorisation, or the formula for simultaneous equations).

$$x = \frac{-b \pm \sqrt{b^2 - 4ac}}{2a} = \frac{16 \pm \sqrt{256 - 156}}{2} = \frac{16 \pm 10}{2}$$

This means that either x = 3 or x = 13.

Determine which value gives a maximum.

$$d^2TR/dx^2 = 6x - 48$$

$$\text{When x = 3, } d^2TR/dx^2 = 18 - 48$$

$$= -30$$

ie, d^2TR/dx^2 is negative when x = 3, proving TR to be a maximum at this value.

Therefore, the price of a unit of production which maximises revenue is when $x = 3$ and is found by substituting in the equation.

$$
\begin{aligned}
p &= x^2 - 24x + 117 \\
&= 9 - 72 + 117 = £54
\end{aligned}
$$

8.6   Activity

Each week a company has fixed costs of £1,800 and variable costs of £$(100x + x^2)$, where x is the quantity of units of Brand Z made and sold. The company's weekly revenue equation is approximately £$(300x - x^2)$. The company has a maximum capacity of just less than 300 units per week and has a monopoly on Brand Z.

You are required to calculate the output level which will maximise profits and the value of profits at that level.

8.7   Activity solution

Method 1 - using the function

Profit = total revenue - total cost

Step 1   Determine the total revenue function.

$$
\begin{aligned}
TR &= P \times Q \\
&= £(300x - x^2) \qquad \text{given}
\end{aligned}
$$

Step 2   Determine the total cost function.

$$
\begin{aligned}
\text{Total cost} &= \text{Total fixed cost} + \text{Total variable cost} \\
&= £1,800 + £(100x + x^2)
\end{aligned}
$$

Step 3   Determine the profit function.

$$
\begin{aligned}
\Pi &= TR - TC \\
&= (300x - x^2) - (1,800 + 100x + x^2) \\
&= 300x - x^2 - 1,800 - 100x - x^2 \\
&= 200x - 2x^2 - 1,800
\end{aligned}
$$

Step 4   Differentiate the profit function with respect to x.

$$
\begin{aligned}
\Pi &= 200x - 2x^2 - 1,800 \\
\frac{d\Pi}{dx} &= 200 - 4x
\end{aligned}
$$

Maximum profit is attained when $200 - 4x = 0$ ie, when $x = 50$ units of output of Brand Z.

Check to ensure a maximum:

$$\frac{d^2\Pi}{dx^2} = -4 \quad \text{negative} \therefore \text{ a maximum point}$$

Step 5   Substitute the value of x calculated above into the profit function.

When   x   =   50

          Π = $200x - 2x^2 - 1{,}800$

                = $10{,}000 - 5{,}000 - 1{,}800$

Profit   =   **£3,200**

Method 2 - using marginal cost = marginal revenue

Step 1   Establish the marginal cost function by differentiating the total cost function.

       TC   =   Total fixed cost + Total variable cost

                = $1{,}800 + 100x + x^2$

    $\dfrac{dTC}{dx}$ = $100 + 2x$

Step 2   Establish the marginal revenue function by differentiating the total revenue function.

       TR   = $300x - x^2$

    $\dfrac{dTR}{dx}$ = $300 - 2x$

Step 3   Equate the marginal revenue with marginal cost to find the profit maximising level of output.

      $300 - 2x$ = $100 + 2x$

$\Rightarrow$ $4x$ =   200

$\therefore$ x   =   50

Step 4   Substitute the value of x into the profit function. This obviously is the same as the previous step 5.

Thus the two methods give the same result and should be used according to what information is given in the question.

8.8   **Activity**

There is a steady, weekly demand for 100 units of a product when the price is £80. If the price is increased to £85 the demand falls to 75 units. The fixed costs of the company selling the product are £2,500 and the variable costs are £40 a unit.

You are required:

(a)   to find the equation of the demand function that links price, P, to the quantity demanded, Q, assuming it to be linear;

                                                  (5 marks)

(b)   to find the price that maximises profit and the level of this profit.

                                                  (8 marks)

                                               (Total: 13 marks)

8.9   Activity solution

(a)

Step 1   State the general form of a demand function.

If the demand function is linear, it will be of the form:

$Q = a + bP$

When P = 80, Q = 100, giving:

$100 = a + 80b$ ....   (1)

When P = 85, Q = 75, giving:

$75 = a + 85b$ ....   (2)

Step 2   Subtract (2) from (1) to eliminate a.

$$25 \quad = \quad -5b$$

$$\therefore b \quad = \quad -\frac{25}{5}$$

$$= \quad -5$$

Step 3   Substitute in (1):

$$100 \quad = \quad a + 80 \times (-5)$$

$$= \quad a - 400$$

$$\therefore a \quad = \quad 500$$

The demand function is therefore:

$$\mathbf{Q = 500 - 5P \text{ or } P = 100 - 0.2Q}$$

Although this part of the question does not involve the use of calculus it is included here for practice as this often forms the first part of a question on profit maximisation.

(b)   Profit Π =   Revenue – Costs

$$= \quad (100Q - 0.2Q^2) - (40Q + 2{,}500)$$

$$= \quad 60Q - 0.2Q^2 - 2{,}500$$

For maximum profit, $\dfrac{d\Pi}{dQ} = 0$ and $\dfrac{d^2\Pi}{dQ^2}$ is negative.

Equating $\dfrac{d\Pi}{dQ}$ to zero:

$$60 - 0.4Q \quad = \quad 0$$

$$\therefore Q \quad = \quad \frac{60}{0.4} \quad = \quad 150$$

$$\text{For } Q = 150, \quad P \quad = \quad £(100 - 0.2Q)$$

$$= \quad £(100 - 0.2 \times 150)$$

$$= \quad £70$$

$$\text{Profit} \quad = \quad £(60Q - 0.2Q^2 - 2,500)$$

$$= \quad £[60 \times 150 - 0.2 \times (150)^2 - 2,500]$$

$$= \quad £(9,000 - 4,500 - 2,500)$$

$$= \quad £2,000$$

Hence   the price that maximises profit is £70
and   the maximum profit is £2,000 per week.

(Tutorial note:

The equating of marginal cost to marginal revenue could be used, but it does not lend itself to verification of maximum by the second differential coefficient, or to calculation of profit.*)*

9   COST MINIMISATION

9.1   Introduction

The same technique can be used in this situation as for revenue maximisation, although this time we are looking for a **minimum** point on the total cost curve, thus the second derivative must be positive.

9.2   Example

In a certain office, examination and analysis of past records shows that there is a relationship between the number of clerks employed and the cost of processing an order for new business. If q is the number of clerks employed, average cost is given by:

$$c = \frac{3}{2(q-4)} + 24q$$

What value of q will minimise this expression and how would you interpret this result?

9.3   Solution

Step 1   Differentiate the cost function with respect to q.

$$c \quad = \quad \frac{3}{2(q-4)} \qquad +24q$$

$$c \quad = \quad \frac{3}{2}(q-4)^{-1} \qquad +24q$$

$$\frac{dc}{dq} \quad = \quad -\frac{3}{2} \times (q-4)^{-2} \quad +24$$

$$= \quad \frac{-3}{2(q-4)^2} + 24$$

Step 2   To find a minimum put $\dfrac{dc}{dq} = 0$.

When $\dfrac{dc}{dq} = 0$, $\dfrac{3}{2(q-4)^2} = 24$

$(q-4)^2 \quad = \quad \dfrac{1}{16}$

$q - 4 \quad = \quad \sqrt{\dfrac{1}{16}} = \dfrac{1}{4}$ or $\dfrac{-1}{4}$

$q \quad = \quad 4\frac{1}{4}$ or $3\frac{3}{4}$

Step 3   To find which value is minimum, calculate the second derivative:

$\dfrac{dc}{dq} = \dfrac{-3}{2}(q-4)^{-2} + 24$

$\dfrac{d^2c}{dq^2} \quad = \quad -2 \times \dfrac{-3}{2}(q-4)^{-3}$

$\quad\quad = \quad 3(q-4)^{-3}$

$\quad\quad = \quad \dfrac{3}{(q-4)^3}$

For $q = 4\frac{1}{4}$, $q - 4$ is positive, thus $\dfrac{3}{(q-4)^3}$ is positive: therefore a minimum value for q has been found.

Step 4   Interpret the result.

As q is $4\frac{1}{4}$, it is apparent that more than four clerks are required. However, at $q = 5$ the cost is rising: therefore some attempt should be made to employ part-time staff so that q is greater that 4 but less than 5.

10   ESTABLISHING A BREAK-EVEN POINT

10.1   Introduction

A firm is said to be producing at break-even point when it is making neither a profit nor a loss, in other words it is that level of output where it is simply covering costs.

ie: Sales = Fixed costs + variable costs

However, in break-even analysis we normally look at the problem in terms of **contribution**.

Definition   Contribution is sales minus variable costs. A linear relationship is assumed in the normal way.

Thus the break-even point is that level of output where

Fixed costs = contribution

To establish the break-even point or points we **do not** use calculus, however we have included this analysis in this chapter as often, questions involving calculus ie, profit maximising, revenue maximising etc, have a small part which asks for the break-even point.

The technique involved is simply one of establishing and manipulating algebraic relationships with the most difficult part being establishing the solution to a quadratic equation ie, finding the value or values of x which satisfy the equation. This is best done using a formula

The formula method

Consider the general quadratic equation

$$ax^2 + bx + c = 0$$

This has the solution

$$x = \frac{-b \pm \sqrt{b^2 - 4ac}}{2a}$$

Example

Solve the following quadratic equation.

$$9x^2 - 30x + 25 = 0$$

$$a = 9, b = -30, c = 25$$

then

$$x = \frac{-(-30) \pm \sqrt{(-30)^2 - 4 \times 9 \times 25}}{2 \times 9}$$

$$= \frac{30 \pm \sqrt{0}}{18}$$

$$= \frac{30}{18} = \frac{5}{3}$$

10.2   Using quadratic equations to establish break-even points - example

Each week a company has fixed costs of £1,800 and variable costs of £$(100x + x^2)$, where x is the quantity of units of Brand Z made and sold. The company's weekly revenue equation is approximately £$(300x - x^2)$. The company has a maximum capacity of just less than 300 units per week.

Find any break-even point.

10.3   Solution

Step 1   Establish the equation for total cost.

The total cost £C is made up of two parts.

$$\therefore \quad C = \text{Fixed costs} + \text{variable costs}$$

$$C = 1,800 + 100x + x^2$$

Step 2   Establish the equation for total revenue, in fact it is given in this question.

The total revenue £R is given by

$$R = 300x - x^2$$

Step 3   Establish the break-even point C = R.

$$\therefore \quad 1,800 + 100x + x^2 = 300x - x^2$$

$$\Rightarrow \quad 1,800 + 100x + x^2 - 300x + x^2 = 0$$

$$\therefore \quad 2x^2 - 200x + 1,800 \qquad = 0 \qquad \text{(dividing by 2)}$$

$$x^2 - 100x + 900 \qquad = 0$$

Step 4   Use the formula to factorise the equation.

$$x = \frac{-b \pm \sqrt{b^2 - 4ac}}{2a}$$

$$a = 1, b = -100, c = 900$$

$$x = \frac{-(-100) \pm \sqrt{(-100)^2 - 4 \times 1 \times 900}}{2 \times 1}$$

$$= \frac{100 \pm \sqrt{10,000 - 3,600}}{2}$$

$$= \frac{100 \pm 80}{2}$$

$$\therefore \quad x = \frac{180}{2} = 90 \qquad \text{or} \qquad x = \frac{20}{2} = 10$$

Therefore the firm will break-even when it produces either 10 or 90 units of Brand Z each week.

11   FULL COST PRICING

11.1   Introduction

A number of studies, most notably an old American study Hall and Hitch in 1939 and a more recent UK study by Hankinson in the early 1980s, showed that the major determinant for the selling price of a product or service was its cost. This may go against the 'demand-based' approaches beloved by economists, but firms do not adopt economists' 'profit-maximising' pricing policies because the necessary information is not always available. In this section we study the pricing policies most usually adopted by businesses in practice.

11.2   Full cost pricing

The principle of cost-plus pricing is to estimate the likely direct costs for a product, then add a percentage to that to cover overheads then a further percentage to provide a profit. Clearly there is a heavy reliance on the correct estimation of costs for a new product; under-estimate and an item will be sold at a loss, over-estimate and a price will be set that is too high to attract demand. However the 'marginalist' approach to pricing is just as dependent on accurate costs information. There are several variations on this basic approach that are discussed later. When a comparison is made between a cost plus approach and that recommended by economists, it is assumed that the pricing process stops there - this is not the case and it would be disastrous if it was. Any pricing policy will require figures to be reviewed to assess the likely effect on customer demand and also the prices that competitors currently charge or are expected to charge. However a review of the advantages and disadvantages are set out below.

11.3   Advantages and disadvantages of cost plus pricing

These comments are based on an approach that takes no notice of other influences.

Advantages

- Inability of organisations to get a complete picture of how selling price affects demand.

- Cost of getting any market information may be prohibitive.

- Easy to produce prices, relies on a formula, so pricing decision can be delegated.

- Gives justification for price rises.

- Said to produce stable prices.

Disadvantages

- Said to ignore demand.

- Thought to ignore competitors.

- Ignores distinction between incremental costs and fixed costs.

- The selling price depends on how fixed costs are apportioned to products (which may depend on estimates of demand which, in turn, will depend on selling price).

11.4   Short-term pricing and marginal cost pricing

In the short-term, a business may accept orders at any price above marginal cost in order to utilise spare capacity, provided that fixed costs are unchanged by the decision, that more profitable work is not displaced, and that other customers will not be encouraged to seek price reductions. Occasionally, businesses will accept work at a price **below** marginal cost in order to keep the work-force employed.

Note that marginal cost pricing is widely employed in practice: BT is able to offer cheap rate telephone calls at evenings and weekends because it is using equipment provided to meet the heavy demand for calls during business hours. In the off-peak period, it need only cover marginal cost and perhaps obtain some contribution towards fixed costs. Similar considerations apply to the off-peak fares available from British Rail.

The Hankinson survey mentioned earlier showed that firms did use an opportunity cost approach to short-term pricing decisions involving disposal of otherwise obsolete stock or using spare capacity. The big danger is that the low selling prices that might be charged under these circumstances must not be allowed to affect the demand for other products or services that the firm produces. This is achieved by some form of product differentiation eg, marking products as 'special reduction' or even 'damaged stock'.

11.5   Pricing policy in inflationary conditions

Inflation presents problems for those responsible for fixing prices, particularly if there is legislation limiting the frequency and extent of price rises. It is desirable to have a system whereby review of a firm's price and cost structure is automatically triggered each time one of its inputs increases in price. However, there will also have to be some anticipation of cost increases, since it will not be practical to raise selling prices each time an input price increases. The Hankinson survey showed evidence of delays between cost increases and increases in selling price.

Price increases should not, of course, be made without considering the effect on demand. Taken over a period, people's wages may rise at least in line with inflation, and, therefore, price increases which are no more than the general level of inflation may have no permanent effect on demand. However, there will almost inevitably be a 'timing difference', with demand being reduced immediately after a price rise but then picking up again. The effect of this on cash flow must be considered. If demand can be stimulated, it might be possible to absorb the effects of input price rises by producing greater output and thereby achieving economies of scale.

Firms undertaking long-term contract work usually insert in the contract a clause governing price escalation. For instance, the contract might specify that 20% of the price is considered fixed and that, of the remaining 80%, half will be inflated in line with an index of wage rates and half in line with a price index (eg, the retail price index or a more specific index related to the type of contract).

11.6   Target pricing

Target pricing is a term which implies that the firm has a sufficient knowledge of the conditions of the market for its product and for the production factors which it uses to be able to set a price which it calculates will achieve a desired target.

Possible targets might include the following:

(a)   **Short or long run profit maximisation**

In practice these are not normally considered to be specific targets and are not usually regarded as being within the scope of target pricing.

(b)   **Sales maximisation**

This may be regarded in a similar light to that of profit maximisation. Strictly it does not represent a specific target.

(c)   **A desired rate of return on capital invested in a product**

This is, perhaps, the most common target, chiefly because investment decisions are based on comparisons of future returns and on estimates of attainable returns. Managers will, therefore, seek to achieve the projections made when the decision was being reached. The techniques and knowledge required to achieve a target rate of return are not too far distant from those required for profit maximisation but greater attention is likely to be paid to the time dimension. Thus, achievement of an overall target may envisage successive sub-targets and successive price changes in the pursuit of a total strategy. For example, a low price may be set initially to break into a market and to secure distribution channels; a higher price may then be charged as the product gains acceptance and demand becomes less price elastic – and shelf space and retailer support is gained. The manager is operating in a dynamic environment and must adapt his tactics as the strategy develops. The setting of an initial low price to achieve a desired level of market acceptance is known as **penetration pricing**.

The important point is that there is a constant awareness of the price/quantity/cost set of relationships and the greater the knowledge of these the more precise the price calculation can become. The manager is seeking that combination of marginal cost, marginal revenue, price and cross elasticity of demand that will achieve the desired target rate of return on the amount invested.

(d)   **Market share**

This is rarely an end in itself; more often it is the necessary pre-condition for the firm to achieve the price and cost combination it desires.

The position, say, of being an acknowledged brand leader may ensure a given amount of shelf-space and selling attention from distribution channels and may give a degree of control over price and perhaps allow the firm to be the price leader in a period of changing costs.

(e)   **Achieve a given rate of growth**

Growth may be an important objective of the firm but because of the costs and risks of obtaining capital, a steady growth rate is desired because this can be obtained from available capital funds. An objective of growth at a particular rate is also likely to require the achievement of a profit rate considered acceptable to the finance markets. The firm cannot go to the capital market for additional finance unless it can prove to that market that it has achieved a satisfactory rate of profit on its existing capital. What is 'satisfactory' depends on a range of influences and conditions at any particular time.

(f)   **Keep out competitors**

This involves the use of price as a barrier to the entry of market competitors. This may mean that some degree of monopoly profit may be sacrificed in the desire to keep price below the level at which it would become profitable for a new firm to enter the market. An example of this policy is seen in the market for UK air passengers (in which less orthodox marketing strategies are also alleged to take place).

12   PRICING AND MARKETING POLICIES

12.1   Introduction

It must be remembered that pricing decisions are not made in a vacuum and there are very few completely new products. Most new products are simply developments of older ones or substitutes for something that already exists.

There is, therefore, a background, or an expected price range, within which a new product will fit. This can sometimes give a completely new product development an enormous opportunity for profit. For example, when the ball-point pen first appeared, it was offered to the public as a competitor to good quality fountain pens, which were then selling for around £1.50. The ballpoint pen sold at around this price until competitors discovered that it cost only a few pence to make, whereupon the price tumbled. For some time, however, the ball-point continued with its fountain pen image being sold as a long lasting holder for which re-fills were supplied. Later the cheap throw-away ball-point became more general.

Occasionally, there are completely new products which create new markets. In this case price tends to follow supply costs. These costs can be expected to fall as mass markets develop, as production becomes more reliable and as initial research, development and fixed equipment costs are recovered. One such product has been the small electronic calculator. Until the development of microprocessors, a calculator was a piece of office equipment outside the price range of most individuals. Early electric calculators were unreliable and prone to breakdown; initially they were expensive.

The microprocessor made possible a cheap, efficient and reliable piece of equipment of value to any individual. There was no price background for such an item because nothing like this had previously existed. Prices were established by a combination of competition and falling supply costs – a good example of the working of a free market economy.

For more normal products the supplier is operating in a known market with a price history. Decisions may be taken with some knowledge of the likely demand within a given possible price range.

12.2   Charging the 'going rate'

There are situations where the producer is satisfied that he can sell a satisfactory quantity at a satisfactory profit at a price which is in line with prices of similar goods or services. The existence of such a situation depends on the nature and strength of competition, especially price competition in the market. The Hall & Hitch survey produced strong evidence for people charging what they felt was 'the fair price'.

Firms are more likely to charge the 'going rate' under the following conditions:

(a)   When the quality or some other feature of a product or a service is more important than price and the price elasticity of demand at the ruling price is largely inelastic. Examples include local hairdressing services, daily and local newspapers, beer and cigarettes.

(b)   When it is believed that a fixed price has become established for a particular product and identified with that product in the market. Inflation, metrication and the economic upheavals of the 1970s and 1980s have upset most of these identities, of which one of the best known examples was probably that of the 6d (2½p) bar of chocolate which lasted for a long period in the 1950s and early 1960s. Fixed prices of this type tend to be associated with 'oligopolies'.

(c)   When price competition will simply reduce revenue for all suppliers without giving additional profits or any other significant market advantage to any individual supplier. This position is associated with oligopolies and with what may be called, perhaps, local oligopolies where local supply is dominated by a small number of traders who are content to retain their local market share. Formal market sharing agreements or collusive behaviour are not necessary under these conditions. Self-interest builds up a form of custom and practice which all established suppliers observe as long as there is no internal or external threat to market stability. It is also likely that all suppliers will share similar cost conditions and will act together to avoid competing for factors and to preserve stable factor costs -- including wages.

12.3   Market penetration

This relates to the attempt to break into a market and to establish that market share which, it has been calculated, will enable the firm to achieve its revenue and profit targets.

Whether the market is an established one which the firm hopes to break open or a new and developing one, the most likely price strategy is to set price as low as possible and substantially below the ruling price of competitors without being so low that the product is thought to be inferior. To achieve this in an established market the firm is likely to need the benefit of a production or marketing innovation thought to give a special advantage.

Once the target market share has been achieved the next stage in the total strategy is likely to be to build up distributor and customer loyalty ie, to reduce the product's price elasticity of demand (make the demand curve steeper). By reducing the relative attraction of substitutes it will also influence the cross elasticity of demand with rival products. This is unlikely to be achieved solely through price changes. There will also have to be changes in advertising, in policies over distribution margins and services and possibly over the availability of services and even of packaging. At this stage there may be a greater emphasis on price stability and stress on quality and availability. This, of course, assumes that successful penetration is now leading to consolidation of the market share and probably an improvement in profitability.

12.4   Market skimming

This is also associated with the launching of a new product but represents a rather different approach – perhaps where the extent of market appeal is uncertain and the firm has not yet committed itself to a major investment programme in the project and its production. The supplier may also be the main or an important supplier of substitutes so that a successful launch will involve a major switch in production investment. Failure will not be too expensive if care is taken.

The skimming approach involves setting a relatively high price stressing the attractions of new features likely to appeal to those with a genuine interest in the product or its associated attractions. Reaction and support is thus solicited from the 'top end' of the particular market. If the launch is successful in this 'cream skimming' exercise, and when the decision has been taken to invest in the necessary new production resources so that larger scale production becomes possible, then the appeal of the new product can be enlarged through a shift in advertising and a reduction in price. The price reduction can be made in stages to coincide with supply side increases as new resources come into use.

One of the conditions necessary for market skimming is the existence of technical barriers to entry into the market, it must be difficult for competitors to come up with a similar product quickly with which they can undercut the price. Such policies are common in 'high-tec' fields which is why one saw calculators, personal computers, domestic stereo sets and videos initially sold at a high price but now those same products are sold for a fraction of their launch price. The same can be said of computer software, although in all of these cases the product life cycle has an influence on longer-term pricing policy.

12.5   Product line promotion

A decision may be taken to promote a particular product line. There may be a number of possible reasons for this eg, it is thought that demand is likely to expand; or profit on this line is found to be greater than others; or the firm attaches particular importance to market leadership in this line thinking that such leadership gives advantages in the marketing of other products. Whatever the reasons for the promotion, pricing will be part of the total promotional package and the price is likely to be set below that of competing brands. A price may also be chosen for its psychological appeal eg, manufacturers of early mass produced small cars in the 1930s made great efforts to achieve a price as near as possible to £100; this is now seen in the need to set the prices of personal computers below £1,000 or multi-media packages below £2,000.

12.6   Tender and sealed bids

It is the function of any market to match supply and demand and to provide a means of communication between those with goods or services to sell and those prepared to pay a price to obtain them. This communication is a two-way process, but it is often easier to find out what is being offered for sale than to find out what people are prepared to pay. Of course, much market research is directed towards establishing this information.

However, under conditions of market uncertainty it is sometimes possible to reverse the normal process of offering goods for sale at a fixed price and then waiting to see which buyers come forward. The goods may be advertised as being for sale and interested buyers are asked to 'tender' ie, make an offer and indicate the price they are willing to pay. An open auction is a market where those wishing to tender are brought together so that they can do so in open competition with each other.

At the other extreme to the open auction, a seller may ask for sealed bids in which tenders are invited but kept sealed (not disclosed to the seller) until a particular day and time when they are opened and decisions made as to selling. The whole process may be administered by a trusted third party or agent of the seller. Property and leases to property, especially farm leases, are sometimes handled in this way.

13   CHAPTER SUMMARY

The formulae to be followed with differentiation can all be proven mathematically, however this is not within the scope of the course.

Differentiation can be used to calculate gradients of curves, with the second derivative used to identify maximum and minimum points.

A wide range of variables may be connected by relationships which appear as curves when graphed. Differentiation is a powerful tool for investigating the properties of these variables, once the basic rules have been mastered. Although a similar approach could be adopted for straight lines of the form $y = a + bx$, there is no need since it is known that the gradient of such lines is the coefficient of x, b.

14   SELF TEST QUESTIONS

14.1   Define the gradient of a curve. (1.2)

14.2   What is the basic rule to differentiate x^n? (1.3)

14.3   What happens to a constant when it is differentiated? (1.13)

14.4   What value is given to the gradient when either the maximum or minimum point is reached? (4.2)

14.5   When is a second derivative used? (5.3)

14.6   How is the second derivative written? (5.3)

14.7   How can the output quantity offering maximum sales revenue be calculated using differential calculus? (8.1)

15   EXAMINATION TYPE QUESTIONS

15.1   Widgets

A manufacturing company producing widgets has weekly fixed costs of £900 and variable costs of £$(10x + x^2)$ where x is the quantity produced. The manufacturing company's capacity is about 70 units.

The demand function for this product is given by $P = $ £$(120 - x)$ where £$P = $ unit price and $x = $ quantity sold.

You are required

(a) to find the level of production at which **revenue** is maximised;

(4 marks)

(b) to find any break-even points;

(6 marks)

(c) to **sketch** a graph of revenue and profit for the range of values $0 < x < 70$;

(4 marks)

(d) to recommend how many widgets the manufacturing company should produce, justifying your answer.

(6 marks)

(Total: 20 marks)

15.2   Hall of residence

A private college has acquired a new hall of residence. Its management accountant estimates that the annual running costs will be as follows:

Fixed costs   £160,000

Variable costs $4N^2$, where N is the number of students in residence.

The college receives from a benefactor an annual grant of £400 for each student in residence. The aims of the college are to minimise the average cost per student and to break even on running the hall.

You are required

(a) to find N, the optimum number of students to be accommodated;

(12 marks)

(b) to find the annual hall fees to be charged to each student; and

(4 marks)

(c) to comment on your method and answer.

(4 marks)

(Total: 20 marks)

(CIMA May 92)

16   ANSWERS TO EXAMINATION TYPE QUESTIONS

16.1   Widgets

(a)   Revenue = price × quantity
                  = $(120 - x)x = 120x - x^2$

Differentiating with respect to x:

$$\frac{dR}{dx} = 120 - 2x = 0 \text{ at a turning point}$$

$$\therefore 120 = 2x$$

$$x = \frac{120}{2} = 60 \text{ widgets}$$

To check it's a maximum

$$\frac{d^2R}{dx^2} = -2 \text{ negative} \therefore \text{ maximum}$$

Revenue will be maximised when 60 widgets are sold.

(b)   The company will break-even when:

revenue = costs

ie, profit = 0

Profit   =   revenue - costs
P = $120x - x^2 - (10x + x^2 + 900)$
P = $-2x^2 + 110x - 900 = 0$ at break-even points

This is a quadratic with:

$a = -2, \quad b = 110, \quad c = -900$

$$x = \frac{-b \pm \sqrt{b^2 - 4ac}}{2a}$$

$$= \frac{-110 \pm \sqrt{110^2 - 4(-2)(-900)}}{2(-2)}$$

$$= \frac{-110 \pm \sqrt{4,900}}{-4} = \frac{-110 \pm 70}{-4}$$

$\therefore x = $ **10 or 45**

(c)   **Graph showing profit (P) and revenue (R) functions: $0 < x < 70$**

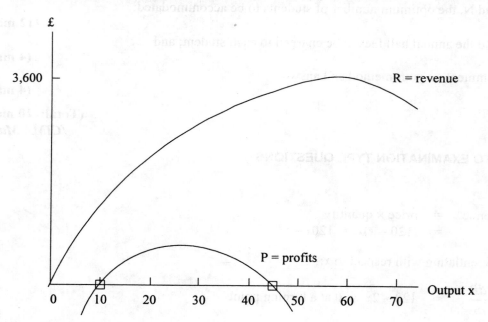

$R = 120x - x^2$. This passes through (0, 0)

and has a maximum at (60, £3,600)

$P = -2x^2 + 110x - 900$. This equals 0 when $x = $ 10 and 45

(d)   To find the profit maximisation point:

$$\frac{dP}{dx} = -4x + 110 = 0$$

$$\therefore \quad 4x = 110$$

$$x = \frac{110}{4} = 27.5 \text{ widgets}$$

$$\frac{d^2P}{dx^2} = -4 \text{ negative} \therefore \text{ maximum}$$

Profit at this point $= -2(27.5)^2 + 110(27.5) - 900$

$= £612.50$

The manufacturing company would be advised to produce 28 widgets a week, as this production level maximises profits.

16.2   Hall of residence

(a)   Total cost $=$ Variable cost + fixed cost

$ =$ $4N^2 + 160,000 \quad (£)$

Average cost per student, A $=$ $\dfrac{\text{Total cost}}{\text{Number of students}}$

$$= \frac{4N^2 + 160,000}{N}$$

$$= 4N + \frac{160,000}{N}$$

$$= 4N + 160,000N^{-1}$$

For minimum, $\dfrac{dA}{dN}$ $=$ 0

$$\frac{dA}{dN} = 4 - 160,000N^{-2} \quad\dotfill\quad \text{(i)}$$

$$= 4 - \frac{160,000}{N^2}$$

Hence for minimum (or maximum), $4 - \dfrac{160,000}{N^2}$ $=$ 0

$$4N^2 - 160,000 = 0$$

$$N^2 = 40,000$$

$$\therefore N = \pm 200$$

To check the minimum, differentiate (i):

$$\frac{d^2A}{dN^2} = -160,000 \times (-2) \times N^{-3}$$

$$= +\frac{320,000}{N^3}$$

When N = +200, $\frac{d^2A}{dN^2}$ is positive, corresponding to a minimum.

Hence to minimise the average cost per student, 200 students should be accommodated.

(b)   The annual fee to break even is the difference between the average cost per student and the £400 grant. Hence,

$$\text{Annual fee} = \frac{4N^2 + 160,000}{N} - 400$$

$$= \frac{4 \times 200^2 + 160,000}{200} - 400 \qquad \text{when N = 200}$$

$$= \underline{\text{£1,200 per student}}$$

(c)   **Comments**

(i)   The hall of residence is only a part of the educational system and to optimise this part may not be in the best interests of the system as a whole. Other considerations, such as size of class and staff-student ratio should be taken into account. This illustrates the danger of sub-optimisation, ie optimisation of one part of the system at the expense of other parts.

(ii)   Other considerations might be:

(1)   Can the hall of residence accommodate 200 students satisfactorily?

(2)   Are students willing or able to pay £1,200?

(3)   Are the cost estimates reliably based?

(4)   Maximisation of profit is better than minimisation of costs.

 **PUBLICATIONS AND DISTANCE LEARNING COURSE ORDER FORM**

	Examination Text £17.00/Text	Examination Kit £8.00/Kit	Examination Notes £5.00/Note	Distance Learning Course £79.00/Subject
Stage 1				
Financial Accounting Fundamentals	☐	☐	☐	☐
Cost Accounting & Quantitative Methods	☐	☐	☐	☐
Economic Environment	☐	☐	☐	☐
Business Environment & Info Technology	☐	☐	☐	☐
Stage 2				
Financial Accounting	☐	☐	☐	☐
Operational Cost Accounting	☐	☐	☐	☐
Management Science Applications	☐	☐	☐	☐
Business & Company Law	☐	☐	☐	☐
Stage 3				
Financial Reporting	☐	☐	☐	☐
Management Accounting Applications	☐	☐	☐	☐
Organisational Management & Development	☐	☐	☐	☐
Business Taxation	☐	☐	☐	☐
Stage 4				
Strategic Financial Management	☐	☐	☐	☐
Strategic Mgt Accountancy & Marketing	☐	☐	☐	☐
Information Management	☐	☐	☐	☐
Management Accounting Control Systems	☐	☐	☐	☐
Postage UK Mainland	£2.00/Text	£1.00/Kit	£1.00/Note	£5.00/Subject
Overseas, NI & ROI	£5.00/Text	£3.00/Kit	£3.00/Note	£15.00/Subject

AT Foulks Lynch Student Number (if applicable) ☐☐☐☐☐☐

CIMA Registration Number ☐☐☐☐☐☐☐☐

Intended Examination Date ☐ November 95 ☐ May 96

Payment details - *please complete section 1, 2 or 3 in accordance with the terms and conditions.*

1 I enclose my cheque (payable to **AT Foulks Lynch Ltd**) for £_____ *(please include postage)*
Signature _____ Date _____

2 Charge Access/Visa card number ☐☐☐☐☐☐☐☐☐☐☐☐☐☐☐☐ Expires ☐☐/☐☐
Signature _____ Date _____

3 Payment by employer. I agree to pay the fees detailed on this form. Please invoice the Company.

Name (*print*) _____ Position _____

Company name _____

Address _____

_____ Postcode _____

☎ _____ Fax number _____

Signature _____ Date _____

Terms and conditions: Employers who sign above are liable for the full fee. Fees include VAT. No refunds for cancelled courses.
All fees in £ Sterling.   ***Note***: Please tick box if you require a monthly report on this student ☐

STUDENT DETAILS
Name _____ ☎ _____

Home address _____

_____ Postcode _____

Please deliver to: Home ☐   Work ☐

Expected delivery: Up to 5 working days UK mainland business addresses
Up to 10 working days UK mainland home addresses (must be someone available to sign)
Up to 6 weeks Overseas addresses
Should you have special delivery requirements please do not hesitate to contact us

Send your completed order to: AT Foulks Lynch Ltd, Number 4, The Griffin Centre,
Staines Road, Feltham, Middlesex, TW14 OHS
VISA/ACCESS Hotline: 0181 831 9990, Fax: 0181 831 9991